GUNS

RECOGNITION GUIDE

Acknowledgements:

Thanks to the MoD Pattern Room, the Infantry Museum, Edgar Brothers, the Royal Military College of Science and the West Midlands Constabulary for their invaluable assistance in providing access to and photography of various weapons in their care.

Colour photography and cover photos: David Hendley
Design: Rod Teasdale

HarperCollinsPublishers
PO Box, Glasgow G4 0BN

First published 2000

Reprint 1 3 5 7 9 10 8 6 4 2

© Jane's Information Group 2000

ISBN 0 00 472453 4

Printed in Italy

DISCLAIMER

The information in the book is derived from examination of weapons, weapon handbooks and other authoritative sources, but it cannot be guaranteed. Neither the authors nor the publisher can be held responsible for any accident arising during the examination of any firearm, whether described in this book or not.

Jane's
GUNS
RECOGNITION GUIDE

Ian Hogg

HarperCollins*Publishers*

Contents

Contents

REVOLVERS

Contents

SUBMACHINE GUNS

Contents

BOLT ACTION RIFLES

Contents

AUTOMATIC RIFLES

Contents

MACHINE GUNS

Contents

Foreword

The object of this book is to enable police, customs officers and others who may be confronted with strange firearms to identify them with a reasonable degree of accuracy. I say 'a reasonable degree' because there are degrees in identification; the manufacturers of the Parabellum pistol recognized about a dozen different models, but collectors divide and sub-divide this into a hundred or more 'variations'. This is doubtless valid in the context of collecting, but for basic identification purposes it is unnecessary; what the makers consider different is sufficient for our purpose.

There is sufficient information to allow anyone unfamiliar with the weapon to ensure that it is unloaded and in a safe condition. In order to keep the book within reasonable bounds, it has been necessary to use some guidelines in selecting the weapons. Firearms rarely wear out; provided that suitable ammunition is available, firearms of over one hundred years of age can be fired and aré lethal, even if their rifling is worn away and their safety is marginal.

The original criteria for inclusion was, broadly, that the weapon was a military or paramilitary design, ammunition was available for it, and/or it was likely to find its way into criminal or terrorist hands. We have extended this slightly in this new edition to cater for weapons which were not intended for military use but which are nevertheless popular with criminals. Representations have been made to us that we have neglected the cheap Spanish automatic of the 1930s and the 'suicide special' revolvers of the early part of this century; to which we can only reply that we could fill two books this size with those classes of weapon, they all look alike anyway, and they are rarely seen today, being deeply unfashionable.

Markings quoted have been taken from actual examples; experience shows that they may vary. Later production may differ from the original, and weapons made to specific contracts may bear different markings. Some discretion must be used where markings do not agree exactly. In the case of some uncommon weapons from Central Europe we have been unable to obtain specimens to examine closely and therefore have omitted any information on markings.

Safety Warning

This book deals with the examination and identification of firearms.

Firearms are designed to kill.

Therefore:

1. Never pick up, accept or hand over a firearm without removing any magazine or emptying any cylinder, and opening the action so as to expose the chamber and demonstrate that the weapon is empty. If you do not know how to do this, leave the weapon alone or ask someone else to do it for you.

2. If circumstances dictate that you must hand over a loaded firearm, make sure that the safety catch is applied and inform the recipient without any ambiguity: "This weapon is loaded. The safety catch is on." If there is no safety catch, ensure the recipient knows.

3. Always assume any firearm to be loaded until you have positively proved that it is not. No matter how old, corroded, rusted, obsolete, decrepit or dirt-covered a firearm may be, it is still possible that it is loaded. And that goes for muzzle-loaded antiques as well.

4. Always use an unloading box if one is available, and always point the firearm in a safe direction while unloading it.

5. Do not be overawed by 'experts' who decry these rules; you will outlive them.

PISTOLS

Glock 17 (Austria)

This pistol appeared in 1983, winning a contract to supply the Austrian Army. Since then it has become enormously popular with police officers, particularly in the USA and has also seen military adoption in several countries. It is a self-cocking automatic using a locked breech relying on the Browning tilting barrel. About 40% of the weapon is made of plastic materials. There are two variant models; the 17L with a longer (153mm) barrel, giving an overall length of 225mm and a weight of 666g. The 19 is the same but in 'compact' form, barrel 102mm, overall 174mm, weight 595g.

SPECIFICATION & OPERATION

CARTRIDGE
9mm Parabellum

DIMENSIONS
Length o/a: 185mm (7.28in)
Barrel: 114mm (4.5in)
Weight: 620g (21.8oz)
Rifling: hexagonal, rh
Magazine capacity: 17 rounds

IN SERVICE DATES 1983-

MARKINGS
'GLOCK 17 AUSTRIA 9X19' Left side of slide. Serial number right side of slide.

SAFETY
There are no manual safety devices; a trigger safety bar protrudes from the trigger face and is automatically pressed in when taking pressure on the trigger. This unlocks an internal safety device, and further pressure on the trigger cocks the striker and then releases it.

UNLOADING
Magazine catch at left side of butt behind trigger. Remove magazine; pull back slide to eject any round in the chamber; inspect chamber through ejection port. Release slide, pull trigger.

Glock Models 20, 21, 22, 23 (Austria)

These four models are large-calibre variants of the 17 and 18. The 20 is in 10mm Auto calibre, the 21 in .45ACP, the 23 in .40 S&W. All are based on the 17 and differ slightly in dimensions. The 24 is in .40 S&W and is the 'compact' version, equivalent to the Model 18.

SPECIFICATION & OPERATION

CARTRIDGE
10mm Auto (20,21) or .40 S&W (22,23)

DIMENSIONS (Model 22)
Length o/a: 185mm (7.28in)
Barrel: 114mm (4.5in)
Weight: 645g (23oz)
Rifling: hexagonal, rh
Magazine capacity: 15

IN SERVICE DATES 1990-

MARKINGS
'GLOCK XX (model number) AUSTRIA 9X19' Left side of slide. Serial number right side of slide.

SAFETY
There are no manual safety devices; a trigger safety bar protrudes from the trigger face and is automatically pressed in when taking pressure on the trigger. This unlocks an internal safety device, and further pressure on the trigger cocks the striker and then releases it.

UNLOADING
Magazine catch at left side of butt behind trigger. Remove magazine; pull back slide to eject any round in the chamber; inspect chamber through ejection port. Release slide, pull trigger.

Steyr 1912 (Austria)

One of the most robust and reliable service pistols ever made, it was hampered by being chambered for a unique cartridge. When Austria was assimilated into the Third Reich in 1938 the service pistols were re-barrelled for the 9mm Parabellum cartridge, and will be found marked ' P-08' on the left side of the slide to indicate their conversion. 9mm Steyr ammunition is still made.

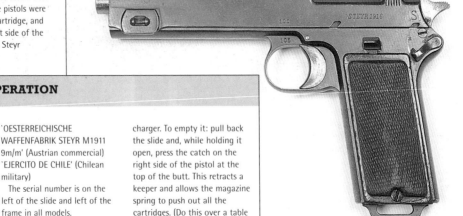

SPECIFICATION & OPERATION

CARTRIDGE
9mm Steyr or 9mm Parabellum

DIMENSIONS
Length o/a: 216mm (8.5in)
Barrel: 128mm (5.0in)
Weight: 1020g (36oz)
Rifling: 4 grooves, rh
Magazine capacity: 8 rounds

IN SERVICE DATES 1912-45

MARKINGS
'STEYR' [date of manufacture] (Austrian military)
'STEYR MOD 1912' (Hungarian military)
'OESTERREICHISCHE WAFFENFABRIK STEYR M1911 9m/m' (Austrian commercial)
'EJERCITO DE CHILE' (Chilean military)

The serial number is on the left of the slide and left of the frame in all models.

SAFETY
Manual safety catch at left rear of frame; forward for safe, DOWN for fire.

UNLOADING
The magazine in this pistol is integral and loaded from a charger. To empty it: pull back the slide and, while holding it open, press the catch on the right side of the pistol at the top of the butt. This retracts a keeper and allows the magazine spring to push out all the cartridges. (Do this over a table or some receptacle to catch the rounds.) Once the magazine is seen to be empty release the slide; if it does not close, depress the cartridge catch again. Then pull the trigger.

Steyr Pi18/GB (Austria)

A high quality pistol using a gas pressure system to delay the opening of the breech. It originally appeared in the 1974 as the Pi18 and a poor-quality license-built version appeared in the USA as the P18. Steyr revoked the license and improved the pistol with a view to meeting an Austrian Army demand; but the Army chose the Glock and apart from moderate commercial sales the GB failed to find a market due to its cost. Military use was restricted to a handful of Special Forces units that took it on trials. Manufacture ceased in 1988.

SPECIFICATION & OPERATION

CARTRIDGE
9mm Parabellum

DIMENSIONS
Length o/a: 216mm (8.5in)
Barrel: 136mm (5.35in)
Weight: 845g (30oz)
Rifling: 4 grooves, polygonal, rh
Magazine capacity: 18

IN PRODUCTION 1974-88

MARKINGS
'Mod GB [Steyr Monogram]
9mm Para' on left side of slide;
'MADE IN AUSTRIA' on right
side of slide. Serial number
right side of frame and slide.

SAFETY
Manual safety catch/de-cocking
lever on left side of slide. When
depressed, it locks the firing pin
and releases the hammer.

UNLOADING
Magazine catch at left side of
butt behind trigger. Remove
magazine; pull back slide to
eject any round in the chamber;
inspect chamber through
ejection port. Release slide, pull
trigger.

Steyr SPP (Austria)

The SPP (Special Purpose Pistol) is a semi-automatic version of the TMP (Tactical Machine Pistol) submachine gun. It uses the same synthetic frame and receiver and operates in the same delayed blowback mode by means of a rotating barrel. The principal difference is that the pistol has no forward handgrip and a slightly greater length of exposed barrel and jacket in front of the receiver. Another prominent feature is a short downward

SPECIFICATION & OPERATION

CARTRIDGE
9 x 19mm Parabellum

DIMENSIONS
Length o/a: 282mm (11.1in)
Barrel: 130mm (5.12in)
Weight: 1300g (2lb 14oz)
Rifling: 6 grooves, rh
Magazine capacity: 15 or 30 rounds

IN PRODUCTION 1993-

MARKINGS
MADE IN AUSTRIA on right side of receiver. STEYR-MANNLICHER and the Steyr badge on the left side of the receiver.

SAFETY
Manual push-through safety catch at the top the pistol grip; push through from left to right for fire.

UNLOADING
Magazine release button on left side of pistol grip behind trigger. Remove magazine. Grasp cocking handle, at rear of receiver and below the rear sight, and pull back to open the breech. Inspect chamber through the ejection port, verifying it to be empty. Release the cocking handle, press the trigger.

spur at the front of the frame, which positions the non-firing hand when using a two-handed hold and also prevents the fingers slipping in front of the barrel when firing.

Browning 1903 (Belgium)

Designed by John Browning, who sold the rights to Colt for the USA and FN for the rest of the world. Colt produced it as a home defence pistol in 7.65mm, FN as a military pistol in 9mm Browning Long calibre. Widely copied in Spain from 1905 onward and in various calibres - most 1905-35 cheap Spanish automatic pistols are copies of this weapon due to its simple design and manufacture.

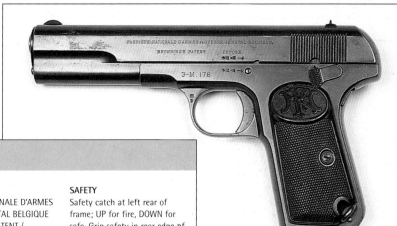

SPECIFICATION & OPERATION

CARTRIDGE
9x 20SR Browning Long, or
7.65mm Browning (.32 ACP)

DIMENSIONS
Length o/a: 205mm (8.07in)
Barrel: 127mm (5.0in)
Weight: 910g (32.1oz)
Rifling: 6 grooves, rh
Magazine capacity: 7 rounds
(9mm) or 8 rounds (7.65mm)

IN SERVICE DATES 1903 -

MARKINGS
'FABRIQUE NATIONALE D'ARMES de GUERRE HERSTAL BELGIQUE / BROWNING'S PATENT / DEPOSE' on left side of slide. Serial number on right side of frame (Belgian model). 'COLT'S PT FA MFG CO HARTFORD CT USA / PATENTED APR 20 1897 DEC 22 1903' on left side of slide. Serial number left side of frame. 'COLT AUTOMATIC / CALIBER .32 RIMLESS SMOKELESS' on right side of slide (US model).

SAFETY
Safety catch at left rear of frame; UP for fire, DOWN for safe. Grip safety in rear edge of butt, must be squeezed in to release the firing mechanism. A magazine safety is fitted.

UNLOADING
Magazine catch in heel of butt. Remove magazine. Pull back slide to eject any round in the chamber and inspect the chamber through the ejection port. Release slide, pull trigger.

Browning 1910 (Belgium)

An improved version of the M1903, in which the recoil spring is placed around the barrel instead of beneath it, giving the unique tubular appearance to the slide. It was copied in Spain in the 1920-35 period, though not to the extent of the M1903, and also in Germany as the 'Rheinmetall' and 'DWM' pistols, easily distinguished by their markings. In 1922 it was given a longer barrel and the slide lengthened by a bayonet-jointed extension, remaining otherwise the same.

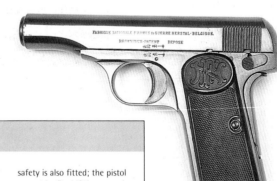

SPECIFICATION & OPERATION

CARTRIDGE
7.65mm Browning (.32 ACP)

DIMENSIONS
Length o/a: 153mm (6.02in)
Barrel: 87.5mm (3.44in)
Weight: 570g (20oz)
Rifling: 6 grooves, rh
Magazine capacity: 7 rounds

IN SERVICE DATES 1910-

MARKINGS
'FABRIQUE NATIONALE D'ARMES de GUERRE HERSTAL BELGIQUE / BROWNING'S PATENT DEPOSE' on left side of slide. `CAL 7m/m.65' on barrel, visible through ejection opening. Serial number on right side of frame, right side of slide and on barrel. On the 1922 model it is also on the slide extension.

SAFETY
Safety catch at left rear of frame. UP for safe, DOWN for fire. Grip safety in rear of pistol grip which must be depressed to permit firing. A magazine safety is also fitted; the pistol cannot be fired if the magazine is withdrawn.

UNLOADING
Magazine catch at heel of butt. Remove magazine, pull back slide to eject any round in the chamber. Release slide. The pistol will remain cocked and the trigger cannot be pressed unless the emptied magazine is replaced.

Browning High Power Model 1935 (Belgium)

Originally produced by FN Herstal in 1935. Wartime German High Powers have approval marks and 'Pist. 640(b)' stamped on the slide. Canadian-made High Powers are marked 'J Inglis'. After 1945 production began again under FN Herstal, and the design was adopted by over 50 armies around the world. The two most innovatory features were the large-capacity magazine and the use of a shaped cam rather than a pinned swinging link to lower the rear end of the barrel during recoil; both these feaures have been widely copied on other designs since 1935. Mark 2 and Mark 3 (illustrated above) versions appeared in the late 1980s. The Mk3 has an automatic firing pin safety device.

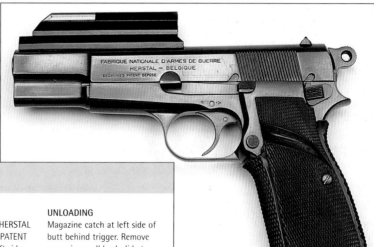

SPECIFICATION & OPERATION

CARTRIDGE
9mm Parabellum

DIMENSIONS
Length o/a: 197mm (7.75in)
Barrel: 118mm (4.65in)
Weight: 920g (32.4oz)
Rifling: 6 grooves, rh
Magazine capacity: 13

IN SERVICE DATES 1935-

MARKINGS
'FABRIQUE NATIONALE HERSTAL BELGIUM BROWNING'S PATENT DEPOSE FN (Year)' on left side of slide. Military models may have the NATO stock number.

SAFETY
Manual at left rear of frame; recent models have it duplicated on both sides of the frame. UP for Safe.

UNLOADING
Magazine catch at left side of butt behind trigger. Remove magazine; pull back slide to eject any round in the chamber; inspect chamber through ejection port. Release slide, pull trigger.

Browning BDA9 (Belgium)

This is derived from the High Power Model 35 above, but uses a double-action lock mechanism and has a de-cocking lever on each side of the frame instead of a safety catch. The magazine catch can be fitted to either side of the grip, and the trigger guard is shaped for two-handed firing. Mechanically, it is the same as the Model 35, operates and strips in the same way except that the slide needs to be pressed back about 1mm to permit removal of the slide stop pin.

SPECIFICATION & OPERATION

CARTRIDGE
9mm Parabellum

DIMENSIONS
Length o/a: 200mm (7.87in)
Barrel: 118mm (4.65in)
Weight: 875g (30.8oz)
Rifling: 6 grooves, rh
Magazine capacity: 14

IN SERVICE DATES 1993-

MARKINGS
'FABRIQUE NATIONALE HERSTAL BELGIUM FN (year)' left side of slide. Serial number right side of frame.

SAFETY
Both sides of frame at rear; UP for safe.

UNLOADING
Magazine catch at left side of butt behind trigger. Remove magazine; pull back slide to eject any round in the chamber; inspect chamber through ejection port. Release slide, pull trigger.

Browning BDA 380 (Belgium)

This is little more than a Beretta 84 with a Belgian accent. FN wanted a blowback pistol for the police market, and since they owned a piece of Beretta it made sense to take an existing successful design and make a few minor cosmetic changes. The most obvious difference is the plastic grip plate with the 'FN' monogram.

SPECIFICATION & OPERATION

CARTRIDGE
9mm Short (.380 Auto) or 7.65mm ACP

DIMENSIONS
Length o/a: 173mm (6.8in)
Barrel: 96mm (3.78in)
Weight: 640g (22.6oz)
Rifling: 6 grooves, rh
Magazine capacity: 13 (9mm) or 12 (7.65mm)

IN SERVICE DATES 1980-

MARKINGS
'FABRIQUE NATIONALE' or 'FN HERSTAL SA' on left side of slide. 'BDA-380' and Serial number left side of frame. If made in the Beretta Factory will have 'PB' monogram on right side of slide.

SAFETY
Manual safety catch at left rear of slide, which acts as a de-cocking lever. Press down to make safe, when the hammer will be released to fall safely on a loaded chamber.

UNLOADING
Magazine catch at left side of butt behind trigger. Remove magazine; pull back slide to eject any round in the chamber; inspect chamber through ejection port. Release slide, pull trigger.

FN Five-seveN (Belgium)

sort of pressure, and thus there is no safety catch of the normal type. The cartridge is considerably longer than the average pistol round, but the grip nevertheless fits the hand well and the recoil impulse is somewhat less than a 9mm Parabellum cartridge, so that the weapon is easily controlled.

The Five-seveN operates on the delayed blowback principle. On firing the barrel and slide both move back, but the barrel is under a forward impulse due to the bullet's friction. The slide is held after a short movement, until the pressure on the barrel is released as the bullet leaves. This allows the barrel to move backwards slightly and release the catch holding the slide, thus allowing the slide to resume its movement and complete the loading cycle.

This is a self-cocking semi-automatic firing the same cartridge as the P-90 personal defence weapon. The trigger action is rather unusual in that pressure on the trigger first loads the firing pin spring and then releases the firing pin. Unless the trigger is pressed, the firing pin is never under any

SPECIFICATION & OPERATION

CARTRIDGE
5.7 x 28mm FN

DIMENSIONS
Length o/a: 208mm (7.8in)
Barrel: 122.5mm (4.42in)
Weight: 618g (2lbs 5oz)
Rifling: 6 grooves rh
Magazine: capacity: 20-rounds

IN PRODUCTION 1998-

MARKINGS
FN HERSTAL BELGIUM on left side of slide; CAL 5.7x28 on right side. Serial number on barrel, visible through ejection port, and on the right side of the slide, below the foresight.

SAFETY
No applied safety. This weapon is safe until the final movement of the trigger.

UNLOADING
Magazine catch in front edge of grip. Remove magazine; pull back slide to empty chamber; verify chamber empty. Release slide. There is no need to pull the trigger.

Imbel M973/MD1 (Brazil)

number have gone to police and some army units. Most parts are interchangeable between all three pistols.

The M973 in its original form was simply a copy of the US Colt M1911A1 in .45 calibre. It was then reworked into 9mm Parabellum calibre but was still known as the M973. In 1990 it was again reworked, this time into .38 Super Auto calibre, primarily for the civil and export markets, though it is believed a

SPECIFICATION & OPERATION

CARTRIDGE
.45 ACP, 9mm Parabellum or .38 Super Auto

DIMENSIONS
Length o/a: 216mm (8.5in)
Barrel: 128mm (5.04in)
Weight: 1035g (36.5oz)
Rifling: 6 grooves, rh
Magazine capacity: 7 rounds (.45); 8 rounds (9mm); 9 rounds (.38 Super)

IN PRODUCTION 1973-

MARKINGS
'FABRICA ITJUBA BRASIL' on left side of slide. 'EXERCITO BRASILIERO' and serial number right side of slide. 'Pist 9 [or 45] M973' and serial number on right side of frame above trigger. Or 'Pist 38 MD1' and serial number on right side of frame.

SAFETY
Manual safety catch on left rear side of frame; UP for safe.

UNLOADING
Magazine catch is a button in the front left side of the butt, behind the trigger. Press in, remove magazine. Pull back slide to eject any round in the breech, inspect chamber through ejection port, release slide. Pull trigger.

Taurus PT 52 S (Brazil)

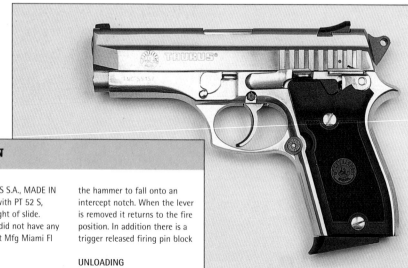

A compact straight blowback pistol modelled on the larger PT 92 AF with identical control levers and takedown. Like the larger 9mm pistols the PT 52 S is available with a stainless steel or carbon steel slide/barrel assembly on an Aluminium frame.

SPECIFICATION & OPERATION

CARTRIDGE
.380 Auto (9mmK)

DIMENSIONS
Length o/a: 180mm (7.1in)
Barrel: 102mm (4.0in)
Weight: 800g (28oz)
Rifling: 6 grooves rh
Magazine capacity: 12

MARKINGS
TAURUS on left of slide along with TAURUS BRASIL in circle with bull's head motif inside, serial number on left of frame, FORJAS TAURUS S.A., MADE IN BRAZIL along with PT 52 S, .380 ACP on right of slide. Earlier models did not have any reference to Int Mfg Miami Fl on the slide.

SAFETY
Manual safety catch/de-cocking lever on both sides of the frame at rear. UP for safe which will lock the hammer in the cocked and uncocked position. DOWN for fire and a continued downward movement releases the hammer to fall onto an intercept notch. When the lever is removed it returns to the fire position. In addition there is a trigger released firing pin block

UNLOADING
Magazine catch at left side of butt behind trigger, pressed in to release magazine. Remove magazine; pull back slide to eject any round in the chamber; inspect chamber through ejection port. Release slide.

China Type 64 (China)

An unusual silenced pistol, easily recognised by the bulbous integral silencer. The breech slide can be locked closed to prevent ejection of the spent case after firing, which could make more noise than the shot itself. Alternatively, it can be unlocked, when the weapon operates in the normal blowback self-loading mode. Note that the cartridge for this weapon is peculiar to it; it will NOT chamber the 7.65mm ACP, which is otherwise of similar dimensions, because the ACP round is semi-rimmed and will prevent the breech closing.

SPECIFICATION & OPERATION

CARTRIDGE
7.65x 17mm rimless

DIMENSIONS
Length o/a: 222mm (8.75in)
Barrel: 95mm (3.74in)
Weight: 810g (28.6oz)
Rifling: 4 grooves, rh
Magazine capacity: 9

IN-SERVICE DATES 1964-

MARKINGS
`64` with factory number in an oval and serial number on left of slide.

SAFETY
Manual safety catch at top of left butt grip; UP for safe. A cross-bolt in the upper part of the slide will lock the slide to the barrel and prevent self-loading action and thus prevent any mechanical noise after firing a silent shot.

UNLOADING
Magazine catch at heel of butt. Remove magazine; pull back slide to eject any round in the chamber; inspect chamber through ejection port. Release slide, pull trigger.

China Type 67 (China)

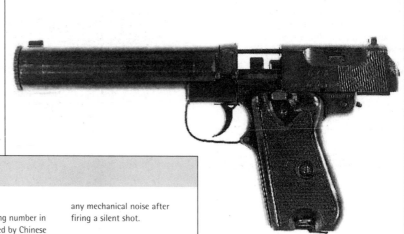

An improved version of the Model 64, this has a rather less clumsy silencing system which fits better into a holster and gives the weapon better balance. There is no provision for locking the breech closed on this model, normal blowback operation being the only option. Note also that not only does this weapon not fire the 7.65mm ACP cartridge, it is not intended to fire the same 7.65mm rimless round used with the Model 64 but needs a special low-powered 7.62mm round known as the Type 64.

SPECIFICATION & OPERATION

CARTRIDGE
7.62 x 17mm Type 64 rimless

DIMENSIONS
Length o/a: 226mm (8.90in)
Barrel: 89mm (3.5in)
Weight: 1050g (37oz)
Rifling: 4 grooves, rh
Magazine capacity: 9

IN SERVICE DATES 1968-

MARKINGS
Factory identifying number in oval; '67' followed by Chinese character; serial number; all on left side of slide.

SAFETY
Manual safety catch at top of left butt grip; UP for safe. A cross-bolt in the upper part of the slide will lock the slide to the barrel and prevent self-loading action and thus prevent any mechanical noise after firing a silent shot.

UNLOADING
Magazine catch at heel of butt. Remove magazine; pull back slide to eject any round in the chamber; inspect chamber through ejection port. Release slide, pull trigger.

CZ99/HS 95 (Croatia)

This pistol was first seen, briefly, in 1991, marketed as the 'CZ99' by Zastava Arms of Yugoslavia. The subsequent civil upheaval closed down communications with that country and nothing more was heard of the pistol until in re-appeared in 1995 with some cosmetic changes and a new owner. It seems to have leaned heavily on the SIG 220 series for its inspiration, using a similar double-action and de-cocking system though with a rather more rounded contour to the butt. The mechanism is also similar, using Browning cam and locking into

SPECIFICATION & OPERATION

CARTRIDGE
9 x 19mm Parabellum

DIMENSIONS
Length o/a: 180mm (7.09in)
Barrel: 102mm (4.0in)
Weight: 990g (2lb 3oz)
Rifling: 6 grooves, polygonal, rh
Magazine: 15-round detachable box

IN PRODUCTION 1995-

MARKINGS
Cal 9mm Para on barrel, visible in ejection port. Made in CROATIA on right side of slide, together with serial number.

SAFETY
De-cocking lever only; there is no manual safety catch. Automatic firing pin safety.

UNLOADING
Magazine catch is duplicated on both sides of the butt, behind the trigger. Remove magazine, draw back slide and inspect chamber through ejection opening. Release slide, press trigger or depress the de-cocking lever.

the ejection opening and with an automatic firing pin safety. It is apparently issued to Croatian army personnel and is also offered for export.

CZ Model 10 (Croatia)

In this case CZ stands for 'Crvena Zastava', the former Yugoslavian government arms factory at Kragujevac, which is probably in Croatia this week. The CZ Model 10 is actually the old Yugoslavian M70 pistol, which was virtually a scaled-down Russian Tokarev TT33. There is no need for a locked breach in this calibre, or in 9mm Short for which the pistol can also be chambered, but it appears to have been a matter of manufacturing convenience to use the same Colt-Browning dropping-barrel lock as did the Tokarev. The pistol is well finished, from good materials, and is widely distributed throughout the Balkans.

SPECIFICATION & OPERATION

CARTRIDGE
7.65mm Browning/ .32 ACP

DIMENSIONS
Length: 165mm
Barrel: 94mm
Weight: 740g
Rifling: 6 groove, rh
Magazine capacity: 8

IN PRODUCTION: 1977 –

MARKINGS
CRVENA ZASTAVA of ZAVOD CRVENA ZASTAVA or ZASTAVA ARMS. Kal (or Cal) 7.65mm Mod 10 (or Mod 70) on left side of slide. Serial number on right side of slide.

SAFETY
Manual safety catch on left side locks firing pin, hammer and slide. There is also a magazine safety which prevents operation of the trigger when the magazine is out.

UNLOADING
Magazine catch on left side of butt, behind trigger. Press in, remove magazine. pull back slide to extract and eject any round in the chamber. Inspect chamber through magazine opening. Release slide. Empty the magazine if necessary, replace empty magazine in pistol, press trigger.

PHP MV 9 (Croatia)

This is another new weapon produced in the Balkans: essentially a Walther P-38 although it looks very different externally. Inside, it is closely modelled on the P-38: breech-locking is done by the same wedge system and the double-action trigger, hammer and decocking lever are the same. The only improvement is the magazine, which now holds 15 rounds. Recent information suggests that manufacture ceased after a short run.

SPECIFICATION & OPERATION

CARTRIDGE
9 x 19 mm Parabellum

DIMENSIONS
Length: 7.67in (195mm)
Barrel: 4.14in (105mm)
Weight: 34.07oz (985g)
Rifling: 6 groove, rh
Magazine capacity: 15

IN PRODUCTION: 1993-1996

MARKINGS
PHP MV CAL 9mm PARA on left side of slide. PAT IMP Made in Croatia (Serial no.) on right.

SAFETY
Manual safety/decocking lever on left. Press down to decock hammer.

UNLOADING
Magazine catch on left side of butt, behind trigger. Remove magazine and empty if necessary. Pull back slide until it locks, examine feedway and chamber. Press slide release catch on left above trigger. Press trigger.

CZ52 (Czechoslovakia)

This replaced the M38 design; it is intended to fire the Czech M48 cartridge, which is more powerful than the normal 7.62mm Soviet pistol round, and thus it uses a complicated roller-locked breech. It can also fire 7.63mm Mauser pistol cartridges.

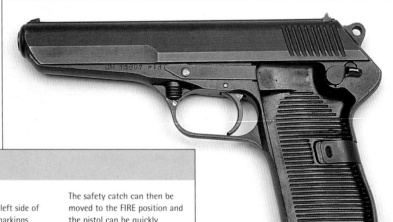

SPECIFICATION & OPERATION

CARTRIDGE
7.62mm Czech M48 (7.62mm Soviet Pistol)

DIMENSIONS
Length o/a: 209mm (8.2in)
Barrel: 120mm (4.7in)
Weight: 860g (30oz)
Rifling: 4 grooves rh
Magazine capacity: 8 rounds

IN SERVICE DATES 1953-70

MARKINGS
Serial number on left side of frame. No other markings

SAFETY
Safety catch at left rear of slide; UP for safe, DOWN for fire. This is a three-position switch; pointing DOWN, the pistol is ready to fire; pointing backward it is safe; and when pushed UP from this position it will drop the cocked hammer safely on to the rebound notch.

The safety catch can then be moved to the FIRE position and the pistol can be quickly brought into use by thumbing back the hammer.

UNLOADING
Magazine catch at the heel of the butt. Remove magazine, pull back slide to eject any round in the chamber, inspect chamber through the ejection port. Release slide, pull trigger.

CZ75 (Czechoslovakia)

One of the best designs to come out of Europe since 1945, the CZ75 has been widely distributed and even more widely copied. It has no unique features, using ideas obviously adopted from many designs; basically it is a Browning-derived design, using the same type of cam-dropped barrel as the Browning High-power. It is simply well put-together of good materials. The fully automatic model has a slightly longer barrel with the end formed into a compensator, and can fire at about 1000 rounds/minute. The CZ85, is similar to the 75 but has ambidextrous safety catch and slide stop.

SPECIFICATION & OPERATION

CARTRIDGE
9mm Parabellum

DIMENSIONS
Length o/a: 203mm (8.0in)
Barrel: 120mm (4.7in)
Weight: 980g (34.5oz)
Rifling: 6 grooves, rh
Magazine capacity: 15 rounds

IN SERVICE DATES 1975-

MARKINGS
'CZ MODEL 75 CAL 9 PARA' on left side of slide. 'MADE IN CZECHOSLOVAKIA' on left side of frame Serial number right side of frame and slide.

SAFETY
Manual safety catch at left rear of frame. UP for safe.

UNLOADING
Magazine catch at left side of butt behind trigger. Remove magazine; pull back slide to eject any round in the chamber; inspect chamber through ejection port. Release slide, pull trigger.

CZ83 (Czechoslovakia)

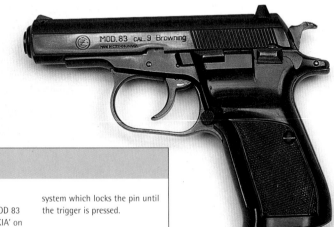

A conventional double-action blowback pocket automatic pistol which can be thought of as Czechoslovakia's answer to the Makarov. It fills the same niche in Czech services and has a few refinements such as an automatic firing pin safety system, ambidextrous safety catch and magazine release, and a trigger guard large enough to take a gloved hand. Note that in 7.65mm and 9mm short calibres the rifling is conventional, but in 9mm Makarov it is of the polygonal form - i.e. the barrel section resembles a circle which has been slightly flattened on four sides.

SPECIFICATION & OPERATION

CARTRIDGE
7.65mm ACP, or 9mm Short (.380 Auto) or 9mm Makarov

DIMENSIONS
Length o/a: 173mm (6.8in)
Barrel: 96mm (3.8in)
Weight: 650g (23oz)
Rifling: 6 grooves, rh
Magazine capacity: 15 (7.65mm) or 13 (9mm)

IN SERVICE DATES 1984-

MARKINGS
`CZ 033 CAL 7,65MM MOD 83 MADE IN CZECHOSLOVAKIA' on left side of slide. Serial number on right side of slide, repeated on barrel.

SAFETY
Ambidextrous manual safety catch at rear of frame which locks hammer and trigger, plus an automatic firing pin safety system which locks the pin until the trigger is pressed.

UNLOADING
Magazine catch at either side of butt behind trigger. Remove magazine; pull back slide to eject any round in the chamber; inspect chamber through ejection port. Release slide, pull trigger.

CZ-85 (Czech Republic)

This is an updated version of the CZ75 in which the general appearance has been retained but the safety catch and slide stop have been duplicated on both sides for ambidextrous operation. Minor changes to the internal dimensions have been made to improve reliability, and the top of the slide is ribbed to reduce shine. Models with fixed or adjustable sights are available.

SPECIFICATION & OPERATION

CARTRIDGE
9mm Parabellum.

DIMENSIONS
Length: 206mm (8.11in)
Weight: 1000g (2 lb 3oz)
Barrel: 120mm (4.74in),
Rifling: 6 grooves, rh
Magazine: 15-round detachable box

IN PRODUCTION 1985–

MARKINGS
CZ MODEL 85 CAL 9 LUGER on left side of slide. MADE IN CZECHOSLOVAKIA on the left side of the frame. Later models may be found with MADE IN THE CZECH REPUBLIC.

SAFETY
Manual safety catch locks slide and hammer and is fitted to both sides of the frame; UP for safe. Automatic firing pin safety.

UNLOADING
Ambidextrous magazine catch on either side of butt; press in, remove magazine. Draw back slide to eject any round in the chamber. Inspect chamber through ejection port. Release slide, pull trigger.

Pistol CZ100/101 (Czech Republic)

Introduced in 1995 this chunky pistol brings synthetic materials into CZ construction. Slide and frame use plastics and steel; the pistol is a self-cocker, the firing system being under no tension unless the trigger is pulled. There is an automatic firing pin safety device. An unusual protrusion on the top of the slide, just behind the ejection port, is intended to permit one-handed cocking by simply placing this part against a hard surface and pushing down on the grip so that the slide is force back to load the first round. The action is the usual

SPECIFICATION & OPERATION

CARTRIDGE
9 x 19mm Parabellum or
.40 S&W

DIMENSIONS
Length o/a: 177mm (6.96in)
Barrel: 95mm (3.74in)
Weight: 645g (1lb 7oz)
Rifling: 6 grooves rh
Magazine: 13-round (9mm) or
10-round (.40) detachable box

IN PRODUCTION 1995-

MARKINGS
CZ 100 Cal .40 &W MADE IN
CZECH REPUBLIC on left side of
slide. CZ and a symbol of a
pistol in a circle moulded into
the lower part of the grips.

SAFETY
Manual safety catch on the
frame locks the trigger.
Automatic firing pin safety.

UNLOADING
Magazine catch in grip, behind
trigger aperture; it may be on
either side. Press to release
magazine. Draw back slide to
empty chamber, verify chamber
empty, release slide. There is no
need to pull the trigger.

Browning cam, locking the chamber top into the ejection port. A laser spot can be fitted into rails provided in the front of the frame.

The Model 101 is similar but has a smaller magazine capacity: 7 rounds of 9mm or 6 rounds of .40.

Lahti L-35 (Finland)

Although resembling the Parabellum, the mechanism is totally different. These pistols were made in small batches which differed in minor details. The Swedish version also differs from the Finnish in minor details. A highly reliable pistol, it became available on the surplus market in the 1970s. DO NOT attempt to dismantle without expert guidance and a full toolkit.

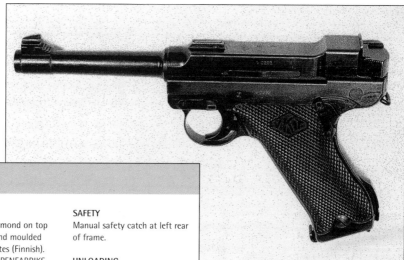

SPECIFICATION & OPERATION

CARTRIDGE
9mm Parabellum

DIMENSIONS
Length o/a: 245mm (9.65in)
Barrel: 107mm (4.21in)
Weight: 1220g (43oz)
Rifling: 6 grooves, rh
Magazine capacity: 8 rounds

IN SERVICE DATES: 1939-85

MARKINGS
'VKT' inside a diamond on top of the receiver and moulded into the butt plates (Finnish). 'HUSQVARNA VAPENFABRIKS AB' on left side of receiver (Swedish).
   Serial number left side of receiver and left side of frame, all models.

SAFETY
Manual safety catch at left rear of frame.

UNLOADING
Magazine catch at the toe of the butt. Remove magazine; grasp the end of the bolt and pull back to eject any round in the chamber. Inspect chamber via ejection port. Release bolt, press trigger.

MAB PA-15 (France)

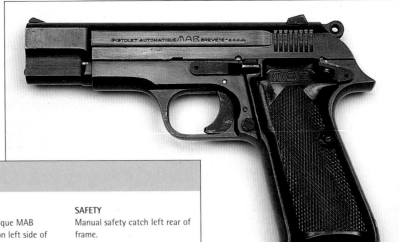

A militarised model of a commercial pistol, adopted by the French Army in the 1960s and also sold commercially. Unusual for its time in using a rotating barrel to lock the barrel and slide together for firing, the barrel turning during recoil to release the slide. A long-barrel target model was also produced.

SPECIFICATION & OPERATION

CARTRIDGE
9mm Parabellum

DIMENSIONS
Length o/a: 203mm (8.0in)
Barrel: 114mm (4.5in)
Weight: 1090g (38.5oz)
Rifling: 6 grooves, rh
Magazine capacity: 15 rounds

IN SERVICE DATES 1975-90

MARKINGS
'Pistol Automatique MAB Brevete SGDG' on left side of slide. 'MODELE PA-15' on right side of slide. Military models: 'P.A.P. Mle F1 Cal 9m/m' on right side of slide; 'MADE IN FRANCE' on right side of frame on both military and commercial models. Serial number on right side of frame above trigger.

SAFETY
Manual safety catch left rear of frame.

UNLOADING
Magazine release button on left side behind trigger. Remove magazine; pull back slide to eject any round in the chamber; inspect chamber through ejection port. Release slide, pull trigger.

Heckler & Koch HK4 (Germany)

This was Heckler & Koch's first firearm, and was based upon the pre-war Mauser HSc pistol. It was available with a kit of four interchangeable barrels, allowing the pistol to be converted to any of the four calibres - 9mm Short, 7.65mm ACP, 6.35mm or .22 rimfire. For the latter, an adjustment was provided to alter the strike of the firing pin.

SPECIFICATION & OPERATION

CARTRIDGE
9mm Browning Short (.380 Auto) or 7.65mm browning (.32ACP)

DIMENSIONS
Length o/a: 157mm (6.18in)
Barrel: 85mm (3.34in)
Weight: 480g (17oz)
Rifling: 6 grooves, lh
Magazine capacity: 7 rounds (9mm); 8 rounds (7.65, 6.35mm and .22)

IN PRODUCTION 1956 -90

MARKINGS
'HECKLER & KOCH GmbH OBERNDORF/N MADE IN GERMANY Mod HK4' on left side of slide.

SAFETY
Safety catch on left rear of slide; DOWN for SAFE, UP for FIRE.

UNLOADING
Set the safety catch to safe. Press back the magazine catch at the heel of the butt and remove the magazine. Pull back the slide to eject any round in the chamber. On releasing the slide it will stay open. Inspect the chamber, then press the trigger; this will allow the slide to close, leaving the hammer cocked. Press the trigger again to drop the hammer.

Heckler & Koch P9/P9S (Germany)

Heckler & Koch's first locked-breech military pistol, this uses a complex roller-locked delayed blowback system similar to that used on the company's rifles and machine guns. The P9 pistol came first but was soon followed and then replaced by the P9S, the difference being that the P9 was single action only, whereas the P9S was double action.

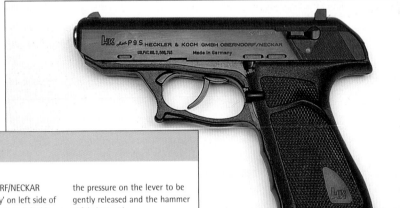

SPECIFICATION & OPERATION

CARTRIDGE
9mm Parabellum

DIMENSIONS
Length o/a: 192mm (7.6in)
Barrel: 102mm (4.01in)
Weight: 880g (31oz)
Rifling: Polygonal, 4 'grooves' rh
Magazine capacity: 9 rounds

IN PRODUCTION 1970 -90

MARKINGS
'HK MOD P9 HECKLER & KOCH GmbH OBERNDORF/NECKAR Made in Germany' on left side of slide. Serial number on left side of slide and right side of frame.

SAFETY
Manual safety catch on left rear of slide, DOWN for SAFE, UP for FIRE A lever beneath the left grip offers control of the hammer. When the hammer is down, pressing this lever will cock it; when the hammer is cocked, pressing this lever, then pulling the trigger, will allow the pressure on the lever to be gently released and the hammer safely lowered.

UNLOADING
Magazine catch at the heel of the butt. Remove magazine. Pull back slide to eject any round from the chamber; inspect chamber through ejection port. Release slide; it will remain open; press down on the cocking lever under the left grip to release the slide; pull the trigger.

Heckler & Koch P7 (Germany)

Developed in response to a German police demand for a pistol which would be safe at all times but without needing to be set to fire before using it. It has a unique grip-catch in the front edge of the butt which, when gripped, engages the trigger with the cocking and firing mechanism. To fire, one simply grips the weapon and pulls the trigger, which then cocks and releases the firing pin. If the weapon is dropped, the grip is released and the weapon is instantly made safe. It uses an unusual gas piston delay system to slow down the opening of the breech after firing.

SPECIFICATION & OPERATION

CARTRIDGE
9mm Parabellum, .40 S&W

DIMENSIONS
Length o/a: 171mm (6.7in)
Barrel: 105mm (4.1in)
Weight: 950g (33.5oz)
Rifling: 4-groove polygonal
Magazine capacity: 8 rounds (P7M8) or 13 (P7M10)

IN SERVICE DATES 1980-

MARKINGS
'HECKLER & KOCH GmbH Oberndorf/Neckar US Pat No 3,566,745 Made in Germany Serial Number'. All on left side of slide. Serial number also on left side of frame. 'P7M8' or 'P7M13' in a panel on the lower part of the butt grip.

SAFETY
No applied safety; a grip control in the butt prevents firing unless the weapon is properly held.

UNLOADING
Magazine catch at left side of butt behind trigger. Remove magazine; pull back slide to eject any round in the chamber; inspect chamber through ejection port. Release slide, squeeze grip and pull trigger.

Heckler & Koch P7K3 (Germany)

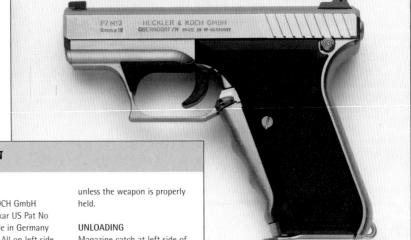

A variation of the basic P7 design, the K3 does away with the gas-retardation system to become a simple fixed-barrel blowback weapon, since it is chambered for the 9mm Short cartridge which does not demand a locked breech. It is also possible to obtain conversion kits for this pistol to adapt it to fire either .22 Long Rifle rimfire cartridges or 7.65mm Browning (.32ACP) cartridges. The kits consist of replacement barrels, magazines and recoil springs and are easily fitted in a few minutes.

SPECIFICATION & OPERATION

CARTRIDGE
9mm Short (.380 Auto) but see above.

DIMENSIONS
Length o/a: 160mm (6.3in)
Barrel: 96.5mm (3.8in)
Weight: 750g (26.5oz)
Rifling: 4-groove polygonal
Magazine capacity: 8 rounds

IN SERVICE DATES 1987-

MARKINGS
'HECKLER & KOCH GmbH Oberndorf/Neckar US Pat No 3,566,745. Made in Germany Serial Number'. All on left side of slide. Serial number also on left side of frame. 'P7K3' in a panel on the lower part of the butt grip.

SAFETY
No applied safety; a grip control in the butt prevents firing unless the weapon is properly held.

UNLOADING
Magazine catch at left side of butt behind trigger. Remove magazine; pull back slide to eject any round in the chamber; inspect chamber through ejection port. Release slide, pull trigger.

Heckler & Koch USP (Germany)

The USP (Universal Self-loading Pistol) was designed with the intention of incorporating all the various features which military and law enforcement agencies appeared to find vital. It uses the Browning cam system of breech locking, together with a patented recoil-reduction system which forms part of the recoil spring and buffer assembly. The frame is of a polymer synthetic material, and metal components are given an anti-corrosion finish.

SPECIFICATION & OPERATION

CARTRIDGE
.40 S&W

DIMENSIONS
Length o/a: 194mm (7.64in)
Barrel: 108mm (4.25in),
Weight: 780g (1lb 11oz)
Rifling: polygonal rifling, rh
Magazine: capacity 13-rounds

IN PRODUCTION 1992-

MARKINGS
H&K USP 9x19mm Serial number on left side of slide Heckler & Koch GmbH Made In Germany on right side of frame.

SAFETY
Safety lever at rear of frame; normally on left, but can be moved to the right side if desires. Lettered S and F, and the appropriate letter should align with a white line on the frame.

UNLOADING
Magazine release lever below trigger-guard. Recesses in the butt permit gripping the magazine to make removal easier. Remove magazine. Draw back slide, inspect chamber through the ejection port. Release slide, press trigger.

The pistol was originally designed and produced in .40 Smith & Wesson caliber, after which variants in .45 ACP and 9 x 19mm Parabellum were produced. All models have a wide variety of options covering the presence or absence of a manual safety catch, of a de-cocking lever, self-cocking only, double action, and ambidextrous controls.

Mauser 1910 and 1934 (Germany)

An enlarged version of a design which appeared in 6.35mm calibre in 1910, this became an officer's pistol during the 1914–18 war and was then sold commercially as the Model 1914. In 1934 a small change in the shape of the butt and some other minor improvements brought the Model 1934 which was sold commercially and then adopted by the German armed forces in 1939-45.

SPECIFICATION & OPERATION

CARTRIDGE
7.65mm Browning (.32 ACP)

DIMENSIONS
Length o/a: 153mm (6.0in)
Barrel: 87mm (3.42in)
Weight: 600g (21oz)
Rifling: 6 grooves, rh
Magazine capacity: 8 rounds

IN PRODUCTION: 1914-34;
1934-45

MARKINGS
`WAFFENFABRIK MAUSER A.G. OBERNDORF aN MAUSER'S PATENT' on left of slide; Mauser badge on left of frame. Serial number on left front of slide and rear of frame (1914). `MAUSER-WERKE AG OBERNDORF aN' on left side of slide. `CAL 7,65 DRPuAP' on right side of slide. Serial numbers on left front of slide and rear of frame (1934).

SAFETY
Manual catch at front edge of left butt grip; UP for fire; when pressed DOWN for safe it locks in this position and can be released by pressing in the button beneath it, when it rises to the FIRE position.

UNLOADING
Magazine catch at heel of butt. Remove magazine; pull back slide to eject any round in the chamber; inspect chamber through ejection port. Release slide, pull trigger.

Mauser Military (c/12) (Germany)

SPECIFICATION & OPERATION

CARTRIDGE
7.63mm Mauser

DIMENSIONS
Length o/a: 318mm (12.5in)
Barrel: 140mm (5.51in)
Weight: 1250g (44oz)
Rifling: 6 grooves, rh
Magazine capacity: 10 rounds

IN SERVICE DATES 1912-45

MARKINGS
'WAFFENFABRIK MAUSER
OBERNDORF A NECKAR' on
right side of frame. Serial
number in full on left side of
chamber and rear of bolt; last
two digits of the number on
almost every removeable part.

SAFETY
Safety lever along side the
hammer; UP for safe, DOWN for
fire. NOTE - Earlier models
worked in the opposite
direction. BE CAREFUL

UNLOADING
This pistol uses an integral box
magazine ahead of the trigger
which is charger-loaded. Unlike
Mannlicher and Roth designs,
there is no short cut to
unloading. Grasp the pistol and
pull back the bolt, gripping the
'wings' at the rear end. This will
eject any round from the
chamber. Release the bolt to
load the next round from the
magazine, pull back to eject,
and carry on loading and
ejecting until the magazine is
empty. Inspect magazine and
chamber, release bolt and pull
the trigger.

There were several variations on the basic
'broomhandle' Mauser (so called because of its
grip), but this M1912 model is probably the most
commonly found and, apart from the safety catch,
is representative of all models. Note that this model
was also made in 9mm Parabellum calibre in 1914-
18 and such weapons have a large figure '9' cut
into the grips and coloured red.

Mauser HSc (Germany)

A double-action weapon introduced in response to Walther's PP model. Most pre-1945 production was taken for military use. Post-1964 production was sold commercially, but in 1984 Mauser ceased manufacture and licensed the design to Renato Gamba of Italy; they ran into difficulties and re-organised in the early 1990s as Societa Armi Bresciana (SAB) and again set about putting the HSc back into production, but few appear to have been made.

SPECIFICATION & OPERATION

CARTRIDGE
7.65mm Browning (.32 ACP)

DIMENSIONS
Length o/a: 152mm (6.0in)
Barrel: 86mm (3.38in)
Weight: 600g (21oz)
Rifling: 6 grooves, rh
Magazine capacity: 8 rounds

IN PRODUCTION 1937-45; 1964-85

MARKINGS
'MAUSERWERKE AG OBERNDORF aN Mod HSc KAL 7,65mm' on left side of slide. Serial number on front edge of butt.

SAFETY
Manual safety catch on left rear of slide; UP for safe, DOWN for fire. There is also a magazine safety.

UNLOADING
Magazine catch at heel of butt. Remove magazine and empty it; pull back slide to eject any round in the chamber; inspect chamber through ejection port. Release slide, replace empty magazine, pull trigger.

Mauser Model 90DA (Germany)

A s with the Mauser 80SA, the Mauser 90DA is also a Hungarian product, finished off in the Mauser factory in Germany. It is the same as the Hungarian FEG P9R but without the ventilated sight rib and also without the option of a light alloy frame. The principal difference between this and the 80SA is that the 90DA is a double-action mechanism, thus the trigger guard is larger and the safety catch doubles as a decocking lever. There is also a Model 90 Compact, the same design but 188mm overall with a 105mm barrel and weighing 950g.

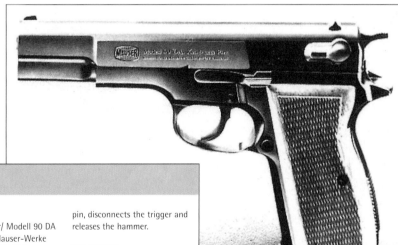

SPECIFICATION & OPERATION

CARTRIDGE
9mm Parabelum

DIMENSIONS
Length o/a: 203mm (8.0in)
Barrel: 118mm (4.65in)
Weight: 1000g (35oz)
Rifling: 6 grooves, rh
Magazine capacity: 14 rounds

IN PRODUCTION 1991-

MARKINGS
'MAUSER Banner/ Modell 90 DA Kal 9mm Para/ Mauser-Werke Oberndorf GmbH D-728 Oberndorf' on left side of slide. Serial number on right side of frame.

SAFETY
Manual safety catch/decocking lever at left rear of slide. Pressing down locks the firing pin, disconnects the trigger and releases the hammer.

UNLOADING
Magazine release button on left side behind trigger. Remove magazine; pull back slide to eject any round in the chamber; inspect chamber through ejection port. Release slide, pull trigger.

Parabellum P'08 (Germany)

There are several variations on the Parabellum (Luger) pistol but the German Army pistole '08 can be taken as representative of the type. Foreign (Persian, Finnish, Portuguese etc) markings can also be found.

SPECIFICATION & OPERATION

CARTRIDGE
9mm Parabellum

DIMENSIONS
Length o/a: 223mm (8.8in)
Barrel: 102mm (4.0in)
Weight: 850g (30oz)
Weight: 850g
Rifling: 8 grooves, rh
Magazine capacity: 8 rounds

IN SERVICE DATES 1908-45

MARKINGS
Maker's name `DWM-ERFUR-KRIEGHOFF-SIMSON' or identifying code `-S/42-42-byf-' engraved on toggle. Year of manufacture engraved over the chamber, Mauser pistols of 1934 and 1935 are marked 'K' and 'G'. Serial number on left side of the barrel extension. Note: these can be duplicated; each of three factories making this pistol used the same numbering system, relying on the factory marking to distinguish them. Each year saw the start of a fresh series of numbers, distinguished by a prefix or suffix letter. It is therefore quite possible to have six pistols all bearing the number 1234, but they would be distinguished by having a letter behind the number and by the maker's mark. Figures stamped on the front end of the barrel extension beneath the rear end of the barrel are the actual (as opposed to the nominal) diameter of the bore across the grooves. Why the makers thought this important enough to stamp on the pistol is a mystery.

SAFETY
Manual safety catch on left side of frame; the operation of this has varied between models, sometimes UP for Safe, sometimes DOWN. However, the frame is stamped with the word `GESICHERT' or `SAFE' or `SEGURANCA' which will be visible when the catch is set to the safe position, and with the word `FEUER' or `FIRE' which will be visible when the catch is set to the fire position. Some models have a grip safety device in the rear edge of the butt which must be squeezed in before the pistol can be fired.

UNLOADING
Magazine catch is a push-button behind the trigger on the left side. Remove magazine. Pull up and back on the two grips on the breech toggle. This will eject any round in the chamber. Inspect the chamber, release the toggle, pull the trigger.

Parabellum 'Long '08' (Germany)

SPECIFICATION & OPERATION

CARTRIDGE
9mm Parabellum

DIMENSIONS
Length o/a: 313mm (12.3in)
Barrel: 200mm (7.9in)
Weight: 1060g (37.3oz)
Rifling: 6 grooves, rh
Magazine capacity: 8 rounds box or 32-round 'snail' magazine

IN SERVICE DATES 1913-45

MARKINGS
Maker's name - `DWM' or `Erfurt' - on the forward toggle link.
Serial numbers on left side of barrel extension, and the last three or four digits will be found repeated on almost every removeable part.

SAFETY
Manual safety catch at left rear of frame; UP for safe, DOWN for fire.

UNLOADING
Magazine catch is a push-button behind the trigger on the left side. Remove magazine. Pull up and back on the two grips on the breech toggle. This will eject any round in the chamber. Inspect the chamber, release the toggle, pull the trigger.

This is simply the standard pistol '08 with a long barrel, introduced for support troops in place of the normal artillery or engineer carbines. They were also used by the German Navy. The 'snail' magazine was not entirely effective and is now rarely encountered with these pistols.

Sauer M38H (Germany)

A modernised version of the M30, of more streamlined appearance and with a double-action trigger.

SPECIFICATION & OPERATION

CARTRIDGE
7.65mm Browning (.32 ACP)

DIMENSIONS
Length o/a: 171mm (6.7in)
Barrel: 83mm (3.25in)
Weight: 720g (25oz)
Rifling: 4 grooves, rh
Magazine capacity: 8 rounds

IN SERVICE DATES 1938-45

MARKINGS
`J.P.SAUER & SOHN SUHL CAL 7,65` on left side of slide; `PATENT` on right side of slide; `S&S` monogram on left butt-grip. `S&S Cal 7,65` on magazine bottom plate. Serial number on rear of frame.

SAFETY
Manual safety catch on left rear of slide; UP for safe, DOWN for fire. A cocking/de-cocking lever lies behind the triggger on the left side of the frame; when the pistol is cocked, pressure on this lever releases the hammer so that it can be lowered safely on to a loaded chamber. When the pistol is uncocked, pressure on this lever will cock the hammer.

Walther P38 (Germany)

Became the German Army official sidearm in 1938 to replace the Luger; was re-adopted when the Bundeswehr reformed in the 1950s, now known as the P1. As with the other Walther pistols, there are slight dimensional differences between the pre- and post-1945 models. There is also a short-barrel model known as the P38K, though this is uncommon. It was the first locked-breech pistol to use the double-action lock, allowing the firer to

SPECIFICATION & OPERATION

CARTRIDGE
9mm Parabellum

DIMENSIONS
Length o/a: 213/218mm (8.38/8.58in)
Barrel: 127/124mm (5.0/4.88in)
Weight: 840/772g (29.6/27.2oz)
Rifling: 6 grooves rh
Magazine capacity: 8 rounds (first figure pre-1945; second figure current production)

IN SERVICE DATES 1938 -

MARKINGS
Pre-1945: (a) 'WALTHER (banner)/Waffenfabrik Walther Zella Mehlis (Thur)/ Walther's {Patent Kal 9m/m/ Mod P38' on left side of slide (very early production); (b) '480 P-38' (late 1939 production) (c) 'ac P-38' (1939-45 production) (d)'WALTHER (banner)/ Carl Walther Waffenfabrik Ulm/Do / P-1' (current production) Serial number left side of slide and left side of frame ahead of trigger guard.

SAFETY
Safety catch on left rear of slide. UP for fire; DOWN for safe, when it locks the safety pin and drops the cocked hammer.

UNLOADING
Magazine catch at heel of butt. Remove magazine; pull back slide to eject any round in the chamber; inspect chamber through ejection port. Release slide, pull trigger.

carry the weapon loaded with the hammer down and then pull through on the trigger to fire the first shot. Surprisingly, the P38 has never ever been copied elsewhere.

Walther PP (Germany)

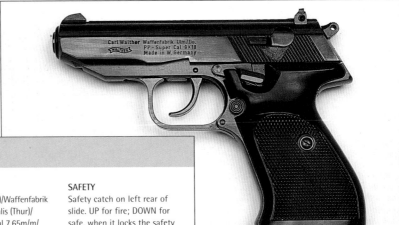

Introduced as a pistol for uniformed police, it was the first successful application of the double-action principle which Walther then adapted to the P38. There is no significant mechanical difference between pre- and post-war models, though the postwar weapons are a few millimetres longer and slightly lighter, and the design has been widely copied, with and without benefit of licence.

SPECIFICATION & OPERATION

CARTRIDGE
7.65mm Browning or 9mm Short

DIMENSIONS
Length o/a: 162/173mm (6.38/6.81in)
Barrel: 85/99mm (3.35/3.90in)
Weight: 710/682g (25/24oz)
Rifling: 6 grooves, rh
Magazine capacity: 8 rounds (first figure pre-1945; second figure current production)

IN SERVICE DATES 1929-

MARKINGS
'WALTHER (banner)/Waffenfabrik Walther Zella-Mehlis (Thur)/ Walther's PatentCal 7.65m/m/ Mod PP' on left side of slide (Pre-1945). 'WALTHER (banner)/ Carl Walther Waffenfabrik Ulm/Do / Model PP Cal 7.65mm' left side of slide, post-1945. Serial number right side of frame behind trigger. May also be found bearing the 'MANURHIN' name; this French company made these pistols under license from about 1948 to 1956.

SAFETY
Safety catch on left rear of slide. UP for fire; DOWN for safe, when it locks the safety pin and drops the cocked hammer.

UNLOADING
Magazine catch at heel of butt. Remove magazine; pull back slide to eject any round in the chamber; inspect chamber through ejection port. Release slide, pull trigger.

Walther PPK (Germany)

This was simply the PP scaled-down for use by plain-clothes police; there are some fundamental design differences in the frame, but mechanically the two work the same way. As with the PP, the post-war models are slightly larger. Easily recognised by the finger-extension on the bottom of the magazine to give a better grip for the hand. A hybrid model, the PPK/S used the slide and barrel of

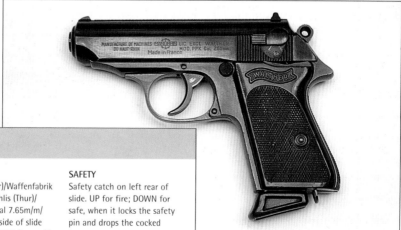

SPECIFICATION & OPERATION

CARTRIDGE
6.35mm Browning, 7.65mm Browning, 9mm Short

DIMENSIONS
Length o/a: 148/155mm (5.70/6.10in)
Barrel: 80/83mm (3.15/3.27in)
Weight: 580/590g (20.46/20.81oz)
Rifling: 6 grooves, rh
Magazine capacity: 7 rounds (first figure pre-1945; second figure current production)

IN SERVICE DATES 1930-

MARKINGS
'WALTHER (banner)/Waffenfabrik Walther Zella-Mehlis (Thur)/ Walther's PatentCal 7.65m/m/ Mod PPK' on left side of slide (Pre-1945). 'WALTHER (banner)/ Carl Walther Waffenfabrik Ulm/Do / Model PPK Cal 7.65mm' left side of slide, post-1945. Serial number right side of frame behind trigger. May also be found bearing the 'MANURHIN' name; this French company made these pistols under license from about 1948 to 1956.

SAFETY
Safety catch on left rear of slide. UP for fire; DOWN for safe, when it locks the safety pin and drops the cocked hammer.

UNLOADING
Magazine catch at heel of butt. Remove magazine; pull back slide to eject any round in the chamber; inspect chamber through ejection port. Release slide, pull trigger.

the PPK and the frame of the PP in order to circumvent the US Gun Control Act of 1968 by increasing its depth dimension, and was restricted to sales in the USA.

Walther P5 (Germany)

This another one of the designs which appeared in response to a German police requirement in the early 1970s for a safe but fast-acting pistol. To achieve this the firing pin of the P5 normally lies lined up with a recess in the hammer; if the hammer falls, it hits the slide but does not touch the firing pin. Only at the instant of hammer release, with the trigger drawn fully back, does a pawl push the entire firing pin up and align it with the solid portion of the hammer. There is also a safety notch in the hammer and the trigger is disconnected from the firing mechanism unless the slide is fully forward.

SPECIFICATION & OPERATION

CARTRIDGE
9mm Parabellum

DIMENSIONS
Length o/a: 181mm (7.125in)
Barrel: 90mm (3.54in)
Weight: 795g (28oz)
Rifling: 6 grooves, rh
Magazine capacity: 8 rounds

IN PRODUCTION 1975-

MARKINGS
'Walther Banner/ P5/Carl Walther Waffenfabrik Ulm/Do.' on left side of slide. Serial number on right side of frame.

SAFETY
There is a de-cocking lever on the left side of the frame which, when pressed, drops the hammer safely on a loaded chamber. All other safety devices are automatic.

UNLOADING
Magazine catch at heel of butt. Remove magazine; pull back slide to eject any round in the chamber; inspect chamber through ejection port. Release slide, pull trigger.

Walther P88 (Germany)

The P88 marked Walther's move away from the wedge system of locking the breech introduced with the P-38 and continued in several other designs. This pistol uses a Browning dropping barrel, controlled by a cam and locking the squared-off area of the chamber into the ejection opening in the slide, a system easier and cheaper to manufacture. The safety system is the same as that adopted in the P5 pistol, described above, and relies upon a non-aligned firing pin; should the hammer accidentally fall, then the end of the firing pin is lined up with a

SPECIFICATION & OPERATION

CARTRIDGE
9mm Parabellum

DIMENSIONS
Length o/a: 187mm (7.36in)
Barrel: 102mm (4.0in)
Weight: 900g (31.75oz)
Rifling: 6 grooves, rh
Magazine capacity: 15 rounds

IN PRODUCTION 1988-

MARKINGS
`Walther Banner/ P88/ Made in Germany' on left side of slide. Serial number on right side of frame.

SAFETY
An ambidextrous de-cocking lever is on both sides of the frame, above the butt. Depressing this allows the hammer to fall safely. All other safety devices are automatic.

UNLOADING
Magazine catch on both sides of butt behind trigger. Remove magazine; pull back slide to eject any round in the chamber; inspect chamber through ejection port. Release slide, pull trigger.

recess in the hammer face. Only by pulling the trigger all the way through will the firing pin be lifted to line up with the solid portion of the hammer.

Desert Eagle (Israel)

A large and heavy pistol which can be found chambered for a variety of cartridges, all of them powerful. It originally appeared in .357 Magnum chambering and others were later added; such powerful loads demand a well-locked breech and the pistol uses a three-lug rotating bolt which is unlocked by gas tapped from the fixed barrel acting on a piston which drives the slide back. This movement of the slide first rotates and then opens the bolt. The pistol may be found with steel or alloy frame and with varying barrel lengths.

SPECIFICATION & OPERATION

CARTRIDGE
.357 Magnum, .44 Magnum, .50 Action Express.

DIMENSIONS (.357 Magnum)
Length o/a: 260mm (10.25in) (with 152mm barrel)
Barrel: 152mm (6in); also 6,10, 14inches (203, 254 and 350mm)
Weight: 1701g (60oz) steel frame; 1474g (52oz) alloy frame.
Rifling: 6 grooves, rh
Magazine: capacity 9 rounds

IN PRODUCTION 1983-

MARKINGS
DESERT EAGLE .357 MAGNUM PISTOL. ISRAEL MILITARY INDUSTRIES. on left side of slide

SAFETY
Ambidextrous manual safety catch on slide locks the firing pin and disconnects the hammer from the trigger.

UNLOADING
Magazine catch on butt, behind trigger. Remove magazine. Pull back slide, exposing chamber. Inspect chamber. Release slide, pull trigger.

Jericho 941 (Israel)

This originally appeared as a 'convertible' pistol in 9mm with a spare barrel, recoil spring and magazine for .41 Action Express cartridges. (The .41AE had the same rim dimensions as 9mm). However, it failed to gain much of a following, and later models dropped the '941' appellation and were convertible to .40 S&W calibre which also has the same rim dimensions but is shorter than the .41AE. There are variant models; the 'F' model has the safety on the frame, while the 'R' Model has it on the slide and uses it as a de-cocking lever.

SPECIFICATION & OPERATION

CARTRIDGE
9mm Parabellum or .41 Action Express

DIMENSIONS
Length o/a: 207mm (8.15in)
Barrel: 120mm (4.7in)
Weight: 1000g (35.3oz)
Rifling: 6 grooves, rh, polygonal
Magazine capacity: 16 (9mm) or 12 (.40) rounds

IN PRODUCTION 1990-

MARKINGS
'JERICHO 941/ ISRAEL MILITARY INDUSTRIES' on left side of slide. 'MADE IN ISRAEL' on right side of frame. Serial number on right side of frame, right side of slide, and last four digits on barrel, visible through the ejection opening.

SAFETY
Manual safety catch/decocking lever at left rear of slide which locks the firing pin, disconnects the trigger and drops the hammer when applied. DOWN for Safe. Later models may have a plain safety catch on the frame or a safety catch/ decocking lever on the slide.

UNLOADING
Magazine catch is a button in the front left side of the butt, behind the trigger. Press in, remove magazine. Pull back slide to eject any round in the breech, inspect chamber through ejection port, release slide. Pull trigger.

Beretta Model 1931 (Italy)

This is an improved version of the Model 1915 with an external hammer. Most were issued to the Italian Navy and have a silver monogram of an anchor and 'RM' let into the wooden butt plates. A few were sold commercially and had plastic grips with 'PB' embossed.

SPECIFICATION & OPERATION

CARTRIDGE
7.65mm ACP

DIMENSIONS:
Length o/a: 152mm (5.0in)
Barrel: 88mm (3.46in)
Weight: 700g (24.6oz)
Rifling: 6 grooves, rh
Magazine capacity: 8 rounds

IN SERVICE DATES 1931-45

MARKINGS
'PISTOLA BERETTA 7.65 BREV 1915-1919 Mo 1931' on left side of slide. Serial numbers right side of frame and slide.

SAFETY
Manual safety catch on left side, above trigger. Forward for SAFE, rearward for FIRE.

UNLOADING
Magazine catch at heel of butt. Remove magazine; pull back slide to eject any round in the chamber; inspect chamber through ejection port. Release slide, pull trigger.

Beretta Model 1934 (Italy)

Probably the most common of the small Berettas, having been widely issued to the Italian armed forces during WWII. Similar to the Model 1931 and best identified by its marking. The year mark in Roman figures indicates the year of the Fascist regime.

SPECIFICATION & OPERATION

CARTRIDGE
9mm Short/.380 Auto

DIMENSIONS:
Length o/a: 150mm (5.9in)
Barrel: 88mm (3.46in)
Weight: 750g (26.5oz)
Rifling: 6 grooves rh
Magazine capacity: 7 rounds

IN SERVICE DATES 1934–45

MARKINGS
`P BERETTA CAL 9 CORTO Mo 1934 BREVETTATO GARDONE V.T. 1937 - XVI' (or other year) on left side of slide. Serial number right side of slide and frame. `PB' monogram bottom of butt-plates.

SAFETY
Manual safety catch on left side, above trigger. Forward for SAFE, rearward for FIRE.

UNLOADING
Magazine catch at heel of butt. Remove magazine; pull back slide to eject any round in the chamber; inspect chamber through ejection port. Release slide, pull trigger.

Beretta M951 (Italy)

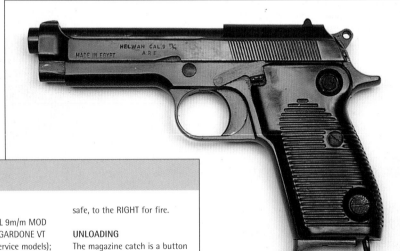

Recognisably Beretta by the cut-away slide top, this was their first locked-breech military pistol. It was also adopted by the Egyptian and Israeli armies, the Nigerian police forces and others.

SPECIFICATION & OPERATION

CARTRIDGE
9mm Parabellum

DIMENSIONS
Length o/a: 203mm (8.0in)
Barrel: 114mm (4.49in)
Weight: 870g (30.7oz)
Rifling: 6 grooves, rh
Magazine capacity: 8 rounds

IN SERVICE DATES 1953-1982
(Italian forces)

MARKINGS
`P BERETTA - CAL 9m/m MOD 1951 - PATENT GARDONE VT ITALIA' (Italian service models); `HELWAN CAL 9 m/m U.A.R.' (Egyptian versions). Serial number on right side of slide.

SAFETY
The safety device is a push-through button at the top of

the grip; push to the LEFT for safe, to the RIGHT for fire.

UNLOADING
The magazine catch is a button at the lower left of the grip; push in and remove magazine. Pull back slide to eject round in the chamber; examine breech; release slide, pull trigger.

Beretta Model 84 (Italy)

The Model 84 represents Beretta's unlocked-breech blowback design in modern form and is accompanied by several variant models. The Model 81 is the same pistol but in 7.65mm ACP calibre; both are double-action pistols and use double-row magazines with a slot in the rear face which allows the contents to be checked. The Models 81BB, 82BB, 83F, 84BB, 84F, 85F, 87BB and 87BB/LB are all variants which differ in the following ways: the BB models have a smaller magazine, a single-column type allowing a thinner butt, a loaded chamber indicator and improved safety by using an automatic

SPECIFICATION & OPERATION

CARTRIDGE
9mm Short (.380 Auto)

DIMENSIONS
Length o/a: 172mm (6.8in)
Barrel: 97mm (3.8in)
Weight: 660g (23oz)
Rifling: 6 grooves, rh
Magazine capacity: 13 rounds

IN SERVICE DATES 1976-

MARKINGS
'PIETRO BERETTA GARDONE V.T.' left side of slide. 'MODEL 84 9m/m' right side of slide; serial number left front of frame.

SAFETY
Manual safety catch at left rear of frame; UP for safe.

UNLOADING
Magazine catch at left side of butt behind trigger. Remove magazine; pull back slide to eject any round in the chamber; inspect chamber through ejection port. Release slide, pull trigger.

firing pin safety system. F models have all the BB features but also have a de-cocking mechanism which allows the hammer to be dropped safely on a loaded chamber. The 87BB/LB has a Long Barrel (150mm). The Model 84 is also made by FN Herstal, as the Browning BDA380.

Beretta Model 92 (Italy)

The Beretta 92, adopted by the US Army as the M9 is offered in many different versions, each denoted by a suffix. The 92S has a decocking lever; the B has an ambidextrous decocking lever; the C is a compact version 197mm long; the F has the trigger guard modified for two-handed grip; the G has no manual safety, just a decocker on the slide. The 92D is double-action only: the hammer cannot be single-action cocked and after each shot the

SPECIFICATION & OPERATION

CARTRIDGE
9mm Parabellum

DIMENSIONS
Length o/a: 217mm (8.54in)
Barrel: 125mm (4.92in)
Weight: 850g (30oz)
Rifling: 6 grooves, rh
Magazine capacity: 15

IN SERVICE DATES 1976-

MARKINGS
'Pist Mod 92 Cal 9 Para BERETTA' left side of slide. Serial number left front of frame.

SAFETY
Manual or other safety depends upon model; see below.

UNLOADING
Magazine catch at left side of butt behind trigger. Remove magazine; pull back slide to eject any round in the chamber; inspect chamber through ejection port. Release slide, pull trigger.

hammer follows the slide back and falls to a safe position. The DS is similar, but without manual safety. The 92M is stainless steel, with a thinner butt and smaller magazine capacity. The Beretta 96 series is a .40 S&W version of the same family and uses the same suffixes.

Beretta Model 93R (Italy)

This is a selective-fire pistol with a selector switch allowing automatic fire at about 1100 rounds per minute in three-round bursts for each pressure of the trigger. There is a fold-down grip in front of the trigger-guard and an extendible steel shoulder stock which can be attached to the rear of the butt. The basic design is that of the Model 92 but with an extended barrel with a muzzle brake. The alternative 20-round magazine extends some distance below the bottom of the butt when fitted.

SPECIFICATION & OPERATION

CARTRIDGE
9mm Parabellum

DIMENSIONS
Length o/a: 240mm (9.45in)
Barrel: 156mm (6.14in) incl muzzle brake
Weight: 1129g (39.8oz)
Rifling: 6 grooves, rh
Magazine capacity: 15 or 20

IN SERVICE DATES 1986-

MARKINGS
'PIETRO BERETTA GARDONE V.T. Cal 9 Parabellum' on left side of slide. Serial number on right side of frame.

SAFETY
Manual safety catch behind trigger. Fire selector lever above left grip: one white dot = single shots, three white dots = three-round burst fire.

UNLOADING
Magazine catch at heel of butt. Remove magazine; pull back slide to eject any round in the chamber; inspect chamber through ejection port. Release slide, pull trigger.

Bernardelli P-018 (Italy)

A conventional double-action semi-automatic. There is also a 'compact' version 109mm long with a 102mm barrel and with a 14-shot magazine. Although specifically designed for police and military use it appears to have had more success on the commercial market.

SPECIFICATION & OPERATION

CARTRIDGE
9mm Parabellum

DIMENSIONS
Length o/a: 213mm (8.38in)
Barrel: 122mm (4.8in)
Weight: 998g (35.2oz)
Rifling: 6 grooves, rh
Magazine capacity: 15

IN SERVICE DATES 1986-

MARKINGS
'VINCENZO BERNARDELLI SpA Gardone V.T. Made in Italy' left side of slide.'Mod P-018 9 Para' left side of frame. Serial number right side of frame and on the barrel, visible in the ejection opening.

SAFETY
Manual safety catch at left rear of frame; UP for safe.

UNLOADING
Magazine catch at heel of butt. Remove magazine; pull back slide to eject any round in the chamber; inspect chamber through ejection port. Release slide, pull trigger.

Tanfoglio TA90 (Italy)

This began more or less as a license-built CZ-75 but improvements have been made and variations introduced, and it is now an independent and original design. The standard model came first; the combat model differs only in its safety arrangements which allow it to be carried 'cocked and locked'. There are also 'Baby Standard' and 'Baby Combat' models which are some 25mm shorter and use 9-round magazines. In addition to 9mm Parabellum, these pistols are available in 9mm IMI, .40 S&W, .41AE, 10mm Auto and .45ACP chamberings.

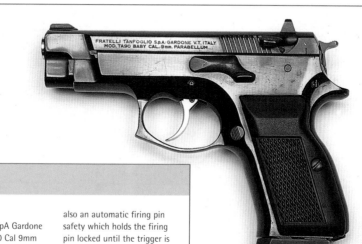

SPECIFICATION & OPERATION

CARTRIDGE
9mm Parabellum

DIMENSIONS
Length o/a: 202mm (7.96in)
Barrel: 120mm (4.7in)
Weight: 1016g (36oz)
Rifling: 6 grooves, rh
Magazine capacity: 15 rounds

IN SERVICE DATES 1983-

MARKINGS
'Fratelli Tanfoglio SpA Gardone V.T. Italy Mod TA-90 Cal 9mm Parabellum' on left side of slide.

SAFETY
Standard models have a manual safety catch on left side of slide which locks firing pin and drops hammer. Combat models have a manual safety catch on left side of frame above butt which simply locks the trigger; there is

also an automatic firing pin safety which holds the firing pin locked until the trigger is correctly pulled through.

UNLOADING
Magazine catch at left side of butt behind trigger. Remove magazine; pull back slide to eject any round in the chamber; inspect chamber through ejection port. Release slide, pull trigger.

Daewoo DP 51 (South Korea)

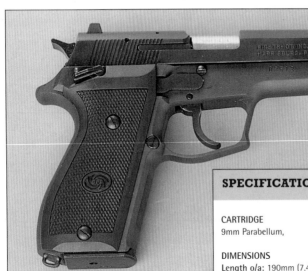

SPECIFICATION & OPERATION

CARTRIDGE
9mm Parabellum,

DIMENSIONS
Length o/a: 190mm (7.48in)
Barrel: 105mm (4.13in)
Weight: 800g (28oz)
Rifling: 6 grooves, rh
Magazine capacity: 13

IN SERVICE DATES 1993-

MARKINGS
'DP51 9MM PARA DAEWOO' on left side of slide. Serial number on right side of frame.

SAFETY
Manual safety catch at left rear of frame; UP for safe.

UNLOADING
Magazine catch at left side of butt behind trigger. Remove magazine; pull back slide to eject any round in the chamber; inspect chamber through ejection port. Release slide, pull trigger.

The DP51 is a semi-automatic pistol in 9mm Parabellum operating on a delayed blowback system. Designed for military and police use, it has a double-action trigger mechanism which is better than most, providing a relatively even trigger pull.

Radom (Poland)

An excellent combat pistol, made for the Polish army pre-1939; during the German occupation it was made for German use but the quality gradually deteriorated. It was reported in late 1994 that it is being put back into production in Poland.

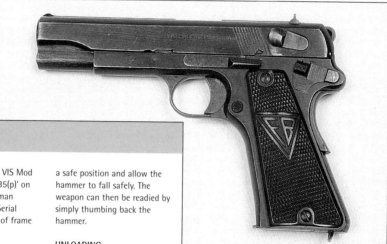

SPECIFICATION & OPERATION

CARTRIDGE
9mm Parabellum

DIMENSIONS
Length o/a: 211mm (8.3in)
Barrel: 115mm (4.52in)
Weight: 1050g (37oz)
Rifling: 6 grooves, rh
Magazine capacity: 8 rounds

IN SERVICE DATES 1936-45

MARKINGS
'F.B. RADOM [year] [Polish eagle] VIS Mo 35 Pat Nr 15567' on left side of slide (Polish models), 'F.B. RADOM VIS Mod 35 Pat Nr 15567 / P. 35(p)' on left side of slide (German occupation models). Serial number on right side of frame above trigger.

SAFETY
The only safety device on this weapon is a grip safety let into the rear of the butt; this must be pressed in before the pistol can be fired. The catch at the left rear of the slide is a de-cocking lever; when depressed it will withdraw the firing pin into a safe position and allow the hammer to fall safely. The weapon can then be readied by simply thumbing back the hammer.

UNLOADING
Magazine catch is a button behind the trigger on the left side. Remove magazine; pull back slide to eject any round in the chamber; inspect chamber through ejection port. Release slide, pull trigger.

Poland P-64 (Poland)

Yet another Walther PP derivative, with elements of the Makarov thrown in, notably the simplified double-action firing mechanism. Like the Makarov, the double-action trigger pull is not very smooth or crisp, but in this type of pistol it is not critical.

SPECIFICATION & OPERATION

CARTRIDGE
9mm Makarov

DIMENSIONS
Length o/a: 155mm (6.1in)
Barrel: 84mm (3.3in)
Weight: 635g (22.4oz)
Rifling: 4 grooves, rh
Magazine capacity: 6 rounds

IN PRODUCTION 1964-84

MARKINGS
'9mm P-64' on left side of slide. Serial number on right side of frame.

SAFETY
Manual safety catch/decocking lever on left rear of slide. Press DOWN to make safe; the firing pin is blocked, the trigger disconnected and the hammer is allowed to fall safely.

UNLOADING
Magazine release on heel of butt. Remove magazine; pull back slide to eject any round in the chamber; inspect chamber through ejection port. Release slide, pull trigger.

Tokarev (Russia)

First produced in 1930, this uses the Browning dropping barrel system of locking and was unusual in having the hammer and its spring and other components in a removable module in the back edge of the butt. It also has the magazine lips machined into the frame, so that slight malformation of the actual magazine does not interfere with feeding. In 1933 the design was modified to have the locking lugs on the barrel all around it, rather then simply on top, a change which

SPECIFICATION & OPERATION

CARTRIDGE
7.62mm Soviet Pistol(also fires 7.63mm Mauser)

DIMENSIONS
Length o/a: 196mm (7.7in)
Barrel: 116mm (4.56in)
Weight: 840q (29.6oz)
Rifling: 4 grooves RH
Magazine capacity: 8 rounds

IN SERVICE DATES 1930-

MARKINGS
Serial number on frame or slide; may have a factory number but generally not.
Copies made in other countries can usually be identified by the badge moulded into the butt grips.

SAFETY
No manual safety; only a half-cock notch on the hammer

UNLOADING
Magazine catch at heel of butt. Remove magazine; pull back slide to eject any round in the chamber; inspect chamber through ejection port. Release slide, pull trigger.

speeded up manufacture and became the TT-33 model It was not in use in large numbers during WWII, but replaced the Nagant revolver thereafter and was widely exported to fellow-Communist countries.

Makarov (Russia)

This is generally assumed to be based upon the Walther PP, though various other versions of its origin exist. The trigger mechanism is simpler than that of the Walther, paid for by a terrible double-action pull. The 9mm Makarov cartridge was designed to obtain the maximum performance from an unlocked breech pistol; though nominally the same size as the western 9mm Police round, the two are not interchangeable. Makarov copies were made in East Germany and China.

SPECIFICATION & OPERATION

CARTRIDGE
9mm Makarov

DIMENSIONS
Length o/a: 161mm (6.3in)
Barrel: 93mm (3.66in)
Weight: 730g (29oz)
Rifling: 4 grooves, rh
Magazine capacity: 8 rounds

IN PRODUCTION 1952-

MARKINGS
Serial number, factory identifying mark and year of manufacture on left side of frame.

SAFETY
Manual safety catch/decocking lever at left rear of slide. Moved UP for safe, it places a block between the hammer and the firing pin, then releases the hammer.

UNLOADING
Magazine release at heel of butt. Remove magazine; pull back slide to eject any round in the chamber; inspect chamber through ejection port. Release slide, pull trigger.

Stechkin (Russia)

This could be considered as an overgrown Walther PP modified to permit selective full-automatic fire; the cyclic rate is about 850 rds/min, though the practical rate is more like 80 rds/min, fired in short bursts. It was issued to officers and NCOs of various Soviet units and also exported to some countries. It was claimed to be an effective submachine gun, but like all such conversions it was difficult to control and was withdrawn in the 1970s when the AKSU shortened version of the AK47 rifle appeared. Terrorists tend to regard it with some favour, and it is likely to appear for a long time to come.

SPECIFICATION & OPERATION

CARTRIDGE
9mm Makarov

DIMENSIONS
Length o/a: 225mm (8.85in)
Barrel: 140mm (5.5in)
Weight: 1030g (36oz)
Rifling: 4 grooves, rh
Magazine capacity: 20 rounds

IN SERVICE DATES 1951-1975

MARKINGS
The serial number and the factory identifying number are stamped on left side of slide.

SAFETY
A safety/selector lever is on the left side of the slide; it has three positions - safe (np), semi-automatic (OA) and full automatic (ABT). When set at safe the slide cannot be retracted.

UNLOADING
Magazine catch at heel of butt. Remove magazine; move selector lever off safe, pull back slide to eject any round in the chamber; inspect chamber through ejection port. Release slide, pull trigger.

PSM (Russia)

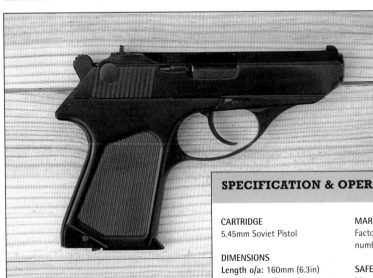

certain specific types of body armour. Although intended strictly as an issue pistol for Soviet security forces, it has become readily available on the black market in Central Europe and might be expected to turn up anywhere in the future.

SPECIFICATION & OPERATION

CARTRIDGE
5.45mm Soviet Pistol

DIMENSIONS
Length o/a: 160mm (6.3in)
Barrel: 85mm (3.35in)
Weight: 460g (16.2oz)
Rifling: 6 grooves, rh
Magazine capacity: 8 rounds

IN PRODUCTION 1980-

MARKINGS
Factory identifier and serial number on left side of slide.

SAFETY
Manual safety catch at the left rear of slide. Pull back to safe.

UNLOADING
Magazine release in heel of butt. Remove magazine; pull back slide to eject any round in the chamber; inspect chamber through ejection port. Release slide, pull trigger.

This is a simple blowback pistol which has been made as slim as possible and without any surface excrescences so that it can be easily concealed. It fires an unusual bottle-necked cartridge at an unremarkable velocity, and yet some reports claim that it has remarkable penetrative powers against

Vektor SP (South Africa)

There are two pistols in this group, the SP1, chambered for the 9mm Parabellum cartridge, and the SP2 chambered for the .40 Smith & Wesson cartridge. Both are to the same design, which uses the same dropping wedge system of breech locking as the Walther P-38 and Beretta 92. The slide of steel, the frame of alloy; an automatic firing pin safety system is used, plus a manual safety catch. The SP2 has an accessory conversion kit, consisting of a barrel, return spring and magazine, allowing it to be reconfigured in 9mm Parabellum calibre.

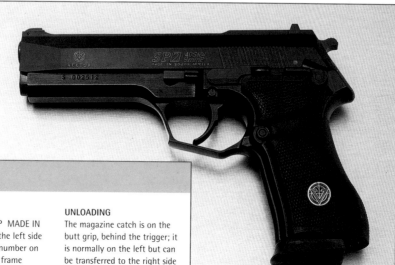

SPECIFICATION & OPERATION

CARTRIDGE
9 x 19mm Parabellum or .40 S&W

DIMENSIONS
Length o/a: 210mm (8.27in)
Barrel: 118mm (4.65in);
Weight: 995g (2lb 3oz)
Rifling: 4 grooves, polygonal, rh
Magazine 15 round detachable box: (11 round in .40 caliber)

IN PRODUCTION 1995-

MARKINGS
VEKTOR SP1 9mm P MADE IN SOUTH AFRICA on the left side of the slide; Serial number on the left side of the frame

SAFETY
There is a manual safety catch which locks both slide and sear, duplicated on both sides of the pistol, and an automatic firing pin safety system.

UNLOADING
The magazine catch is on the butt grip, behind the trigger; it is normally on the left but can be transferred to the right side if required. Remove the magazine. Pull back the slide, to eject any round remaining in the chamber. Inspect the chamber, verifying it to be empty. Release the slide, pull the trigger.

Two compact versions, known as the SP-1 and SP-2 General Officer's Pistols, are also produced. These are 20mm shorter in overall length, with 103mm barrels and weigh 850g, but are otherwise identical with the full-sized weapons.

Astra 300 (Spain)

Smaller version of the Astra 400 introduced in
9mm in 1922 for Spanish Prison Service; in
7.65mm and 9mm in 1923 for commercial sales.
Adopted by Spanish Navy in 9mm in 1928. Total of
85,390 (both calibres) supplied to German Army in
1939–44; these will have German property marks
(WAA and Nazi eagle). Manufacture ceased in 1947,
171,300 having been made.

SPECIFICATION & OPERATION

CARTRIDGE
9mm Short (1922-); 7.65mm ACP
(1923-)

DIMENSIONS
Length: 165mm (6.5in)
Barrel: 90mm (3.54in)
Weight: 560g (19.75oz)
Rifling: 6 grooves, rh
Magazine capacity: 7 rounds

IN SERVICE DATES 1922-50

MARKINGS
'UNCETA y COMPANIA'. Serial
number right rear of frame,
right rear of slide. Astra
trademark behind front sight
blade.

SAFETY
Manual, above trigger; UP for
safe, DOWN for fire. Magazine
safety. Grip safety.

UNLOADING
Magazine catch at heel of butt.
Remove magazine; pull back
slide to eject any round in the
chamber; inspect chamber
through ejection port. Release
slide, pull trigger.

Astra 400 (Spain)

Spanish service pistol 1921-50, sold commercially, also used by French Army in 1920s. Total production 106,175. Based on an earlier Campo-Giro model which it resembles in its tubular receiver and barrel. Copies of this pistol were made during the Spanish Civil War and may be found marked `F. ASCASO TARASA' or simply `RE'(Republica Espana). Although chambered for the 9mm Largo cartridge, these pistols, when in good condition, would chamber and fire 9mm Parabellum, 9mm Steyr, 9mm Browning Long and .38 Super cartridges. It is not

SPECIFICATION & OPERATION

CARTRIDGE
9mm Largo (Bergmann-Bayard); 7.65mm ACP (rare); 7.63mm Mauser (rare)

DIMENSIONS
Length: 235mm (9.25in)
Barrel: 150mm (5.9in)
Weight: 880g (31oz)
Rifling: 6 grooves, rh
Magazine capacity: 8 rounds

IN SERVICE DATES 1921-50

MARKINGS
`UNCETA Y COMPANIA' on slide top; Astra trademark behind front sight. Serial number right rear of frame.

SAFETY
Manual behind trigger, UP for safe; DOWN for fire. Magazine safety. Grip safety.

UNLOADING
Magazine catch at heel of butt. Remove magazine; pull back slide to eject any round in the chamber; inspect chamber through ejection port. Release slide, pull trigger.

recommended in worn pistols. Pistols in 7.65mm and 7.63mm calibres are known but extremely rare and were probably only made as samples.

Astra A-50 (Spain)

This is an updated version of an earlier model known as the 'Constable' and in spite of its appearance is a simple single-action design of fixed-barrel blowback. It can also be found chambered for the 7.65mm Browning cartridge.

SPECIFICATION & OPERATION

CARTRIDGE
9mm Short (.380 Auto)

DIMENSIONS
Length: 168mm (6.6in)
Barrel: 89mm (3.5in)
Weight: 650g (23oz)
Rifling: 6 grooves, rh
Magazine capacity: 7

IN SERVICE DATES 1960-

MARKING
'ASTRA UNCETA CIA Guernica Spain Mod A-50' on left side of slide. Serial number right side of frame.

SAFETY
Manual safety catch at left rear of frame. UP for safe.

UNLOADING
Magazine catch at left side of butt behind trigger. Remove magazine; pull back slide to eject any round in the chamber; inspect chamber through ejection port. Release slide, pull trigger.

Astra A-75 (Spain)

This is more or less a double-action version of the A-70, a compact and robust weapon firing a pair of potent cartridges. Primarily intended for police and military use it has seen some success in the commercial market. In 1994 an aluminium-framed version was announced and a version in .45ACP chambering is expected in late 1995.

SPECIFICATION & OPERATION

CARTRIDGE
9mm Parabellum or .40 S&W

DIMENSIONS
Length o/a: 166mm (6.54in)
Barrel: 89mm (3.50in)
Weight: 880g (31oz)
Rifling: 6 grooves, rh
Magazine capacity: 8 (9mm) or 7 (.40)

IN SERVICE DATES 1993-

MARKINGS
'ASTRA GUERNICA SPAIN A-75' on left side of slide; serial number on right side of frame.

SAFETY
Manual safety catch at left rear of frame; UP for safe. Half-cock notch on the hammer, and automatic firing pin safety device.

UNLOADING
Magazine catch at left side of butt behind trigger. Remove magazine; pull back slide to eject any round in the chamber; inspect chamber through ejection port. Release slide, pull trigger.

Astra A-100 (Spain)

With the introduction of the A-90, the A-80 was discontinued, but there was still a demand for a pistol without manual safety. In addition, overseas markets preferred the magazine release in the butt, behind the trigger. The A-100 attended to these requirements, improved the safety mechanisms and introduced the .45 chambering. It also adopted the larger magazine of the A-90.

SPECIFICATION & OPERATION

CARTRIDGE
9mm Parabellum or .45 ACP

DIMENSIONS
Length o/a: 180mm (7.1in)
Barrel: 96.5mm (3.8in)
Weight: 985g (35oz)
Rifling: 6 grooves, rh
Magazine capacity: 15 (9mm); 9 (.45)

IN SERVICE DATES 1990-

MARKINGS
'ASTRA UNCETA CIA SA GUERNICA SPAIN MOD A-100', on left side of slide. Serial number on left side of frame.

SAFETY
No manual safety is provided; there is a de-cocking lever and an automatic firing pin safety, allowing the pistol to be carried loaded with the hammer down and fired by simply pulling the trigger.

UNLOADING
Magazine catch at left side of butt behind trigger. Remove magazine; pull back slide to eject any round in the chamber; inspect chamber through ejection port. Release slide, pull trigger.

Star M40 Firestar (Spain)

An extremely compact pistol for this calibre, the M40 is slimmer than a comparable revolver and smaller than most automatics of this power. It is easily concealed. It also has the slide running in internal rails in the frame, which helps reliability and accuracy and was among the first of the new generation Star pistol to have this feature. There is also an M45 Firestar, which is the same pistol but chambered for the .45ACP cartridge; the only

SPECIFICATION & OPERATION

CARTRIDGE
.40 S&W

DIMENSIONS
Length o/a: 165mm (6.5in)
Barrel: 86mm (3.4in)
Weight: 855g (30oz)
Rifling: 6 grooves, rh
Magazine capacity: 6 rounds

IN PRODUCTION 1993-

MARKINGS
'STAR EIBAR ESPANA' on left side of slide. Serial number on right side of frame.

SAFETY
Manual safety catch on both sides of the frame above the butt; UP for safe. If the hammer is down, applying this catch locks both hammer and slide. If the hammer is cocked, only the hammer is locked and the slide

can be withdrawn to check on the chamber. There is also an automatic firing pin safety, a magazine safety and a half-cock notch on the hammer.

UNLOADING
Magazine catch at left side of butt behind trigger. Remove magazine; pull back slide to eject any round in the chamber; inspect chamber through ejection port. Release slide, pull trigger.

noticeable difference lies in the slide; the M45 slide is the same width end to end, while the M40 slide has the front section rebated. However the .45 model is some 5mm longer and weighs 1025g.

Star Megastar (Spain)

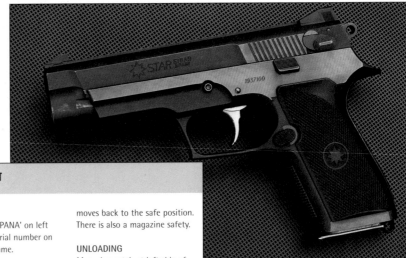

This is a full-sized heavy calibre weapon which has an unusually large magazine capacity; the data for the .45 version is given above, and the 10mm holds 14 rounds and is fractionally heavier. As with the Firestar models, the slide runs inside the frame, giving it good support and contributing to the accuracy.

SPECIFICATION & OPERATION

CARTRIDGE
.45 ACP or 10mm Auto

DIMENSIONS
Length o/a: 212mm (8.35in)
Barrel: 116mm (4.57in)
Weight: 1360g (48oz)
Rifling: 6 grooves rh
Magazine capacity: 12

IN PRODUCTION 1993-

MARKINGS
'STAR EIBAR ESPANA' on left side of slide. Serial number on right side of frame.

SAFETY
Manual safety catch/de-cocking lever on both sides of slide at rear. UP for fire, DOWN for safe, and a continued downward movement will lock the firing pin and release the hammer. When the lever is released it moves back to the safe position. There is also a magazine safety.

UNLOADING
Magazine catch at left side of butt behind trigger. Remove magazine; pull back slide to eject any round in the chamber; inspect chamber through ejection port. Release slide, pull trigger.

SIG P210 (Switzerland)

One of the world's finest pistols, this was developed during WWII by SIG and was adopted by the Swiss Army in 1949, and by the Danish Army shortly afterward. Widely sold, particularly in target versions, further military adoption has evaded it due to the high price. The slide runs in rails inside the frame, one of the first production pistols to use this system, which contributes to its renowned accuracy and reliability. There are several variations; the P-210 has a polished finish and wooden grips; P-210-2

SPECIFICATION & OPERATION

CARTRIDGE
9mm Parabellum

DIMENSIONS
Length o/a: 215mm (8.46in)
Barrel: 120mm (4.7in)
Weight: 900g (31.7oz)
Rifling: 6 grooves, rh
Magazine capacity: 8 rounds

IN PRODUCTION 1949-

MARKINGS
SIG badge, model number (eg P-210-2) and serial number on right side of slide.

SAFETY
Manual safety catch on left side, behind trigger. UP for safe.

UNLOADING
Magazine release at heel of butt. Remove magazine; pull back slide to eject any round in the chamber; inspect chamber through ejection port. Release slide, pull trigger.

sand-blasted finish and plastic grips; P-210-4 was a special model for the West German Border Police; and P-210-5 and -6 are target models, the -5 having an extended barrel.

SIG P220 (Switzerland)

Sales of the SIG P-210 suffered because of its high price, due to the design and method of manufacture, so the company set about simplifying these attributes, resulting in the P220. Even so, the quality is still outstanding. This, and subsequent models, are properly known as 'SIG-Sauer' pistols because SIG collaborated with JP Sauer of Germany, so enabling them to sell Swiss-designed but German-made pistols to the rest of the world,

SPECIFICATION & OPERATION

CARTRIDGE
9mm Parabellum

DIMENSIONS
Length o/a: 198mm (7.8in)
Barrel: 112mm (4.4in)
Weight: 750g (26.5oz)
Rifling: 6 grooves, rh
Magazine capacity: 9 rounds

IN PRODUCTION 1975-

MARKINGS
'SIG SAUER' on left forward area of slide. P220 and serial number on right side of slide. Serial number on right side of frame.

SAFETY
There is a de-cocking lever in the left side of the butt, with its thumb-piece just behind the trigger. Pressing DOWN on this will drop the hammer into a safety notch. There is an automatic firing pin safety which locks the pin at all times except during the last movement of the trigger when firing. Note that the catch above the left grip is a slide lock, used when dismantling the pistol, and not a safety device.

UNLOADING
Magazine release at heel of the butt. Remove magazine; pull back slide to eject any round in the chamber; inspect chamber through ejection port. Release slide, pull trigger.

something not permitted had the pistols been made in Switzerland. Swiss companies are only permitted to sell weapons to people who do not want them.

SIG P225 (Switzerland)

This model, which is more or less a compact version of the P220, was developed in response to a German police demand in the mid-1970s for a 9mm pistol which could be safely carried but brought into action without the need to set or operate any safety devices. It relies on the same automatic firing pin safety and de-cocking lever as do the other SIG models, which was sufficient to meet the German requirement, and it was adopted by a number of Swiss and German police forces.

SPECIFICATION & OPERATION

CARTRIDGE
9mm Parabellum

DIMENSIONS
Length o/a: 180mm (7.1in)
Barrel: 98mm (3.85in)
Weight: 740g (26oz)
Rifling: 6 grooves, rh
Magazine capacity: 8 rounds

IN PRODUCTION 1978-

MARKINGS
'SIG SAUER' on left forward area of slide. P220 and serial number on right side of slide. Serial number on right side of frame.

SAFETY
There is a de-cocking lever in the left side of the butt, with its thumb-piece just behind the trigger. Pressing DOWN on this will drop the hammer into a safety notch. There is an automatic firing pin safety which locks the pin at all times except during the last movement of the trigger when firing. Note that the catch above the left grip is a slide lock, used when dismantling the pistol, and not a safety device.

UNLOADING
Magazine release at heel of the butt. Remove magazine; pull back slide to eject any round in the chamber; inspect chamber through ejection port. Release slide, pull trigger.

SIG P226 (Switzerland)

The P226 was developed in late 1980 as an entrant for the US Army's pistol contest and came within an ace of winning it, being beaten solely on price. In effect, it was the P220 with an enlarged magazine and an ambidextrous magazine release in the forward edge of the butt, behind the trigger, instead of at the base of the butt. About 80 percent of the parts are from the P220 and P225 pistols. Although turned down by the US Army,

SPECIFICATION & OPERATION

CARTRIDGE
9mm Parabellum

DIMENSIONS
Length o/a: 196mm (7.7in)
Barrel: 112mm (4.4in)
Weight: 750g (26.5oz)
Rifling: 6 grooves, rh
Magazine capacity: 15 rounds

IN PRODUCTION 1981-

MARKINGS
'SIG SAUER' on left forward area of slide. 'P226' and serial number on right side of slide. Serial number on right side of frame.

SAFETY
There is a de-cocking lever on the left side of the butt, with its thumb-piece just behind the trigger. Pressing DOWN on this will drop the hammer into a safety notch. There is an automatic firing pin safety which locks the pin at all times except during the last movement of the trigger when firing. Note that the catch above the left grip is a slide lock, used when dismantling the pistol, and not a safety device.

UNLOADING
Magazine release at heel of the butt. Remove magazine; pull back slide to eject any round in the chamber; inspect chamber through ejection port. Release slide, pull trigger.

several US Federal agencies have purchased this pistol and it has been sold widely in the commercial market, almost half a million having been made by 1995.

SIG-Sauer P-228 (Switzerland)

The P-228 appeared in 1988 and was intended to round off the SIG line with a compact pistol having a large magazine capacity. The majority of the parts are from the P-225 and P-226 pistols and it uses the same automatic firing pin safety and de-cocking double-action system. The magazine catch can be mounted on either side of the frame to suit the user's preference.

SPECIFICATION & OPERATION

CARTRIDGE
9 x 19mm Parabellum

DIMENSIONS
Length o/a: 180mm (7.08in)
Barrel: 98mm (3.86in)
Weight: 830g (1lb 13oz)
Rifling: 6 grooves, rh
Magazine: 13-round detachable box

IN PRODUCTION 1988-

MARKINGS
SIG-SAUER on left forward part of slide. P228 MADE IN GERMANY (or W.GERMANY) on right side of slide with serial number. Serial number on right side of frame. CAL 9 PARA in barrel, visible in ejection port.

SAFETY
There is a de-cocking lever on the left side of the butt, with a thumb-piece just behind the trigger. Pressing DOWN on this will drop the hammer into a safety notch. There is an automatic firing pin safety which locks the firing pin at all times except during the final movement of the trigger when firing. Note that the catch above the left grip is a slide lock, used when dismantling the pistol, and is not a safety device.

UNLOADING
Magazine release is normally on the left side of the butt, behind the trigger, but can be moved to the right. Remove the magazine; pull back the slide to eject any round in the chamber. Inspect the chamber through the ejection port. Release the slide, pull the trigger or depress the decocking lever.

SIG-Sauer P-229 (Switzerland)

The P-229 is, except for slight changes in the contours of the slide, the P228 chambered for the .40 Smith & Wesson cartridge. The standard model uses a steel slide and alloy frame; a variant is the P-229SL with stainless steel slide. The principal visible change is the upper surface of the slide which is distinctly rounded rather than the usual SIG angular appearance. The frame and controls are

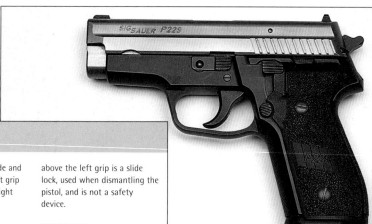

SPECIFICATION & OPERATION

CARTRIDGE
.40 Smith & Wesson or 9mm Parabellum

DIMENSIONS
Length o/a: 180mm (7.08in)
Barrel: 98mm (3.86in)
Weight: 870g (30.7oz)
Rifling: 6 grooves, rh
Magazine capacity: 12 rounds

IN PRODUCTION 1991-

MARKINGS
SIG-SAUER MADE IN GERMANY (or W.GERMANY on early production) on left side of slide.

P229 on right slide of slide and also moulded into the left grip plate, Serial number on right side of slide and frame.

SAFETY
There is a de-cocking lever on the left side of the butt, with a thumb-piece just behind the trigger. Pressing DOWN on this will drop the hammer into a safety notch. There is an automatic firing pin safety which locks the firing pin at all times except during the final movement of the trigger when firing. Note that the catch

above the left grip is a slide lock, used when dismantling the pistol, and is not a safety device.

UNLOADING
Magazine release is normally on the left side of the butt, behind the trigger, but can be moved to the right. Remove the magazine; pull back the slide to eject any round in the chamber. Inspect the chamber through the ejection port. Release the slide, pull the trigger or depress the decocking lever.

exactly as for other SIG pistols, so that familiarity with any one of them ensures easy operation of the remainder. It may be found with alloy frame and carbon steel slide, or alloy frame and stainless steel slide. The latter version is also produced in 9mm Parabellum chambering.

SIG P-230 (Switzerland)

The P-230 is the baby of the SIG family, a blowback pocket or small holster pistol widely used by police and security forces. It was originally produced in 7.65mm Browning caliber, but the 9mm Short version proved more popular and production of the smaller caliber ceased in the 1980s. The pistol is double action, with a de-cocking lever on the left grip, and is fitted with the usual SIG automatic firing pin safety system. Production of the 9mm model ended in 1996.

SPECIFICATION & OPERATION

CARTRIDGE
9 x 17mm Short (.380 Auto)

DIMENSIONS
Length o/a: 168mm (6.61in)
Barrel: 92mm (3.62in)
Weight: 460g (16.2oz)
Rifling: 6 grooves, rh
Magazine: 7-round detachable box

IN PRODUCTION 1972-

MARKINGS
MADE IN W.GERMANY (or GERMANY) P230 with serial number on right side of slide. Late production merely has P230 and the serial number. On the left side of the slide SIG-SAUER 9mm KURZ.

SAFETY
There is no manual safety catch. A de-cocking lever on the left side of the frame allows the cocked hammer to be lowered safely, and there is an automatic firing pin safety system which only allows the firing pin to move during the last movement of the trigger when firing.

UNLOADING
Magazine release is at the heel of the butt. Remove the magazine; pull back the slide to eject any round in the chamber. Inspect the chamber through the ejection port. Release the slide, pull the trigger or depress the decocking lever.

SIG P-232 (Switzerland)

The design was introduced in 1997 as the replacement for the P-230 and is really little more than a re-design of the 230 to take advantage of modern manufacturing techniques. The general shape is the same, with very slight changes in the slide contours. Variant models include one with a stainless steel slide, one with black slide and blued steel frame, and one which is self-cocking ('double action only'). The 7.65mm caliber has also been re-introduced.

SPECIFICATION & OPERATION

CARTRIDGE
7.65mm Browning; 9 x 17mm Short

DIMENSIONS
Length o/a: 168mm (6.61in)
Barrel: 92mm (3.62in),
Weight: 500g (18oz)
Rifling: 6 grooves, rih
Magazine capacity: 7-rounds (8 rounds in 7.65mm calibre)

IN PRODUCTION 1997-

MARKINGS
SIG-SAUER MADE IN GERMANY P232 on left side of slide. Serial number on right side of slide and frame.

SAFETY
There is no manual safety catch. A de-cocking lever on the left side of the frame allows the cocked hammer to be lowered safely, and there is an automatic firing pin safety system which only allows the firing pin to move during the last movement of the trigger when firing.

UNLOADING
Magazine release is at the heel of the butt. Remove the magazine; pull back the slide to eject any round in the chamber. Inspect the chamber through the ejection port. Release the slide, pull the trigger or depress the decocking lever.

Sphinx AT2000 (Switzerland)

This originally appeared in the early 1980s as the 'ITM AT 84'; the ITM company was absorbed by Sphinx Engineering in the late 1980s and the pistol was re-named accordingly. Originally it was little more than a copy of the CZ 75 but the Swiss makers made a number of minor changes and improvements which have resulted in an entirely fresh design, and most of the component parts are no longer interchangeable with the CZ 75 or any of its many clones. Among various patented improvements are

SPECIFICATION & OPERATION

CARTRIDGE
9 x 19mm Parabellum or 9 x 21 IMI or .40 S&W.

DIMENSIONS
Length o/a: 204mm (8.03in)
Barrel: 115mm (4.53in)
Weight: 1030g (36.3oz)
Rifling: 6 grooves, rh
Magazine capacity: 15 rounds

IN PRODUCTION 1985-

MARKINGS
+ SOLOTHURN + AT 2000 on left side of slide. SPHINX MADE IN SWITZERLAND on left side of frame, with serial number.

SAFETY
Manual safety catch on left side of frame can be applied when the hammer is cocked or uncocked. On production after 1990 the safety catch is duplicated on the right side of the frame. There is also an automatic firing pin safety which locks the firing pin except during the final movement of the trigger to release the hammer when firing.

UNLOADING
Magazine release is on the left side of the butt, behind the trigger. Remove the magazine; pull back the slide to eject any round in the chamber. Inspect the chamber through the ejection port. Release the slide, pull the trigger.

an automatic firing pin safety system and a magazine dimensioned so that it can readily digest a variety of cartridges, so that changing calibre merely requires a change of barrel and/or slide, without touching the magazine. There are a number of different options of firing system and finish available.

Kirrikale (Turkey)

This is a Turkish-made copy of the Walther PP and is almost identical to the German product. Kirrikale Tufek became Makina ve Kimya Endustrisi in 1952 and the final two years production carried the MKE badge. Frequently found with American dealer's name `FIREARMS CENTER INC VICTORIA, TEXAS' marked on left side of slide.

SPECIFICATION & OPERATION

CARTRIDGE
7.65mm Browning or 9mm Short

DIMENSIONS
Length o/a: 168mm (6.6in)
Barrel: 95mm (3.74in)
Weight: 700g (24.5oz)
Rifling: 6 grooves, rh
Magazine capacity: 7 rounds

IN PRODUCTION 1948-1954

MARKINGS
`Kirrikale Tufek FB Cap 7,65 [9]mm' on left side of slide. Serial number and year of manufacture on right side of slide. Late models marked `MKE MADE IN TURKEY' on left side of slide.

SAFETY
Safety catch/decocking lever on left rear of slide; press DOWN to make safe and drop hammer.

UNLOADING
Magazine catch at heel of butt. Remove magazine, pull back slide to eject any round in the chamber, release slide. Pull trigger.

Welrod Mark 1 (UK)

The Welrod was a very efficient silent assassination pistol developed by the British Special Operations Executive at their workshops in Welwyn Garden City in 1942 and subsequently manufactured by BSA Ltd. It was a single shot weapon, with a magazine in the butt. To operate it, the knurled cap at the rear end of the receiver was turned

SPECIFICATION & OPERATION

CARTRIDGE:
7.65mm Browning/ .32 ACP

DIMENSIONS
Length: o/a 312mm
Barrel: 111mm
Weight: 1.11kg
Rifling: 6 grooves, rh
Magazine capacity: 6

IN PRODUCTION 1942 – 45

MARKINGS
Serial number on front face of silencer and underneath the rear end of the receiver. No other identifying marks.

SAFETY
Grip safety at top rear of butt must be pressed in to permit trigger movement.

UNLOADING
Magazine catch is the horizontal lever beneath the trigger. Press down, and the entire butt will come away from the receiver, the magazine being a fixture inside the butt. Now grasp the silencer portion, rotate the rear cap anti-clockwise until it unlocks, pull sharply back to extract and eject any round in the chamber. Examine the chamber and feed way via the ejection port ; close the bolt, rotate the end cap to lock, press forward the grip safety and press back the trigger to release the striker. Empty the magazine if necessary and replace the butt unit on to the gun.

and drawn back, opening the bolt, and then pushed forward to load a cartridge and cock the striker, after which it was turned to lock. Grasping the pistol depressed the grip safety at the rear of the butt, and pulling the trigger fired the cartridge. An integral silencer in the forward part of the gun body ensured that the sounds of both propellant and bullet were effectively muffled. There was also a Mark 2 model, similar to the Mark 1 shown here but without a trigger-guard and with the magazine release at the back of the butt.

Smith & Wesson Model 39 (USA)

Smith & Wesson's first modern automatic pistol, this was accompanied by the Model 44, essentially similar but single-action only. It was the progenitor of several similar improved models which followed it. Numbers were taken into service by the US Navy and Special Forces.

SPECIFICATION & OPERATION

CARTRIDGE
9mm Parabellum

DIMENSIONS
Length o/a: 188mm (7.4in)
Barrel: 101mm (4.0in)
Weight: 750g (26.5oz)
Rifling: 6 grooves, rh
Magazine capacity: 8

IN SERVICE DATES 1954-80

MARKINGS
'SMITH & WESSON MADE IN U.S.A. MARCAS REGISTRADAS SMITH & WESSON SPRINGFIELD MASS' and S&W monogram on left side of slide. Serial number left side of frame above trigger.

SAFETY:
Magazine safety. Manual safety catch at rear left of slide which retracts the firing pin and lowers the hammer when applied.

UNLOADING
Magazine catch at left side of butt behind trigger. Remove magazine; pull back slide to eject any round in the chamber; inspect chamber through ejection port. Release slide, pull trigger.

Smith & Wesson Model 59 (USA)

B asically the same pistol as the Model 39 but with a larger magazine; can be quickly distinguished because the rear edge of the butt is straight, and not curved as is that of the Model 39.

SPECIFICATION & OPERATION

CARTRIDGE
9mm Parabellum

DIMENSIONS
Length o/a: 189mm (7.4in)
Barrel: 101mm (4.0in)
Weight: 785g (27.7oz)
Rifling: 6 grooves, rh
Magazine capacity: 14 rounds

IN SERVICE DATES 1954-80

MARKINGS
`SMITH & WESSON MADE IN U.S.A. MARCAS REGISTRADAS SMITH & WESSON SPRINGFIELD MASS' on left side of slide. Serial number left side of frame above trigger.

SAFETY
Magazine safety. Manual safety catch at rear left of slide which retracts the firing pin and lowers the hammer when applied.

UNLOADING
Magazine catch at left side of butt behind trigger. Remove magazine; pull back slide to eject any round in the chamber; inspect chamber through ejection port. Release slide, pull trigger.

Smith & Wesson Third Generation Pistols 9mm (USA)

This series appeared in 1989 and consists of models in 9mm Parabellum, 10mm Auto, .40 Smith & Wesson and .45 ACP calibres. They are identified by a numbering system, the first two digits indicating the calibre, the third indicating features such as compact size or the presence of a decocking lever, and the final figure the material and finish. Thus the 4043 is a .40 S&W with double-action only and an alloy frame with stainless steel slide. The Model 1076 was a special 10mm model developed for the FBI.

SPECIFICATION & OPERATION

CARTRIDGE
9mm Parabellum, 10mm Auto, .40 Smith & Wesson or .45 ACP

DIMENSIONS (Model 4000)
Length o/a: 190.5mm (7/5in)
Barrel: 101.6mm (4.0in)
Weight: 1091g (38.5oz)
Rifling: 6 grooves, rh
Magazine capacity: 11 rounds

IN PRODUCTION 1989-

MARKINGS
'SMITH & WESSON SPRINGFIELD MA. USA' on left side of slide. 'MOD 40XX' and serial number left side of frame.

SAFETY
Ambidextrous safety catch on both sides of the slide at the rear. UP for safe. There are also an automatic firing pin safety system and a magazine safety system. Some models may have a de-cocking lever, some may be double-action only.

UNLOADING
Magazine catch at left side of butt behind trigger. Remove magazine; pull back slide to eject any round in the chamber; inspect chamber through ejection port. Release slide, pull trigger.

Smith & Wesson Third Generation (USA)

This is a generic title for a series of automatic pistols developed by Smith & Wesson and introduced in 1988. Designed in consultation with law enforcement and military experts, these pistols incorporate double-action triggers, triple safety systems, fixed barrel bushings for greater accuracy and simpler take-down, three-dot sights for quick alignment, bevelled magazine well for quicker changing, and a greatly improved trigger pull. The pistols are available in a variety of calibres and

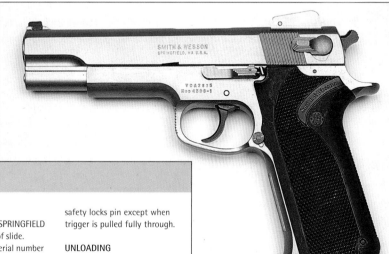

SPECIFICATION & OPERATION

CARTRIDGE
.45ACP

DIMENSIONS
Length: 7.875in
Barrel: 4.0 in
Weight: 39oz
Rifling: 6 grooves, rh
Magazine capacity: 11

IN PRODUCTION: CA 1990 -

MARKINGS
SMITH & WESSON SPRINGFIELD MA. U.S.A. on left of slide. MODEL 4506 and serial number on left of frame S&W monogram on right side of frame

SAFETY
Ambidextrous manual safety catch at rear of frame; UP for SAFE Magazine safety prevents firing when magazine is removed. Automatic firing pin safety locks pin except when trigger is pulled fully through.

UNLOADING
Magazine catch in front left edge of butt, behind trigger. Press in, remove magazine; empty magazine if necessary. Draw back slide, ejecting any round in the chamber. Inspect chamber to ensure the weapon is empty. Release slide. Replace magazine. Pull trigger.

finishes. The pistol illustrated is the Model 4506, the number indicating .45 calibre and a stainless steel slide and frame.

Smith and Wesson Sigma .40 (USA)

The Sigma is Smith & Wesson's venture into using synthetic materials in gun construction, using high-strength polymer material for the frame. It also incorporates the currently-fashionable self-cocking (or 'double-action only') firing mechanism, so that the pistol can be fired without delay or preparation. The basic model is chambered for the .40 S&W cartridge, but it is also available in 9mm Parabellum and a sub-compact model in 9mm Short is also manufactured.

SPECIFICATION & OPERATION

CARTRIDGE
.40 S&W

DIMENSIONS:
Length: 188mm
Barrel: 114mm
Weight: 737g
Rifling: 6 groove, rh
Magazine Capacity: 15

IN PRODUCTION: 1994 -

MARKINGS
SMITH & WESSON Model SW40 on left side of slide. Serial number on right side of frame.

SAFETY
There is no manual safety catch, all safety being automatic. There is a safety device built in to the trigger, and there is also an automatic firing pin safety system such that the firing pin cannot move unless the trigger is fully pulled through.

UNLOADING
Magazine catch on left front edge of butt, behind trigger. Remove the magazine and empty it is necessary. Pull back the slide so as to eject any round left in the chamber. Examine the chamber through the ejection port and ensure it is empty. Release the slide. Replace the magazine.

Smith & Wesson Model 2213 (USA)

The smallest automatic pistols of the Smith & Wesson range, the 2213 is a simple blowback in .22 calibre but produced with a stainless steel slide and alloy frame and intended for serious outdoor use. Its partner is the Model 2214 which is exactly the same pistol but with a blued carbon steel slide in an alloy frame. While both are advertised as being for the 'casual plinker and outdoorsman' they would, of course, be useful home defence weapons.

SPECIFICATION & OPERATION

CARTRIDGE
.22 Long Rifle rimfire

DIMENSIONS
Length: 6.125in
Barrel: 3.0in
Weight: 18oz
Rifling: 6 grooves, rh
Magazine capacity: 8

IN PRODUCTION: CA 1989 –

MARKINGS
MODEL 2213 and serial number on left side of frame. S&W monogram on right side of frame.

SAFETY
Manual safety catch at left rear of frame. UP for SAFE

UNLOADING
Magazine catch at heel of butt; remove magazine and empty it if required. Pull back slide to eject any round in the chamber. Inspect chamber through ejection opening. Release slide, pull trigger. Replace empty magazine in pistol.

AMT Hardballer (USA)

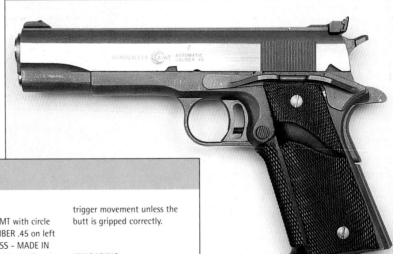

A faithful stainless steel copy of the full sized Colt Government 1911A1 pistol with a magazine capacity of 7 rounds of .45 ACP. Also available in a 'Long slide' version with a 178mm barrel and weight of 1303g.

SPECIFICATION & OPERATION

CARTRIDGE
.45 ACP

DIMENSIONS
Length: 216mm (8.5in)
Barrel: 127mm (5in)
Weight: 1076g (38oz)
Rifling: 6 grooves rh
Magazine capacity: 7

IN PRODUCTION 1977 -

MARKINGS
HARDBALLER , AMT with circle AUTOMATIC CALIBER .45 on left of slide, STAINLESS - MADE IN USA on right of slide, AMT and serial number on right of frame.

SAFETY
Manual safety catch lever on top left of frame at the rear. UP for safe, DOWN for fire. A grip safety is incorporated into the rear of the frame which blocks trigger movement unless the butt is gripped correctly.

UNLOADING
Magazine catch at left side of butt behind trigger, pressed in to release magazine. Remove magazine; pull back slide to eject any round in the chamber; inspect chamber through ejection port. Release slide, pull trigger.

AMT On Duty (USA)

A new design pistol making extensive use of machined Aluminium (frame) and steel investment castings (trigger group and internal parts) as well as a stamped sheet metal slide. Based on the .40 S&W cartridge with a 9mm Parabellum version also produced that is slightly heavier. Both

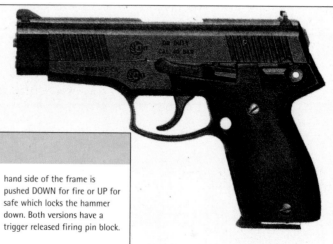

SPECIFICATION & OPERATION

CARTRIDGE
9mm Parabellum, .40 S&W

DIMENSIONS
Length: 203mm (8in)
Barrel: 114mm (4,5in)
Weight: 840g (29.5oz)
Rifling: 6 grooves rh
Magazine capacity: 15 (9mm), 11 (.40 S&W)

IN PRODUCTION 1991 -

MARKINGS
AMT Motif, ON DUTY (9mm), or AMT Motif, ON DUTY CAL .40 S&W (.40 S&W) on left of slide, IRWINDALE CA on left of frame, MADE IN USA on right of slide, serial number and AMT motif on right of frame.

SAFETY
There are two versions of the AMT On Duty. The 'decocker' model has a manual decocking lever at rear of the left hand side of the frame which is pushed UP to decock. The 'double action only' can only be fired by trigger cocking. The safety lever at rear of the left hand side of the frame is pushed DOWN for fire or UP for safe which locks the hammer down. Both versions have a trigger released firing pin block.

UNLOADING
Magazine catch at left side of butt behind trigger, pressed in to release magazine. Remove magazine; pull back slide to eject any round in the chamber; inspect chamber through ejection port. Release slide.

models used double column high capacity magazines. Both are available in two versions, 'double action only' and 'decocker' (see safety operation above).

AMT Automag II (USA)

Gas-assisted action, stainless steel self loading pistol in an unusual pistol calibre, .22 WMR made by Arcadia Machine & Tool, Inc in California. The Automags model were briefly branded IAI (Irwindale Arms Inc) in 1990. Three models are made with varying length slides and barrels. The shortest pistol also has a cropped grip and a magazine capacity of 7 rounds. A number of larger calibre 'Automag' pistols are also made with calibres up to .50 Action Express

SPECIFICATION & OPERATION

CARTRIDGE
.22 WMR

DIMENSIONS with 153mm Barrel
Length: 235mm (9.25in)
Barrel: 152mm (6in). 114mm (4.5in) and 86mm (3.35in) barrelled models available.
Weight: 907g (32oz)
Rifling: 6 grooves rh
Magazine capacity: 9

IN PRODUCTION 1986 -

MARKINGS
AMT Motif, AUTOMAG II, .22 RIMFIRE MAGNUM on left of slide, IRWINDALE CA. on left of frame, STAINLESS - MADE IN USA, PAT PENDING on right of slide, serial number on right of frame.

SAFETY
Thumb operated safety lever on left of slide at the rear, UP for fire, DOWN for safe.

UNLOADING
Magazine catch at bottom of butt, pressed back to release

Browning BDM (USA)

This is a variant of the FN-Browning BDA and is a double-action version of the original Browning High-Power. The slide has a more rounded top, and the barrel locks into the ejection opening. The rear sight is micrometer adjustable, and the hammer is a rounded and serrated thumb-spur rather than the usual tapering spur. The safety catch is ambidextrous,. and it is possible to modify the action to provide single-action only.

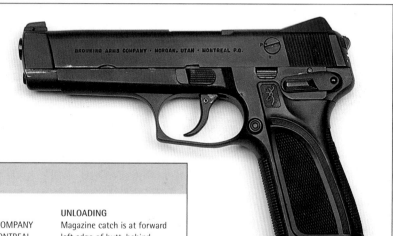

SPECIFICATION & OPERATION

CARTRIDGE
9mm Parabellum

DIMENSIONS
Length: 200mm
Barrel: 119mm
Weight: 930g
Rifling: 6 grooves, rh
Magazine capacity: 15

IN PRODUCTION: 19909 –

MARKINGS
BROWNING ARMS COMPANY
MORGAN UTAH . MONTREAL
P.Q. on left side of slide

SAFETY
Manual safety catch on both
sides of the frame. UP for SAFE

UNLOADING
Magazine catch is at forward
left edge of butt, behind
trigger. Remove magazine. Pull
back slide to eject any round in
the chamber. Inspect chamber
via ejection port. Release slide,
pull trigger. Empty magazine
and replace in pistol.

Colt M1911/M1911A1 (USA)

Also made commercially, when it will carry the Colt name and 'prancing pony' badge. There are many look-alikes: the Spanish Llama and Star, Argentine Hafdasa and Mexican Obregon can be confused with this pistol; the easiest method of distinguishing is to look at the markings. The Norwegian forces used a modified version, made under license, and marked 'Mo 1912'; the slide release catch (on the left side of the frame above the trigger)

SPECIFICATION & OPERATION

CARTRIDGE .45 ACP

DIMENSIONS
Length o/a: 216mm (8.5in)
Barrel: 127mm (5.0in)
Weight: 1105g (39oz)
Rifling: 6 grooves, lh
Magazine capacity: 7 rounds

IN SERVICE DATES 1911-90

MARKINGS
'MODEL OF 1911 U.S.ARMY PATENTED APRIL 29 1907 COLT'S PAT FA MFG CO'
'M1911A1 U.S.ARMY ITHACA GUN CO INC ITHACA N.Y.'
'REMINGTON RAND INC SYRACUSE N.Y. U.S.A.'
'M1911A1 U.S.ARMY U.S.& S.CO SWISSVALE PA USA'
All models will also be marked 'UNITED STATES PROPERTY'. Serial number right side of frame.

SAFETY
Grip safety. Manual safety catch at left rear of frame; UP for safe, DOWN for fire. The hammer may be drawn to the half-cock position.

UNLOADING
Magazine catch on left side, behind trigger; press in to release magazine. Remove magazine, pull back slide to eject any round in the chamber; inspect chamber through ejection opening in slide; release slide, pull trigger.

is longer. A model marked 'RAF' or 'ROYAL AIR FORCE' may be found; this is chambered for the .455 Webley & Scott cartridge NOT interchangeable with .45 ACP!

Colt Delta Elite (USA)

Colt's Government model re-chambered for the powerful 10mm Auto cartridge with a small internal modification to the frame above the slide stop and a recoil absorbing polymer recoil spring guide. Produced in blued carbon steel and stainless steel.

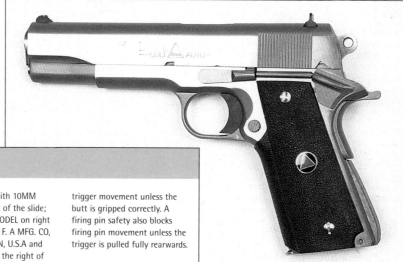

SPECIFICATION & OPERATION

CARTRIDGE
10mm Auto

DIMENSIONS
Length o/a: 216mm (8.5in)
Barrel: 127mm (5.5in)
Weight: 1077g (38oz)
Rifling: 6 grooves lh
Magazine capacity: 8

IN PRODUCTION 1987 -

MARKINGS
DELTA ELITE, COLT AUTO and 'Delta' triangle with 10MM inside on the left of the slide; GOVERNMENT MODEL on right of slide; COLT PT. F. A MFG. CO, HARTFORD, CONN, U.S.A and serial number on the right of the frame.

SAFETY
Manual safety catch lever on top left of frame at the rear. UP for safe, DOWN for fire. A grip safety is incorporated into the rear of the frame which blocks trigger movement unless the butt is gripped correctly. A firing pin safety also blocks firing pin movement unless the trigger is pulled fully rearwards.

UNLOADING
Magazine catch at left side of butt behind trigger, pressed in to release magazine. Remove magazine; pull back slide to eject any round in the chamber; inspect chamber through ejection port. Release slide.

Colt MkIV Series 80 (USA)

A continuation of the powerful .45 ACP Colt 1911/1911A1 pistol line with the inclusion of a firing pin block safety. Available in .38 Super with a higher magazine capacity and 28 grams greater weight. Models have been manufactured from blued carbon steel and stainless steel. A low priced, matte finish, carbon steel version was introduced in 1993 as the model 1991 with slightly different markings, most notably COLT M1991 A1 on the left of the slide.

SPECIFICATION & OPERATION

CARTRIDGE
.45 ACP, .38 Super

DIMENSIONS
Length o/a: 216mm (8.5in)
Barrel: 127mm (5.5in)
Weight: 1078g (38oz)
Rifling: 6 grooves lh
Magazine capacity: 8 (.45), 9 (.38 Super)

IN PRODUCTION 1983 -

MARKINGS
COLT MK IV - SERIES 80 - on left of slide, GOVERNMENT MODEL on right of slide, COLT'S P.T.F.A. MFG. CO. HARTFORD, CONN, U.S.A. and serial number on right of frame.

SAFETY
Manual safety catch lever on top left of frame at the rear. UP for safe, DOWN for fire. A grip safety is incorporated into the rear of the frame which blocks trigger movement unless the butt is gripped correctly. A firing pin safety also blocks firing pin movement unless the trigger is pulled fully rearwards.

UNLOADING
Magazine catch at left side of butt behind trigger, pressed in to release magazine. Remove magazine; pull back slide to eject any round in the chamber; inspect chamber through ejection port. Release slide.

Colt Officer's ACP, Colt Officer's ACP LW (USA)

A very compact version of the .45 ACP Colt Mk IV Government Model with a 37.5mm shorter slide and 10mm shorter frame. The standard models are produced in carbon steel and stainless steel with the lightweight version having an aluminium alloy frame which reduces the weight by 283g. This makes for a potent combination: extremely light and concealable yet still chambered for a major calibre round.

SPECIFICATION & OPERATION

CARTRIDGE
.45 ACP

DIMENSIONS (ACP LW)
Length o/a: 184mm (7.25in)
Barrel: 89mm (3.5in)
Weight: 680g (24oz)
Rifling: 6 grooves lh
Magazine capacity: 6

IN PRODUCTION 1985 -

MARKINGS

COLT MK IV - SERIES 80 - on left of slide, OFFICERS ACP right of slide, COLT'S PT.F.A. MFG. CO. HARTFORD, CONN, U.S.A. and serial number on right of frame.

SAFETY
Manual safety catch lever on top left of frame at the rear. UP for safe, DOWN for fire. A grip safety is incorporated into the rear of the frame which blocks trigger movement unless the butt is gripped correctly. A firing pin safety also blocks firing pin movement unless the trigger is pulled fully rearwards.

UNLOADING
Magazine catch at left side of butt behind trigger, pressed in to release magazine. Remove magazine; pull back slide to eject any round in the chamber; inspect chamber through ejection port. Release slide.

Colt Government Model .380 (USA)

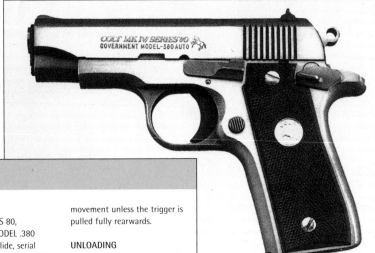

Derived from the .45 ACP Colt Government Model with a similar barrel locking system, the Government .380 is built with a much smaller frame, slide and barrel. The characteristic Model 1911 grip safety is not fitted. A number of variations of the Model .380 are made: with a shorter slide (Mustang Plus II) or shorter slide and frame (.380 Mustang). In addition aluminium alloy framed versions are available with the suffix 'Pocketlite', the heaviest of which weighs only 418g.

SPECIFICATION & OPERATION

CARTRIDGE
.380 Auto (9mmK)

DIMENSIONS
Length o/a: 152mm (5.0in)
Barrel: 82.6mm (3.25in)
Weight: 730g (26oz)
Rifling: 6 grooves lh
Magazine capacity: 7

IN PRODUCTION 1983 -

MARKINGS
COLT MKIV SERIES 80, GOVERNMENT MODEL .380 AUTO on left of slide, serial number on left of frame, COLT'S PT. F .A. MFG. CO. HARTFORD, CONN, U.S.A. on right of frame.

SAFETY
Manual safety catch lever on top left of frame at the rear. UP for safe, DOWN for fire. A firing pin safety also blocks firing pin movement unless the trigger is pulled fully rearwards.

UNLOADING
Magazine catch at left side of butt behind trigger, pressed in to release magazine. Remove magazine; pull back slide to eject any round in the chamber; inspect chamber through ejection port. Release slide.

Colt Double Eagle (USA)

This is based on the Government Model M1911A1 but has the added feature of double-action firing. The shape is slightly different, being more 'streamlined' and with a reverse-curved trigger guard for two-handed firing. Variations include the 'Combat Commander'; version, more compact (114mm barrel) and also available in .40 S&W calibre, and an 'Officer's Model' with an 89mm barrel available only in .45 calibre.

SPECIFICATION & OPERATION

CARTRIDGE
10mm Auto or .45 ACP

DIMENSIONS
Length o/a: 216mm (8.5in)
Barrel: 127mm (5.0in)
Weight: 1092g (38.5oz)
Rifling: 6 grooves, lh
Magazine capacity: 8 rounds

IN PRODUCTION 1990-

MARKINGS
'COLT DOUBLE EAGLE/ MK II SERIES 90' on left side of slide. Serial number on right side of frame.

SAFETY
Safety and de-cocking lever behind the left grip. Pressing down secures the safety pin and drops the hammer, after which pulling the trigger will cock and fire.

UNLOADING
Magazine catch on left side, behind trigger; press in to release magazine. Remove magazine, pull back slide to eject any round in the chamber; inspect chamber through ejection opening in slide; release slide, pull trigger.

Colt 2000 (USA)

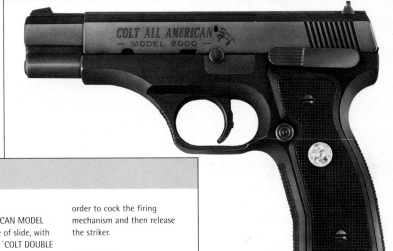

The Model 2000 was to be the Colt for the 21st century; designed by Reid Knight and Eugene Stoner, it broke away from the familiar dropping barrel system of breech locking and adopted a rotating barrel. The trigger mechanism was self-cocking, the object being to duplicate the trigger 'feel' of a double-action revolver. Unfortunately for Colt it failed to attract interest and production ended in 1994.

SPECIFICATION & OPERATION

CARTRIDGE
9mm Parabellum

DIMENSIONS
Length o/a: 192mm (7.5in)
Barrel: 114mm (4.5in)
Weight: 810g (28.6oz)
Rifling: 6 grooves, lh
Magazine capacity: 15

IN PRODUCTION 1991-94

MARKINGS
'COLT ALL AMERICAN MODEL 2000' on left side of slide, with Colt pony badge. 'COLT DOUBLE ACTION 9mm' on right side of slide. Serial number underneath the front end of the frame.

SAFETY
There are no manual safety devices on this pistol. Like a double-action revolver, it is necessary to pull the trigger in order to cock the firing mechanism and then release the striker.

UNLOADING
Magazine catch at either side of butt behind trigger. Remove magazine; pull back slide to eject any round in the chamber; inspect chamber through ejection port. Release slide, pull trigger.

Coonan (USA)

An all stainless steel pistol built on the Colt Government pattern but lengthened and internally modified to accommodate the rimmed .357 Magnum revolver cartridge. Approximately 5000 made in the first ten years of production, mainly with the 'B' series linkless barrel. A limited number were produced to order with a 153mm bull barrel and standard slide. Other options included a shortened and cropped Cadet model.

SPECIFICATION & OPERATION

CARTRIDGE
.357 Magnum

DIMENSIONS
Length o/a: 211mm (8.3in)
Barrel: 127mm (5.0in)
Weight: 1180 (41,6oz)
Rifling: 6 grooves rh
Magazine capacity: 7

IN PRODUCTION 1980 -

MARKINGS
COONAN .357 MAGNUM AUTOMATIC on left of slide, serial number on right of frame.

SAFETY
Manual safety catch lever on top left of frame at the rear. UP for safe, DOWN for fire. A grip safety is incorporated into the rear of the frame which blocks trigger movement unless the butt is gripped correctly.

UNLOADING
Magazine catch at left side of butt behind trigger, pressed in to release magazine. Remove magazine; pull back slide to eject any round in the chamber; inspect chamber through ejection port. Release slide.

L.A.R. Grizzly Win Mag (USA)

As is very obvious from the shape, this is based upon the Colt M1911A1 pistol, the significant external differences being the extended barrel, the squared-off trigger-guard and the micrometer-adjustable rear sight. The pistol is chambered for a unique cartridge, which is arrived at by necking-down the .45 ACP case to accept a .357 bullet, Conversion kits are available to permit changing the calibre top .357 Magnum, .45 ACP, .44 Magnum and various 9mm cartridges. The pistol can also be found

SPECIFICATION & OPERATION

CARTRIDGE
.357/44 Grizzly Win Mag

DIMENSIONS
Length: 266mm
Barrel: 165mm
Weight: 1.350
Rifling: 6 grooves rh
Magazine capacity: 7

IN PRODUCTION: CA. 1985 –

MARKINGS
L.A.R. MFG INC WEST JORDAN UT 84084 U.S.A. and serial number on right rear side of frame. L.A.R. logo and GRIZZLY IN MAG on left side of slide.

SAFETY
Manual safety catch on both sides of frame; Up for SAFE

UNLOADING
Magazine catch at left front edge of butt, behind trigger/ Remove magazine and empty it if necessary. Pull back the slide so as to eject any round left in the chamber, examine the chamber through the ejection port to ensure it is empty. Release the slide, pull the trigger. Replace the empty magazine in the pistol.

with the frame, slide and barrel extended to cater for 8- and 10-inch barrels, and the barrel may also be cut into the form of a compensator.

High Standard (USA)

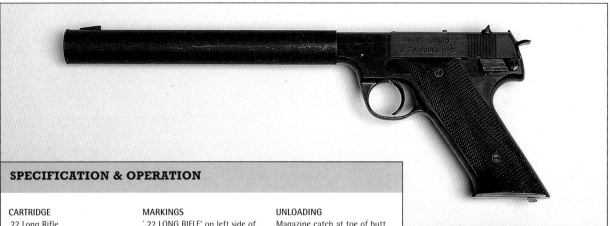

SPECIFICATION & OPERATION

CARTRIDGE
.22 Long Rifle

DIMENSIONS
Length o/a: 279mm (11.0in)
Barrel: 171mm (6.7in)
Weight: 1135g (40oz)
Rifling: 6 grooves, rh
Magazine capacity: 10 rounds

IN PRODUCTION 1932-84

MARKINGS
'.22 LONG RIFLE' on left side of
barrel. 'HIGH STANDARD' on left
side of slide. 'SUPERMATIC
CITATION' on left side of frame.
Serial number on right side of
frame.

SAFETY
Manual safety catch on left rear
of frame; UP for safe.

UNLOADING
Magazine catch at toe of butt.
Remove magazine; pull back
slide to eject any round in the
chamber; inspect chamber
through ejection port. Release
slide, pull trigger.

High Standard produced a wide range of models over the years, but they were all very similar in appearance, differing in sights, grips, barrel contours, finish and so forth but all to the same basic design. Only one was ever produced in a calibre other than .22, and that was the 9mm Short Model G of 1947. Recent information is that the design has been revived by the Mitchell Arms Co of California and will enter production in 1995. The description and data provided here apply to the 'Olympic' model of 1950.

Liberator (USA)

This was a mass-produced assassination pistol which was dropped to resistance groups and guerilla forces in various theatres of war in 1944-45. A short-range, single-shot weapon, a million were made and distributed freely, and will continue to turn up for years. Five loose cartridges can be carried in the hollow butt; ejection of the empty case must be done by using a pencil or some similar implement.

SPECIFICATION & OPERATION

CARTRIDGE
.45 ACP

DIMENSIONS
Length o/a: 141mm (5.55in)
Barrel: 102mm (4.0in)
Weight: 445g (15.6oz)
Rifling: None; smoothbore.
Magazine capacity: Nil; single-shot weapon

IN SERVICE DATES 1942-45

MARKINGS
None.

SAFETY
None.

UNLOADING
Pull back the striker, at the rear end of the pistol, and turn through 90 degrees to lock. Lift the plate closing the rear end of the barrel and check that the chamber is empty. Replace the plate. Turn the striker back through 90 degrees. Press the trigger. Pull out the sliding plate at the bottom of the butt and check that there are no loose cartridges inside.

US Pistol .45in, Mark 23 Mod0 (SOCOM)

In 1990 the US Special Operations Command (SOCOM) requested proposals for an automatic pistol in .45 caliber which was to be of superior accuracy to the M1911A1 and be provided with an accessory silencer and a laser aiming spot projector. The SOCOM pistol is generally similar to the Heckler & Koch USP which formed the basis of the design. It is a double-action design, hammer fired, with the breech locked by the Browning dropping barrel system. An additional recoil buffer is incorporated into the buffer spring assembly to reduce the felt recoil and thus improve the accuracy. The muzzle protrudes from the slide and is threaded to

SPECIFICATION & OPERATION

CARTRIDGE
.45 ACP

DIMENSIONS
Length o/a: 245mm (9.65in);
with suppressor 421mm (16.57in)
Barrel: 149mm (5.87in),
Weight: 1210g (2 lb 10oz); with suppressor and full magazine: 1920g (4lb 4oz)
Rifling: 4 grooves, polygonal, rh

Magazine capacity: 12-rounds

IN PRODUCTION 1995-
MARKINGS
U.S.PROPERTY Mk 23 Mod 0
Serial number on left side of slide

SAFETY
Manual safety on both sides of the frame; there is also, in front of the safety, a manual de-

cocking lever which will lower the cocked hammer silently.

UNLOADING
Magazine catch at rear edge of trigger guard. Remove magazine. Ensure slide lock is unlocked. Draw back slide, inspect chamber through ejection opening. Release slide, press trigger or depress de-cocking lever.

accept the sound suppressor, which is said to give a reduction of 25dB in noise. A slide lock is provided so that the pistol can be fired without the slide recoiling when the silencer is fitted, so that the noise of the slide and the ejected cartridge do not negate the silencing of the shot. The front of the frame is grooved to accept the laser spot projector, which can project either visible or infra-red light. The normal iron sights are also fitted with three tritium markers for firing in poor light.

113

Ruger P-85 (USA)

This first appeared as the P-85, but since then the model number has changed periodically with the year as minor improvements have been made. There are now several variations on the basic design, offering single action, double action, double-action only, and de-cocker models in which the safety catch also releases the hammer. Models in .45 ACP and .40 S&W chambering are also available, differing only slightly from the basic model's dimensions, and there is also a 'convertible' model which allows changing the calibre to 7.65mm Parabellum.

SPECIFICATION & OPERATION

CARTRIDGE
9mm Parabellum

DIMENSIONS
Length o/a: 200mm (7.87in)
Barrel: 114mm (4.48in)
Weight: 910g (32oz)
Rifling: 6 grooves, rh
Magazine capacity: 15

IN PRODUCTION 1987-

MARKINGS
'RUGER P[XXX]' (according to model number) on left side of slide. Serial number on right side of frame. 'BEFORE USING THIS GUN READ WARNINGS IN INSTRUCTION MANUAL AVAILABLE FREE FROM STURM, RUGER & Co INC' on right side of frame. 'STURM, RUGER & CO INC/SOUTHPORT CONN USA' on right side of slide.

SAFETY
Ambidextrous safety catch at rear of slide. When pressed DOWN it secures the firing pin, interposes a block between hammer and pin, and disconnects the trigger.

UNLOADING
Magazine release latch on both sides behind trigger. Remove magazine; pull back slide to eject any round in the chamber; inspect chamber through ejection port. Release slide, pull trigger.

Ruger Standard (USA)

This was the pistol which founded Ruger's business and it has been in constant production since 1949. A Mark 2 introduced in 1982 has some small improvements, including a hold-open latch and a new magazine catch, a new safety catch and a modified trigger system. Both pistols were supplemented by target models with longer barrels, and a 'bull barrel' model with a heavier cylindrical barrel replacing the normal tapered barrel. The 'Government Target Model Mark 2' has a heavy 175mm barrel.

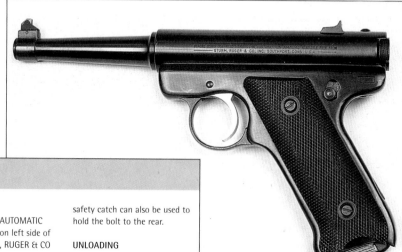

SPECIFICATION & OPERATION

CARTRIDGE
.22 Long Rifle rimfire

DIMENSIONS
Length o/a: 222mm (8.66in)
Barrel: 120mm (4.7in)
Weight: 1020g (36oz)
Rifling: 6 grooves, rh
Magazine capacity: 9 rounds

IN PRODUCTION 1949-

MARKINGS
'RUGER .22 CAL AUTOMATIC PISTOL MARK 1' on left side of receiver. 'STURM, RUGER & CO SOUTHPORT CONN USA' and serial number on right side of receiver.

SAFETY
Sliding button on the left rear side of the frame; push UP for safe. Note that this only works when the gun is cocked. The safety catch can also be used to hold the bolt to the rear.

UNLOADING
Magazine release at heel of butt. Push backwards to remove magazine; pull back bolt, using the 'wings' at the rear end of the receiver, to eject any round in the chamber; inspect chamber through ejection port. Release bolt, pull trigger.

Para Ordnance P14 (Canada)

A high-capacity Canadian-made version of the Colt Government pistol with a double column magazine and supported chamber barrel. The company originally produced aftermarket high capacity frame kits in aluminium and later carbon steel. Complete pistols are available with aluminium alloy or steel frames. Compact models are also listed (P13-45 and P12-45) along with a similar sized range in .40 S&W with slightly higher capacities. The combination of high capacity and powerful cartridges makes a formidable if weighty pistol with the steel frame.

SPECIFICATION & OPERATION

CARTRIDGE
.45 ACP

DIMENSIONS
Length o/a: 216mm (8.5in)
Barrel: 127mm (5.0in)
Weight: 1070g (37.7oz)
Rifling: 6 grooves rh
Magazine capacity: 13

IN PRODUCTION 1991 -

MARKINGS
PARA-ORDNANCE on left of slide, P-14-45 on right of slide, PARA-ORDNANCE INC, FT. LAUDERDALE FL, MADE IN CANADA and serial number on right of frame.

SAFETY
Grip safety. Manual safety catch lever on top left of frame at the rear. UP for safe, DOWN for fire. A firing pin safety also blocks firing pin movement unless the trigger is pulled fully rearwards.

UNLOADING
Magazine catch at left side of butt behind trigger, pressed in to release magazine. Remove magazine; pull back slide to eject any round in the chamber; inspect chamber. Release slide.

Savage (USA)

All Savage pistols look similar, though there are three different models: the 1907 with large grip serrations on the slide and a serrated hammer; the 1915 with similar slide serrations, a grip safety and no hammer; and the 1915 with thinner grip serrations, a spur hammer and a wedge-shaped grip. An American commercial product, numbers of 1915 models were bought by the Portuguese Army and passed on to the Guarda Nacional de Republica, being sold off in the 1950s, so that they are rather more common in Southern Europe than might otherwise be expected.

SPECIFICATION & OPERATION

CARTRIDGE
7.65mm Browning (.32 ACP) or 9mm Short (.380 Auto)

DIMENSIONS
Length o/a: 167mm (6.6in)
Barrel: 96mm (3.77in)
Weight: 625g (22oz)
Rifling: 6 grooves, rh
Magazine capacity: 10 rounds

IN PRODUCTION 1907-28

MARKINGS
'SAVAGE' on left side of frame or top of slide. 1917 models have 'Savage 1917 Model' on left side of frame. All have company trade-mark (an Indian head) with 'Savage Quality' around it moulded into the butt grips.

SAFETY
Manual safety catch left rear of frame; UP for safe.

UNLOADING
Magazine catch at toe of butt. Remove magazine; pull back slide to eject any round in the chamber; inspect chamber through ejection port. Release slide, pull trigger.

Springfield P9 (USA)

This was actually the Czech CZ75 pistol made for Springfield Armory (a private company, not the government establishment, which had closed in1975). There were some slight differences, such as the adoption of a ring hammer instead of the spur type used on the CZ75, and some changes in the frame contours, and it was available in three calibres, and in compact and longslide versions too.

SPECIFICATION & OPERATION

CARTRIDGE
9mm Parabellum

DIMENSIONS
Length o/a: 206mm (8.1in)
Barrel: 120mm (4.7in)
Weight: 1000g (35.25oz)
Rifling: 6 grooves, rh
Magazine capacity: 16 rounds

IN PRODUCTION 1989-93

MARKINGS
'MODEL P9 Cal 9mm' on left side of slide. 'SPRINGFIELD ARMORY' on right side of slide. Serial number on right side of frame.

SAFETY
Manual safety catch on left side of frame above butt. UP for Safe.

UNLOADING
Magazine catch at left side of butt behind trigger. Remove magazine; pull back slide to eject any round in the chamber; inspect chamber through ejection port. Release slide, pull trigger.

REVOLVERS

Taurus 76 (Brazil)

Primarily a target revolver with a Patridge frontsight and adjustable rearsight, the Taurus Model 76 is built on a medium frame the equivalent of Smith & Wesson's 'K' frame revolvers of which is an external copy. Internal parts of the trigger group are different however with a coil mainspring, floating firing pin and transfer bar safety.

SPECIFICATION & OPERATION

CARTRIDGE
.32 S&W Long

DIMENSIONS
Length o/a: 284mm (11.2in)
Barrel: 155mm (6.1in)
Weight: 1190g (42oz)
Rifling: 5 grooves rh
Magazine capacity: 6

MARKINGS
TAURUS BRASIL on left of barrel, .32 LONG on right of barrel, serial number and MADE IN BRAZIL on right of frame below front of cylinder, TAURUS BRASIL in circle with bull's head motif inside on right of frame behind recoil shield.

SAFETY
Trigger operated transfer bar to transmit hammer force to floating firing pin.

UNLOADING
The cylinder latch is on the left of the frame behind the cylinder. Push cylinder latch forwards, swing out the cylinder to the left, eject any live or spent cartridges by pushing the cylinder ejector rod to the rear.

Manurhin MR73 (France)

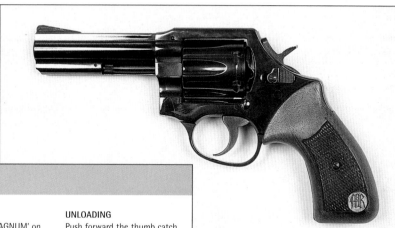

Manurhin were primarily machinery manufacturers but took to making Walther automatic pistols under license after the 1939-45 war. In the early 1970s they began developing a line of revolvers of which the MR73 is the backbone. Though generally based on Smith & Wesson's pattern, it has a few features of its own such as a roller-bearing trigger system which gives a remarkably smooth action. There are various models - the 'Defense' is detailed above - for competition, sport and service use. They are widely sold in Europe and used by many French police forces.

SPECIFICATION & OPERATION

CARTRIDGE
.357 Magnum

DIMENSIONS
Length o/a: 195mm (7.7in)
Barrel: 63mm (2.5in) Other barrel lengths available.
Weight: 880g (31oz)
Rifling: 6 grooves, rh
Chambers: 6

IN PRODUCTION 1973-

MARKINGS
'MR 73 Cal 357 MAGNUM' on right or left side of barrel. Manurhin (MR) monogram badge let into grips.

SAFETY
There is no applied safety device on this revolver.

UNLOADING
Push forward the thumb catch on the left side of the frame, behind the cylinder, and allow the cylinder to swing out to the left of the frame. Press in the ejector rod so as to force out the ejector plate and thus eject the contents of the chambers. Return the cylinder to the frame, ensuring the catch locks.

Korth Combat Magnum (Germany)

Probably the most expensive revolver in the world, and certainly one of the most carefully made, this would be unusual to find in the wrong hands. A conventional double-action revolver with ventilated rib, it has such refinements as an adjustable firing pin and adjustable trigger pull, and its automatic ejection feature is unique.

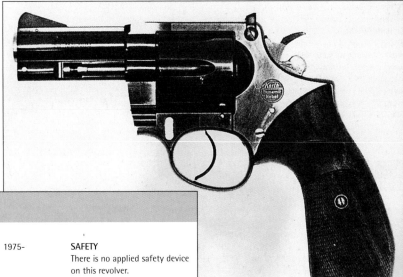

SPECIFICATION & OPERATION

CARTRIDGE
.357 Magnum

DIMENSIONS
Length o/a: 230mm (9.0in)
Barrel: 100mm (3.93in)
Weight: 980g (34.5oz)
Rifling: 6 grooves, rh
Chambers: 6

IN PRODUCTION 1975-

MARKINGS
'.357 MAGNUM' on left side of barrel. 'KORTH' in a circle on the left side of the frame, above the butt.

SAFETY
There is no applied safety device on this revolver.

UNLOADING
Press the release catch alongside the hammer and the cylinder will swing out of the frame and automatically eject the contents of the chambers.

Arminius Model 10 (Germany)

This is shown as an example of a wide range of cheap revolvers made by Friedrich Pickert of Zella St Blasii/Zella Mehlis, Germany, from the 1890s until 1945. Although cheap and simple, they were made of sound material and untold numbers survive in working order. They can be found in 'hammerless' (actually with a concealed hammer) or hammer designs, with varying barrel lengths, and in calibres of .22RF, 5.5mm Velo-Dog, 6.35mm ACP, 7.65mm ACP, .320, 7.5mm Swiss, 7.62mm Nagant and .380.

SPECIFICATION & OPERATION

CARTRIDGE
7.65mm Browning

DIMENSIONS
Length o/a: 155mm (6.1in)
Barrel: 65mm (2.55in)
Weight: 460g (16.2oz)
Rifling: 4 grooves, rh
Chambers: 5

IN PRODUCTION 1895-1945

MARKINGS
'F PICKERT DEUTSCHE INDUSTRIE' on top strap. 'Kal .380' on left side of barrel. Warrior's head trademark moulded into butt grips.

SAFETY
Manual safety catch on left side of frame, above butt. Press forward to fire, back for safe. Locks hammer when applied and also disconnects it from the cylinder to permit unloading.

UNLOADING
Apply the safety catch. Depress the latch on the right side beneath the barrel and pull out the ejector rod from the hollow cylinder axis pin. Swing the ejector about its hinge until it is aligned with the 'one-o-clock' chamber, then thrust out the empty case. Retract the ejector rod, turn the cylinder to the next chamber and repeat until the cylinder is empty.

Cylinders can be 5, 7 or 8 shot, according to calibre, and some models have no ejector rod but require the removal of the cylinder (by pulling out the axis rod) to unload.

Weihrauch HW-9 (Germany)

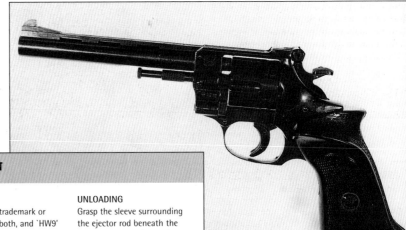

This is actually a .38 frame carrying a .22 barrel, which makes for a heavy pistol of good accuracy. An inexpensive weapon, it and its various derivatives (different barrel lengths, sights and grips) are highly popular throughout Europe .

SPECIFICATION & OPERATION

CARTRIDGE
.22LR

DIMENSIONS
Length o/a: 295mm (11.6in)
Barrel: 150mm (5.9in)
Weight: 1100g (39oz)
Rifling: 8 grooves, rh
Chambers: 6

IN PRODUCTION 1970-

MARKINGS
Warrior's head trademark or `ARMINIUS' or both, and `HW9' on left side of frame. Serial number on right side of frame. `CAL .22 LR' on left side of barrel.

SAFETY
There is no applied safety device on this revolver.

UNLOADING
Grasp the sleeve surrounding the ejector rod beneath the barrel and pull it forward to unlock the cylinder, which will then swing out to the left on a crane. Push the ejector rod back so as to eject the contents of the chambers, then swing the cylinder back into the frame, where it will lock and the spring sleeve will re-engage.

Em-Ge Model 323 'Valor' (Germany)

This is a cheap, but reasonably well made revolver which started life as a starting pistol firing .22 blank cartridges and was then improved into a .22 rimfire revolver and then to a .32 calibre centre-fire model. It can also be found with longer barrels. These were widely exported, particularly to the USA, where they were sold under the 'Valor' name in the middle 1960s until the 1968 Gun Control Act outlawed them. They are still widely found throughout Europe.

SPECIFICATION & OPERATION

CARTRIDGE
.32 S&W Long

DIMENSIONS
Length o/a: 155mm (6.1in)
Barrel: 45mm (1.77in)
Weight: 700g (24.5oz)
Rifling: 6 grooves, rh
Chambers: 6

IN PRODUCTION 1965-

MARKINGS
`CAL 32 S&W lg' on left side of barrel. `MADE IN GERMANY' and serial number right side of barrel. `Gerstenberger & Eberwein Gersetten-Gussenstadt' on left side of frame. Serial number on right side of frame.

SAFETY
There is no applied safety device on this revolver.

UNLOADING
Draw back the hammer to half-cock. Open the loading gate on the right side of the frame, and push out the contents of the chambers one by one by using the ejector rod.

Miroku .38 Special Police (Japan)

This appears to have been intended to attract Japanese police, who had been armed with revolvers during the US occupation after 1945. They preferred to return to automatics once they were given the chance, and Miroku therefore exported almost their entire output to the USA under the EIG and Liberty Chief badges. Cheap but serviceable, they survived for about twenty years. There was also a six-shot model, slightly larger, using the same names.

SPECIFICATION & OPERATION

CARTRIDGE
.38 Special

DIMENSIONS
Length o/a: 195mm (7.7in)
Barrel: 64mm (2.5in)
Weight: 485g (17oz)
Rifling: 6 grooves, rh
Chambers: 5

IN PRODUCTION 1967-1984

MARKINGS
Japanese markings unknown, but those exported carry either an 'EIG' monogram on the left side of the frame or the name 'LIBERTY CHIEF' on the left side of the frame over the trigger. '.38 SPECIAL CALIBER' on left side of barrel. Serial number on right side of frame.

SAFETY
There is no applied safety device on this revolver.

UNLOADING
Pull back the thumb catch on the left side of the frame, behind the cylinder, and allow the cylinder to swing out to the left of the frame. Press in the ejector rod so as to force out the ejector plate and thus eject the contents of the chambers. Return the cylinder to the frame, ensuring the catch locks.

Nagant: Russian Model 1895 (Belgium/Russia)

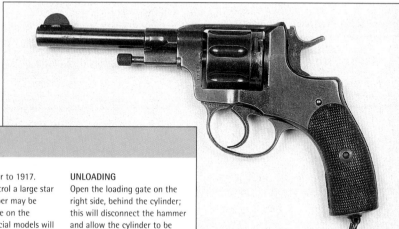

A solid-frame revolver which may be found as a single-action or double-action, the latter being the more common. An unusual weapon; as the hammer is cocked, the cylinder is pushed forward so that the mouth of the chamber engages around the rear of the barrel. This, together with a specially long cartridge with the bullet concealed inside the case, makes a gas-tight joint between cylinder and

SPECIFICATION & OPERATION

CARTRIDGE
7.62mm Russian Revolver

DIMENSIONS
Length o/a: 230mm (9.1in)
Barrel: 114mm (4.5in)
Weight: 750g (26.5oz)
Rifling: 4 grooves, rh
Chambers: 7

IN SERVICE DATES 1895-1950

MARKINGS
Russian inscription in an oval form, with the date of manufacture beneath on left side of frame prior to 1917. Under Soviet control a large star and factory number may be stamped anywhere on the weapon. Commercial models will be marked `L NAGANT BREVETE LIEGE' with a date prior to 1902. Serial number on frame in front of cylinder and possibly on barrel; some commercial models also have it on the cylinder, trigger-guard and butt.

SAFETY
There is no safety device on this revolver.

UNLOADING
Open the loading gate on the right side, behind the cylinder; this will disconnect the hammer and allow the cylinder to be rotated freely by hand. Withdraw the ejector rod forward from its resting place in the axis of the cylinder, swing it to the right and then push back to eject the cartridge from the chamber. Repeat this for all chambers. Replace ejector rod, close loading gate.

barrel. This revolver can be found all over Europe and in any other country which has been subjected to Soviet influence. Modern revolvers using the same principle are produced for target shooting in Russia and the Czech Republic, and ammunition is available in many countries.

Astra Model 960 (Spain)

This is a modern double action revolver for police or commercial use. It is a re-work of the earlier Cadix model (see below) to conform to the US 1968 Gun Control Act, the essential change being the adoption of a transfer bar mechanism to prevent the hammer striking the firing pin unless the trigger is correctly pulled through. The front sight has a larger ramp, the trigger-guard is somewhat more smoothly streamlined and the hammer was made larger. The back sight is adjustable and the mainspring can be regulated for strength of hammer blow. It can be found with a 152mm barrel.

SPECIFICATION & OPERATION

CARTRIDGE
.38 Special

DIMENSIONS
Length o/a: 241mm (9.5in)
Barrel: 102mm (4.0in)
Weight: 1150g (40.5oz)
Rifling: 6 grooves, rh
Chambers: 6

IN PRODUCTION 1973-

MARKINGS
'ASTRA SPAIN' with badge, on right side of frame.'.38 SPECIAL' on left side of barrel. Serial number bottom of butt grip.

SAFETY
There is no safety device on this revolver.

UNLOADING
Press forward the thumb catch on the left side of the frame, behind the cylinder, and allow the cylinder to swing out to the left of the frame. Press in the ejector rod so as to force out the ejector plate and thus eject the contents of the chambers. Return the cylinder to the frame, ensuring the catch locks.

Astra Cadix (Spain)

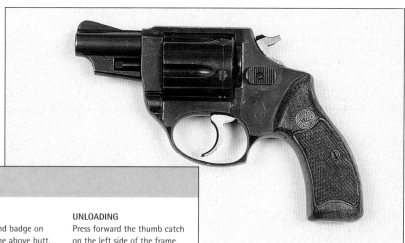

The Cadix is a double-action revolver with swing-out cylinder and can be found in the four calibres quoted below. The dimensions differing accordingly; data given here is for the .38 Special model. Models in .22 calibre have a 9-chambered cylinder, .32 models a 6-chambered cylinder. The ejector rod shroud and trigger guard have very distinctive shapes.

SPECIFICATION & OPERATION

CARTRIDGE
.22LR, .22 Magnum, .32 S&W Long or .38 Special

DIMENSIONS
Length o/a: 229mm (9.0in)
Barrel: 102mm (4.0in)
Weight: 715g (25.2oz)
Rifling: 6 grooves, rh
Chambers: 5

IN PRODUCTION 1958-73

MARKINGS
'ASTRA SPAIN' and badge on right side of frame above butt. Calibre at left front of ejector rod shroud beneath barrel. Serial number on left side of frame behind trigger. Astra badge on grips.

SAFETY
There is no safety device on this revolver.

UNLOADING
Press forward the thumb catch on the left side of the frame, behind the cylinder, and allow the cylinder to swing out to the left of the frame. Press in the ejector rod so as to force out the ejector plate and thus eject the contents of the chambers. Return the cylinder to the frame, ensuring the catch locks.

Astra 357 Police (Spain)

This replaced an earlier model, the 357, and has a stronger hammer, smoothed-out front sight which is less liable to snag in the holster, and a non-adjustable rear sight better adapted to instinctive shooting. The short barrel tends to deliver a good deal of muzzle blast due to the powerful cartridge.

SPECIFICATION & OPERATION

CARTRIDGE
.357 Magnum

DIMENSIONS
Length o/a: 212mm (8.35in)
Barrel: 77mm (3.0in)
Weight: 1040g (36.6oz)
Rifling: 6 grooves, rh
Chambers: 6

IN PRODUCTION 1980-

MARKINGS
`ASTRA SPAIN' and badge on right side of frame, above butt. `357 MAGNUM CTG' on left side of barrel. Serial number left side of frame behind trigger. Astra badges on grips.

SAFETY
There is no safety device on this revolver.

UNLOADING
Press forward the thumb catch on the left side of the frame, behind the cylinder, and allow the cylinder to swing out to the left of the frame. Press in the ejector rod so as to force out the ejector plate and thus eject the contents of the chambers. Return the cylinder to the frame, ensuring the catch locks.

Llama Ruby Extra (Spain)

'Ruby' was a brand name of the Gabilondo Company of Eibar, Spain, first applied to a cheap copy of the Browning 1903 pistol made for the French Army in 1915. The name was allowed to lapse and was replaced by 'Llama' in the 1920s. It was revived in the early 1950s for a series of revolvers which were of generally cheaper construction and finish that their regular Llama range. The 'Ruby Extra' appeared as Models 12, 13 and 14, varying in calibre from .22 to .38 Special and with barrel lengths from 2 to 6 inches. Some

SPECIFICATION & OPERATION (MODEL 14 ILLUSTRATED)

CARTRIDGE
.32 Smith & Wesson Long

DIMENSIONS
Length: 6.4in
Barrel: 2 in
Weight: 1.12lbs
Rifling: 5 grooves, rh
Chambers: 6

IN PRODUCTION: CA 1953 – 1970

MARKINGS
GABILONDO y CIA ELGOEIBAR ESPANA on barrel; RUBY EXTRA in oval on left side of frame,. RUBY in medallions at top of grips.
.32 S & W L on left side of barrel.

SAFETY
None; double-action revolver

UNLOADING
Press forward catch on left side of frame, alongside hammer and swing cylinder out to the left side. Push back on the ejector rod to expel any rounds or empty cases in the chambers. Inspect chambers, swing cylinder back into frame and ensure it locks. Lower hammer if cocked.

had ventilated ribs on the barrel and micrometer sights, other had plain barrels with fixed sights. Manufacture of this particular range of revolvers appears to have ended around 1970.

Llama Comanche (Spain)

A thoroughly conventional modern revolver, quite obviously based upon the Smith & Wesson design and none the worse for that. It is well made of good material and excellently finished, and it enjoys a wide sale throughout Europe as well as being widely exported. It can be met almost anywhere in the world. The company makes several similar revolvers which only differ in size and calibre.

SPECIFICATION & OPERATION

CARTRIDGE
.357 Magnum

DIMENSIONS
Length o/a: 235mm (9.25in)
Barrel: 102mm (4.0in)
Weight: 1035g (36.5oz)
Rifling: 6 grooves, rh
Chambers: 6

IN PRODUCTION 1970-

MARKINGS
'GABILONDO y CIA VITORIA ESPANA' on left side of barrel. 'LLAMA .357 MAG CTG' on right side of barrel. Serial number on bottom of grip frame.

SAFETY
There is no applied safety device on this revolver.

UNLOADING
Push forward the thumb catch on the left side of the frame, behind the cylinder, and allow the cylinder to swing out to the left of the frame. Press in the ejector rod so as to force out the ejector plate and thus eject the contents of the chambers. Return the cylinder to the frame, ensuring the catch locks.

Bulldog revolvers (UK)

This is a class of revolver rather than a specific make. Originated by Webley as a small, heavy-calibre personal defence weapon, it was widely copied by European makers, especially in Belgium. All exhibit the same appearance, a solid frame double-action revolver with a large butt and short, stubby barrel, often oval in section, though round

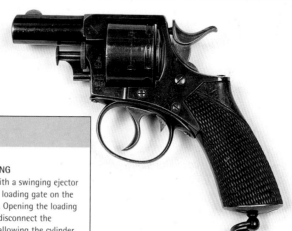

SPECIFICATION & OPERATION

CARTRIDGE
.44 or .45

DIMENSIONS
Length o/a: 159mm (6.25in)
Barrel: 64mm (2.5in)
Weight: 525g (18.5oz)
Rifling: 7 grooves, rh
Chambers: 6

IN PRODUCTION 1878-1939

MARKINGS
Various. Original Webley designs have 'WEBLEY PATENT' on the left side of the frame in front of the cylinder and may also have the Webley 'Winged Bullet' trademark. Others will have their maker's name, usually on top of the barrel, or simply 'BULLDOG' or 'BRITISH BULLDOG' on the barrel.

SAFETY
Not usually found on these revolvers, though some continental makes can be found with a safety catch on the left side of the frame above the butt.

UNLOADING
Usually with a swinging ejector rod and a loading gate on the right side. Opening the loading gate will disconnect the hammer, allowing the cylinder to be rotated, and pushing the ejctor rod back will empty each chamber in turn. Cheaper models will have no ejector system and require the axis pin to be removed to allow the cylinder to drop out of the frame, after which the axis pin is used to punch the case out of each chamber.

and octagonal barrels will be met. Usually in .44 or .45, specimens in .380 are not uncommon, and some European versions may be found chambered for 10.6 German Ordnance and similar metric calibres.

Webley .320 Pocket Hammerless (UK)

In addition to being chambered for the .320 revolver cartridge, these pistols could also be chambered and regulated for the .32 Long or Short Colt or .32 Smith & Wesson cartridges if desired. Nickel plating and mother-of-pearl grips are also to be found. Although produced for several years, it is doubtful if more than 10,000 were made, but they still turn up quite regularly.

SPECIFICATION & OPERATION

CARTRIDGE
.320 Revolver, or similar cartridges

DIMENSIONS
Length o/a: 178mm (7.0in)
Barrel: 76mm (3.0in)
Weight: 480g (17oz)
Rifling: 7 grooves, rh
Chambers: 6

IN PRODUCTION 1901-36

MARKINGS
'WEBLEY'S PATENT' and serial number on right side of frame.

SAFETY
A sliding manual safety catch is fitted over the hammer position. Sliding this back locks the hammer and exposes the word 'SAFE'.

UNLOADING
Press down the thumb catch on the left side of the frame, so withdrawing the stirrup lock and allowing the top strap to rise. Hinge down the barrel, and the ejector plate will be forced out, ejecting the contents of the chambers. Hinge the barrel back until the top strap locks beneath the stirrup catch once more.

Enfield Pistol, Revolver, No2 Mk1 or Mk1* (UK)

After WWI the British Army decided to adopt a .38 revolver, easier for trainees to master. Provided with a 200-grain bullet, it promised sufficient stopping power. Webley produced a design, but one from the Royal Small Arms Factory at Enfield was selected. It was, in fact, little more than a copy of the Webley Mark VI revolver scaled down and with a slightly different trigger mechanism. The Mark I version had a conventional

SPECIFICATION & OPERATION

CARTRIDGE
.38 Mark 1 or 2 British service. Will also chamber .38 S&W, .38 Short Colt, .380 Revolver.

DIMENSIONS
Length o/a: 260mm (10.23in)
Barrel: 127mm (5.0in)
Weight: 780g (27.5oz)
Rifling: 7 grooves, rh
Chambers: 6

IN SERVICE DATES 1931-55

MARKINGS
'ENFIELD/ No 2 [crown] Mk I [or I*]/[year]' on right side of frame below hammer. These pistols were also made by the Albion Motor Company and may be found marked 'ALBION' instead of Enfield. Parts may be found stamped SSM, indicating manufacture of these parts by the Singer Sewing Machine Company. Serial number on bottom of butt frame.

SAFETY
There is no safety device on this revolver.

UNLOADING
Press down the thumb-catch alongside the hammer to release the 'stirrup lock' above the standing breech, and hinge the barrel down to expose the cylinder. This will cause the extractor plate to come out of the cylinder and extract any rounds or cases. Once clear, raise the barrel until the top strap engages with the stirrup lock once more.

hammer with spur; this was inconvenient for tank crews, and the Mark I* had the hammer spur removed; most Mk I were converted to Mk I* on repair, so few originals remain.

Webley .38 Pocket Pistol No 3 (UK)

A popular weapon (it cost £3 when introduced) some 55,000 were made. Although primarily intended for commercial sale, numbers went to government and police agencies and various additional markings can be found. Longer barrels and adjustable sights could also be provided, and there is also a rare variation with no trigger guard and a folding trigger. Small numbers of a version in

SPECIFICATION & OPERATION

CARTRIDGE
.38 S&W

DIMENSIONS
Length o/a: 205mm (8.1in)
Barrel: 76mm (3.0in)
Weight: 540g (19oz)
Rifling: 7 grooves, rh
Chambers: 6

IN PRODUCTION 1896-1939

MARKINGS
'WEBLEY'S PATENT' and serial number on right side of frame.

'MK III .38' on left side of top strap. May have 'MADE IN ENGLAND' on right side of top strap. Weapons purchased by the Indian government will have the Broad Arrow and 'I' mark with the year of purchase on the right side of the frame in front of the trigger.

SAFETY
Not normally fitted, but could be obtained as an optional extra, in which case it is a small lever on the right side of the

frame alongside the hammer. Push UP for safe.

UNLOADING
Press down the thumb catch on the left side of the frame, so withdrawing the stirrup lock and allowing the top strap to rise. Hinge down the barrel, and the ejector plate will be forced out, ejecting the contents of the chambers. Hinge the barrel back until the top strap locks beneath the stirrup catch once more.

.32 calibre were also made; this can be easily recognised by the cylinder having the front half of slightly smaller diameter than the rear half.

Webley Mark IV service revolver (UK)

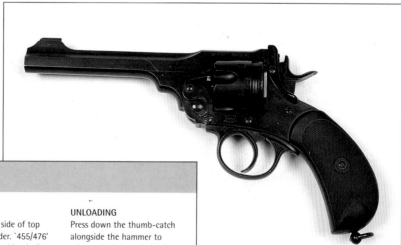

This revolver was widely issued during the South African War and a total of 36,700 were made before production stopped in 1904. It was also sold on the commercial market, where it could be provided with 3, 5 or 6 inch barrels as well as the service 4 inch type. The changes between the earlier Mark III pistol and this one were small improvements found desirable by reports from users, such as a lighter hammer, improved cylinder catch and locks and so on. It is still quite recognisably a Webley.

SPECIFICATION & OPERATION

CARTRIDGE
.455 British Service

DIMENSIONS
Length o/a: 235mm (9.25in)
Barrel: 102mm (4.0in)
Weight: 1020g (36oz)
Rifling: 7 grooves, rh
Chambers: 6

IN SERVICE DATES 1899-

MARKINGS
'MARK IV' on left side of top strap, above cylinder. '455/476' on left side of barrel lug in front of cylinder. 'WEBLEY PATENTS' and winged bullet trademark on left side of frame below cylinder. Serial number right side of frame above trigger.

SAFETY
There is no safety device on this revolver.

UNLOADING
Press down the thumb-catch alongside the hammer to release the 'stirrup lock' above the standing breech, and hinge the barrel down to expose the cylinder. This will cause the extractor plate to come out of the cylinder and extract any rounds or cases. Once clear, raise the barrel until the top strap engages with the stirrup lock once more.

Webley Mark 5 service revolver (UK)

The Mark V differed from the Mark IV by having a slightly larger and stronger cylinder to withstand the additional force generated by smokeless powder cartridges; previous models had been developed around the existing black powder designs, but Cordite had been adopted during the life of the Mark IV pistol, and Webley's felt it better to be on the safe side. It is notable that many earlier revolvers, on repair, were fitted with the Mark V

SPECIFICATION & OPERATION

CARTRIDGE
.455 British Service

DIMENSIONS
Length o/a: 235mm (9.25in)
Barrel: 102mm (4.0in)
Weight: 1005g (35.5oz)
Rifling: 7 grooves, rh
Chambers: 6

IN SERVICE DATES 1913-

MARKINGS
'WEBLEY/MARK V/PATENTS' on left side of frame below cylinder. 'MARK V' on left side of top strap above cylinder. Serial number right side of frame above trigger.

SAFETY
There is no safety device on this revolver.

UNLOADING
Press down the thumb-catch alongside the hammer to release the 'stirrup lock' above the standing breech, and hinge the barrel down to expose the cylinder. This will cause the extractor plate to come out of the cylinder and extract any rounds or cases. Once clear, raise the barrel until the top strap engages with the stirrup lock once more.

cylinder, which necessitated machining away some of the frame to allow it to fit. These cylinders can be recognised by the rear edge being radiused, whereas previous cylinders had a sharp edge.

Webley .38 Mark IV service revolver (UK)

Webley developed this revolver to meet the British requirement for a .38 model, but the Army chose the Enfield design, and therefore Webley produced this commercially. But in World War Two over 100,000 were taken by the British Army and remained in use until 1956. It differs from the Enfield - which was based on the Webley design - only in its lockwork and some minor details, and the two can be easily confused at first glance. A target model, with adjustable backsight, was also sold commercially.

SPECIFICATION & OPERATION

CARTRIDGE
.38 British Service or .38 S&W or similar

DIMENSIONS
Length o/a: 266mm (10.5in)
Barrel: 127mm (5.0in)
Weight: 760g (27oz)
Rifling: 7 grooves, rh
Chambers: 6

IN SERVICE DATES 1929-56

MARKINGS
'MARK IV .38 145/200' on left side of top strap, above cylinder. Webley 'winged bullet' trademark or 'PAT 186131' on right side of frame, below cylinder. Serial number on right side of frame below cylinder.

SAFETY
There is no safety device on this revolver.

UNLOADING
Press down the thumb-catch alongside the hammer to release the 'stirrup lock' above the standing breech, and hinge the barrel down to expose the cylinder. This will cause the extractor plate to come out of the cylinder and extract any rounds or cases. Once clear, raise the barrel until the top strap engages with the stirrup lock once more.

Webley .455 WG model (UK)

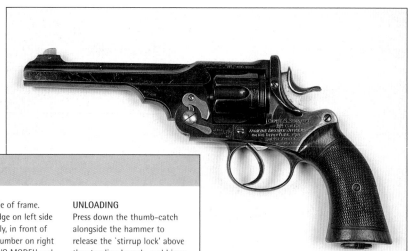

These revolvers were due to a new Webley designer, Michael Kaufman, and his initials and a number are stamped on, largely to ensure that he got his royalties for every pistol. Many improvements which later became standard on other Webley designs first appear on this model, and it was widely bought by British officers and travellers going to the wilder parts of the world in those days. The WG is generally held to mean 'Webley

SPECIFICATION & OPERATION

CARTRIDGE
.455 Webley

DIMENSIONS
Length o/a: 286mm (11.25in)
Barrel: 152mm (6.0in)
Weight: 1138g (40oz)
Rifling: 7 grooves, rh
Chambers: 6

IN SERVICE DATES 1885-1912

MARKINGS
'WEBLEY PATENTS' and Winged Bullet on left side of frame. Calibre of cartridge on left side of barrel assembly, in front of cylinder. Serial number on right side of frame. 'WG MODEL' and year on left side of top strap. The letters 'MK' in a triangle, together with a number will be found on the right side of the frame.

SAFETY
There is no applied safety device on this revolver.

UNLOADING
Press down the thumb-catch alongside the hammer to release the 'stirrup lock' above the standing breech, and hinge the barrel down to expose the cylinder. This will cause the extractor plate to come out of the cylinder and extract any rounds or cases. Once clear, raise the barrel until the top strap engages with the stirrup lock once more.

Government' model, though others say it means 'Webley-Green', Green being the original designer of the stirrup lock.

Charter Arms Pathfinder (USA)

This design is typical of a number of small revolvers made by Charter Arms in calibres from .22 to .44 under names such as 'Undercover', 'Undercoverette', 'Off Duty', 'Pathfinder' and 'Bulldog'. All were side-opening double-action weapons of high quality, intended for concealed carriage by police officers or for personal defence.

SPECIFICATION & OPERATION

CARTRIDGE
.22LR

DIMENSIONS
Length o/a: 188mm (7.48in)
Barrel: 76mm (3.0in)
Weight: 525g (18.5oz)
Rifling: 6 grooves, rh
Chambers: 6

IN PRODUCTION 1964-

MARKINGS
'PATHFINDER .22' on left side of barrel. 'CHARTER ARMS CORP/BRIDGEPORT CONN' on left side of barrel. Serial number on right side of frame.

SAFETY
There is no safety device on this revolver.

UNLOADING
Press forward the thumb catch on the left side of the frame, behind the cylinder, and allow the cylinder to swing out to the left of the frame. Press in the ejector rod so as to force out the ejector plate and thus eject the contents of the chambers. Return the cylinder to the frame, ensuring the catch locks.

Colt New Navy/Army/Marine Revolvers (USA)

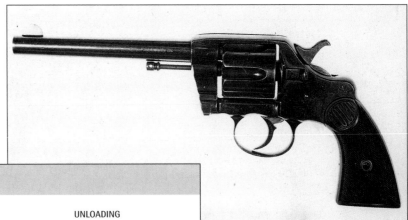

Three variant models; New Army has smooth walnut butt plates, New Navy has hard rubber; New Marine Corps has chequered walnut, slightly rounded butt. New Navy had five rifling grooves. Marine Corps chambered .38 Special cartridge instead of .38 Long Colt. All cylinders revolve anti-clockwise. Distinguishable from Smith & Wesson revolvers by the unsupported ejector rod.

SPECIFICATION & OPERATION

CARTRIDGE
.38 Long Colt

DIMENSIONS
Length o/a: 280mm (11.0in)
Barrel: 152mm (6.0in)
Weight: 965g (34oz)
Rifling: 6 grooves lh
Cylinder: 6 chambers

IN SERVICE DATES 1889-1919

MARKINGS
'COLT .38 DA' left side of barrel;
'US ARMY/NAVY/MARINE CORPS' top of barrel. Serial number: bottom of butt frame.

SAFETY
No manual safety devices but trigger will not operate unless cylinder is closed and locked.

UNLOADING
Pull back the thumb catch on left side of frame, which releases cylinder to open to the left. Push back on ejector rod to eject cases; load chambers individually; swing chamber into frame.

Colt Detective Special (USA)

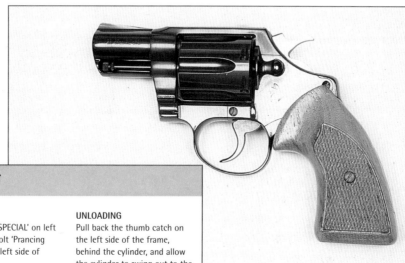

The Detective Special was simply a shortened version of the standard Police Positive Special revolver, designed to provide plain-clothes police with a concealable but powerful pistol. It is very similar to the 'Banker's Special' which appeared in 1928, the principal difference being that the Banker had a full-sized butt with squared-off end, whereas the Detective had a smaller butt with rounded end, again for better concealment. With something in the order of a million and a half of these two models made, they are relatively common.

SPECIFICATION & OPERATION

CARTRIDGE
.38 Special

DIMENSIONS
Length o/a: 171mm (6.73in)
Barrel: 54mm (2.12in)
Weight: 595g (21oz)
Rifling: 6 grooves, lh
Chambers: 6

IN PRODUCTION 1927-86

MARKINGS
'.38 DETECTIVE SPECIAL' on left side of barrel. Colt 'Prancing Pony' badge on left side of frame.

SAFETY
There is no safety device on this revolver.

UNLOADING
Pull back the thumb catch on the left side of the frame, behind the cylinder, and allow the cylinder to swing out to the left of the frame. Press in the ejector rod so as to force out the ejector plate and thus eject the contents of the chambers. Return the cylinder to the frame, ensuring the catch locks.

Colt Pocket Positive (USA)

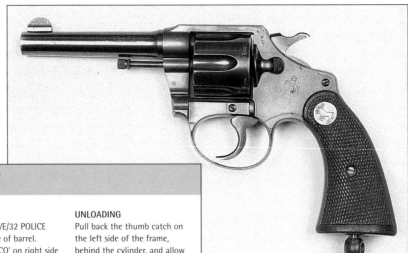

This was the continuance of an earlier mode, the New Pocket Model, but with the addition of the Positive Safety feature described under 'Police Positive'. Serial numbers continued, but any serial number above 30,000 has the Positive Safety device. These pistols can be found chambered either for the .32 Long Colt, or for the .32 Police Positive and .38 S&W Long cartridges. The chambers differ slightly in order to obtain the optimum performance from each round; it is possible to interchange ammunition quite safely.

SPECIFICATION & OPERATION

CARTRIDGE
.32 Long Colt

DIMENSIONS
Length o/a: 215mm (8.5in)
Barrel: 115mm (4.5in)
Weight: 455g (16oz)
Rifling: 6 grooves, lh
Chambers: 6

IN PRODUCTION 1895-1943

MARKINGS
'POCKET POSITIVE/32 POLICE CTG' on left side of barrel. 'COLT'S PAT FA CO' on right side of barrel. Colt 'Prancing Pony' badge on left side of frame.

SAFETY
There is no applied safety device on this revolver.

UNLOADING
Pull back the thumb catch on the left side of the frame, behind the cylinder, and allow the cylinder to swing out to the left of the frame. Press in the ejector rod so as to force out the ejector plate and thus eject the contents of the chambers. Return the cylinder to the frame, ensuring the catch locks.

Colt New Service revolver (USA)

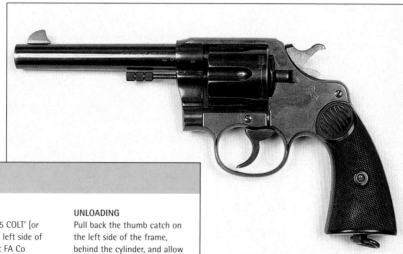

Developed in the 1890s primarily as a military revolver, it was not officially adopted until 1917 (see below) but then continued in production until 1944, some 360,000 being made. The greater part were in .45 Colt or .44 S&W Russian, though such odd calibres as .44/40 Winchester and .476 Eley were produced in small numbers.

SPECIFICATION & OPERATION

CARTRIDGE
.45 Colt and 17 other calibres

DIMENSIONS
Length o/a: 275mm (10.8in)
Barrel: 140mm (5.5in)
Weight: 1162g (41oz)
Rifling: 6 grooves, lh
Chambers: 6

IN SERVICE DATES 1898-1944

MARKINGS
'NEW SERVICE 45 COLT' [or other calibre] on left side of barrel. 'Colt's Pat FA Co Hartford Conn' and various patent dates on top of barrel. Serial number bottom of butt frame.

SAFETY
There is no applied safety device on this revolver.

UNLOADING
Pull back the thumb catch on the left side of the frame, behind the cylinder, and allow the cylinder to swing out to the left of the frame. Press in the ejector rod so as to force out the ejector plate and thus eject the contents of the chambers. Return the cylinder to the frame, ensuring the catch locks.

Colt Model 1917 revolver (USA)

In 1917 the US Army, short of pistols, called on Colt (and Smith & Wesson) to fill the gap using their stock heavy revolver but chambering it for the .45 Auto cartridge fired by the Colt automatic pistol which was the approved sidearm. The M1917 is therefore the New Service but with a shortened cylinder so that the rimless .45 ACP cartridge will load with the aid of two three-shot clips, positioning the rounds in the chamber and giving the ejector something to push against. It remained in service throughout World War II.

SPECIFICATION & OPERATION

CARTRIDGE
.45 ACP

DIMENSIONS
Length o/a: 273mm (10.75in)
Barrel: 140mm (5.5in)
Weight: 1134g (40oz)
Rifling: 6 grooves, lh
Chambers: 6

IN SERVICE DATES 1917-45

MARKINGS
'COLT D.A. 45' on left side of barrel. 'COLT'S PAT FA CO HARTFORD CONN' on top of barrel, with various patent dates.'UNITED STATES PROPERTY' on right side of frame. Serial number bottom of butt.

SAFETY
There is no applied safety device on this revolver.

UNLOADING
Pull back the thumb catch on the left side of the frame, behind the cylinder, and allow the cylinder to swing out to the left of the frame. Press in the ejector rod so as to force out the ejector plate and thus eject the contents of the chambers. Return the cylinder to the frame, ensuring the catch locks.

Colt Python (USA)

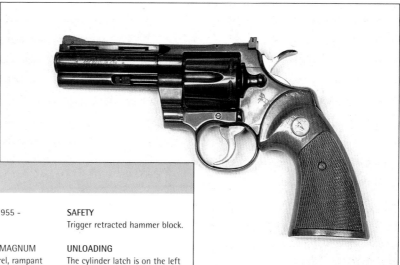

Colt's premier double-action revolver in post war year with a fine reputation for accuracy with its 1:14 twist rifling. Early models were available with a nickel plated finish but this was dropped with the introduction of stainless steel to supplement the existing blued carbon steel models. A very limited number were made with 203mm (8") barrels and chambered for .38 S&W Special only.

SPECIFICATION & OPERATION

CARTRIDGE
.357 Magnum (&.38 S&W Special)

DIMENSIONS
Length o/a: 343mm (13.5in)
Barrel: 203mm (8.0in). Also available 102mm (4in) and 152mm (6in) barrels
Weight: 1360g (48oz)
Rifling: 6 grooves rh
Magazine capacity: 6

IN PRODUCTION 1955 -

MARKINGS
PYTHON 357, 357 MAGNUM CTG on left of barrel, rampant Colt motif on left of frame, COLT'S PT. F. A. MFG. CO. HARTFORD, CONN, USA on right of barrel, serial number on frame under cylinder crane.

SAFETY
Trigger retracted hammer block.

UNLOADING
The cylinder latch is on the left of the frame behind the cylinder. Pull cylinder latch to the rear, swing out the cylinder to the left, eject any live or spent cartridges by pushing the cylinder ejector rod to the rear.

Colt King Cobra (USA)

A budget double-action stainless steel revolver with two barrel lengths and adjustable sights introduced to succeed the Trooper series. Built on a rugged frame with extensive use of cast parts the Cobra was a competitor for the Ruger GP 100 and Smith & Wesson L frame .357 Magnum revolvers.

SPECIFICATION & OPERATION

CARTRIDGE
.357 Magnum

DIMENSIONS: With 153mm (6") barrel
Length o/a: 280mm (11.0in)
Barrel: 152mm (6.0in). Also available with 102mm (4in) barrel.
Weight: 1303g (46oz)
Rifling: 6 grooves lh
Magazine capacity: 6

IN PRODUCTION 1986 -

MARKINGS
KING COBRA and Cobra head motif on left of barrel, rampant Colt motif on left of frame, - 357 MAGNUM CARTRIDGE - & COLT'S PT. F. A. MFG. CO. HARTFORD, CONN, USA on right of barrel, serial number on frame under cylinder crane.

SAFETY
Trigger retracted hammer block

UNLOADING
The cylinder latch is on the left of the frame behind the cylinder. Pull cylinder latch to the rear, swing out the cylinder to the left, eject any live or spent cartridges by pushing the cylinder ejector rod to the rear.

Colt Anaconda (USA)

Colt's largest double-action revolver and made entirely from stainless steel. Chambered for the formidable .44 Magnum cartridge with 6" and 8" barrelled versions also produced chambered for 45 Colt.

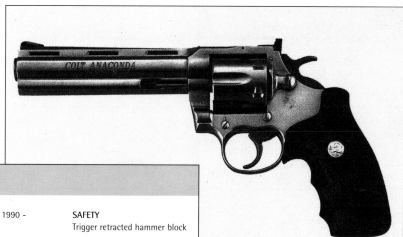

SPECIFICATION & OPERATION

CARTRIDGE
.44 Magnum

DIMENSIONS: With 203mm (8") barrel
Length o/a: 345mm (13.56in)
Barrel: 203mm (8.0in). Also with 102mm (4in) and 152mm (6in) barrels
Weight: 1672g (59oz)
Rifling: 6 grooves lh
Magazine capacity: 6

IN PRODUCTION 1990 -

MARKINGS
COLT ANACONDA 44 MAGNUM on left of barrel, rampant Colt motif on left of frame, DOUBLE-ACTION REVOLVER, COLT'S PT. F. A. MFG. CO. HARTFORD, CONN, USA on right of barrel, serial number on frame under cylinder crane.

SAFETY
Trigger retracted hammer block

UNLOADING
The cylinder latch is on the left of the frame behind the cylinder. Pull cylinder latch to the rear, swing out the cylinder to the left, eject any live or spent cartridges by pushing the cylinder ejector rod to the rear.

Forehand & Wadsworth .38 Hammerless (USA)

As can be seen there is very little to distinguish this from the other popular 1890s pistols, the Smith & Wesson, Harrington & Richardson, Iver Johnson and Hopkins and Allen pocket ejectors. Apart from small details of the triggers and hammers, and perhaps a frame contour or two, they are as alike as peas in a pod. And fragile as they may look, they are sufficiently robust to have lasted for a century and still work well. There must be tens of thousands of them out there.

SPECIFICATION & OPERATION

CARTRIDGE
.38 S&W

DIMENSIONS
Length o/a: 165mm (6.5in)
Barrel: 80mm (3/15in)
Weight: 515g (18oz)
Rifling: 6 grooves, lh
Chambers: 5

IN PRODUCTION 1890-1902

MARKINGS
'FOREHAND ARMS CO WORCESTER MASS' on barrel rib, together with various patent dates. Serial number bottom of butt.

SAFETY
There is no applied safety device on this revolver. Like almost all so-called 'hammerless' revolvers it does have a hammer, concealed under a shroud.

UNLOADING
Press on the hammer shroud to disengage it from the top strap, then hinged the barrel down; this will cause the central ejector plate to empty the chamber. Hinge the barrel back and ensure it snaps into place under the spring catch.

Harrington & Richardson .38 Auto Ejector (USA)

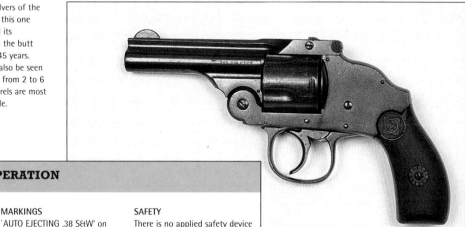

Another of the popular pocket revolvers of the early years of the century, though this one lasted in production for longer than all its competitors and, with some changes in the butt contours, even re-appeared in post-1945 years. Commonly found nickel-plated, it can also be seen in .22 and .32 calibres and with barrels from 2 to 6 inches, though the 3.35 and 4 inch barrels are most common since they are more pocketable.

SPECIFICATION & OPERATION

CARTRIDGE
.38 S&W

DIMENSIONS
Length o/a: 187mm (7.35in)
Barrel: 83mm (3.25in)
Weight: 420g (15oz)
Rifling: 5 grooves, rh
Chambers: 5

IN PRODUCTION 1897-1940

MARKINGS
'AUTO EJECTING .38 S&W' on left side of barrel. 'HARRINGTON & RICHARDSON ARMS COMPANY WORCESTER MASS USA' and various patent dates on top of barrel rib. 'H&R' trademark, a pierced target, on both grips. Serial number on the left side of the butt frame, concealed by the grips.

SAFETY
There is no applied safety device on this revolver.

UNLOADING
Grasp the knurled ends of the spring catch above the standing breech, lift, and hinge the barrel down. This will cause the ejector plate to move out and eject the contents of the chambers. Close the barrel and ensure the spring catch engages.

Hopkins & Allen .38 Safety Police (USA)

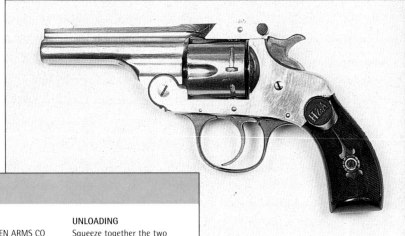

Apart from the catch securing the barrel closed, there is little to distinguish this from any of its contemporaries, but the trigger action is unique; the hammer is mounted on an eccentric axis pin and if it is thumbed back and released it strikes the pistol frame and not the firing pin in the standing breech. Pulling the trigger rotates the axis pin and lowers the hammer so that it will strike the firing pin. It was this which inspired the 'Safety' portion of the name. It was a well-made and sound design, but is less common than the others shown here since it was only made for seven years.

SPECIFICATION & OPERATION

CARTRIDGE
.38 S&W

DIMENSIONS
Length o/a: 185mm (7.28in)
Barrel: 83mm (3.25in)
Weight: 460g (16oz)
Rifling: 6 grooves, rh
Chambers: 5

IN PRODUCTION 1907-14

MARKINGS
'HOPKINS & ALLEN ARMS CO NORWICH CONN' and various patent dates on top barrel rib. Serial number of butt frame beneath grips.

SAFETY
There is no applied safety device on this revolver.

UNLOADING
Squeeze together the two ribbed catches on each side of the top strap to release, then hinge down the barrel to eject the contents of the cylinder. Return the barrel, ensuring that the spring catch engages.

Iver Johnson Safety Automatic (USA)

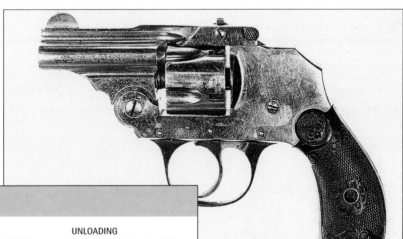

A s with most revolvers of this period, the word 'automatic' means automatic ejection of the spent cases as the barrel is opened. Also as usual, the word 'hammerless' means a concealed hammer, though in this case the frame of the pistol is designed to conceal it, while other makers often used the frame of their hammer models and added a light metal shroud. The 'Safety' title comes from the Iver Johnson 'Hammer the Hammer' transfer bar system which prevents the hammer striking the frame-mounted firing pin unless the trigger is

SPECIFICATION & OPERATION

CARTRIDGE
.32 S&W

DIMENSIONS
Length o/a: 191mm (7.52in)
Barrel: 76mm (3.0in)
Weight: 440g (15.5oz)
Rifling: 5 grooves, rh
Chambers: 6

IN PRODUCTION 1894-1917

MARKINGS
`IVER JOHNSON'S ARMS & CYCLE WORKS FITCHBURG MASS USA' on left side of barrel. Serial number on butt frame beneath grips.

SAFETY
There is no applied safety device on this revolver.

UNLOADING
Grasp the knurled ends of the spring catch above the standing breech, lift, and hinge the barrel down. This will cause the ejector plate to move out and eject the contents of the chambers. Close the barrel and ensure the spring catch engages.

correctly pulled so as to slide a transfer bar between the two and thus transfer the blow. Dropping the pistol or letting the hammer slip during cocking could not cause the weapon to fire.

153

Ruger Security Six (USA)

Sturm, Ruger & Co got into the revolver business in the early 1950s, making single-action Western guns for the 'quick-draw' craze of the time. These were so popular that they persuaded Colt to restart making single action guns and many others joined in. Ruger then moved to the police market with this extremely sound and reliable revolver, since when, as they say, he has never looked back. The 'Speed Six' is the same pistol but with a rounded butt.

SPECIFICATION & OPERATION

CARTRIDGE
.357 Magnum

DIMENSIONS
Length o/a: 235mm (9.25in)
Barrel: 102mm (4.0in)
Weight: 950g (33.5oz)
Rifling: 6 grooves, rh
Chambers: 6

IN PRODUCTION 1968-

MARKINGS
`STURM RUGER & CO INC SOUTHPORT CONN USA' on left side of barrel. `.38 SPECIAL CAL [or .357 MAGNUM CAL]' on right side of barrel. `RUGER SECURITY SIX' on right side of frame.

SAFETY
There is no applied safety device on this revolver.

UNLOADING
Press in the recessed catch on the left side of the frame, behind the cylinder, and allow the cylinder to swing out to the left of the frame. Press in the ejector rod so as to force out the ejector plate and thus eject the contents of the chambers. Return the cylinder to the frame, ensuring the catch locks.

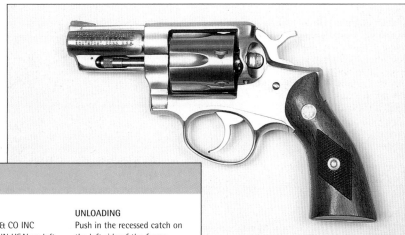

This is simply the Security Six (above) with slightly modified grips and with a sighting groove in the backstrap instead of a separate rear sight, a modification intended to provide adequate sights for rapid combat firing at short range and avoid getting the sights deranged by careless insertion into the holster or other rough handling. A highly successful weapon, it was widely adopted by US police forces and sold for home defense.

SPECIFICATION & OPERATION

CARTRIDGE
.357 Magnum

DIMENSIONS
Length o/a: 254mm (10.0in)
Barrel: 102mm (4.0in)
Weight: 950g (33.5oz)
Rifling: 6 grooves, rh
Chambers: 6

IN PRODUCTION 1969-87

MARKINGS
`STURM RUGER & CO INC SOUTHPORT CONN USA' on left side of barrel. `.38 SPECIAL CAL [or .357 MAGNUM CAL]' on right side of barrel. `RUGER POLICE SERVICE SIX' on right side of frame.

SAFETY
There is no applied safety device on this revolver.

UNLOADING
Push in the recessed catch on the left side of the frame, behind the cylinder, and allow the cylinder to swing out to the left of the frame. Press in the ejector rod so as to force out the ejector plate and thus eject the contents of the chambers. Return the cylinder to the frame, ensuring the catch locks.

Ruger GP 100 (USA)

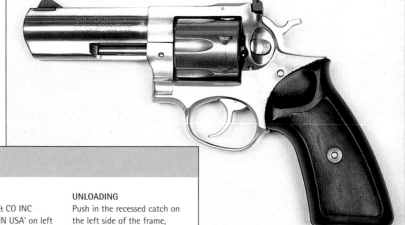

The SP-100 replaced the Security Six as the standard police revolver in 1987 and incorporated a number of improvements which experience had suggested, such as the full-length ejector shroud to give a slight degree of muzzle preponderance and the construction of the trigger guard and mechanism as a separate inserted sub-assembly. It is a robust revolver and will be around for many years to come.

SPECIFICATION & OPERATION

CARTRIDGE
.357 Magnum

DIMENSIONS
Length o/a: 238mm (9.35in)
Barrel: 102mm (4.0in)
Weight: 1247g (44oz)
Rifling: 5 grooves, rh
Chambers: 6

IN SERVICE DATES 1987-

MARKINGS
'STURM RUGER & CO INC SOUTHPORT CONN USA' on left side of barrel. 'RUGER GP 100 .357 MAGNUM CAL [or .38 SPECIAL CAL]' on right side of barrel. Serial number right side of frame.

SAFETY
There is no applied safety device on this revolver.

UNLOADING
Push in the recessed catch on the left side of the frame, behind the cylinder, and allow the cylinder to swing out to the left of the frame. Press in the ejector rod so as to force out the ejector plate and thus eject the contents of the chambers. Return the cylinder to the frame, ensuring the catch locks.

Dan Wesson (USA)

Although of conventional appearance, the Dan Wesson revolvers are quite unique in having interchangeable barrels and grips, so that the owner can change the configuration of the pistol to suit his particular requirements of the moment, whether it be hunting, target shooting or self-defence. Basic calibres available run from .22 Long Rifle to .45 Colt, and the range of barrels from 2 inches (52mm) to 15 inches, though all lengths are not necessarily available in all calibres. The system uses a removable barrel, screwed into the frame in the usual manner, with a removable shroud, all locked in place by a

SPECIFICATION & OPERATION

CARTRIDGE
.22LR, .22WMR, .32 S&W, .38Special,. .357 Magnum, .41 Magnum, .44 Magnum, .45 Colt

DIMENSIONS: (Model 15-2 .357 MAG)
Length o/a: 305 mm (12.0in)
Barrel: 152mm (6.0in). Also 2.5, 4 and 8inch available.
Weight: 1077g (38oz)
Rifling: 6 grooves, rh
Chambers: 6

IN PRODUCTION 1968-

MARKINGS
None

SAFETY
Double-action revolver; no applied safety.

UNLOADING
Press down on the thumb latch on the left side of the frame in front of the cylinder, to release the cylinder. Swing the cylinder out to the left and press in on the ejector rod to eject any rounds in the chambers. Inspect the chambers and verify they are empty. Return the cylinder to its place, allowing the catch to spring back and lock.

special key. When properly assembled the cylinder-breech clearance is ensured by feeler gauges, and the barrel is held in tension by the shroud. The rest of the revolver is a conventional solid-frame with side-opening cylinder.

Smith & Wesson Hand Ejector (USA)

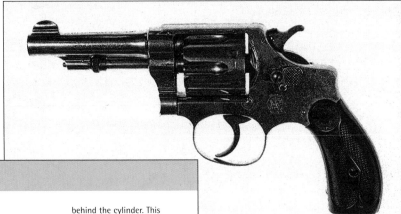

The .32 Hand Ejector was the first S&W revolver to employ the side-opening cylinder, and it went through three models, the second of which (shown here) adopted the innovations of the Military and Police such as the now-familiar push-catch for releasing the cylinder and the front anchorage for the ejector rod. The third model added the safety hammer block and a few refinements to the trigger mechanism. It was a popular weapon, widely used by police forces and for home defence, over 300,000 of the three models being made.

SPECIFICATION & OPERATION

CARTRIDGE
.32 Smith & Wesson Long

DIMENSIONS
Length o/a: 190mm (7.5in)
Barrel: 83mm (3.25in)
Weight: 505g (18oz)
Rifling: 5 grooves, rh
Chambers: 5

IN PRODUCTION 1896-1942

MARKINGS
'SMITH & WESSON' on left side of barrel. '.32 S&W LONG CTG' on right side of barrel. Serial number bottom of butt frame.

SAFETY
There is no safety device on this revolver.

UNLOADING
Press forward the thumb-catch on the left side of the frame, behind the cylinder. This releases the cylinder which can then be swung out to the left side on its crane. Push back on the ejector rod and a central ejector plate emerges from the cylinder to remove the cases from the chambers. Release the ejector rod, swing the cylinder back into the frame until it locks safe.

Smith & Wesson Safety Hammerless (USA)

This is more or less the same revolver as the contemporary standard 'Double Action' model but with the hammer concealed under a rise in the frame and with a grip safety bar let into the rear edge of the butt. It is not actually hammerless. A popular weapon, it went through a number of minor changes during its life, though it finalised in 1907 and remained unchanged until 1940. Commonly called the 'Lemon Squeezer', for obvious reasons.

SPECIFICATION & OPERATION

CARTRIDGE
.38 Smith & Wesson

DIMENSIONS
Length o/a: 190mm (7.5in)
Barrel: 83mm (3.25in)
Weight: 510g (18oz)
Rifling: 5 grooves rh
Chambers: 6

IN PRODUCTION 1887-1940

MARKINGS
'S&W' Monogram on right rear side of frame. '*.38 S&W CTG' on left side of barrel.

SAFETY
Grip safety which must be depressed to unlock the hammer mechanism.

UNLOADING
Grasp the two knurled buttons above the standing breech, pull back and up. This will unlock the frame latch and pivot the barrel/cylinder assembly about its pivot on the frame, so raising the rear of the cylinder. A cam forces out an extractor plate to empty the chambers. Once emptied, swing the barrel up with sufficient force to snap the frame latch into engagement.

This began production in 1899 and, with improvements and modifications, has continued to the present day. Prior to 1902 the ejector rod was unsupported at its front end; after that date the familiar socket was used, supporting the ejector rod at the front end. Production stopped in 1942, about 800,000 having been made, and was resumed after the war as the `Model 10'. Various barrel lengths have been produced, from two to 6.5 inches, though four and five inches appear to have been the most

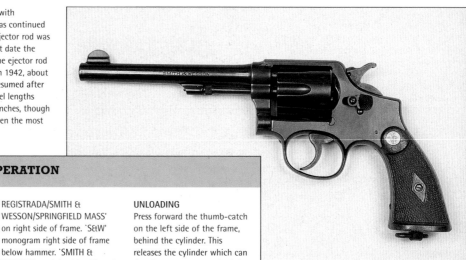

SPECIFICATION & OPERATION

CARTRIDGE
.38 Special

DIMENSIONS
Length o/a: 235mm (9/25in)
Barrel: 101mm (4.0in)
Weight: 865g (30.5oz)
Rifling: 5 grooves rh
Chambers: 6

IN SERVICE DATES 1899-

MARKINGS
`MADE IN U.S.A./MARCA REGISTRADA/SMITH & WESSON/SPRINGFIELD MASS' on right side of frame. `S&W' monogram right side of frame below hammer. `SMITH & WESSON' on right side of barrel. `.38 S&W SPECIAL CTG' on right side of barrel. Serial number on bottom of butt grip.

SAFETY
There is no safety device on this revolver.

UNLOADING
Press forward the thumb-catch on the left side of the frame, behind the cylinder. This releases the cylinder which can then be swung out to the left side on its crane. Push back on the ejector rod and a central ejector plate emerges from the cylinder to remove the cases from the chambers. Release the ejector rod, swing the cylinder back into the frame until it locks safe.

popular. An `Airweight' model, with alloy frame, appeared in 1952 (Model 12) and a stainless model in 1970 (Model 64).

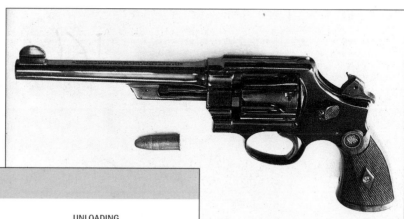

The flagship of the S&W line in its day, this was also called the 'Triple Lock' model since it incorporated a third cylinder lock in the shroud beneath the barrel. About 20,000 were made in all, over 13,000 in .44 S&W calibre. Small numbers were also made in .45 Colt, .44 S&W Russian, .450 Eley and .44-40 Winchester calibres, and 5000 were made in .455 Webley for the British Army in 1915-17.

SPECIFICATION & OPERATION

CARTRIDGE
.44 S&W Special and others (see remarks)

DIMENSIONS
Length o/a: 298mm (11.75in)
Barrel: 165mm (6.5in)
Weight: 1075g (38oz)
Rifling: 5 grooves, rh
Chambers: 6

IN PRODUCTION 1907-15

MARKINGS
'SMITH & WESSON SPRINGFIELD MASS USA' and patent dates on top of barrel. 'S&W DA 44' on left side of barrel. Serial number on bottom of butt frame.

SAFETY
There is no safety device on this revolver.

UNLOADING
Press forward the thumb-catch on the left side of the frame, behind the cylinder. This releases the cylinder which can then be swung out to the left side on its crane. Push back on the ejector rod and a central ejector plate emerges from the cylinder to remove the cases from the chambers. Release the ejector rod, swing the cylinder back into the frame until it locks.

Smith & Wesson US Model 1917 (USA)

The Model 1917, like the similar Colt, was a standard S&W product (the .45 Hand Ejector) modified to accept the .45 automatic pistol cartridge for the sake of ammunition commonality. The cartridges were loaded into semi-circular clips, three at a time, and two clips loaded the cylinder. It is possible to load the cartridges without the clips, and they will chamber satisfactorily, being held at the correct point by a slight step in the chamber. But they will not eject without the clip. The pistol was released to the commercial market in the 1920s

SPECIFICATION & OPERATION

CARTRIDGE
.45 Auto Colt

DIMENSIONS
Length o/a: 274mm (10.78in)
Barrel: 140mm (5.5in)
Weight: 1020g (36oz)
Rifling: 6 grooves, rh
Chambers: 6

IN SERVICE DATES 1917-45

MARKINGS
'SMITH & WESSON SPRINGFIELD MASS USA' and patent dates on top of barrel. 'S&W DA 45' on left side of barrel. Serial number on bottom of butt frame.

SAFETY
There is no safety device on this revolver.

UNLOADING
Press forward the thumb-catch on the left side of the frame, behind the cylinder. This releases the cylinder which can then be swung out to the left side on its crane. Push back on the ejector rod and a central ejector plate emerges from the cylinder to remove the cases from the chambers. Release the ejector rod, swing the cylinder back into the frame until it locks.

and a special cartridge with a thick rim, to reproduce the thickness of the clip and so fill the space between the cylinder and the standing breech, was made under the name '.45 Auto Rim', but this has been obsolete for many years.

Smith & Wesson .38/200 British service (USA)

Like the M1917, this was another standard commercial model (the Military & Police) modified to meet a British order. The only difference between it and the M&P is the dimensioning of the chamber for the British service .38 200-grain round; this dimension is such that the standard .38 S&W and .38 Colt New Police cartridges will also fit. About 890,000 were made, and early orders were filled with a mixture of 4, 5 and 6 inch barrel

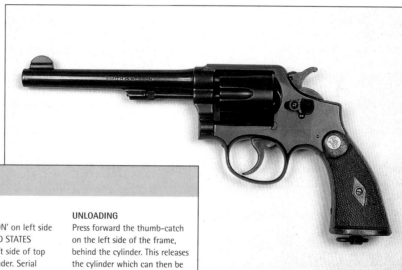

SPECIFICATION & OPERATION

CARTRIDGE
.38 British Service or .38 S&W and similar

DIMENSIONS
Length o/a: 258mm (10.15in)
Barrel: 127mm (5.0in)
Weight: 680g (24oz)
Rifling: 5 grooves, rh
Chambers: 6

IN SERVICE DATES 1940-54

MARKINGS
`SMITH & WESSON' on left side of barrel. `UNITED STATES PROPERTY' on left side of top strap, above cylinder. Serial number at bottom of butt frame.

SAFETY
There is no safety device on this revolver.

UNLOADING
Press forward the thumb-catch on the left side of the frame, behind the cylinder. This releases the cylinder which can then be swung out to the left side on its crane. Push back on the ejector rod and a central ejector plate emerges from the cylinder to remove the cases from the chambers. Release the ejector rod, swing the cylinder back into the frame until it locks.

models. All were blued and polished, with chequered butts and S&W medallions. After April 1942 production was standardised on a 5 inch barrel, sand-blast blue finish and plain walnut butt grips.

Smith & Wesson Model 60 (USA)

The 'J' frame Smith & Wesson Model 60 was the first stainless steel revolver produced anywhere in the world. Designed to combat the corrosion found on blued carbon steel firearms which are carried close to the body, the Model 60 was based on the popular Model 36 'Chief's Special'.

SPECIFICATION & OPERATION

CARTRIDGE
.38 S&W Spl

DIMENSIONS: With 76mm (3")
barrel
Length o/a: 191mm (7.5in)
Barrel: 76mm (3.0in) Also with 63mm (2.5in) barrel.
Weight: 694g (24.5oz)
Rifling: 6 grooves rh
Magazine capacity: 5

IN PRODUCTION 1965 –

MARKINGS
SMITH & WESSON on left of barrel, .38 S&W SPL on the right of the barrel, Smith & Wesson motif on right of frame behind recoil shield, MADE IN USA, MARCAS REGISTRADAS SMITH & WESSON, SPRINGFIELD, MASS on right of frame below cylinder, model number and serial number on frame under cylinder crane.

SAFETY
Trigger retracted hammer block.

UNLOADING
The cylinder latch is on the left of the frame behind the cylinder. Push cylinder latch forwards, swing out the cylinder to the left, eject any live or spent cartridges by pushing the cylinder ejector rod to the rear.

Smith & Wesson 36 'Chiefs Special' (USA)

Smith & Wesson's steel framed Model 36 Chief's Special was the first of their small 'J' frame five-shot double-action revolvers. The name originated at a police officers' conference held in Colorado in 1950 where the revolver was first shown publicly. An ultra lightweight version was known as the Chief's Special Airweight was introduced in 1952 with an Aluminium frame and cylinder and an unloaded weight of 298g. This was discontinued in 1954 with an improved steel cylinder derivative, the Model 37, launched in 1957 using the same name and a weight

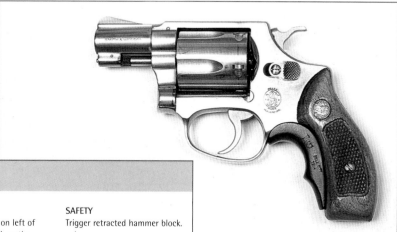

SPECIFICATION & OPERATION

CARTRIDGE
.38 S&W Spl

**DIMENSIONS: With 76mm (3")
barrel**
Length o/a: 191mm (7.5in)
Barrel: 76mm (3.0in). Also with
63mm (2.5in) barrel.
Weight: 694g (24.5oz)
Rifling: 6 grooves rh
Magazine capacity: 5

IN PRODUCTION 1950 -

MARKINGS
SMITH & WESSON on left of
barrel, .38 S&W SPL on the
right of the barrel, Smith &
Wesson motif on right of frame
behind recoil shield, MADE IN
USA, MARCAS REGISTRADAS
SMITH & WESSON, SPRINGFIELD,
MASS on right of frame below
cylinder, model number and
serial number on frame under
cylinder crane.

SAFETY
Trigger retracted hammer block.

UNLOADING
The cylinder latch is on the left
of the frame behind the
cylinder. Push cylinder latch
forwards, swing out the cylinder
to the left, eject any live or
spent cartridges by pushing the
cylinder ejector rod to the rear.

of 354g. Other J frame Chiefs' Special derivatives are the shrouded hammer Model 38 Bodyguard Airweight and Model 49 Bodyguard along with the Model 40 and Model 42 enclosed hammer double-action only Centennials. In 1989 the J frame range were repackaged as 'LadySmith' revolvers and gained more barrel and grip options

Smith & Wesson Model 29 & 629 (USA)

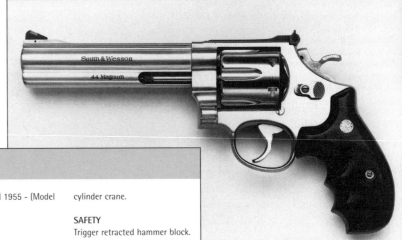

Smith & Wesson launched the carbon steel 'N' frame Model 29 as the first .44 Magnum revolver in 1955. In 1972 it won a awesome reputation as the 'Most Powerful Handgun In The World' following its discovery by Hollywood. The stainless steel equivalent, the Model 629 was first produced in 1979. Both models have been made in a number of styles and barrel lengths, the early versions only having a shrouded ejector rod. Recent production

SPECIFICATION & OPERATION

CARTRIDGE
.44 Magnum (& .44 Spl)

Rifling: 6 grooves rh
Magazine capacity: 6

IN PRODUCTION 1955 - (Model 629 1979 -)

MARKINGS
SMITH & WESSON on left of barrel, 44 MAGNUM on the right of the barrel, Smith & Wesson motif on right of frame behind recoil shield, MADE IN USA, MARCAS REGISTRADAS SMITH & WESSON, SPRINGFIELD, MASS on right of frame below cylinder, model number and serial number on frame under

cylinder crane.

SAFETY
Trigger retracted hammer block.

UNLOADING
The cylinder latch is on the left of the frame behind the cylinder. Push cylinder latch forwards, swing out the cylinder to the left, eject any live or spent cartridges by pushing the cylinder ejector rod to the rear.

models designated the Model 629 Classic have the ejector rod shroud extended into a full length barrel under-lug. A lightweight barrel model known as the Mountain Gun has a 4" barrel.

Smith & Wesson 586/686 (USA)

The 'L' frame Smith & Wesson .357 Magnums in blued carbon steel (Model 586) and stainless steel (Model 686) have been among their fastest selling revolvers since their introduction and are available in a wide range of barrel lengths. Their heavy medium frame with heavy barrel lug have contributed to low recoil and good reliability even when used continuously with full power ammunition.

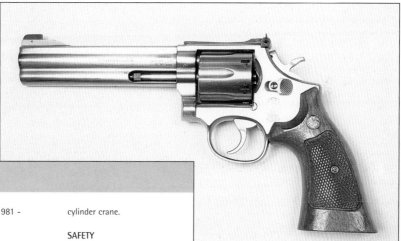

SPECIFICATION & OPERATION

CARTRIDGE
.357 Magnum (&.38 S&W Spl)

DIMENSIONS: With 213mm (8.375in) barrel

Rifling: 6 grooves rh
Magazine capacity: 6

IN PRODUCTION 1981 -

MARKINGS
SMITH & WESSON on left of barrel, S.&W. 357 MAGNUM on the right of the barrel, Smith & Wesson motif on left of frame behind recoil shield, MADE IN USA, MARCAS REGISTRADAS SMITH & WESSON, SPRINGFIELD, MASS on right of frame below cylinder, model number and serial number on frame under

cylinder crane.

SAFETY
Trigger retracted hammer block.

UNLOADING
The cylinder latch is on the left of the frame behind the cylinder. Push cylinder latch forwards, swing out the cylinder to the left, eject any live or spent cartridges by pushing the cylinder ejector rod to the rear.

Smith & Wesson 625 (USA)

The stainless steel 'N' frame Model 625 was introduced in 1987 as a limited edition of 5000 based on a carbon steel revolver made in 1917 for use with the rimless .45 ACP pistol cartridge. The ammunition is secured in 'half moon' three round clips or 'full moon' six round clips before inserting into the cylinder. With a quantity of prepared full moon clips reloading is extremely swift. The success of the 'Model of 1987' limited edition as a

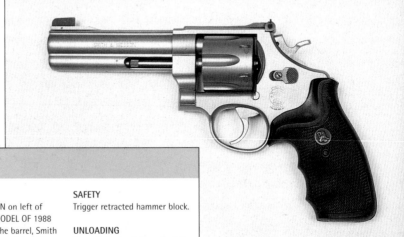

SPECIFICATION & OPERATION

CARTRIDGE
.45 ACP

DIMENSIONS
Length o/a: 264mm (10.375in)
Barrel: 127mm (5.0in)
Weight: 1276g (45oz)
Rifling: 6 grooves rh
Magazine capacity: 6

IN PRODUCTION 1987 -

MARKINGS
SMITH & WESSON on left of barrel, 45 CAL MODEL OF 1988 on the right of the barrel, Smith & Wesson motif on right of frame behind recoil shield, MADE IN USA, MARCAS REGISTRADAS SMITH & WESSON, SPRINGFIELD, MASS on right of frame below cylinder, model number and serial number on frame under cylinder crane.

SAFETY
Trigger retracted hammer block.

UNLOADING
The cylinder latch is on the left of the frame behind the cylinder. Push cylinder latch forwards, swing out the cylinder to the left, eject any live or spent cartridges by pushing the cylinder ejector rod to the rear.

moderately powerful and reliable double-action revolver prompted Smith & Wesson to change the 625 to a catalogued product known as the Model of 1988.

SUB-MACHINE GUNS

Owen (Australia)

An unusual weapon, firstly because of the top-mounted magazine and secondly for the quick-release barrel attachment. This is not in order to change barrels, but to allow the weapon to be dismantled quickly, since the bolt and spring have to be removed from the front of the receiver. Although heavy it was utterly reliable and much preferred to the Austen by Australian troops. It was retained in use well into the 1960s. Early models had a solid frame and cooling fins around the rear of the barrel;

SPECIFICATION & OPERATION

CARTRIDGE
9mm Parabellum

DIMENSIONS
Length o/a: 813mm (32.0in)
Barrel: 250mm (9.84in)
Weight, empty: 4.21kg (9lb 4oz)
Rifling: 7 grooves, rh
Magazine capacity: 33 rounds
Rate of fire: 700 rds/min

IN PRODUCTION 1941-44

MARKINGS
`OWEN 9mm Mk I LYSAGHT PK AUSTRALIA Patented 22/7/41 serial number' all on right side of frame.

SAFETY
A combined safety catch and selector lever on the right side of the frame. Rotate backwards to set safe, when the bolt is locked. In the central position the weapon gives single shots, and in the forward position automatic fire.

UNLOADING
Magazine catch on rear of magazine housing. Remove magazine, pull back cocking handle to eject any round in the chamber. Inspect chamber via ejection port, release cocking handle, press trigger.

from early 1943 a skeleton frame and plain barrel were used. These models were also issued painted in green/ochre camouflage colours.

Submachine gun F1 (Australia)

Although extremely popular with the troops the Owen gun was somewhat out of date by the early 1960s and a new gun - the X3 - was therefore designed and the first models produced in 1962: the X3 could be described as an Australian version of the Sterling type, but this might be carrying the similarity too far. It has many features of the Sterling, particularly internally, though there are obvious differences in the trigger housing. and the bolt handle is on the left side. The rearsight is a special design and the top-mounted magazine of

SPECIFICATION & OPERATION

CARTRIDGE
9 x 19mm Parabellum

DIMENSIONS
Length o/a: 715mm (28.15in)
Barrel: 203mm (8.00in)
Weight: 3.26kg (7 lb 3oz)
Rifling: 6 grooves, rh
Magazine capacity: 34 rounds
Rate of Fire: 600 rds/min.

IN PRODUCTION   1963-87

MARKINGS
F1 LITHGOW and serial number of right side of receiver.

SAFETY
There is a combined safety and fire selector switch on the left side of the trigger mechanism housing. The safety, when applied, locks the bolt if it is in the forward position, preventing it moving should the weapon be dropped. If the bolt is cocked, the safety will move the bolt away from the sear and lock it.

UNLOADING
Magazine catch at rear of magazine housing. Remove magazine. Pull back bolt until cocked. Inspect chamber through ejection port to ensure it is empty. Hold cocking hand and press trigger, allowing bolt to go forward under control.

the Owen has been retained in response to the army's demands. An interesting feature is the way in which the small of the butt fits into the rear of the receiver, which is possible with the straight-line layout of the X3. It is a simple and effective gun which performed well in the jungle war in Vietnam and was then formally adopted as the 9mm submachine-gun F1. Manufacture ceased in the late 1980s with the advent of the AUG rifle.

Steyr MPi69 (Austria)

The MPi69 was adopted by the Austrian Army in 1969 and remains in wide use by several other armies and security forces. An excellent weapon, its only peculiarity is the attachment of the sling to the cocking system; some people do not like this, and for them the Steyr company makes the MPi81, which is the same weapon but with a conventional

SPECIFICATION & OPERATION

CARTRIDGE
9mm Parabellum

DIMENSIONS
Length, stock extended:
670mm (26.38in)
Length, stock retracted:
465mm (18.31in)
Barrel: 260mm (10.24in)
Weight, empty: 3.13kg (6lb 14oz)
Magazine capacity: 25 or 32 rounds
Rate of fire: 550 rds/min

IN PRODUCTION 1969-90

MARKINGS
STEYR-DAIMLER-PUCH AG MADE IN AUSTRIA and serial pressed into plastic stock.

SAFETY
Cross-bolt passing through the receiver; one end is marked 'S' in white and protrudes when the weapon is safe, the other is marked 'F' in red and protrudes when the weapon is set to fire. If the button is pushed only half-way in either direction, the gun will fire single shots only.

UNLOADING
Magazine release in the heel of the butt. Withdraw the magazine. Cock the weapon by holding the pistol grip in one hand and grasping the sling with the other. Hold the sling out sideways, disengage the cocking slide catch from the front sight, then pull back the bolt by pulling back on the sling. Examine the chamber via the ejection port, ensuring it is empty, then press the trigger and allow the sling and bolt to go forward.

cocking handle and with the rate of fire increased to about 700 rds/min. There is also a special long-barrel version of the MPi81, designed for firing out of the ports of an armoured personnel carrier and known as the 'Loop-Hole' model.

Steyr AUG Para (Austria)

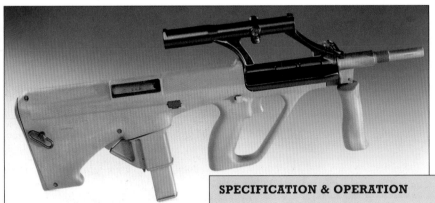

producing a submachine gun with the minimum requirement for new parts manufacture, and to date it is the most successful. For some time the company also sold a kit of parts from which any AUG rifle could be converted into the submachine gun version.

This is simply the Steyr AUG assault rifle, described elsewhere, converted to 9mm Parabellum calibre by fitting a new barrel, new bolt and a magazine adapter to take the MPi69 magazines. The gas operating system of the rifle is disabled and the AUG Para is a blowback weapon. The long barrel gives it excellent accuracy and a higher velocity than is usual from this cartridge. Steyr were one of the first to adapt an existing assault rifle design to the 9mm cartridge, so

SPECIFICATION & OPERATION

CARTRIDGE
9mm Parabellum

DIMENSIONS
Length o/a: 665mm (26.18in)
Barrel: 420mm (16.54in)
Weight, empty: 3.30kg
(7lb 4oz)
Rifling: 6 grooves, rh
Magazine capacity: 25 or
32 rounds
Rate of fire: 700 rds/min

IN PRODUCTION 1988-

MARKINGS
STEYR-DAIMLER-PUCH AG
MADE IN AUSTRIA and serial
pressed into plastic stock.

SAFETY
A cross-bolt safety catch above the trigger. Press in from left to right to make safe; press from right to left to fire. Fire selection is performed by the trigger; the first pressure gives single shots, further pressure gives automatic fire.

UNLOADING
Remove magazine. Pull back cocking handle, inspect chamber, release it and pull trigger.

Steyr TMP (Austria)

The TMP (Tactical Machine Pistol) has replaced the MPi69 and MPi 81 as the standard Steyr production submachine gun. The receiver is almost entirely of synthetic material, and so tough that steel inserts to guide the bolt are not required. There is a folding forward handgrip, and a sound suppressor can be fitted. There are plans to adopt a modular system of construction, similar to that of the AUG rifle, which will permit changing a few parts to convert the TMP to other calibres such as

SPECIFICATION & OPERATION

CARTRIDGE
9mm Parabellum

DIMENSIONS
Length o.a: 270mm (10.63in)
Barrel: 150mm (5.90in)
Weight, empty: 1.30kg (2lb 14oz)
Rifling: 6 grooves, rh
Magazine capacity: 15, 20 or 25 rounds
Rate of fire:

IN PRODUCTION 1993-

MARKINGS
'Steyr-Mannlicher' and serial number on left side of receiver.

SAFETY
A cross-bolt safety catch lies in the top of the grip, behind the trigger. Pushed from left to right, the weapon is safe. Pushed from right to left, the weapon is set for automatic fire. Pushed half-way the weapon is set for single shots.

UNLOADING
Magazine catch is a button in the left front edge of the butt, just behind the trigger. Remove magazine. Grasp cocking handle, a pair of wings beneath the rear sight, and pull back to eject any round in the chamber. Inspect chamber via the ejection port, pull trigger and allow cocking handle and bolt to run forward.

10mm Auto. The same weapon, without the forward hand grip, and firing single shots only, is marketed as the SPP (Special Purpose Pistol).

FMK Mod 2 (Argentina)

An Argentine army weapon, this was originally called the 'PA3(DM)' for Pistola Ametralladora 3, Domingo Matheu factory. It replaced the earlier PA2(DM), which was simply a copy of the US M3A1 gun, in the early 1970s and is still in production. There is also a version with a solid wooden butt. The FMK is reliable and well-balanced; it can be fired quite easily single-handed.

SPECIFICATION & OPERATION

CARTRIDGE
9mm Parabellum

DIMENSIONS
Length, stock extended:
693mm (27.3in)
Length, stock retracted:
523mm (20.5in)
Barrel: 290mm (11.4in)
Weight, empty: 3.40kg
(7lb 8oz)
Rifling: 6 grooves, rh
Magazine capacity: 25 rounds

Rate of fire: 650 rds/min

IN PRODUCTION 1974-

MARKINGS
FMK 2 CAL 9MM FABRICA MILITAR DE ARMAS PORTATILES ROSARIO ARGENTINA and serial on right of receiver. Serial repeated on bolt.

SAFETY
Grip safety with selector on the left side of the receiver; UP for safe; midway for single shots, DOWN for automatic fire.

UNLOADING
Remove magazine, squeeze in the grip safety, pull back the cocking handle to eject any round in the chamber. Inspect the chamber through the ejection port, release the bolt, press the trigger.

FN P-90 (Belgium)

It is unlikely that the P-90 will turn up in the wrong hands for some years yet, as production only got underway in the early 1990s and the entire output is destined for military use. Of unconventional appearance but entirely conventional internal blowback operation, the magazine is unique in lying above the weapon with the cartridges at 90 degrees. The penetrative power of the bullet is formidable. Empty cases are ejected downward through the hollow pistol grip.

SPECIFICATION & OPERATION

CARTRIDGE
5.7 X 28mm

DIMENSIONS
Length o/a: 500mm (19.68in)
Barrel: 263mm (10.35in)
Weight, empty: 2.54kg (5lb 90z)
Rifling: 6 grooves, rh
Magazine capacity: 50 rounds
Rate of fire: 900 rds/min

IN PRODUCTION 1990-

MARKINGS
'P-90 Cal 5.7 X 28' and serial number on left side of sight mount. 'FN HERSTAL SA BELGIUM' on left side of receiver.

SAFETY
A manual safety in the form of a serrated catch in the rear edge of the trigger guard. Push forward for fire, back for safe.

UNLOADING
The magazine catch is at the rear of the magazine, which lies on top of the receiver. Squeeze in, and remove the magazine by drawing the rear end up and back. Pull back the cocking lever to eject any round in the chamber; repeat to be sure, since the chamber cannot be examined through the ejection port. Release the cocking handle, press trigger.

Vigneron (Belgium)

A Belgian design, this was issued to the Belgian Army in 1953 and then to the Belgian forces in the Belgian Congo. After the Congo became independent these weapons were taken over by Congo troops, after which they were undoubtedly dispersed all over Central Africa. Numbers also appear to have been acquired by the Portuguese, who took it into service as the M/961, and these were probably left in Angola. As a result, the Vigneron can be expected to turn up anywhere in Africa for some years to come.

SPECIFICATION & OPERATION

CARTRIDGE
9mm Parabellum

DIMENSIONS
Length, stock extended:
872mm (34.33in)
Length, stock retracted:
695mm (27.36in)
Barrel: 300mm (11.8in)
Weight, empty: 3.28kg (7lb 4oz)
Rifling: 6 grooves, rh
Magazine capacity: 32 rounds
Rate of fire: 600 rds/min

IN PRODUCTION 1952-62

MARKINGS
'ABL52 VIG M1' and serial number on right side of magazine housing.
'Licence Vigneron' cast into right side of receiver.

SAFETY
A combined safety catch and fire selector lever is on the left side of the receiver. Turned to the rear makes the weapon safe; forward one notch for single shots, forward and DOWN for automatic fire. There is also a grip safety on the pistol grip which must be squeezed in to unlock the bolt.

UNLOADING
Magazine catch on right side of magazine housing. Remove magazine. Pull back cocking handle to eject any round in the chamber, inspect chamber via the ejection port. Release cocking handle, pull trigger.

SAF (Chile)

SPECIFICATION & OPERATION

CARTRIDGE
9mm Parabellum

DIMENSIONS
Length, stock extended:
640mm (25.2in)
Length, stock retracted: 410mm
(16.15in)
Barrel: 200mm (7.88in)
Weight, empty: 2.90kg (6lb 6oz)
Rifling: 6 grooves, rh
Magazine capacity: 20 or 30
rounds
Rate of fire: 1200 rds/min
IN PRODUCTION 1990-

MARKINGS
'FAMAE Mod SAF Cal 9mm serial
number' on left side of receiver.

SAFETY
Combined safety catch and fire
selector on left side of receiver,
above pistol grip. UP for safe;
DOWN one notch for single
shots, two notches for three-
round burst.

UNLOADING
Magazine catch on front edge
of trigger guard, behind
magazine housing. Remove
magazine. Pull back cocking
handle to eject any round in the
chamber, inspect chamber via
ejection port, release cocking
handle., pull trigger.

This is the Chilean Army issue weapon and is also exported. The weapon is based
upon the SIG 550 rifle design, which is made under licence in Chile, and the
designer's object was to utilise as many parts of the rifle as possible to save
production costs. The standard model has a folding butt; there is also a fixed butt
model, a version with an integral silencer, and the 'Mini-SAF', a shortened version
with no butt and a fixed forward grip. The 30-round magazine is of translucent
plastic, enabling the ammunition to be visually checked, and there are studs and slots
allowing two or more magazines to be connected together.

China Type 64 (China)

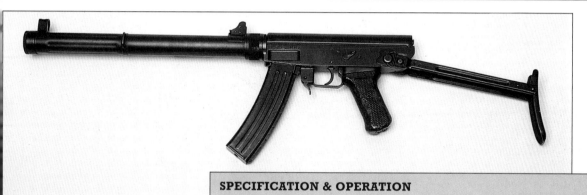

The Type 64 has an integral silencer and uses a special cartridge based on the 7.63mm Mauser but with a pointed, heavy bullet fired at subsonic velocity. The mechanism combines the blowback action and bolt of the Soviet PPS-43 submachine gun, the trigger mechanism of the Czech ZB26 machine gun and the silencer is a classical Maxim pattern full of baffles and with a perforated barrel. With the special cartridge it is reasonably silent, but with standard full-charge pistol ammunition it is almost as noisy as an unsilenced weapon.

SPECIFICATION & OPERATION

CARTRIDGE
7.62 x 25mm Type P Subsonic

DIMENSIONS
Length, stock extended:
843mm (33.3in)
Length, stock retracted:
635mm (25.0in)
Barrel: 244mm (9.6in)
Weight, empty: 3.40kg
(7lb 8oz)
Rifling: 4 grooves, rh
Magazine capacity: 30 rounds

Rate of fire: 1300 rds/min

IN PRODUCTION 1966-

MARKINGS
Factory identifier and serial on
top of receiver.

SAFETY
Safety catch on the right side
of the receiver: a hinged plate
which moves up to block the
bolt.

UNLOADING
Magazine catch behind
magazine. Remove magazine,
press down safety plate, pull
back cocking handle to eject
any round in the chamber.
Inspect the chamber via the
ejection port, release bolt,
press trigger.

179

China Type 79 (China)

A somewhat unusual weapon of which full details are not yet known, this is gas operated, using a short-stroke tappet above the barrel which forces back an operating rod to drive a rotating bolt; the system is broadly that of the AK series of rifles, as are the outer controls such as the safety and pistol grip, making it easier to train soldiers already familiar with the rifle. It is remarkably light for a submachine gun, no doubt due to the rotating bolt system which removes the need for the heavy bolt needed in a simple blowback weapon.

SPECIFICATION & OPERATION

CARTRIDGE
7.62 x 25mm Soviet Pistol

DIMENSIONS
Length, stock extended:
740mm (29.13in)
Length, stock retracted:
470mm (18.50in)
Barrel: 225mm (8.86in)
Weight, empty: 1.90kg
(4lb 3oz)
Rifling: unknown
Magazine capacity: 20 rounds

Rate of fire: 650 rds/min

IN PRODUCTION 1980-

MARKINGS
Factory identifier and serial on top of receiver.

SAFETY
Manual safety catch/fire selector on right side of receiver; UP for safe, central for automatic fire, DOWN for single

shots.

UNLOADING
Magazine catch at front of magazine housing. Remove magazine, pull back cocking lever to eject any round in the chamber. Inspect chamber via ejection port, release cocking lever, press trigger.

AGRAM 2000 (Croatia)

The Agram 2000 is a locally-manufactured submachine gun constructed principally of metal stampings and plastic mouldings. The muzzle is threaded and a protecting sleeve is screwed on; this can be removed and a silencer fitted. There is no provision for a shoulder stock, and the sights are a simple front blade and rear flip-over marked for 50 and 150 metres, so the practical accuracy of this weapon is questionable. An alternative model, the Agram 2002, is said to have an adjustable rear sight

SPECIFICATION & OPERATION

CARTRIDGE
9 x I 9 mm Parabollum

DIMENSIONS
Length o/a: 350 mm (13.8in);
with suppressor, 4B2 mm
(18.57in)
Weight: 1.9 kg (4lb 3oz)
Barrel: 152 mm (6.0in)
Rifling: 4 grooves rh
Magazine capacity: 20 of 32
rounds
Rate of Fire: 750 rds/min

IN PRODUCTION 1997-

MARKINGS
Not known; only specimen
examined had all markings
defaced by acid.

SAFETY
Manual safety /selector switch
on left side above trigger.
'S' for safe, 'R' for automatic.
'1' for single shots.

UNLOADING
Magazine catch at bottom rear
of magazine housing. Remove
magazine, pull back cocking
handle to eject any round in the
chamber, inspect chamber.
Release cocking handle.

with settings to 250 metres, but in the absence of a
shoulder stock this appears to be rather pointless.
The magazine is interchangeable with that of the Uzi
submachine gun, as are some other local designs.

ERO (Croatia)

This is an unashamed direct copy of the Uzi submachine gun. It uses the same wrap-around bolt, grip safety, pistol grip magazine housing, top cocking handle and every other Uzi feature and the end result is indistinguishable from the Uzi. It is, one supposes, one way of obtaining a reliable weapon without having to go to the trouble to design and develop one. It is said to be on general issue to Croatian military and police forces. There is also a 'Mini-ERO' which, naturally enough, is a copy of the Mini-Uzi.

SPECIFICATION & OPERATION

CARTRIDGE
9 x 19mm Parabellum

DIMENSIONS
Length o/a: 650mm (25.6in)
Barrel: 260mm (10.23in)
Weight: 3.73kg (8lb 4oz)
Rifling: 4 grooves, rh
Magazine capacity: 32 rounds
Rate of Fire: 600 rds/min

IN PRODUCTION 1995 -

MARKINGS
ERO Zagred and serial number on left side of receiver

SAFETY
Combined safety and fire selector switch on left side of receiver, above the grip. Pulled to the rear for SAFE, pushed forward to the central position for single shots, fully forward for automatic fire. In addition there is a grip safety which must be squeezed in by gripping the pistol grip before the bolt can be cocked or released.

UNLOADING
Magazine release at the bottom of the grip/magazine housing on the left side. Remove magazine. Holding grip so as to squeeze the grip safety, pull back the bolt to eject any round in the chamber. Inspect the empty chamber via the ejection port. Release the cocking handle and allow the bolt to close.

Sokacz (Croatia)

This cheap, simple submachine gun is clearly influenced by the old Russian PPSh and PPS designs. The trigger mechanism, with switch-like safety/fire selector catch inside the trigger guard is similar to that of the PPSh; the simple interior with breechblock, recoil spring and buffer, is based on the PPS. The side-folding butt is as basic as can be and still survive. The only part that shows original thought is the magazine housing and release catch. The perforated jacket is long enough to act as a fore-end grip. The weapon is made from pressed steel and stamped metal welded together.

SPECIFICATION & OPERATION

CARTRIDGE
9 x 19mm Parabellum

DIMENSIONS
Length o/a: 880mm (34.65in) butt extended; 605mm (23.81in) butt folded.
Barrel: 300mm (11.81in)
Weight: 3.58kg (7lb 4oz)
Rifling: 6 grooves, rh
Magazine capacity: not known
Rate of Fire: not known

IN PRODUCTION 1997 -

MARKINGS
Serial number only.

SAFETY
Finger-operated safety inside trigger guard. Press to rear for safe. Forward one notch for single shots; fully forward for automatic fire.

UNLOADING
Magazine catch behind magazine housing. Press in, remove magazine and empty if necessary. Pull back cocking handle and examine feedway and chamber through ejection port. Release bolt. Press trigger.

alongside the receiver. It has a curiously short butt pad. There is a push-through safety catch but no provision for firing single shots.

This is a reasonably well-made weapon, which shows signs of original thinking. The receiver and jacket are of the same diameter and the jacket is perforated. The magazine housing is unusually deep and can act as a fore-grip without putting strain on the magazine, something that can otherwise cause stoppages. There is a knurled surface on the lower receiver which can be used as an alternate fore-grip. The stock is of steel rod which slides into sheaths

SPECIFICATION & OPERATION

CARTRIDGE
9 x 19mm Parabellum

DIMENSIONS
Length o/a: 850mm (33.46in) butt extended; 565mm (22.25in) butt folded.
Barrel: 220mm (8.66in)
Weight: 3.41kg (7lb 8oz)
Rifling: 4 grooves, rh
Magazine capacity: 32 rounds
Rate of Fire: not known

IN PRODUCTION 1991 - ?

MARKINGS
ZAG M-91 on left of receiver above trigger. PHTO BS7 9mm PARA on left above magazine housing.

SAFETY
Push-through button in front of and above trigger. Push to left for safe.

UNLOADING
Magazine catch on left side of magazine. Remove magazine and empty if necessary. Pull back cocking handle until sear engages and examine feedway and chamber through ejection port. Grasp cocking handle, draw back slightly, press trigger and allow bolt to go forward under control.

CZ Model 25 (Czechoslovakia)

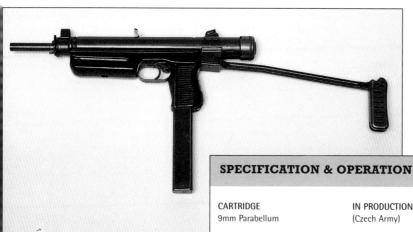

This is one of a family of four similar weapons; the Model 23 (bottom right) has a wooden stock, the Model 25 (right) a folding stock, and both fire the 9mm Parabellum cartridge. The Model 24 has a wooden stock, the Model 26 a folding stock, and both fire the 7.62mm Soviet pistol cartridge, and will usually fire the 7.63mm Mauser pistol cartridge. They were produced in large numbers, liberally supplied to revolutionaries and will be found anywhere in the world.

SPECIFICATION & OPERATION

CARTRIDGE
9mm Parabellum

DIMENSIONS
Length, stock extended:
686mm (27.0in)
Length, stock retracted:
445mm (17.5in)
Barrel: 284mm (11.2in)
Weight, empty: 3.09kg (6lb 13oz)
Magazine capacity: 24 or 40 rounds.
Rate of fire: 600 rds/min

IN PRODUCTION 1949-68 (Czech Army)

MARKINGS
'ZB 1949 she' with serial number on left side of receiver behind pistol grip.

SAFETY
A metal switch inside the trigger guard behind the trigger. Push to the RIGHT to lock the bolt open or closed. Push to the LEFT to fire. For

single shots, press the trigger to the first resistance; for automatic fire press the trigger as far as possible.

UNLOADING
Press the magazine catch, in the bottom of the pistol-grip, and remove the magazine. Pull back the cocking handle in the top of the receiver to eject Release the bolt, press the trigger.

Skorpion (Czechoslovakia/Yugoslavia)

SPECIFICATION & OPERATION

CARTRIDGE
7.65mm Browning (.32 ACP)

DIMENSIONS
Length, stock extended:
513mm (20.2in)
Length, stock retracted:
269mm (10.59in)
Barrel: 112mm (4.40in)
Weight, empty: 1.59kg (3kb 8oz)
Magazine capacity: 10 or 20 rounds
Rate of fire: 850 rds/min

IN PRODUCTION ca 1960-75

MARKINGS
Serial number on left side of receiver.

SAFETY
There is a manual safety catch and fire selector on the left side, above the pistol grip. Back, to the notch marked `1', gives single shots. Central, the notch marked `0' is safe; forward to the notch marked `20' gives automatic fire.

UNLOADING
Magazine catch is a button on the left side of the frame just behind the magazine housing. Remove the magazine. Grasp the cocking knobs on each side of the upper receiver and pull back to eject any round in the chamber. Inspect the chamber via the ejection port. Release the cocking knobs, press the trigger.

This was originally developed as a replacement for the pistol for the crews of armoured vehicles, though the choice of cartridge is peculiar. Reports say that other models in 9mm Short (.380 Auto) and 9mm Parabellum were made, but none have been seen in the west. The Yugoslav Zastava company manufacture the 7.65mm model for export as their M84. It has been widely distributed to various Communist countries and in central Africa, and is a popular weapon with terrorists. It can be expected to appear anywhere in the world.

Madsen Models 1946 and 1951 (Denmark)

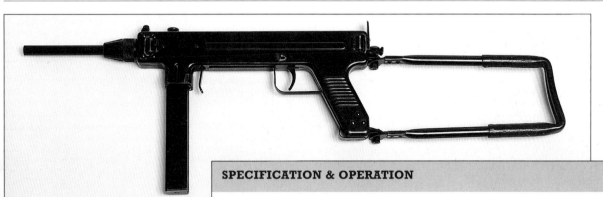

The first of a series of Madsen designs which are all very similar. The receiver is made of two pressings, hinged down the back, and by removing the barrel retaining nut and barrel it is possible to open the receiver up like a book, exposing all the parts inside. The cocking handle on this model is actually a plate on top of the receiver which has `wings' on the sides and can be grasped and pulled back. The Model 1946 was used by the Danish Army and also sold to some South American countries and to Thailand. The Model 1951 is similar but has the cocking handle in the form of a round knob on top of the receiver.

SPECIFICATION & OPERATION

CARTRIDGE
9mm Parabellum

DIMENSIONS
Length, stock extended:
780mm (30.7in)
Length, stock retracted:
550mm (21.65in)
Barrel: 200mm (7.87in)
Weight, empty: 3.15kg
(6lb 15oz)
Rifling: 4 grooves, rh
Magazine capacity: 32 rounds
Rate of fire: 500 rds/min

IN PRODUCTION 1945-53

MARKINGS
'MADSEN' on right side of receiver. Serial number on top of receiver.

SAFETY
Manual safety catch on the left side of receiver, a sliding button. Push forward for safe, rearward for fire. In addition there is a grip safety device behind the magazine housing which must be gripped and squeezed towards the housing to permit the bolt to close.

UNLOADING
Magazine catch at rear of magazine housing. Remove magazine, pull back cocking handle to eject any round in the chamber. Inspect chamber via ejection port. Grip magazine housing and squeeze the grip safety, pull trigger.

Jati-Matic/GG-95 PDW (Finland)

The Jati-Matic uses a patented design in which the bolt recoils up an inclined plane at an angle to the barrel. This upward movement of the bolt allows the pistol grip to be set higher than normal so that the firer's hand lies almost on the axis of the barrel. This, it is claimed, reduces the usual lifting effect of the muzzle, allowing the firer to keep the weapon aligned on the target more easily.

The weapon consists of a pressed-steel receiver with hinged top cover. A forward folding grip beneath the

SPECIFICATION & OPERATION

CARTRIDGE
9 x 19mm Parabellum

DIMENSIONS
Length o/a: 375mm (14.75in)
Barrel: 203mm (8.0in)
Weight: 1.65kg (3lb 10oz)
Rifling: 6 grooves, rh
Magazine capacity: 20 or 40 rounds
Rate of Fire: 600 rds/min

IN PRODUCTION 1993-

MARKINGS
JatiMatic Made in Finland 9.00 Para and serial number, left side of receiver.

SAFETY
Push-through safety button above and in front of the trigger. Press to the Right for SAFE. to the left for fire. Single shots and automatic fire are controlled by the trigger-text above.

UNLOADING
Magazine release is at the rear of the magazine housing, below the trigger guard. Remove the magazine. Grasp the forward handle, unclip it from the rest position if necessary, unfold and then pull sharply back to retract the bolt and cock the weapon. Examine the chamber via the ejection port and verify that it is empty. Pull the trigger to release the bolt, return the forward handle to the folded position.

barrel also acts as the cocking lever and, when closed, as a positive bolt lock. The trigger is pulled against a stop for single shots; pulling it past the stop gives automatic fire. The magazine is a double-column design and the Carl Gustav magazine will also fit. Various accessories were offered, such as silencer, different sizes of magazine and a laser pointing device.

The Jati-Matic appeared in the early 1980s, but in spite of assessment by various countries, found no takers. In the early 1990s it appeared again, offered by a Chinese company, but it rapidly disappeared again and re-appeared in Finland in the mid-1990s as the GG-95 Personal Defence Weapon, made by the Golden Gun Company.

Suomi M1931 (Finland)

One of the earliest non-German submachine guns, the Suomi was developed in Finland and saw use in Scandinavian armies, the Swiss Army, South America and Poland, and was built under license in Denmark and Switzerland. It was generally considered to be among the best designs available in 1939 when the British Army tried to acquire some (without luck - the Russians attacked Finland and the Finns had no guns to spare). It remained in Finn service until well after 1945, most of their guns being modified to accept the Carl Gustav magazine, upon which the other Scandinavian countries had standardised.

SPECIFICATION & OPERATION

CARTRIDGE
9mm Parabellum

DIMENSIONS
Length o/a: 870mm (34.25in)
Barrel: 314mm (12,36in)
Weight, empty: 4.60kg (10lb 2oz)
Rifling: 6 grooves, rh
Magazine capacity: 71 round drum, or 20 or 50 round box
Rate of fire: 900 rds/min

IN PRODUCTION 1931-44

MARKINGS
Serial number on end cap and on left side of receiver.

SAFETY
Manual safety lever in the front edge of the trigger guard. Push backwards, into the guard, to make safe; this locks the bolt in either the forward or rearward position.

UNLOADING
Magazine release behind the magazine housing. Remove magazine. Pull back cocking lever to eject any round in the chamber. Examine chamber via the ejection port, release cocking lever, press trigger.

This replaced the MAS 38 submachine gun and fires a far more practical cartridge. It is a very compact design and the magazine housing, complete with magazine, can be folded forward to lie under the barrel and make it more convenient for carrying. It was more or less replaced in the French Army by the adoption of the 5.56mm FA-MAS rifle, but is still widely used by reserve forces and by police and other para-military forces. It will also be encountered in former French colonies.

SPECIFICATION & OPERATION

CARTRIDGE
9mm Parabellum

DIMENSIONS
Length, stock extended:
660mm (26.0in)
Length, stock retracted:
404mm (15.9in)
Barrel: 230mm (9.05in)
Weight, empty: 3.63kg (8lb 0oz)
Rifling: 4 grooves, lh
Magazine capacity: 32 rounds
Rate of fire: 600 rds/min

IN PRODUCTION 1949-

MARKINGS
'M.A.T. Mle 49 9m/m serial number' on left side of receiver.

SAFETY
A grip safety in the rear edge of the pistol grip must be squeezed in to allow the bolt to move. There is no other form of safety device.

UNLOADING
Magazine catch behind the magazine housing. Remove magazine, pull back cocking handle to eject any round in the chamber. Inspect chamber via ejection port. Release cocking handle, press trigger.

H&K MP5SD (Germany)

This is the silenced member of the MP5 family; the mechanism is exactly the same as the standard MP5 but the short barrel is drilled with 30 holes and surrounded by a large silencer casing. This casing is divided into two chambers; the first surrounds the barrel and receives the propellant gas via the 30 holes, which serve also to reduce the bullet's velocity

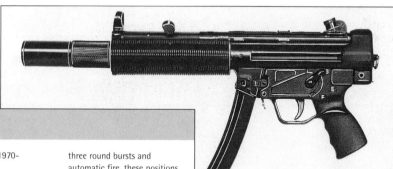

SPECIFICATION & OPERATION

CARTRIDGE
9 x 19mm Parabellum

DIMENSIONS
Length o/a: SD1 550mm (1.65in); SD2 780mm (30.70in); SD3, butt extended 780mm (30.70in), butt retracted 610mm (24.0in)
Barrel: 146mm (5.75in)
Weight: SD1 2.9kg (6lb 6oz); SD2 3.2kg (7lb 1oz); SD3 3.5kg (7lb 11oz)
Rifling: 6 grooves, rh
Magazine capacity: 15 or 30 rounds
Rate of Fire: 800 rds/min

IN PRODUCTION 1970-

MARKINGS
Kal 9mm x 19 on left side of magazine housing.

SAFETY
Combined safety and fire selector switch on the left side of the receiver. In the SD1, 2 and 3 this is a three-position switch, UP for SAFE (S) down one notch for single shots (E) and to the bottom for automatic fire (F), In the SD4,5 and 6 it is a four-position switch, UP for SAFE and down in succession for single shots, three round bursts and automatic fire, these positions being marked by representations of one, three and several bullets.

UNLOADING
Magazine release behind and below magazine housing, Remove magazine, pull back handle and cock the weapon. Examine the breech to ensure the chamber is empty. Grasp the cocking handle and pull the trigger, allowing the cocking handle to go forward under control.

to below the speed of sound. The gases swirl around in this chamber and lose some of their velocity and heat, and then pass to the second chamber where they expand and are again swirled around before being released to the atmosphere.

There are six versions of this weapon; the MP5SD1 has the end of the receiver closed by a cap and has no butt-stock; the SD2 has a fixed plastic butt; the SD3 has a sliding retractable butt; all three can fire either single shots or automatic. The SD4 is as for the SD1 but with the addition of a three-round burst facility; the SD5 is the SD2 with three-round burst; and the SD6 is the SD3 with three-round burst.

H&K MP5K (Germany)

This is a special short version of the MP5 intended for use by police and anti-terrorist squads who require very compact firepower. The weapon can be carried concealed under clothing or in the glove compartment of a car, and it can also be concealed in, and fired from, a specially fitted briefcase. Mechanically it is the same as the MP5 but with a shorter barrel and smaller magazines. Four versions are made; the MP5K is fitted with adjustable iron sights or a telescope if desired; the MP5KAI has a smooth upper surface with very small iron sights so that there is little to catch in clothing or a holster in a quick draw; the MP5KA4 is similar to the MP5K but has an additional three-round burst facility; and the MP5KA5 is similar to the Al with the addition of the three-round burst fitment. No butt is fitted, but there is a robust front grip which gives good control when firing.

SPECIFICATION & OPERATION

CARTRIDGE
9 x 19mm Parabellum

DIMENSIONS
Length o/a: 325mm (12.67in)
Barrel: 115mm (4.5in)
Weight: 1.99kg (4lb 6oz)
Rifling: 6 grooves, rh
Magazine capacity: 15 or 30 rounds
Rate of Fire: 900 rds/min

IN PRODUCTION 1972-

MARKINGS
Kal 9mm x 19 on left side of magazine housing.

SAFETY
Combined safety and fire selector switch on the left side of the receiver. In the MP5K and KA1 this is a three-position switch, UP for SAFE (S) down one notch for single shots (E) and to the bottom for automatic fire (F), In the KA4 and KA5 it is a four-position switch, UP for SAFE and down in succession for single shots, three round bursts and automatic fire, these positions being marked by representations of one, three and several bullets. Post 1990 production will have this switch duplicated on both sides of the weapon.

UNLOADING
Magazine release behind and below magazine housing, Remove magazine, pull back handle and cock the weapon. Examine the breech to ensure the chamber is empty. Grasp the cocking handle and pull the trigger, allowing the cocking handle to go forward under control.

H&K HK53 (Germany)

SPECIFICATION & OPERATION

CARTRIDGE
5.56 x 45mm NATO

DIMENSIONS
Length, stock extended: 755mm (29.72in)
Length, stock retracted: 563mm (22,17in)
Barrel: 211mm (8.31in)
Weight, empty: 3.05kg (6lb 12oz)
Rifling: 6 grooves, rh
Magazine capacity: 25 rounds
Rate of fire: 700 rds/min

IN PRODUCTION 1975-

MARKINGS
'MP53 Kal 5.56mm x 45 serial number (month/year)' along top rib of receiver. 'Kal 5.56mm x 45' on left side of magazine housing.

SAFETY
Manual safety catch/fire selector on left side of receiver, above trigger. UP for safe, central for single shots, DOWN for automatic fire.

UNLOADING
The magazine catch is behind the magazine housing. Remove magazine, pull back cocking handle to clear any round from the breech, inspect the chamber via the ejection port, release cocking handle, pull trigger.

'Sub machine gun' means different things to different people; several countries classify the Kalashnikov rifle as a submachine gun, while most people consider that firing a pistol cartridge is the sole entree to the class. True, it is hard to say where a weapon in this calibre ceases to be a compact assault rifle and becomes a submachine gun, but if the makers classify as such, then we can only follow suit. Certainly a number of armies and security forces have adopted the HK53 and appear to be happy with it. It has to have a very efficient flash suppressor to satisfy the demands of firing a rifle cartridge in a 211mm barrel.

MP5K-PDW Personal Defence Weapon (Germany/USA)

This was designed by the Heckler & Koch subsidiary in the USA as a weapon for aircrew or vehicle-borne troops who need something extremely compact. It is, in effect, the MP5K fitted with a folding butt and with the muzzle modified to accept a silencer. There is also provision for fitting a laser spot projector. Should the butt not be

SPECIFICATION & OPERATION

CARTRIDGE
9 x 19mm Parabellum

DIMENSIONS
Length, with butt-cap: 349mm (13.75in)
Length, with butt extended: 603mm (23.75in)
Length, with butt folded: 368mm (14.50in)
Barrel: 5.0in (127mm)
Weight with butt: 2.79kg (6lb 2oz)
Weight with butt-cap: 2.09kg (4lb 10oz)
Rifling: 6 grooves, rht

Magazine capacity: 30-rounds
Rate of Fire: 900 rds/min

IN PRODUCTION 1991-

MARKINGS
Made in Germany for HK Inc Chantilly Va on right side of magazine housing. Kal 9mm x 19 on left side of magazine housing.

SAFETY
Combined safety and fire selector switch on both the left and right sides of the receiver. This is a four-position switch, UP for SAFE and down in succession for single shots, three round bursts and automatic fire, these positions being marked by representations of one, three and several bullets.

UNLOADING
Magazine release behind and below magazine housing, Remove magazine, pull back handle and cock the weapon. Examine the breech to ensure the chamber is empty. Grasp the cocking handle and pull the trigger, allowing the cocking handle to go forward under control.

needed, it can be easily removed and a butt cap fitted on the end of the receiver. Selective fire is standard, but a two or three-round burst unit can be fitted to the trigger mechanism if required.

Numbers of these weapons were converted by modifying the cocking handle so that it could be pushed in, through the bolt, to engage on a hole in the receiver, so as to lock the bolt in the forward position. When so modified, the weapon became the MP38/40.

his is the familiar German army weapon generally, and wrongly, called the 'Schmeisser'. It as made by the Erma company and designed by ollmer, and like all his designs has the characteristic elescoping casing around the recoil spring and bolt ssembly. It was later replaced in production by the IP40 which simplified some features and made anufacture easier and quicker. The MP38 is istinguished by the corrugated surface of the achined steel receiver, the hole in the magazine ousing and the machined aluminium grip frame.

SPECIFICATION & OPERATION

CARTRIDGE
9mm Parabellum

DIMENSIONS
Length, stock extended:
833mm (32.80in)
Length, stock retracted:
630mm (24.80in)
Barrel: 251mm (9.88in)
Weight, empty: 4.08kg
(9lb 0oz)
Rifling: 6 grooves, rh
Magazine capacity: 32 rounds

Rate of fire: 500 rds/min

IN PRODUCTION 1938-40

MARKINGS
`MP38 (Year)' on rear receiver cap. Serial number on left side of rear cap. May have the factory code '27' stamped on the top of the receiver.

SAFETY
Pull back the cocking handle

and turn it up into a notch in the receiver slot. There is no selector device; the MP38 fires only in the automatic mode.

UNLOADING
Magazine catch on rear of magazine housing. Remove magazine, pull back cocking handle to eject any round in the chamber. Inspect chamber via ejection port, release cocking handle, press trigger.

MP41 (Germany)

The MP41 is a rare example of wartime German private enterprise; it was an attempt by Schmeisser to produce a submachine gun to compete with the MP40, and he did it by simply taking the MP40 receiver and barrel and grafting it on to a wooden stock similar to that of the Schmeisser-designed Bergmann MP28. He also added a fire selector so that single shots could be fired. However, the German Army was not interested and never adopted it. A small quantity was made and found their way into various military units as substitute standard weapons, but they are now relatively uncommon.

SPECIFICATION & OPERATION

CARTRIDGE
9mm Parabellum

DIMENSIONS
Length o/a: 864mm (34.0in)
Barrel: 251mm (9/88in)
Weight, empty: 3.70kg (8lb 3oz)
Rifling: 6 grooves, rh
Magazine capacity: 32 rounds
Rate of fire: 600 rds/min

IN PRODUCTION 1941-42

MARKINGS
'MP41 Patent Schmeisser C.G.Haenel Suhl' on top of receiver. Serial number on rear of receiver, left side of barrel and left side of receiver.

SAFETY
Pull back cocking handle and turn up into a notch in the receiver slot. The cocking handle can be pushed into the bolt, in its forward position, and into a hole in the receiver to lock the bolt.

UNLOADING
Magazine catch on rear of magazine housing. Remove magazine, pull back cocking handle to eject any round in the chamber. Inspect chamber via ejection port, release cocking handle, press trigger.

Steyr-Solothurn MP34 (Germany)

A solid and extremely well-made weapon, designed in Germany, perfected by a German-owned company in Switzerland and manufactured in Austria. It was used by the Austrian Army, was also taken into limited use by the German Army, and bought by the Portuguese in 1942, where it remained in use by their Fiscal Guards until the late 1970s. A number were also made in 9mm Parabellum calibre for the Germany Army in 1938-39. An unusual feature is a magazine loading device built into the magazine housing.

SPECIFICATION & OPERATION

CARTRIDGE
9 x 23mm Steyr

DIMENSIONS
Length o/a: 808mm (31.8in)
Barrel: 200mm (7.87in)
Weight, empty: 4.36kg
(9lb 10oz)
Rifling: 6 grooves, rh
Magazine capacity: 32 rounds
Rate of fire: 500 rds/min

IN PRODUCTION 1934-39

MARKINGS
Serial number & year over chamber. Steyr monogram (SSW) may also be above the chamber.

SAFETY
A sliding safety catch is on top of the receiver in front of the rear sight. Slide forward to make the weapon safe by locking the bolt whether in the open or closed position.

UNLOADING
Magazine catch on magazine housing. Remove magazine, pull back cocking handle to eject any round in the chamber. Inspect chamber via ejection port, release cocking handle, press trigger.

Walther MPK and MPL (German)

SPECIFICATION & OPERATION

CARTRIDGE
9mm Parabellum

DIMENSIONS (MPK)
Length, stock extended:
659mm (25.94in)
Length, stock retracted:
373mm (14.69in)
Barrel: 173mm (6.81in)
Weight, empty: 2.80kg
(6lb 3oz)
Rifling: 6 grooves, rh
Magazine capacity: 32 rounds
Rate of fire: 550 rds/min

IN PRODUCTION 1963-85
MARKINGS
Serial number on left side of
receiver.

SAFETY
There is a manual safety catch
on both sides of the receiver,
behind the trigger. When turned
UP and to the rear, the weapon
is safe; then turned forward and
DOWN, the weapon is ready to
fire. The original design had no
provision for single shots; as an
option, a different mechanism

with a third position on the
safety catch could be fitted to
give single shots, but how many
of these were actually made is
not known.

UNLOADING
Magazine release is behind the
magazine housing, below the
trigger guard. Remove the
magazine, pull back the cocking
handle to eject any round in the
chamber. Inspect the chamber
via the ejection port, release the
cocking handle, pull the trigger.

The MPK and MPL are simply the same weapon
with either long (L) or short (K) barrels. The long
model has a 260mm barrel., which increases the
overall length to 749mm. In spite of its excellent
quality and performance it was never adopted by
any army, but some German naval units and various
European police forces took it into use in the 1960s.
A silencer-equipped model was later developed but
this apparently attracted few customers.

KGP-9 (Hungary)

This was first revealed in the latter 1980s and is the standard submachine gun of the Hungarian military and police forces. It is a conventional blowback weapon, principally assembled from pressed steel components stiffened with castings. It fires from an open bolt, but the bolt carries a floating firing pin and the actual firing is done by a hammer mechanism. An unusual feature is that the standard barrel can be removed and replaced by a longer one, presumably to convert the weapon into a form of carbine with a longer range.

SPECIFICATION & OPERATION

CARTRIDGE
9 x 19mm Parabellum

DIMENSIONS
Length, butt extended: 615mm (24.21in)
Length, butt folded: 355mm (13.97in)
Barrel: 190mm 97.48in)
Weight: 2.75kg (6lb 1oz)
Rifling: 6 grooves, rh
Magazine capacity: 25 rounds
Rate of Fire: 900 rds/min

IN PRODUCTION 1987-

MARKINGS
F.E.G. Hungary Cal 9mm P and serial number on right side of receiver.

SAFETY
Combined safety catch and fire selector switch on left side above and in front of trigger. To the REAR for SAFE; forward and down for single shots, fully forward for automatic fire.

UNLOADING
Magazine release is behind the magazine housing, below trigger guard. Remove magazine. Pull back cocking handle and hold bolt open while verifying that the chamber is empty. Release bolt. Pull trigger.

Uzi (Israel)

One of the most famous of submachine guns and one which is likely to appear anywhere in the world. The Uzi has been made under license in Belgium and Germany, and the general layout and principles of its mechanism have been copied in several countries. It is still in production in Israel,

SPECIFICATION & OPERATION

CARTRIDGE
9mm Parabellum

DIMENSIONS
Length, fixed stock: 640mm (25.2in)
Length, stock extended: 640mm (25.2in)
Length, stock retracted: 440mm (17.3in)
Barrel: 260mm (1-.24in)
Weight, empty: 3.50kg (7lb 11oz)
Rifling: 4 grooves, rh
Magazine capacity: 25, 32 or 40 rounds
Rate of fire: 600 rds/min

IN PRODUCTION 1953-

MARKINGS
Serial number left rear side of receiver on Israeli models; may also have Hebrew markings. 'M.P. UZI Kal 9mm serial number' on left rear side of receiver on German models.

SAFETY
A combined safety catch and fire selector is fitted into the top of the pistol grip on the left side. Pulled back, the weapon is safe with the bolt locked; in the central position single shots are possible, and in the forward position automatic fire is possible. There is also a grip safety on the pistol grip which must be squeezed in so as to release the bolt.

UNLOADING
The magazine catch is at the bottom left side of the pistol grip. Remove the magazine. Pull back the cocking handle so as to eject any round in the chamber, inspect the chamber via the ejection port, release the cocking handle and pull the trigger.

and has been joined in the past decade by two smaller models, the Mini-Uzi and the Micro-Uzi; these resemble the Uzi but are simply smaller in all dimensions except the calibre. They are easily identifiable by their similarity with the basic Uzi and by their names, which are marked on the left side of the receiver.

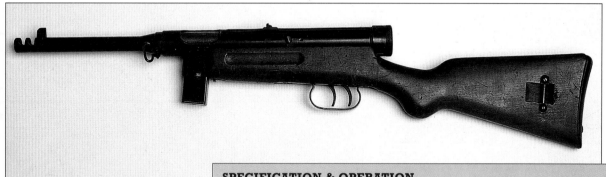

This is a simplified model of the 38/42, differing in the size of the bolt and details of the mainspring. A visual distinction is the absence of the small spring housing which projects from the rear of the receiver in earlier models. This weapon was entirely exported, users being Pakistan, Syria, Costa Rica and Iraq among many others.

SPECIFICATION & OPERATION

CARTRIDGE
9mm Parabellum

DIMENSIONS
Length o/a: 798mm (31.4in)
Barrel: 210mm (8.25in)
Weight, empty: 3.98kg
(8lb 12oz)
Rifling: 6 grooves, rh
Magazine capacity: 20 or 40 rounds
Rate of fire: 550 rds/min

IN PRODUCTION 1945-55

MARKINGS
MOSCH. AUTOM. BERETTA MOD 38/A44 CAL 9- and serial number on top of receiver.

SAFETY
Manual safety catch on the left side of the receiver, marked 'F' for fire and 'S' for safe. Move the catch to 'S' (rearwards) to make safe. Two triggers; front trigger for single shots, rear trigger for automatic fire.

UNLOADING
Magazine catch on magazine housing. Remove magazine, pull back cocking handle to eject any round in the chamber. Inspect chamber, release cocking handle, pull trigger.

Beretta Model 12 (Italy)

SPECIFICATION & OPERATION

CARTRIDGE
9mm Parabellum

DIMENSIONS
Length, stock extended:
645mm (25.4in)
Length, stock retracted:
418mm (16.45in)
Barrel: 200mm (7.87in)
Weight, empty: 3.0kg (6lb 10oz)
Rifling: 6 grooves, rh
Magazine capacity: 20, 30, 40 rounds

Rate of fire: 550 rds/min

IN PRODUCTION 1959-78

MARKINGS
P.M. BERETTA Mod 12-Cal 9/m Parabellum and serial number on top of receiver

SAFETY
There is a grip safety let into the rear of the pistol grip, which must be pressed in to unlock the bolt for either cocking or firing. A push-button safety catch above the grip on the left side, when pushed in, locks the grip safety in the safe position.

UNLOADING
Magazine catch behind the magazine housing. Remove magazine, grasp the grip and press in the grip safety, pull back the bolt. Inspect the chamber, release the bolt, press the trigger.

The Model 12 is considerably different to earlier Beretta submachine guns, due to the retirement of the designer Marengoni in 1956 and the appearance of a new designer, Salza. It is primarily made of metal stampings and uses a 'telescoping' or 'overhung' bolt which wraps around the barrel and thus reduces the length of the weapon. It has a front hand grip and the stock may be a hinged, tubular metal type folding around to the right side of the weapon, or a detachable wooden type. The Model 12 was adopted by the Italian forces in 1961 and by various South American and African countries. It has also been made under licence in Brazil and Indonesia.

Socimi Type 821 (Italy)

This appears to be based upon the CZ25 pattern though with modern precision castings rather than sheet metal for the receiver and a generally more angular shape. The Socimi company promoted it for some years and claimed sales in various parts of the world, but they eventually went into liquidation and the design was then taken over by Franchi, who marketed it as the LF821. What success they have had with it is not currently known.

SPECIFICATION & OPERATION

CARTRIDGE
9mm Parabellum

DIMENSIONS
Length, stock extended:
600mm (23.62)
Length, stock retracted:
400mm (15.75in)
Barrel: 200mm (7.88in)
Weight, empty: 2.45kg
(5lb 7oz)
Rifling: 6 grooves, rh
Magazine capacity: 32 rounds

Rate of fire: 600 rds/min

IN PRODUCTION ca 1984-89

MARKINGS
'SOCIMI SpA Mod 821 9mm' and serial number on top of receiver.

SAFETY
There is a combined safety catch and fire selector on the left side, above the pistol grip.

In its rearmost position the weapon is safe; central, single shots; forward automatic fire.

UNLOADING
Magazine catch is at the bottom left side of the pistol grip. Remove magazine; pull back cocking handle to eject any round in the chamber. Inspect chamber via the ejection port, release cocking handle, press trigger.

Spectre (Italy)

This unusual weapon is the only double-action submachine gun in existence and it has been widely adopted by European police forces since, like many modern pistols, it can be de-cocked, carried loaded but safely, and then fired in the double-action mode by simply pressing the trigger. The magazines are also unusual, having four columns of cartridges and thus compressing 50 rounds into less vertical space than is usually taken by a 30 rounds magazine. Semi-automatic long-barrelled versions can also be found.

SPECIFICATION & OPERATION

CARTRIDGE
9mm Parabellum

DIMENSIONS
Length, stock extended: 580mm (22.83in)
Length, stock retracted: 350mm (13.78in)
Barrel: 130mm (5.12in)
Weight, empty: 2.90kg (6lb 6oz)
Rifling: 6 grooves, rh
Magazine capacity: 30 or 50 rounds
Rate of fire: 850 rds/min

IN PRODUCTION ca 1984-

MARKINGS
'SITES Mod SPECTRE Cal 9mm made in Italy patented' on right side of receiver.

SAFETY
There is no conventional safety catch. There is a de-cocking lever on each side at the top of the pistol grip, and a fire selector lever on each side above the trigger. The weapon can be loaded and cocked and the de-cocking lever is then pressed to release the bolt without firing. To fire, all that is necessary is to pull the trigger which then cocks and releases the firing pin. The fire selector gives single shots in the UP position, automatic fire in the DOWN position.

UNLOADING
Magazine catch is in the front edge of the trigger guard. Remove magazine. Pull back cocking handle to remove any round in the chamber, inspect chamber via the ejection port. Release the cocking handle. Press trigger.

This is one of the growing number of submachine guns actually chambered for a rifle cartridge, being based on components of the Daewoo company's assault rifle. Capable of automatic fire and three-round bursts, it has been given a large and efficient muzzle compensator and flash hider in order to reduced the defects of firing a rifle

SPECIFICATION & OPERATION

CARTRIDGE
5.56 x 45mm M193

DIMENSIONS
Length: (butt extended)
838mm (33.0in)
Length: (butt folded)
653mm (25.71in)
Barrel: 263mm (10.35in)
Weight: 2.87kg (6lb 5oz)
Rifling: 6 grooves, rh
Magazine capacity: 20 or
30 rounds
Rate of Fire: 850 rds/min

IN PRODUCTION 1990-

MARKINGS
DAEWOO PRECISION
INDUSTRIES LTD on left side
of receiver. 5.56MM K1A1
and serial number on left
side of magazine housing.

SAFETY
Combined safety and fire
selector switch on left side
of receiver above pistol
grip. Turn to the REAR for
SAFE. Turn forward to the
vertical for three-round
bursts, and forward again
for automatic fire. The

cocking handle can also be
locked into the receiver to
prevent movement.

UNLOADING
Magazine release is on the
left side of the magazine
housing. Press in and
remove magazine; pull back
cocking handle until it
locks. Inspect chamber
through ejection port and
ensure it is empty. Press
trigger to release bolt.

cartridge from a short barrel, and it is claimed that this reduces muzzle climb and flash by a considerable amount. The sights are provided with Tritium inserts for night shooting, and the weapon has an extremely simple sliding wire butt-stock. It seems, though, that the idea of a submachine gun firing a 5.56mm cartridge did not gain many adherents, and in about 1996 the weapon was re-named a 'short assault rifle'. which is perhaps a more accurate title.

Sola Super (Luxembourg)

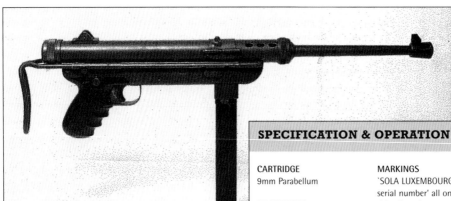

This is a simple but well-made weapon which seems to have some affinity with an earlier, Belgian, design known as the RAN. The Sola was made in Luxembourg and was reputedly sold to some African and South American countries, so it could turn up anywhere. It failed to attract any major military contracts, since it appeared at a time when there was a glut of surplus submachine guns on the world markets. The makers developed a simplified version - the Sola Light - but this found no takers either, and they then abandoned the weapons business for something more profitable.

SPECIFICATION & OPERATION

CARTRIDGE
9mm Parabellum

DIMENSIONS
Length, stock extended:
875mm (34.45in)
Length, stock retracted:
600mm (23.62in)
Barrel: 300mm (11.81in)
Weight, empty: 2.90kg
(6lb 6oz)
Rifling: 6 grooves, rh
Magazine capacity: 32
rounds
Rate of fire: 550 rds/min

IN PRODUCTION 1954-57

MARKINGS
'SOLA LUXEMBOURG [Year] serial number' all on left side of receiver.

SAFETY
A combined safety catch/fire selector is on the left side of the receiver, above the pistol grip. UP and forward for safe, DOWN one notch for single shots, fully down for automatic fire. The hinged ejection port cover also acts as a safety device, preventing bolt movement when closed.

UNLOADING
The magazine catch is a large button let into the left side of the receiver behind the magazine housing. Press in and remove the magazine. Pull back the cocking handle to eject any round in the chamber. Inspect the chamber via the ejection port, release the cocking handle, pull the trigger.

MGP-15 (Peru)

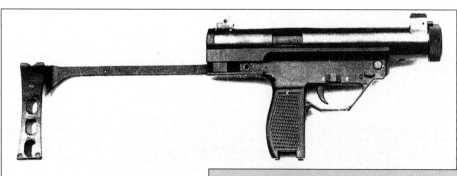

An exceptionally small weapon made in Peru and designed for use by special forces and security guards; it is well-balanced and can be fired one-handed if necessary. A screwed cap around the muzzle can be removed, leaving a screwed section available for the attachment of a suppressor, which is provided as an accessory. The magazine is based upon that of the Uzi submachine gun and Uzi magazines are interchangeable.

SPECIFICATION & OPERATION

CARTRIDGE
9mm Parabellum

DIMENSIONS
Length, stock extended:
490mm (19.3in)
Length, stock retracted:
271mm (10.66in)
Barrel: 162mm (6.38in)
Weight, empty: 2.31kg
(5lb 1oz)
Rifling: 12 grooves, rh
Magazine capacity: 20 or

32 rounds
Rate of fire: 700 rds/min

IN PRODUCTION 1990-

MARKINGS
`SIMA-CEFAR 9mm MGP-15`
and serial number on left side
of receiver.

SAFETY
Manual safety catch/selector
lever on left side of receiver,

above trigger guard. UP for
safe, to the rear for automatic
fire, forward for single shots.

UNLOADING
Magazine catch at left bottom
of pistol grip. Remove
magazine, pull back cocking
handle to eject any round in the
chamber. Inspect chamber via
ejection port, release cocking
handle, press trigger.

MGP-79A (Peru)

This is the service submachine gun of the Peruvian armed forces, a simple and robust blowback design. The butt folds alongside the receiver so that the butt-plate can be grasped by the hand holding the magazine for extra grip. A threaded portion in the front end of the receiver is to allow a perforated barrel jacket to be fitted, allowing a better grip to be taken when talking deliberate aim, and the barrel can be removed and replaced by a combined barrel/silencer assembly.

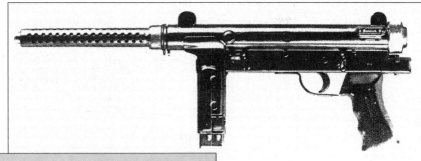

SPECIFICATION & OPERATION

CARTRIDGE
9mm Parabellum

DIMENSIONS
Length, stock extended: 809mm (31.85in)
Length, stock retracted: 544mm (21.4in)
Barrel: 237mm (9.33in)
Weight, empty: 3.08kg (6lb 13oz)
Rifling: 12 grooves, rh
Magazine capacity: 20 or 32 rounds

Rate of fire: 850 rds/min

IN PRODUCTION 1979-85

MARKINGS
'SIMA-CEFAR 9mm MGP-79A' and serial number on left side of receiver.

SAFETY
Manual safety catch on left side of receiver, above trigger. Rearward for safe, DOWN for fire. A manual fire selector switch is on the left side of the receiver just behind the magazine housing.

UNLOADING
Magazine catch at left bottom of magazine housing. Remove magazine, pull back cocking handle to eject any round from the chamber. Inspect chamber via the ejection port, release cocking handle, pull trigger.

MGP-87 (Peru)

This is more or less the same mechanism as the MGP-79A weapon, but slightly smaller by having a shorter barrel and shorter butt. The barrel can be removed by unscrewing the knurled retaining cap at the front of the receiver, and a combined barrel and suppressor can be screwed on to the receiver as a complete replacement unit. It has been adopted by the Peruvian armed forces and will gradually replace the MGP-79A as the standard service weapon.

SPECIFICATION & OPERATION

CARTRIDGE
9mm Parabellum

DIMENSIONS
Length, stock extended:
766mm (30.15in)
Length, stock retracted:
500mm (19.68in)
Barrel: 194mm (7.64in)
Weight, empty: 2.90kg
(6lb 6oz)
Rifling: 12 grooves, rh
Magazine capacity: 20 or

32 rounds
Rate of fire: 800 rds/min

IN PRODUCTION 1987-

MARKINGS
`SIMA-CEFAR 9mm MGP-87'
and serial number on left side
of receiver.

SAFETY
A combined safety catch and
fire selector on the left side of

the receiver. Back for safe,
down to the first stop for
automatic, forward to the
second notch for single shots.

UNLOADING
Magazine catch at left bottom
of magazine housing. Remove
magazine, pull back cocking
handle to eject any round from
the chamber. Inspect chamber
via the ejection port, release
cocking handle, pull trigger.

Poland pz-63 (Poland)

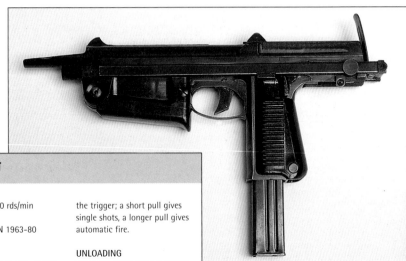

This is a peculiar weapon which resembles an over-grown automatic pistol. Instead of a bolt moving inside the receiver, it uses a moving slide, just like a pistol. The lower portion of the slide is extended beneath the muzzle to act as a compensator, deflecting the muzzle gases upwards to counteract the natural rise of the weapon when firing automatic. It is almost impossible to make accurate aimed automatic fire since the slide and sights are constantly moving during firing.

SPECIFICATION & OPERATION

CARTRIDGE
9mm Parabellum

DIMENSIONS
Length, stock extended:
583mm (22.95in)
Length, stock retracted:
333mm (13.11ub)
Barrel: 152mm (6.0in)
Weight, empty: 1.80kg
(3lb 15oz)
Rifling: 6 grooves, rh
Magazine capacity: 25 or
40 rounds

Rate of fire: 600 rds/min

IN PRODUCTION 1963-80

MARKINGS
Serial number right side of side and frame. Factory number (11) in oval.

SAFETY
Manual safety catch on left side top of pistol grip; turn UP to make safe, turn DOWN to fire. Fire selection is performed by

the trigger; a short pull gives single shots, a longer pull gives automatic fire.

UNLOADING
Magazine catch at heel of butt. Remove magazine, grasp the serrated rear section of the slide and pull it to the rear, so ejecting any round in the chamber. Inspect the chamber through the ejection port, release the slide and pull the trigger.

A Portuguese service weapon, developed in Portugal and based upon features of other designs, combining the stock and firing mechanism of the US M3 and the bolt and general construction of the German MP40. A reliable and robust weapon, it was widely used in Africa and many found their way into the hands of insurgents of one sort or another. It could also turn up in the Far East, due to its use in Portuguese Timor. A slightly improved version of this weapon will be found marked as the M63 pattern, and this was superseded by the M1973 model which a perforated barrel jacket. All are mechanically almost identical.

SPECIFICATION & OPERATION

CARTRIDGE
9mm Parabellum

DIMENSIONS
Length, stock extended:
813mm (32.1in)
Length, stock retracted:
625mm (24.6in)
Barrel: 250mm (9/85in)
Weight, empty: 3.77kg
(8lb 5oz)
Rifling: 6 grooves, rh
Magazine capacity: 32 rounds
Rate of fire: 500 rds/min

IN PRODUCTION 1948-55

MARKINGS
'FBP M/48' and serial number on left side of magazine housing.

SAFETY
Pull back cocking handle and turn up into a cut-out in the receiver slot to lock it in the rear position. When the bolt is forward, pushing the cocking handle in will lock the inner end into a cut in the receiver wall and thus lock the bolt forward.

UNLOADING
Magazine catch on side of magazine housing. Remove magazine, pull back cocking handle to eject any round in the chamber. Release cocking handle, press trigger.

Lusa A2 (Portugal)

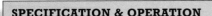

SPECIFICATION & OPERATION

CARTRIDGE
9mm Parabellum

DIMENSIONS
Length, stock extended: 585mm
(23.0in)
Length, stock retracted: 458mm
(18.0in)
Barrel: 160mm (6.3in)
Weight, empty: 2.85kg
(6lb 5oz)
Rifling: 6 grooves, rh
Magazine capacity: 30 rounds
Rate of fire: 900 rds/min
IN PRODUCTION 1992-

MARKINGS
`INDEP LUSA A2 [year] serial
number' on right side of receiver.

SAFETY
A combined safety catch and fire
selector lever is mounted on the
left side of the receiver, above the
pistol grip. This is marked `0' for
safe, `1' for single shots, `3' for
three-round bursts and `30' for
automatic fire.

UNLOADING
Magazine catch on left side of
receiver, behind magazine housing.
Remove magazine. Pull back
cocking handle to eject any round
in the chamber, inspect chamber via
the ejection port. Release cocking
handle, press trigger.

This weapon was developed by the Portuguese INDEP company to replace the
earlier FBP models. A robust and compact design, is has an unusual double-
cylinder form of receiver, with the bolt and barrel in the lower section and the
overhung section of the bolt, together with its recoil spring, in the top. The fire
selector gives the full choice of options, and there are such things as sound
suppressors and laser sighting aids provided as accessories.

Probably the best of the three wartime Soviet submachine guns, the PPS was designed and manufactured inside Leningrad during the 900-day siege; the weapon was designed so as to be made on existing machinery using existing materials, since nothing could be brought in from outside. After the war the Soviets got rid of them to fellow-travelling nations, largely because of political ill-feeling between Moscow and Leningrad. They were extensively used by the North Korean and Chinese armies during the Korean War and they are particularly common in the Far East.

SPECIFICATION & OPERATION

CARTRIDGE
7.62mm Soviet Pistol

DIMENSIONS
Length, stock extended: 808mm (31.81in)
Length, stock retracted: 606mm (23.86in)
Barrel: 254mm (10.0in)
Weight, empty: 3.33kg (7lb 6oz)
Rifling: 4 grooves, rh
Magazine capacity: 35 rounds
Rate of fire: 700 rds/min

IN PRODUCTION 1943-45

MARKINGS
Serial number and factory identifying mark on top or side of receiver.

SAFETY
Manual safety catch in front edge of trigger guard. Push forward to make safe; this locks the bolt in either the fully forward or fully rearward position. There is no fire selector lever; the weapon fires only at full-automatic.

UNLOADING
Magazine catch is around the rear of the magazine housing. Remove magazine, pull back cocking handle to eject any round in the chamber. Inspect chamber via ejection port, release cocking handle, pull trigger.

PPSh-41 (Russia)

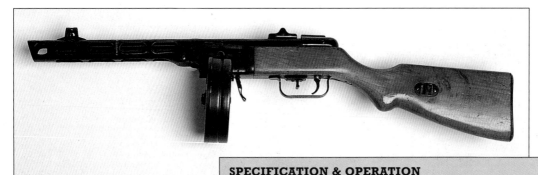

The third wartime Soviet submachine gun and the most common, some five million having been made. They were widely distributed to Communist countries after 1947 and can be found all over the world. Conversions to 9mm Parabellum chambering have been done, though they are unlikely to be encountered in any number. This superseded the PPS-40 to provide a weapon capable of using box or drum magazines and which was simpler and quicker to manufacture. Early models have an adjustable tangent backsight; later models, the majority of production, have a simple two-position flip-over notch backsight.

SPECIFICATION & OPERATION

CARTRIDGE
7.62mm Soviet Pistol

DIMENSIONS
Length o/a: 828mm (32.6in)
Barrel: 265mm (10.43in)
Weight, empty: 3.56kg
(7lb 13oz)
Rifling: 4 grooves, rh
Magazine capacity: 71 round drum or 35 round box
Rate of fire: 900 rds/min

IN PRODUCTION 1941-47

MARKINGS
Serial number and factory identifying code on receiver.

SAFETY
Manual safety latch on the cocking handle; this can be pushed into notches cut into the receiver wall when the bolt is either fully forward or fully back, and locks the bolt in that position. There is a fire selector switch inside the trigger guard, in front of the trigger; push forward for automatic fire, back for single shots.

UNLOADING
Magazine release is behind the magazine housing and folds up under the stock. Fold down, press forward and slide the magazine out. Pull back cocking handle to eject any round in the chamber, inspect the chamber via the ejection port, release the cocking handle, press trigger.

SPECIFICATION & OPERATION

CARTRIDGE
5.45 x 39.5mm Soviet

DIMENSIONS
Length, stock extended:
730mm (28.75in)
Length, stock retracted:
490mm (19.3in)
Barrel: 206.5mm (8.13in)
Weight empty: 2.70kg
(5lb 15oz)
Rifling: 4 grooves, rh
Magazine capacity: 30 rounds

Rate of fire: 700 rds/min

IN PRODUCTION 1975-

MARKINGS
Factory identification, serial
number and year of
manufacture on left side of
receiver.

SAFETY
Manual safety catch/fire
selector on right side of
receiver; UP for safe, central for
automatic fire, DOWN for single
shots.

UNLOADING
Magazine catch in front of
trigger guard. Remove
magazine, pull back cocking
lever on right side of receiver to
eject any round in the chamber,
examine chamber through the
ejection port, release cocking
lever, pull trigger.

This weapon first saw action in Afghanistan in
1982. It is simply a shortened version of the
standard AK 74 rifle, intended for use by armoured
troops, special forces and others requiring a more
compact weapon. There is a bulbous muzzle
attachment which compensates for firing a rifle
cartridge in a much shorter barrel than that for
which it was originally designed. The design has
been copied in Yugoslavia, though chambered for
the 5.56mm NATO cartridge and probably intended
for export rather than for adoption by local forces.

BXP (South Africa)

A South African design, used by their army and police and which may yet find its way to other places. The BXP is a versatile weapon which can be fitted with a silencer, a grenade launching attachment, or various types of muzzle compensator. It is made from steel pressings, and the bolt is hollowed out to wrap around that portion of the barrel which is inside the receiver, so that it has a full-length barrel even though only a part of it is visible.

SPECIFICATION & OPERATION

CARTRIDGE
9mm Parabellum

DIMENSIONS
Length, stock extended:
607mm (23.9in)
Length, stock retracted:
387mm (15.24in)
Barrel: 208mm (8.19in)
Weight, empty: 2.50kg
(5lb 8oz)
Rifling: 6 grooves, rh
Magazine capacity: 22 or 32
rounds
Rate of fire: 1000 rds/min

IN PRODUCTION 1988-

MARKINGS
G.D.P.S. and serial number on
top of receiver.

SAFETY
Manual safety catch on the
left and right sides of the
receiver, above the pistol grip.
UP (green dot) for safe, DOWN
(red dot) for fire. There is no
fire selector; pulling the
trigger to its first stop gives
single shots; pulling it beyond
this point produces automatic
fire. There is a safety notch on
the bolt which will catch the
sear should the bolt be jarred
back or should the hand slip
during cocking.

UNLOADING
Magazine catch in pistol grip.
Remove magazine, pull back
cocking handle (top of
receiver) to eject any round in
the chamber. Inspect the
chamber through the ejection
port. Release cocking handle,
pull trigger.

Sanna 77 (South Africa)

This weapon appeared in South Africa in the 1970s and is based upon the Czech CZ25, though whether it was actually made in South Africa or whether the guns were refurbished CZ 75s bought from Czechoslovakia and modified so as to fire only in the semi-automatic mode is not certain. It was not a military weapon, but was sold for self-defence by farmers and others who felt the need for it, and it can be assumed that several of them have passed into other hands by this time and are liable to appear anywhere in Africa.

SPECIFICATION & OPERATION

CARTRIDGE
9mm Parabellum

DIMENSIONS
Length, stock extended:
650mm (25.6in)
Length, stock retracted:
450mm (17.72in)
Barrel: 290mm (11.4in)
Weight, empty: 2.80kg
(6lb 3oz)
Rifling: 6 grooves, rh
Magazine capacity: 40 rounds

Rate of fire: single shots

IN PRODUCTION 1977-80

MARKINGS
Serial number on left side of receiver.

SAFETY
A manual safety catch is inside the trigger guard, behind the trigger. Pushed from left to right it locks the bolt rendering the weapon safe.

UNLOADING
Magazine catch at the heel of the pistol grip. Remove magazine. Pull back cocking handle to eject any round in the chamber. Inspect chamber via the ejection port. Release cocking handle, press trigger.

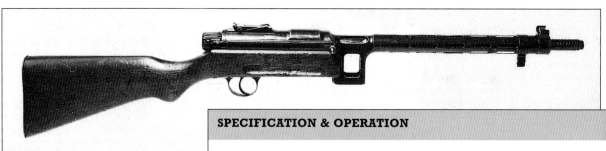

Developed during the Spanish Civil War, this was one of three weapons which were similar except for their firing arrangements; the others were the RU35 which fired only at 300 rds/min, and the TN 35 which fired at 700 rds/min. As seen above the SI 35 fired at either rate, but the process of setting the speed was far too involved for practical use in battle and although the weapon was reliable and accurate, it never achieved much popularity. It was offered in the USA and Britain during the 1939-45 war and both countries tested it before turning it down in favour of something more simple.

SPECIFICATION & OPERATION

CARTRIDGE
9 x 23mm Largo (Bergmann-Bayard)

DIMENSIONS
Length o/a: 900mm (35.43in)
Barrel: 270mm (10.63in)
Weight, empty: 3.80kg
(8lb 6oz)
Rifling: 6 grooves, rh
Magazine capacity: 30 or 40 rounds
Rate of fire: 300 or 700 rds/min
IN PRODUCTION 1936-44

MARKINGS
'STAR - SUB-FUSIL AMETRALLADORA MODELO SI 1935 CAL 9MM' on left side of receiver. Serial number on right side of receiver.

SAFETY
There are two switches on the left side of the receiver, a three-position switch above the trigger and a two-position switch in front of it. To set the weapon safe, the forward switch is pushed forward and the rear switch pushed all the way to the rear. To fire single shots, the forward switch remains forward, and the rear switch is pushed fully forward. To fire automatic at 300 rds/ min, the forward switch is pulled back and the rear switch left all the way forward. To fire automatic at 700 rds/min the forward switch is back and the rear switch in its central position.

UNLOADING
Magazine catch behind the magazine housing. Remove magazine, pull back cocking handle to eject any round in the chamber, and inspect the chamber via the ejection port. Release the cocking handle, press the trigger.

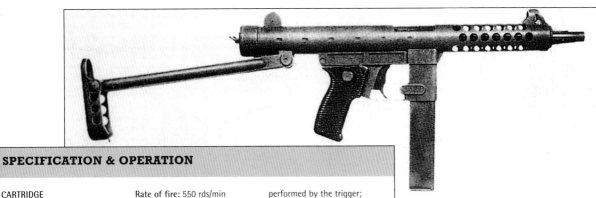

SPECIFICATION & OPERATION

CARTRIDGE
9 x 23mm Largo (Bergmann-Bayard)

DIMENSIONS
Length, stock extended:
701mm (27.6in)
Length, stock retracted:
480mm (18.9in)
Barrel: 201mm (7.91in)
Weight, empty: 2.87kg
(6lb 5oz)
Rifling: 6 grooves, rh
Magazine capacity: 20 or 30
rounds

Rate of fire: 550 rds/min

IN PRODUCTION 1963-70

MARKINGS
'STAR EIBAR ESPANA MODEL Z-62' and serial number on left side of magazine housing.

SAFETY
A manual cross-bolt safety in the upper part of the pistol grip. When pushed from right to left it blocks the sear and the weapon is safe. Fire selection is

performed by the trigger; pulling the upper part of the trigger produces single shots, pulling on the lower part produces automatic fire.

UNLOADING
Magazine catch at the rear of the magazine housing. Remove magazine, pull back cocking handle to eject any round in the chamber. Inspect chamber via the ejection port, release cocking handle, pull trigger.

This was developed for the Spanish Army, replaced the Z-45 in 1953 and remained in service until 1971, when it was replaced by the Z-70B; this looks the same but has a conventional trigger and a selector lever above it to give single shots or automatic fire. Both weapons were offered on the export market and were also offered in 9mm Parabellum chambering, but whether any were adopted by other countries is not known.

219

The Z-84 replaced the earlier Z-70B in Spanish service in the middle 1980s and is a thoroughly modern and compact design using pressed metal for lightness. The centre of balance is above the pistol grip, so that it can be easily fired one-handed if necessary. As well as being used by Spain, numbers have been sold to security forces in several countries, though no details are forthcoming from the manufacturers.

SPECIFICATION & OPERATION

CARTRIDGE
9mm Parabellum

DIMENSIONS
Length, stock extended:
615mm (24.2in)
Length, stock retracted:
410mm (16.14in)
Barrel: 215mm (8.46in)
Weight, empty: 3.00kg
(6lb 10oz)
Rifling: 6 grooves, rh
Magazine capacity: 25 or 30 rounds
Rate of fire: 600 rds/min

IN PRODUCTION 1985-

MARKINGS
'STAR EIBAR ESPANA MOD Z-84' and serial number on right of receiver.

SAFETY
A cross-bolt safety button is set inside the trigger-guard. Pushed from right to left, the weapon is safe. Pushed from left to right it exposes a red mark and indicates the weapon is ready to fire. A sliding fire selector on the left side of the receiver which is pushed forward for single shots, rearward for automatic fire.

UNLOADING
The magazine release is in the heel of the pistol grip. Remove the magazine. Pull back the cocking handle to eject any round in the chamber. Inspect the chamber via the ejection port, release the cocking handle, pull the trigger.

Carl Gustav 45 (Sweden)

One of the oldest submachine guns still in service, the Carl Gustav is a robust weapon which is likely to last a long time. The original models had no magazine housing and used a drum magazine, but in 1948 a box magazine was developed, leading to all guns being modified by having a magazine housing added. The Carl Gustav is used by the Swedish, Irish and Indonesian armies and was also made under licence in Egypt as the 'Port Said'. A highly modified version, with an integral silencer replacing the usual barrel, was used by US Special Forces in Vietnam.

SPECIFICATION & OPERATION

CARTRIDGE
9mm Parabellum

DIMENSIONS
Length, stock extended:
808mm (31.8in)
Length, stock retracted:
552mm (21.7in)
Barrel: 213mm (8.39in)
Weight, empty: 3.90kg
(8lb 9oz)
Rifling: 6 grooves, rh
Magazine capacity: 36 rounds

Rate of fire: 600 rds/min

IN PRODUCTION 1945-

MARKINGS
Serial number on top of
receiver.

SAFETY
Pull back the cocking handle
and turn it up into a notch in
the cocking handle slot. When
the bolt is forward, it can be
locked in place by pushing the
cocking handle into the bolt so
that its other end passes
through the bolt and into a
hole in the receiver.

UNLOADING
Remove the magazine, pull back
the cocking handle. Inspect the
chamber, release the cocking
handle and press the trigger.

SIG MP310 (Switzerland)

SPECIFICATION & OPERATION

CARTRIDGE
9mm Parabellum

DIMENSIONS
Length, stock extended:
735mm (28.9in)
Length, stock retracted:
610mm (24.0in)
Barrel: 200mm (7.88in)
Weight, empty: 3.15kg
(6lb 15oz)
Rifling: 6 grooves, rh
Magazine capacity: 40 rounds
Rate of fire: 900 rds/min

IN PRODUCTION 1958-72

MARKINGS
'SIG NEUHAUSEN MOD 310
9mm' and serial number on top
of receiver.

SAFETY
There is no applied safety device
on this weapon; the only safety
measure that can be taken is to
press in the catch on the left
side of the magazine housing
and pivot the entire magazine
forward to lie underneath the
barrel. This permits the weapon
to be carried safely, provided
there is no round in the
chamber, and it can be brought
into action simply by swinging
the magazine back into
position. Fire selection is done
by trigger pressure; the first
pressure gives single shots,
harder pressure automatic fire.

UNLOADING
The magazine release is behind
the magazine housing. Remove
magazine. Pull back cocking
handle to eject any round in the
chamber. Inspect chamber via
the ejection port, release
cocking handle, press trigger.

This is based upon an earlier design which proved
too expensive to make, and became the Swiss
police submachine gun in the early 1960s. However
it was still too expensive to become a popular
military weapon and only a small quantity were sold
in various parts of the world before the production
line was dismantled in 1978. An extremely well-
made gun, like all SIG products, it was a pioneer in
the use of precision castings rather than machined
forgings.

Rexim-Favor (Turkey)

SPECIFICATION & OPERATION

CARTRIDGE
9mm Parabellum

DIMENSIONS
Length o/a: 870mm (34,25in)
Barrel: 340mm (13.38in0
Weight, empty: 3.79kg
(8lb 6oz)
Rifling: 6 grooves, rh
Magazine capacity: 32 rounds
Rate of fire: 600 rds/min

IN PRODUCTION 1953-70

MARKINGS
No markings have been seen on any Rexim-Favor weapon apart from those produced in Turkey, which carry Turkish markings and a serial number on the left side of the receiver; `XXXX A2 MOD 1968 ANKARA CAP 9MM'.

SAFETY
A combined safety catch/fire selector is on the left side of the receiver, above the pistol grip. To the rear for safe, DOWN and central for single shots, forward for automatic.

UNLOADING
The magazine catch is a thumb switch on the left side of the receiver, behind the magazine housing. Remove the magazine; pull back the cocking handle to eject any round in the chamber; inspect chamber via the ejection port, release the cocking handle, pull the trigger.

This weapon has an odd history; it is reputed to have been a French design, stolen by a glamorous female spy, which then passed to a Swiss company, who had the weapons made in Spain in the 1950s. The Swiss went bankrupt in 1957, the Spanish factory took over the guns, and where they went to after that is anybody's guess. A number were either made, modified or refurbished in Turkey in the late 1960s and used by the Turkish Army for some years. It has a somewhat complicated mechanism, which was one reason for the lack of military interest in the original design, but seems to be well made and accurate. It can be found with a wooden butt or with a folding butt.

This was the original Sten, designed at the Royal Small Arms Factory, Enfield, and made by BSA and various ordnance factories. It is recognisable by the spoon-like muzzle compensator and the wooden cover to the trigger mechanism, and also the folding forward grip. A Mark I* version appeared late in 1941 using a metal cover for the trigger mechanism and without the grip or muzzle compensator. About 100,000 of these models were made and most went to the regular forces. Various patterns of metal stock can be found

SPECIFICATION & OPERATION

CARTRIDGE
9mm Parabellum

DIMENSIONS
Length o/a: 896mm (35.27in)
Barrel: 198mm (7.8in)
Weight, empty: 3.26kg (7lb 30z)
Rifling: 6 grooves, rh
Magazine capacity: 32 rounds
Rate of fire: 550 rds/min

IN PRODUCTION 1941-42

MARKINGS
`STEN Mk I' on top of magazine housing.

SAFETY
Pull back cocking handle and turn down into a notch in the operating slot. Fire selection is done by a cross-bolt passing through the trigger mechanism housing; pushed in from left to right it gives single shots, pushed from right to left gives automatic fire.

UNLOADING
Magazine catch on top of magazine housing. Press down and remove magazine, pull back cocking handle to eject any round in the chamber, and inspect the chamber via the ejection port. Release the cocking handle, press the trigger.

Sten Mk II (UK)

SPECIFICATION & OPERATION

This was the most common version of the Sten, over two million being made in the UK, Canada and New Zealand. The mechanism is the same as the Mark I but the barrel and stock are removable for easier packing and storage. The magazine housing can also be rotated to close the ejection port. Used by British forces, it was also dropped to resistance movements all over Europe and the Far East, so that it can be encountered anywhere in the world. It was also copied by the resistance (notably in Denmark) and by the Germans.

CARTRIDGE
9mm Parabellum

DIMENSIONS
Length o/a: 952mm (37.48in)
Barrel: 197mm (7.76in)
Weight, empty: 3.00kg
(6lb 10oz)
Rifling: 2 or 6 grooves, rh
Magazine capacity: 32 rounds
Rate of Fire: 550 rds/min

IN PRODUCTION 1942-44

MARKINGS
'STEN MK II' on top of magazine housing. Weapons made in Canada may also have 'LONG BRANCH' and year.

SAFETY
Pull back cocking handle and turn up into a notch in the operating slot. Fire selection is done by a cross-bolt passing through the trigger mechanism housing; pushed in from left to right it gives single shots,

pushed from right to left gives automatic fire.

UNLOADING
Magazine catch on top of magazine housing. Press down and remove magazine, pull back cocking handle to eject any round in the chamber, and inspect the chamber via the ejection port. Release the cocking handle, press the trigger.

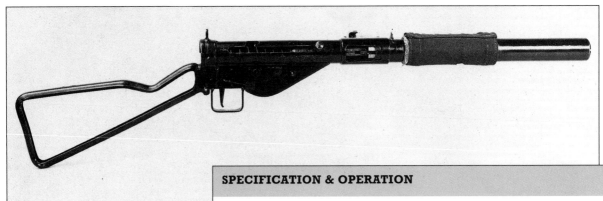

This is the 'Silent Sten', originally produced for clandestine forces but then taken into use by the British Army for use by patrols and raiding parties. The mechanism is that of the Mark II weapon, though using a lighter bolt, and the barrel and silencer are a special integral unit which screws into the receiver in place of the normal barrel and retaining sleeve. The canvas sleeve around the silencer is to protect the hand from heat, and it was not recommended to fire this weapon at full automatic except in the gravest emergencies.

SPECIFICATION & OPERATION

CARTRIDGE
9mm Parabellum

DIMENSIONS
Length o/a: 900mm (35.4in)
Barrel: 90mm (3.54in)
Weight, empty: 3.48kg
(7lb 11oz)
Rifling: 6 grooves, rh
Magazine capacity: 32 rounds
Rate of fire: 450 rds/min

IN PRODUCTION 1943-45

MARKINGS
'STEN M.C. Mk IIS' on top of magazine housing.

SAFETY
Pull back cocking handle and turn up into a notch in the operating slot. Fire selection is done by a cross-bolt passing through the trigger mechanism housing; pushed in from left to right it gives single shots, pushed from right to left gives automatic fire.

UNLOADING
Magazine catch on top of magazine housing. Press down and remove magazine, pull back cocking handle to eject any round in the chamber, and inspect the chamber via the ejection port. Release the cocking handle, press the trigger.

Sten Mk V (UK)

The Mark V Sten was an attempt to improve the quality of the weapon and produce something which looked less cheap and nasty than the Mark II. The mechanism remained unchanged, but the gun now had a wooden stock, a wooden pistol grip and had the muzzle formed in the same manner as the service No 4 rifle, so that the standard bayonet could be fitted. The gun was finished in stove enamel and the butt on early models had a brass butt-plate with a trap for carrying cleaning equipment; later models have a steel butt-plate without the trap. However, the greatest design defect of the Sten - the magazine - remained the same, so that the Mark V was little more reliable than the patterns which had gone before.

SPECIFICATION & OPERATION

CARTRIDGE
9mm Parabellum

DIMENSIONS
Length o/a: 7.62mm (30.0in)
Barrel: 198mm (7.8in)
Weight, empty: 3.90kg
(8lb 9oz)
Rifling: 6 grooves, rh
Magazine capacity: 32 rounds
Rate of fire: 600 rds/min

IN PRODUCTION 1944-46

MARKINGS
`STEN M.C. Mk V' on top of magazine housing.

SAFETY
Pull back cocking handle and turn up into a notch in the operating slot to lock the bolt in the cocked position. Press in the cocking handle when the bolt is forward to lock it to the receiver. Fire selection is done by a cross-bolt passing through the trigger mechanism housing; pushed in from left to right it gives single shots, pushed from right to left gives automatic fire.

UNLOADING
Magazine catch on top of magazine housing. Press down and remove magazine, pull back cocking handle to eject any round in the chamber, and inspect the chamber via the ejection port. Release the cocking handle, press the trigger.

Sterling (UK)

The Sterling has been used by some 50 or more countries; it is the Canadian C1, and forms the basis of the Australian F1 submachine gun, and although Sterling collapsed in 1988 the gun is still made under license in India; there must be tens of thousands of them in existence and they could appear anywhere. There is a silenced version, known as the L34 in British service, which bears the same relationship to the L2A3 as did the Sten IIS to the Mark II. There are also innumerable semi-automatic versions of the L2 pattern used by police and security forces around the world.

SPECIFICATION & OPERATION

CARTRIDGE
9mm Parabellum

DIMENSIONS
Length, stock extended: 710mm (27.95in)
Length, stock retracted: 480mm (18.90in)
Barrel: 198mm (7.80in)
Weight, empty: 2.70kg (5lb 15oz)
Rifling: 6 grooves, rh
Magazine capacity: 34 rounds
Rate of fire: 550 rds/min

IN PRODUCTION 1953-88

MARKINGS
'STERLING SMG 9mm' and serial number on top of magazine housing on standard production. 'Gun Submachine 9mm L2A3', serial number, NATO Stock Number, on top of magazine housing on weapons produced for the British Army.

SAFETY
Combined safety catch and fire selector lever on left side of frame, above the pistol grip. To the rear for safe; central for single shots; forward for automatic fire.

UNLOADING
Magazine catch at rear of magazine housing. Press down and remove magazine, pull back cocking handle to eject any round in the chamber, and inspect the chamber via the ejection port. Release the cocking handle, press the trigger.

Sterling L34A1 (UK)

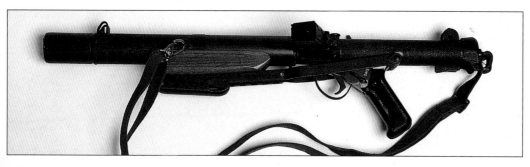

When the Sten was replaced by the Sterling, it became necessary to replace the Sten Mark 6 silenced version as well, and the L2 Sterling was therefore re-designed into this L34 model, using the silent Sten as a guide but improving the technology. The mechanism is similar to that of the L2 weapon but the barrel has 72 radial holes to permit the escape of gas and thus reduce the emergent velocity of the bullet. This escaping gas is contained within an expanded metal wrapping around the barrel, and after seeping through this is expands into the cylindrical silencer casing. The front part of this contains a spiral diffuser, through the centre of which the bullet passes but which causes the gases to swirl and slow down further before escaping at a velocity too low to cause a loud report. The reduced gas pressure necessitates the use of a lighter bolt than standard.

SPECIFICATION & OPERATION

CARTRIDGE
9 x 19mm Parabellum

DIMENSIONS
Length, butt extended: 864mm (34.0in); butt folded: 660mm (26.00in)
Weight: unloaded: 3.60kg (7lb 15oz)
Barrel: 198mm (7.80in)
Rifling: 6 grooves, rh
Magazine capacity: 34 rounds
Rate of fire: 550 rds/min

IN PRODUCTION 1966-85

MARKINGS
Gun, Submachine, 9mm L34A1, serial number and NATO Stock Number on top of magazine housing.

SAFETY
Combined safety catch and fire selector lever on left side of frame above the pistol grip. To the rear for safe, centre for single shots, forward for automatic fire.

UNLOADING
Magazine catch is at the rear of the magazine housing. Remove magazine. Pull back cocking handle to eject any round in the chamber and inspect the chamber via the ejection port. Release the cocking handle and press the trigger.

Thompson M1928 and M1 (USA)

SPECIFICATION & OPERATION

CARTRIDGE
.45 ACP

DIMENSIONS
Length o/a: 857mm (33.74in)
with compensator
Barrel: 267mm (10.5in)
Weight, empty: 4.88kg
(10lb 12oz)
Rifling: 6 grooves, rh
Magazine capacity: 20 or 30
rounds box, 50 or 100 round
drum
Rate of fire: 700 rds/min

IN PRODUCTION 1919-42

MARKINGS
'THOMPSON SUBMACHINE
GUN/CALIBER .45 COLT
AUTOMATIC CARTRIDGE/
MANUFACTURED BY/ COLT'S
PATENT FIREARMS MFG
CO/HARTFORD, CONN, USA/
MODEL OF 1928\serial number'
all on left side of receiver.

SAFETY
Manual safety catch above the
pistol grip on the left side of
the receiver. Back for safe,
forward for fire. The weapon
can only be set to safe when
the bolt is drawn back. A fire

selector switch is further
forward on the left side of the
receiver; move forward for
automatic fire, back for single
shots.

UNLOADING
Magazine catch is a thumb-
operated latch just behind the
trigger on the left grip. Release
the magazine. Pull back the
cocking handle to eject any
round in the chamber, inspect
the chamber via the ejection
port. Release the cocking
handle, pull the trigger.

This can claim to be the first submachine gun
insofar as Thompson was the man who invented
the word, though it was not the first such weapon to
see service. It did not appear until 1921, well after
the Bergmann and Beretta designs, and the 1928
version was much the same as the 1921 except for
some minor changes to the bolt to reduce the rate of
fire. But it was this model which was adopted by the
US Marines as the M1 (illustrated above) and
initiated the submachine gun in American service,
and its association with Chicago and the gangster era
was also responsible for much of the distaste with
which many armies viewed this class of weapon. But
for reliability and solid construction, very few guns
have ever come close to the Thompson.

US M3 (USA)

safety mechanism and the unnecessarily complicated bolt retraction and cocking handle on the right-hand side, which soon gave problems due to breakages in action.

This could be called America's answer to the Sten gun, since it was their examination of the Sten which prompted the demand for a cheap and simple weapon to replace the Thompson. Designed by George Hyde assisted by a metal-pressing expert from General Motors, the M3 was designed so as to be capable of being changed to 9mm calibre by changing the bolt, barrel and magazine, though it seems very few such changes were ever made in the field. Its principal defects were its rudimentary

SPECIFICATION & OPERATION

CARTRIDGE
.45 ACP or 9mm Parabellum

DIMENSIONS
Length, stock extended:
745mm (29.33in)
Length, stock retracted:
570mm (22.44in)
Barrel: 203mm (8.0in)
Weight, empty: 3.67kg
(8lb 2oz)
Rifling: 4 grooves, rh
Magazine capacity: 30 rounds
Rate of fire: 400 rds/min

IN PRODUCTION 1942-44

MARKINGS
'GUIDE LAMP DIV OF GENERAL MOTORS/ US MODEL M3/ serial number' on top of receiver.

SAFETY
A hinged cover over the ejection port carries a lug which, when the cover is closed, engages with a recess in the bolt if the bolt is forward, or with the front edge of the bolt when the bolt is to the rear,

locking the bolt in either position.

UNLOADING
Magazine catch is on the left side of the magazine housing. Open ejection port cover; remove magazine. Pull back bolt retracting lever on right side of receiver to cock the bolt. Inspect the chamber through the ejection port, press the trigger, close the ejection port cover.

SPECIFICATION & OPERATION

CARTRIDGE
9mm Parabellum

DIMENSIONS
Length, stock extended:
835mm (32.9in)
Length, stock retracted:
647mm (35.47in)
Barrel: 330mm (13,0in) with
compensator
Weight, empty: 2.17kg
(4lb 12oz)
Rifling: 6 grooves, rh
Magazine capacity: 50 or 100
rounds
Rate of fire: 750 rds/min
IN PRODUCTION 1990-

MARKINGS
'CALICO M-900' on left side of
magazine mounting. Serial
number on left side of frame.

SAFETY
Selector in the front edge of
the trigger guard, with levers
on both sides of the weapon.
When to the rear, and
projecting into the trigger
guard, the system is safe.
Pushed forward one notch
permits single shots, all the
way for automatic fire. Safety
can be set by using the outside
levers, removed by pressing
forward with the trigger finger.

UNLOADING
Magazine catch on top of
receiver. Squeeze in, then
remove magazine by
withdrawing back and up. Pull
back cocking lever to remove
any round in the chamber,
inspect chamber via the
ejection slot, release cocking
handle, pull trigger.

One of several similar weapons in the Calico range, the M960A is known as the 'Mini Sub Machine Gun'; there is also a 'Light' model with a solid butt-stock and a 'Concealable' model in which the barrel does not extend beyond the fore-end. All use the same receiver and the same helical-feed magazines. The 50 round magazine is shown here; the 100 round is similar but longer, stretching over the rear end of the receiver.

Colt (USA)

This is based upon the well-known M16 rifle configuration, so that the training time is greatly reduced when soldiers already familiar with the rifle are given this weapon. The butt-stock is telescoping, and the only outward difference between this and various short M16 type rifles is the thin and long magazine. Note that purchasers had the option of full automatic fire or three-round bursts, and the fire selector switch marking will indicate which mechanism is in place. It is also possible to have a purely semi-automatic model with no automatic or burst-fire capability.

SPECIFICATION & OPERATION

CARTRIDGE
9mm Parabellum

DIMENSIONS
Length, stock extended: 730mm (28.75in)
Length, stock retracted: 650mm (25.6in)
Barrel: 260mm (10.25in)
Weight, empty: 2.59kg (5lb 11oz)
Rifling: 6 grooves, rh
Magazine capacity: 20 or 32 rounds
Rate of fire: 900 rds/min

IN PRODUCTION 1990-
MARKINGS
Colt 'prancing pony' trademark, 'COLT' in script form, 'SMG' and serial number on left side of magazine housing.

SAFETY
Selector switch on left side above the pistol grip. When the switch is to the rear and its associated pointer to the front, the weapon is safe. With the switch forward and the pointer to the rear, the weapon is set for either automatic fire or three-round bursts. The intermediate position, with the switch down, gives single shots.

UNLOADING
Magazine release on both sides of the weapon, a shrouded button on the right and a hinged tab on the left. Press either to remove magazine. Pull back the cocking handle ('wings' at the base of the carrying handle) inspect the chamber via the ejection slot, release bolt, press trigger.

Something like 10,000 of these guns were produced and supplied to US police forces, US Army, Cuba and Peru, and it was also made under licence in Peru. Most were in .45 ACP calibre, though some were also made in 9mm Parabellum and in .38 Super Auto chambering. Two improved models, the Model 7 which fired from a closed bolt, and the Model 8 which had a long fore-end rather than a forward pistol grip, were developed but it is doubtful if many of either type were made. Thailand bought the design of the Model 8 and invited the designer to assist in setting up a factory, but there is no record of any production.

SPECIFICATION & OPERATION

CARTRIDGE
.45 ACP

DIMENSIONS
Length o/a: 750mm (29,5in)
Barrel: 225mm (8.85in)
Weight, empty: 3.27kg (7lb 3oz)
Rifling: 6 grooves, rh
Magazine capacity: 30 rounds
Rate of fire: 600 rds/min

IN PRODUCTION 1949-52

MARKINGS
'INGRAM 6 POLICE ORDNANCE CO LOS ANGELES CALIF. U.S.A.' above the chamber. Serial number on right side of chamber

SAFETY
Pull back cocking handle and turn it up into a recess in the cocking handle slot. Some later models are said to have a manual safety catch on the left side of the receiver. Fire selection is done by the trigger; first pressure produces single shots, more pressure brings automatic fire.

UNLOADING
The magazine catch is behind the magazine housing. Remove magazine, pull back cocking handle to clear any round from the breech, inspect the chamber via the ejection port, release cocking handle, pull trigger.

Ruger MP-9 (USA)

This weapon was designed by Uzi Gal, designer of the Uzi submachine gun, in the early 1980s. It was originally to be manufactured in Canada, but this fell through and the design was eventually sold to Sturm, Ruger who made some minor changes and put the weapon into production in 1994.

The frame and lower receiver are of Zytel synthetic material, the upper portion of the receiver being of steel. Internally the operation is similar to that of the Uzi, using a telescoping bolt, but firing

SPECIFICATION & OPERATION

CARTRIDGE
9 x 19mm Parabellum

DIMENSIONS
Length, butt extended: 556mm
(21.89in)
Length, butt folded: 376mm
(14.80in)
Barrel: 173mm (6.81in)
Weight: 3.0kg (6lb 10oz)
Rifling: 6 grooves, rh
Magazine: 34 rounds
Rate of Fire: 600 rds/min

IN PRODUCTION : 1994-

MARKINGS

SAFETY
Three-position sliding safety catch/selector switch on the left side, above the pistol grip, as on the Uzi submachine gun. Rearward position is safe, mid position single shots, forward for full automatic fire.

UNLOADING
Magazine release is at the bottom of the pistol grip. Remove magazine, pull back cocking handle and hold bolt on sear. Examine the chamber through the ejection port and verify that it is empty. Grasp the cocking handle, pull the trigger and allow the bolt to close under control.

from a closed bolt. The pistol grip is at the centre of balance and acts as the magazine housing, and behind the grip is an openwork frame which runs back and up to the rear of the receiver. The folding butt is hinged and jointed so as to fold down and lie alongside this fixed openwork frame when not required.

Vietcong K-50M (Vietnam)

In 1950 the Chinese produced a copy of the Soviet PPSh-41 submachine gun, calling it the Type 50. Numbers of these were supplied to North Vietnam, who then redesigned it and produced it as this K-50M. The major changes were the removal of the original fold-over butt, replacing it with a telescoping wire butt, shortening the barrel jacket and removing the muzzle compensator, and adding a pistol grip. The curved magazine is similar to the Chinese pattern. The result is quite a distinctive weapon, unlikely to be mistaken for anything else. So far as mechanism goes, though, it is still a Soviet PPSh.

SPECIFICATION & OPERATION

CARTRIDGE
7.62mm Soviet Pistol (or 7.63mm Mauser)

DIMENSIONS
Length, stock extended: 756mm (29.76in)
Length, stock retracted: 571mm (22.46in)
Barrel: 269mm (10.59in)
Weight, empty: 3.40kg (7lb 8oz)
Rifling: 4 grooves, rh
Magazine capacity: 25, 32 or 40 rounds
Rate of fire: 600 rds/min

IN PRODUCTION 1958-65

MARKINGS
Serial number on top of receiver.

SAFETY
Manual safety latch on the cocking handle; this can be pushed into notches cut into the receiver wall when the bolt is either fully forward or fully back, and locks the bolt in that position. There is a fire selector switch inside the trigger guard, in front of the trigger; push forward for automatic fire, back for single shots.

UNLOADING
Magazine release is behind the magazine housing and folds up under the stock. Fold down, press forward and slide the magazine out. Pull back cocking handle to eject any round in the chamber, inspect the chamber via the ejection port, release the cocking handle, press trigger,

Zastava M85 (Yugoslavia)

This is obviously a Yugoslavian copy of the Soviet AKSU-74 submachine gun, differing in being chambered for the Western 5.56mm cartridge rather than the Soviet 5.45mm round, probably in order to attract the export market. Due to the current political situation in ex-Yugoslavia we have no idea of how many of these weapons have been made, or where they may have been distributed, but the possibility of their appearance should be borne in mind, and a weapon of this shape should not be automatically identified as the AKSU.

SPECIFICATION & OPERATION

CARTRIDGE
5.56 x 45mm

DIMENSIONS
Length, stock extended:
790mm (31.10in)
Length, stock retracted:
570mm (22.44in)
Barrel: 315mm (12.40in)
Weight, empty: 3.20kg
(7lb 1oz)
Rifling: 6 grooves, rh
Magazine capacity: 20 or 30 rounds
Rate of fire: 700 rds/min

IN PRODUCTION 1987-

MARKINGS
`CRVENA ZASTAVA M/85; [year]; serial number' on right side of receiver.

SAFETY
This uses the standard Kalashnikov type of safety lever/fire selector on the right side of the receiver; in the top position it locks the trigger and blocks movement of the cocking handle and the weapon is safe; the first position DOWN gives automatic fire and the fully DOWN position gives single shots.

UNLOADING
Magazine release is behind the magazine housing. Remove magazine, set the fire selector to one of the fire positions, pull back the cocking handle to eject any round in the chamber. Inspect the chamber via the ejection port, release the cocking handle, pull the trigger.

The Model 56 was a replacement for the elderly Model 49 and was a simpler design to manufacture. It was basically similar in outline to the German MP40 and followed some of the internal design layout. The folding butt was a direct copy of the MP40, as was the pistol grip. The bolt was simplified and the return spring was a single large coil. A bayonet was fitted, and overall effect was of a modern well designed weapon. In fact, it suffered from using the 7.62mm Soviet pistol round, and something with more stopping power would have made it a more effective weapon. As a result, a later version, known as the M65 was developed in 9mm Parabellum calibre for export, but it is not thought that many were ever sold.

SPECIFICATION & OPERATION

CARTRIDGE
7.62mm Soviet Pistol

DIMENSIONS
Length o/a: 870mm (34.25in)
Weight: unloaded: 2.98kg (6lb 9oz)
Barrel: 250mm (9.84in)
Rifling: 4 grooves, rh
Magazine capacity: 32 rounds
Rate of fire: 600 rds/min

IN PRODUCTION 1957-

MARKINGS
M56, factory identification number and serial number on left side of receiver.

SAFETY
There is a cross-bolt safety catch in the receiver above the trigger; pushed to the right for fire, to the left for safe. In front of this catch, on the left side, is a two position selector giving single shots or automatic fire.

UNLOADING
Magazine catch is on the magazine housing. Depress and remove the magazine. Pull back cocking handle until it catches on the sear. Examine the chamber via the ejection port to ensure it is empty. Grasp cocking handle, press trigger, and allow the bolt to go forward under control.

BOLT ACTION RIFLES

Bolt Action Rifles

There have only been a handful of successful bolt actions; there have been a number of unsuccessful ones , and there are some which appear to be different simply to avoid patent litigation, but knowledge of the principal systems will probably be a sufficient guide to anything which may be encountered. Bolt systems are divided into two - turn-bolts and straight-pull bolts:

TURN-BOLTS

so-called because to open them it is necessary to lift the handle and so rotate the body of the bolt in order to unlock it from the chamber or action:-

MAUSER

The most widely used, because it is undoubtedly the strongest and generally considered to be the most reliable and accurate. The bolt carries lugs with which it locks firmly into the chamber so that there can be no movement of the bolt during firing. The drawback is that the bolt must revolve sufficiently to disengage these lugs before it can move backwards, and on loading it must close completely before it can be rotated to lock. Together with this bolt came the charger-loading system, adopted by many other bolt actions, in which the ammunition is held in some form of spring clip. This clip is positioned above the magazine and the cartridges are pushed from the clip, into the magazine, after which the clip is discarded. In order to avoid confusion between this system and the system developed by Mannlicher, the Mauser (and Lee, and others,) system is called 'charger loading', while the Mannlicher system is called 'clip loading'

LEE

The Lee turnbolt is theoretically weaker and less accurate than the Mauser, but it is undoubtedly the fastest and smoothest of all bolt actions; a trained soldier with a Lee-Enfield rifle can deliver aimed fire twice as fast as one with a Mauser. The fundamental difference is that the bolt lugs lock into recesses in the action body; these have curved surfaces so that as soon as the bolt begins to turn, it also begins to open and move backwards, and on closing it can begin rotation before it is completely closed. The theoretical disadvantage is that since the bolt is not locked into the chamber it can compress slightly under the pressure of the explosion and so affect the chamber pressure and ballistics. In practice this is scarcely noticeable.

KRAG-JORGENSEN

The Krag system, from Norway, is less a bolt system than a magazine system, since the bolt is of no great interest but the magazine lies laterally beneath the bolt and feeds up and around the left side to deliver the cartridge to the boltway on the left-hand side of the action. Loading is done by opening a hinged trap-door and pushing loose rounds in; on closing the door a magazine spring bears on the rounds and forces them up to the feedway. It is a reliable enough system, particularly with rimmed ammunition, but, as with so many other systems, one wonders whether avoiding existing patents was the major reason for its development.

LEBEL

The French Lebel bolt system uses two forward locking lugs plus a large rectangular lug on the outside of the bolt body which locks into a recess in the action. A screw passes through this lug to retain the

Bolt Action Rifles

bolt head; the screw must be removed and the head detached in order to remove the bolt, since the head will not pass through the boltway and out of the back of the action. It also has a unique magazine, tubular in form, lying beneath the barrel, from which rounds are lifted up to the breech by a linkage operated by the movement of the bolt.

MANNLICHER

The essence of the Mannlicher system is not so much the bolt, which is comparable to that of the Mauser, but the magazine, since Mannlicher invented the clip-loading system. In this system the cartridges are held in a clip, and clip and cartridges are dropped into the magazine as a unit. The clip is locked in place and a spring-loaded arm pushes the cartridges up as they are loaded. When the last shot is fired the clip can be expelled; in some later designs it expels itself.

MOSIN-NAGANT

Developed by Captain Mosin of the Russian Army, this bolt is a complex three-piece device which appears to have been designed primarily to avoid patent litigation.

STRAIGHT-PULL BOLTS

so-called because to open them it is only necessary to grasp the handle and pull it straight back without lifting.

MANNLICHER

The founder of the straight-pull system, Mannlicher developed two kinds. His first used a wedge beneath the bolt which was pushed down and lifted up by a sleeve attached to the bolt handle. The second also used a sleeve with helical grooves inside which connected with lugs on the bolt body, carried inside the sleeve, so that as the handle was pulled back the sleeve rode over and forced the lugs to turn the bolt and unlock it.

SCHMIDT

This resembles the Mannlicher second type, but uses a bolt sleeve which carries the bolt body. A rod is driven back and forth by the handle and engages in a cam track in the bolt sleeve to rotate the sleeve. The locking lugs are actually on the sleeve, and the bolt body does not rotate. It was later modified to become much shorter but the principle remained the same. It has only ever been used on Swiss Army rifles and carbines.

LEE

The Lee straight pull is similar to the first Mannlicher system, using a wedge beneath the bolt which is controlled by the bolt handle; as the handle is pulled back it first lifts the wedge and then pulls on the bolt. It is unlikely to be encountered; almost all Lee straight-pull rifles are museum pieces.

ROSS

The Ross resembles the second Mannlicher but uses a screw-thread in the bolt sleeve which engaged with a helical screw-thread on the bolt body, so that reciprocal movement of the sleeve rotates the bolt and its locking lugs. Unfortunately it proved susceptible to dirt on active service, and the bolt can be assembled wrongly, still close and fire, but is then blown open violently. Not to be recommended.

Steyr-Mannlicher SSG-69 (Austria)

D eveloped as a sniping rifle for the Austrian Army in 1969, this was later put on the commercial market and was also adopted by numerous military and police forces. Minor changes have been made such as a heavier and larger bolt knob, a short-barrelled version, a special 'Police Version' which will accept a silencer, but they all use the same basic mechanism, a turnbolt locking by lugs on the bolt turning into recesses in the receiver behind the magazine. The magazine is now the Schoenauer type, though for some years a ten-round detachable box was offered as an alternative.

SPECIFICATION & OPERATION

CARTRIDGE
7.62 x 51mm NATO

DIMENSIONS
Length o/a: 1140mm (44.9in)
Weight: 3.90kg (8lb 9oz)
Barrel: 650mm (25.6in)
Rifling: 4 grooves, rh
Magazine capacity: 5 rounds

IN PRODUCTION 1969-

MARKINGS
'STEYR-MANNLICHER SSG69' and serial number on left side of receiver.

SAFETY
Manual safety catch on right rear of receiver. Push forward to fire, back for safe.

UNLOADING
Squeeze in the two sides of the magazine release catch at the bottom edge of the stock and withdraw the rotary magazine; the rear end is transparent and reveals the contents; empty out any ammunition by pushing the top round out and allowing the spool to turn and present the next round. Open the bolt to extract any round in the chamber. Examine the chamber and feedway, close the bolt, press the trigger, replace the empty magazine.

The essential difference between the Mannlicher and other turn-bolt systems lay in his pioneering of the clip loading system. The bolt is opened and a complete clip of ammunition is dropped into the magazine. An arm forces the cartridges up in the clip to be collected by the bolt, and when the last round is loaded, the clip drops out of the magazine through a hole in the bottom, or, in some designs, was ejected upwards when the bolt was opened after the last round was fired. Note that the clip is an essential part of the magazine system; without a clip the rifle is a single-shot weapon, since the magazine is unusable.

SPECIFICATION & OPERATION

CARTRIDGE
6.5 x 53R (Dutch); 6.5 x 53mm (Romanian)

DIMENSIONS: (Dutch M1895 rifle)
Length o/a: 1295mm (51.0in)
Weight: 4.30kg (9lb 8oz)
Barrel: 790mm (31.10in)
Rifling: 4 grooves, rh
Magazine capacity: 5 rounds

IN PRODUCTION 1895-1940

MARKINGS
Manufacturer ('STEYR' or 'HEMBRUG'), year and serial number above chamber.

SAFETY
A thumb-switch at the top rear of the bolt. Turned to the right, the rifle is safe. Turned to the left, the rifle is ready to fire. Note that on the Romanian M1893 rifle the safety can only be applied when the striker is cocked; on the Dutch M1895 it can be applied in any condition of the bolt.

UNLOADING
Open bolt to extract any cartridge in the chamber. Examine the magazine aperture; if there are cartridges in the magazine, press forward the clip release button in the front edge of the trigger guard. This will allow the clip, with any remaining ammunition, to be ejected upwards through the action. Check the chamber and magazine are both empty, close the bolt, press the trigger.

Mannlicher straight-pull bolt rifles (Austria)

There are two varieties of straight-pull bolt used in Mannlicher rifles; the first has a wedge beneath the bolt which is forced down by movement of the handle, and is found on the M1886 Austrian rifle. The second uses a bolt sleeve with helical grooves, inside which is a bolt body with lugs; as the bolt handle, attached to the sleeve, is pulled back, the grooves in the sleeve force the bolt body to turn and unlock. This was used on the Austrian M1895 service rifle. Both are designed so that if the bolt is not securely locked, the firing pin cannot go forward.

SPECIFICATION & OPERATION

CARTRIDGE
8 X 50R Austrian Service

DIMENSIONS: (Austrian M1895 rifle)
Length o/a: 1272mm (50.0in)
Weight: 3.78kg (8lb 6oz)
Barrel: 765mm (30.11in)
Rifling: 4 grooves, rh
Magazine capacity: 5 rounds

IN PRODUCTION 1895-1918

MARKINGS
'STEYR M.95' over chamber. Serial number on left of chamber.

SAFETY
Manual safety catch on the left rear side of the action. When turned up it engages with the bolt, locking it in place, and also partly withdraws the striker. Turned down, to the left, the rifle is made ready to fire.

UNLOADING
Place safety catch to the 'fire' position. Open the bolt to extract any round in the chamber. Examine the magazine aperture; if there is ammunition in the magazine, press the clip release button in the front edge of the trigger guard. This will eject the clip and any ammunition upwards through the action. Check the chamber and magazine are both empty, close the bolt, pull the trigger.

Mannlicher-Schoenauer Greek M1903 (Austria)

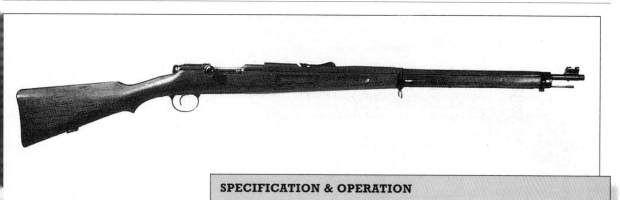

This was a combination of the Mannlicher turn-bolt breech with a rotary spool magazine developed by Otto Schoenauer. The magazine consists of a spindle with five grooves for cartridges around its circumference, held under tension by a spring. As the cartridges are fed into the magazine from a charger they slot into the grooves and turn the spindle, placing more tension on the spring. As the bolt is operated, so the spring turns the spindle to present each cartridge to the bolt in turn. The Greek 1903 rifle was the only service weapon to use this magazine, but it was widely used on sporting rifles and carbines and is still used today on the Steyr-Mannlicher SSG69 (below).

SPECIFICATION & OPERATION

CARTRIDGE
6.5 x 54mm Greek Service

DIMENSIONS
Length o/a: 1226mm (48.25in)
Weight: 3.77kg (8lb 5oz)
Barrel: 725mm (28.54in)
Rifling: 4 grooves, rh
Magazine capacity: 5 rounds

IN PRODUCTION 1903-30

MARKINGS

Year and place of manufacture ('BREDA' or 'STEYR') above breech. Serial number on right side of action.

SAFETY
Manual safety catch at the rear of the bolt. Turn to the left to fire, to the right for safe.

UNLOADING
Place the safety catch to 'fire'. Open the bolt to extract and eject any round in the chamber. Examine the chamber and magazine aperture; if there is ammunition remaining in the magazine, press down the knurled catch on the right-hand side of the action. This will release the cartridges remaining in the magazine and cause them to be ejected through the action. Check chamber and magazine again, close the bolt, pull the trigger.

FN 30-11 Sniping rifle (Belgium)

SPECIFICATION & OPERATION

CARTRIDGE
7.62 x 51mm NATO

DIMENSIONS
Length o/a: 1117mm (43.97in)
Weight: 4.85kg (10lb 10oz)
Barrel: 502mm (19.76in)
Rifling: 4 grooves, rh
Magazine capacity: 10 rounds

IN PRODUCTION 1978-86

MARKINGS
`FABRIQUE NATIONALE
HERSTAL` on left side of barrel.
Serial number on right side of
action.

SAFETY
Manual safety catch on the end
of the bolt. To the left for fire,
to the right for safe.

UNLOADING
Place safety catch to `fire`. Open
the bolt to eject any round in
the chamber. Inspect the
magazine aperture; if
ammunition is in the magazine,
work the bolt to load and
unload cartridges until the
magazine is empty. Check both
chamber and magazine, then
depress the magazine platform
and close the bolt. Press the
trigger.

Developed as a sniping rifle for police and
military use, this used a standard Mauser bolt
action and integral magazine in a heavy receiver and
barrel. Aperture sights were fitted but a telescope
was the more usual sighting method. Accessories
such as a firing sling and bipod were usually
supplied with the rifle.

Sako TRG (Finland)

SPECIFICATION & OPERATION

CARTRIDGE
7.62 x 51mm NATO or .308
Lapua Magnum

DIMENSIONS: (TRG21)
Length o/a: 1150mm (45.27in)
Weight: 4.70kg (10lb 6oz)
Barrel: 660mm (26.0in)
Rifling: 4 grooves, rh
Magazine capacity: 10 rounds

IN PRODUCTION 1992-

MARKINGS
'SAKO TRG21' and serial number
on left side of receiver.

SAFETY
Manual safety catch inside the
trigger guard. Press forward to
fire, pull back to make safe,
which locks the bolt, trigger
and firing pin.

UNLOADING
Magazine release at rear of
magazine. Remove magazine,
empty out any ammunition.
Open bolt to extract any
cartridge left in the chamber.
Examine chamber and feedway,
close bolt, press trigger, replace
empty magazine.

The TRG is a specialised sniping rifle. The receiver
is of forged steel and the heavy barrel is also
cold-forged and fitted with a combined flash hider
and muzzle brake. The action and barrel are mounted
to an aluminium skeleton frame, to which is
attached the synthetic stock and fore-end. The
muzzle brake can be removed and replaced with a
silencer. The stock is fully adjustable in every
direction and is also capable of adaptation to right-
or left-handed firers. The TRG21 is the 7.62mm
model; there is also a TRG41 which fires .308 Lapua
Magnu; it has a 690mm barrel and a 5 round
magazine.

TOKKA M65-A308 (Finland)

The M65 was a popular sporting and hunting rifle for many years and can be found in a variety of chamberings and finishings from 6.5mm to 7.62mm. The model shown here, the A308 is so-called because it is chambered for .308 Winchester, the commercial version of 7.62mm NATO. A heavy barrel rifle with bipod and pistol grip, it is designed for precision shooting, either big game or sniping. The depth of the wooden stock conceals and protects the 10-round magazine. Other M65s have a five-round magazine.

SPECIFICATION & OPERATION

CARTRIDGE
7.62 x 51mm NATO

DIMENSIONS:
Length o/a: 1210mm (47.63in)
Weight: 5.15kg (11lb 6oz)
Barrel: 475mm (18.70in)
Rifling: 6 grooves, rh
Magazine capacity: 10 rounds

IN PRODUCTION 1985-1989

MARKINGS
TIKKA M65 and serial number on left side of receiver.

SAFETY
Mauser-type manual safety catch at rear of bolt.

UNLOADING
Magazine release at base of magazine well in front of the trigger. Remove magazine and empty if necessary. Open the bolt. Examine feedway and chamber. Close bolt and press trigger.

SPECIFICATION & OPERATION

CARTRIDGE
7.5 x 54mm French Service

DIMENSIONS
Length o/a: 1022mm (40.25in)
Weight: 3.75kg (8lb 4oz)
Barrel: 575mm (22.6in)
Rifling: 4 grooves, rh
Magazine capacity: 5 rounds

IN PRODUCTION 1936-55

MARKINGS
'ST ETIENNE' and year of
manufacture on left side of
action. Serial number on right
side of action.

SAFETY
There is no manual safety device
on this weapon. BE CAREFUL.

UNLOADING
Open the bolt to extract any
cartridge in the chamber. Then
press in the magazine floor
plate release button on the
right side of the action body, at
the front edge of the magazine,
and allow the magazine
contents to fall into the hand.
Check that the magazine space
and chamber are empty, close
the bolt, press the trigger.
Replace the magazine follower,
spring and floor-plate.

Ugly, roughly made, but immensely strong and
reliable, this was the French Army's rifle to
match the 7.5mm cartridge introduced in 1929. A
folding-butt model was also made for paratroops
and Alpine troops, though this is rarely encountered.
Late models (converted in the 1950s) have an
extended barrel with concentric rings to permit
launching rifle grenades. The finish varies from
phosphated, to browned to enamelled, according to
when it was made and for which arm of the service.

GIAT FR-F1 & FR-F2 (France)

SPECIFICATION & OPERATION

This is a precision sniping rifle based on the action of the MAS36 service rifle; it was actually designed first as a target rifle, and then modified for the sniping role. The F1 was issued first in 7.5mm calibre, and then changed to 7.62mm calibre in the late 1970s. The FR-F2 model is an improved version; the fire-end is of plastic-covered metal instead of wood, the bipod is stronger, and there is a thermal insulating sleeve over the barrel to prevent warping due to heat and reduce the infra-red signature.

CARTRIDGE
7.5 x 54mm or 7.62 x 51mm

DIMENSIONS
Length o/a: 1138mm (44.8in)
Weight: 5.20kg (11lb 7oz)
Barrel: 552mm (22.9in)
Rifling: 4 grooves. rh
Magazine capacity: 10 rounds

IN PRODUCTION 1966-80 (F1); 1984- (F2).

MARKINGS
'FR-F1 7.62 N M.A.S.' and serial number on left side of receiver.

SAFETY
Manual safety catch inside the trigger guard, behind the trigger. Press down to make safe; press up and to the left to fire.

UNLOADING
Magazine catch on the right side of the receiver above the front end of the magazine. Remove magazine. Place safety catch to 'fire' and open the bolt to eject any round in the chamber. Inspect the chamber, close the bolt, pull the trigger.

12.7mm PGM Hecate II (France)

PGM Precision are well-known makers of sporting rifles, and in the late 1980s they developed a range of sniping rifles, largely adopted by French and other continental police forces. The 'Hecate' is more or less a scaled-up version of their 'Intervention' sniping rifle and is a conventional bolt action repeating rifle. The wooden butt, with cheek-piece, can be removed for transportation and has a monopod beneath it; there is a bipod attached to the receiver fore-end, and a pistol grip. A large single-baffle muzzle brake reduces the recoil to a reasonable amount, and it cane be removed and replaced by a silencer. The rifle has been taken into use by the French Army.

SPECIFICATION & OPERATION

CARTRIDGE
50 Browning

DIMENSIONS
Length o/a: 1380mm (54.33in)
Barrel: 700mm (27.56in)
Weight: 13.50kg (29lb 12oz)
Rifling: 8 grooves, rh
Magazine capacity: 7 rounds

IN PRODUCTION 1988-

MARKINGS
None.

SAFETY
Manual safety catch on right side of receiver, locks sear and trigger.

UNLOADING
Remove magazine. Open bolt to extract any cartridge in the chamber. Examine magazine aperture and chamber to ensure both are empty. Close bolt, pull trigger.

Mauser Gewehr 98 (Germany)

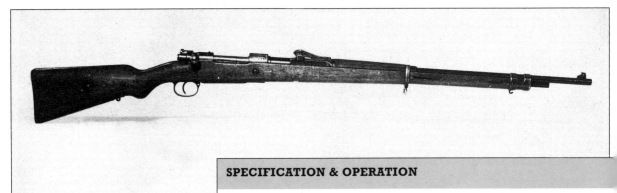

Mauser made many military rifles for various nations, but most of them were variations of this, the perfected Mauser rifle which armed the German Army for half a century; understand this and you understand them all. Robust, well-made, accurate and reliable, these rifles will last for years to come and still be serviceable. The Gew 98 improved on the basic Mauser design by having a third locking lug beneath the bolt, locking into a recess in the left action sidewall. The bolt sticks out at right-angles; a variation with a turned-down bolt was provided for cyclist troops in 1904 but is unlikely to be met.

SPECIFICATION & OPERATION

CARTRIDGE
7.92 x 57mm Mauser

DIMENSIONS
Length o/a: 1250mm (49.21in)
Weight: 4.09kg (9lb 0oz)
Barrel: 740mm (29.13in)
Rifling: 4 grooves, rh
Magazine capacity: 5 rounds

IN PRODUCTION 1898-1918

MARKINGS
'Mod 98', manufacturer's name and serial number on top of chamber.

SAFETY
A manual safety catch on the rear of the bolt. Turned to the left, the rifle is ready to fire. Turned to the right the rifle is safe.

UNLOADING
Place the safety catch to 'fire' and open the bolt to extract any round in the chamber. Examine the magazine aperture. If there is ammunition in the magazine, press the magazine floor-plate catch in the front edge of the trigger guard. This allows the magazine floor plate to hinge at its front end, open, and dump the contents of the magazine. Examine the chamber and magazine aperture again, close the bolt, press the trigger, and then close the magazine floor plate.

Mauser Karabiner 98k (Germany)

This is the 'short rifle' version of the Gewehr 98, developed in time for World War Two and is immediately recognisable by its shorter length, turned-down bolt, and recess in the woodwork to allow the bolt to be grasped. Rifles made from 1942 to 1945 are often of lesser quality - using stamped metal for the barrel bands and trigger-guard, for example, and laminated plywood for the furniture. They shot just as well, since there was no diminution in the quality of the bolt, barrel and action. About 1.5 million were made in ten years, so there will be Kar 98k's around for a long time yet.

SPECIFICATION & OPERATION

CARTRIDGE
7.92 x 57mm Mauser

DIMENSIONS
Length o/a: 1110mm (43.7oin)
Weight: 3.92kg (8lb 11oz)
Barrel: 600mm (23.6in)
Rifling: 4 grooves, rh
Magazine capacity: 5 rounds

IN PRODUCTION 1935-45

MARKINGS
'Kar 98k', manufacturer's code and serial number on sides of chamber.

SAFETY
A manual safety catch on the rear of the bolt. Turned to the left, the rifle is ready to fire. Turned to the right the rifle is safe.

UNLOADING
Place the safety catch to 'fire' and open the bolt to extract any round in the chamber. Examine the magazine aperture. If there is ammunition in the magazine, press the magazine floor-plate catch in the front edge of the trigger guard. This allows the magazine floor plate to hinge at its front end, open, and dump the contents of the magazine. Examine the chamber and magazine aperture again, close the bolt, press the trigger, and then close the magazine floor plate.

Mauser SP66 (Germany)

This is a heavy-barrelled rifle using the 'short-throw' Mauser bolt so as to reduce the amount of movement required of the firer; it is purely a sniper rifle and thus various refinements can be accommodated which would not be found on hunting or military weapons. The stock is adjustable in several directions, the 'lock time' between pulling the trigger and the bullet leaving the muzzle is extremely short, and there is a combined muzzle brake and flash hider. Optical sights are obligatory - there are no iron sights - and night sights can be very easily fitted.

SPECIFICATION & OPERATION

CARTRIDGE
7.62 x 51mm NATO or .300 Winchester Magnum

DIMENSIONS
Length o/a: 1120mm (44.29in)
Weight: 6.25kg (13lb 12oz)
Barrel: 730mm (28.75in)
Rifling: 4 grooves, rh
Magazine capacity: 3 rounds

IN PRODUCTION 1976-

MARKINGS
'MAUSER-WERKE OBERNDORF GmbH' and serial number on left side of receiver.

SAFETY
A manual safety catch on the rear of the bolt. Turned to the left, the rifle is ready to fire. Turned to the right the rifle is safe.

UNLOADING
Place the safety catch to 'fire' and open the bolt to extract any round in the chamber. Examine the magazine aperture. If there is ammunition in the magazine, press the magazine floor-plate catch in the front edge of the trigger guard. This allows the magazine floor plate to hinge at its front end, open, and dump the contents of the magazine. Examine the chamber and magazine aperture again, close the bolt, press the trigger, and then close the magazine floor plate.

This was developed by Mauser as a somewhat less expensive sniping rifle than the SP66 described above, principally for police use. The bolt design is new, though it adheres to the well-tried Mauser double front lug system, and the barrel is cold forged and provided with a muzzle brake and flash hider. The stock is of laminated wood and ventilated so as to avoid warping of the barrel due to heat concentration. No iron sights are fitted, optical sights being the rule.

SPECIFICATION & OPERATION

CARTRIDGE
7.62 x 51mm NATO

DIMENSIONS
Length o/a: 1210mm (47.63in)
Weight: 4.90kh (10lb 13oz)
Barrel: 730mm (28.75in)
Rifling: 4 grooves, rh
Magazine capacity: 9 rounds

IN PRODUCTION 1990-

MARKINGS
'MAUSER-WERKE OBERNDORF GmbH' and Serial Number on left of receiver.

SAFETY
A manual safety catch on the rear of the bolt. Turned to the left, the rifle is ready to fire. Turned to the right the rifle is safe.

UNLOADING
Withdraw the magazine from the bottom of the stock by pressing in the bottom catch. Empty the magazine of ammunition. Open the bolt, extracting any round remaining in the chamber. Examine the magazine aperture and the chamber to ensure both are empty, close the bolt, pull the trigger.

12.7mm Gepard M1, M1A1 (Hungary)

This is a single-shot anti-materiel rifle firing the Russian 12.7mm cartridge. The barrel is carried in a tubular cradle, which also mounts the bipod, and a barrel extension carried the padded butt plate. The pistol grip acts as the bolt handle; to load, the grip is twisted up, unlocking the interrupted-thread breech-block which can then be withdrawn completely from the rifle. A round is loaded into the chamber and the breech-piece is replaced, and the pistol grip turned down to lock. A hammer in the pistol grip unit is now manually cocked and the trigger pressed to fire the rifle. Aiming is done by means of a 12x telescope, and the cartridge is sufficiently accurate to deliver a 300mm (11.8inch) group at 600 meters range. The armour-piercing bullet will defeat 15mm of steel armour at the same range.

The M1A1 is the same weapon but mounted on a back-pack frame which also serves as a firing mount for use in soft ground or snow; the bipod is still attached to the cradle but folded up when the frame is used. The M1A1 weighs 48lb 8oz (22kg).

SPECIFICATION & OPERATION

CARTRIDGE
12.7 x 107mm Soviet

DIMENSIONS
Length o/a: 1570mm (61.81in)
Barrel: 1100mm (43.30in)
Weight: 19.0kg (41lb 14oz)
Rifling: 8 grooves, rh
Magazine: none; single shot.
IN PRODUCTION 1992-

MARKINGS

SAFETY
A thumb-operated catch on the pistol grip locks the hammer.

UNLOADING
Grasp the pistol grip and twist anti-clockwise until it unlocks, then remove the breech unit, together with any round which may be held by the extractor. Remove the cartridge, inspect the chamber, replace the breech piece and pull the trigger.

Mannlicher-Carcano TS Carbine M1891 (Italy)

The Mannlicher-Carcano family formed the Italian service weapons from 1891 to 1945. The TS (Truppo Special) carbine is one of the more common examples of the system; the other weapons - rifle M1891, cavalry carbine M1891, carbine M91/24 and rifle M91/38 - are identical in their mechanism. The bolt is basically Mauser, the magazine Mannlicher, with its associated clip, and the Carcano part of the title comes from the Italian who designed the bolt safety system. They were mostly sold off after 1945 and spread throughout the world; President Kennedy was shot with a Mannlicher-Carcano carbine.

SPECIFICATION & OPERATION

CARTRIDGE
6.5 x 52mm Mannlicher

DIMENSIONS
Length o/a: 920mm (36.22in)
Weight: 3.13kg (6lb 14oz)
Barrel: 450mm (17.72in)
Rifling: 4 grooves, rh
Magazine capacity: 6 rounds

IN PRODUCTION 1891-1918

MARKINGS
Year of manufacture and 'TERNI' and serial number on side of breech.

SAFETY
Manual safety catch in the form of a collar with a knurled 'flag' around the end of the bolt. Turned DOWN to the right, the rifle is ready to fire. Turned UP so that it is visible in the line of sight, the rifle is set to safe.

UNLOADING
Place safety catch to 'fire' and open the bolt, thus ejecting any round which may be in the chamber. Inspect the chamber and magazine. If there is ammunition in the magazine, press the clip latch in the front edge of the trigger guard; this will release the ammunition clip and it, together with any cartridges it contains, will be ejected upwards through the top of the action. Check again, close the bolt and press the trigger.

Mannlicher-Carcano M1938 (Italy)

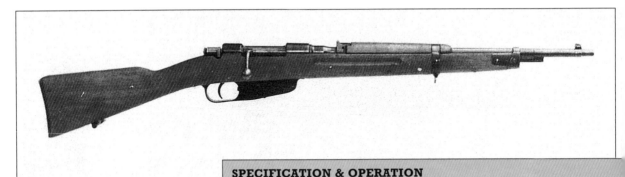

The 1914-18 war suggested that the Italian 6.5mm cartridge was insufficiently powerful, and experience in North Africa and Abyssinia reinforced this view, and the Model 1938 rifle and carbine were built around a new 7.5mm cartridge. However, they left it too late, and when Italy entered the war in 1940 it was decided to withdraw these new weapons and give them to the militia so as to simplify ammunition supply in the field. A handful of the carbines were modified in 1944 to fire German 7.92mm Mauser ammunition. These can be recognised by 7.92 S stamped into the top of the chamber; it is unwise to fire these converted weapons.

SPECIFICATION & OPERATION

CARTRIDGE
7.35 x 51mm Italian M38

DIMENSIONS
Length o/a: 1021mm (40.2in)
Weight: 3.40kg (7lb 8oz)
Barrel: 530mm (29.85in)
Rifling: 4 grooves, rh
Magazine capacity: 6

IN PRODUCTION 1937-40

MARKINGS
Year of manufacture, 'TERNI', and serial number on right side of chamber.

SAFETY
Manual safety catch in the form of a collar with a knurled `flag' around the end of the bolt. Turned DOWN to the right, the rifle is ready to fire. Turned UP so that it is visible in the line of sight, the rifle is set to safe.

UNLOADING
Place safety catch to 'fire' and open the bolt, thus ejecting any round which may be in the chamber. Inspect the chamber and magazine. If there is ammunition in the magazine, press the clip latch in the front edge of the trigger guard; this will release the ammunition clip and it, together with any cartridges it contains, will be ejected upwards through the top of the action. Check again, close the bolt and press the trigger.

Beretta Sniper (Italy)

This is a conventional Mauser-type bolt action, with a heavy free-floating barrel and an harmonic balancer contained within a tube concealed by the wooden fore-end. This is vibrated by the shot being fired and is so designed as to damp out vibrations in the barrel, ensuring the maximum accuracy. There is a flash hider on the muzzle, and the tube of the balanced forms a point of attachment for a bipod. Fully adjustable iron sights are provided but it also carries a NATO-standard mount for telescope and electro-optical sights.

SPECIFICATION & OPERATION

CARTRIDGE
7.62 x 51mm NATO

DIMENSIONS
Length o/a: 1165mm (45.9in)
Weight: 5.55kg (12lb 4oz)
Barrel: 586mm (23.05in)
Rifling: 4 grooves, rh
Magazine capacity: 5 rounds

IN PRODUCTION 1985-

MARKINGS
`P.BERETTA` above chamber.
Serial number right side of receiver.

SAFETY
Thumb-catch behind bolt handle

UNLOADING
Magazine catch behind magazine. Push safety catch to `fire`, remove magazine, open bolt to eject any round in the chamber. Inspect chamber, close bolt, press trigger.

Arisaka 38th Year rifle (Japan)

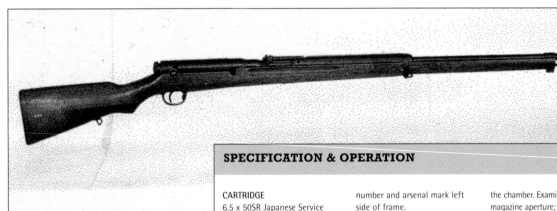

Japanese service rifle, based on the Mauser system, also supplied to Britain, Mexico, Russia, Indonesia and Thailand at various times. Can be found converted to fire the US .30-06 cartridge, done in the 1950s to provide weapons for South Korea, or for the 7.92mm Mauser, a conversion done by the Chinese. Something like three million were made and they can be found almost anywhere. Japanese nomenclature can confuse; `38th Year' refers to the reign of the Emperor at the time of introduction; it equates to 1905. The system changed in the 1930s (see p306).

SPECIFICATION & OPERATION

CARTRIDGE
6.5 x 50SR Japanese Service

DIMENSIONS
Length o/a: 1275mm (50.2in)
Weight: 4.12kg (9lb 1oz)
Barrel: 799mm (31.46in)
Rifling: 4 or 6 grooves, rh
Magazine capacity: 5 rounds

IN PRODUCTION 1907-44

MARKINGS
Japanese ideographs for `38 Year' above chamber; serial number and arsenal mark left side of frame.

SAFETY
Knurled cap at the rear end of the bolt is the safety catch. With the rifle cocked, press in this cap with the palm of the hand and twist it to the right to make safe, to the left to fire. It only works with the rifle cocked.

UNLOADING
Set safety catch to `fire'. Open bolt to extract any round left in the chamber. Examine the magazine aperture; if there is ammunition in the magazine, place one hand underneath the magazine plate under the stock, and with the other hand press forward the magazine catch in the front edge of the trigger guard. This will release the magazine floor plate and the contents of the magazine. Replace the magazine spring and plate (front edge first), check there is no ammunition in magazine or chamber, close bolt, press trigger.

Arisaka Type 99 short rifle (Japan)

This began as a conversion of the 38th Year rifle to a 7.7mm cartridge. That proved unwieldy and the design was changed to a short rifle which did away with the need for carbines. Early models were excellent but those made in the last year of the war were crude; few have survived. The 'Paratroop' version is similar but has either an interrupted thread or wedge joint between barrel and action, allowing it to be dismantled into two pieces. 'Type 99' now refers to the year in the Japanese calendar and equates to 1939 in western chronology.

SPECIFICATION & OPERATION

CARTRIDGE
7.7 x 58mm Japanese Service

DIMENSIONS
Length o/a: 1150mm (45.27in)
Weight: 3.80kg (8lb 6oz)
Barrel: 657mm (25.9in)
Rifling: 4 grooves, rh
Magazine capacity: 5 rounds

IN PRODUCTION 1940-45

MARKINGS
Japanese ideographs for 'Type 99' above chamber; serial number and arsenal mark left side of frame.

SAFETY
Knurled cap at the rear end of the bolt is the safety catch. With the rifle cocked, press in this cap with the palm of the hand and twist it to the right to make safe, to the left to fire. It only works with the rifle cocked.

UNLOADING
Set safety catch to 'fire'. Open bolt to extract any round left in the chamber. Examine the magazine aperture; if there is ammunition in the magazine, place one hand underneath the magazine plate under the stock, and with the other hand press forward the magazine catch in the front edge of the trigger guard. This will release the magazine floor plate and the contents of the magazine. Replace the magazine spring and plate (front edge first), check there is no ammunition in magazine or chamber, close bolt, press trigger.

Krag-Jorgensen rifles (Norway)

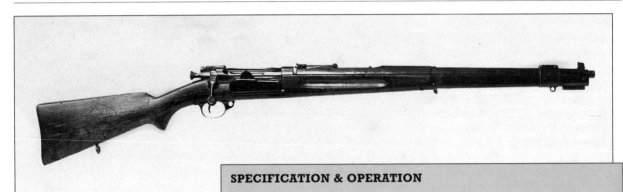

The Krag-Jorgensen was developed in Norway and is unusual because of its side-loading magazine. The door flap is opened, loose rounds placed inside, and the door closed, which puts pressure on the rounds and feeds them under and around the bolt to appear on the left side of the boltway. It was adopted by Denmark then Norway and then the USA, but only Norway stayed with it, developing their last version as late as 1930. Many thousands of these rifles and carbines were sold off for hunting purposes in Scandinavia and the USA and are still in use in both areas.

SPECIFICATION & OPERATION

CARTRIDGE
6.5 x 55mm (Norway; .30 Krag (USA); 8 x 56R (Denmark)

DIMENSIONS: (Norway, M1930)
Length o/a: 1219mm (48.0in)
Weight: 5.19kg (11lb 7oz)
Barrel: 750mm (29.53in)
Rifling: 4 grooves, lh
Magazine capacity: 5 rounds

IN PRODUCTION 1888-1935

MARKINGS
`(USA): MODEL 1894 SPRINGFIELD ARMORY' and serial number on left side of receiver.

SAFETY
Manual safety catch on the end of the bolt. Turn to the left for fire, to the right for safe.

UNLOADING
Open the magazine by hinging the door forward (Danish weapons) or down (US and Norwegian), tipping the rifle to the right and allowing the cartridges to fall out on to some convenient surface. Close the magazine, set the safety catch to `fire' and open the bolt to eject any round in the chamber. Inspect the chamber and the magazine aperture to the left of the boltway to ensure no ammunition remains in the weapon. Close the bolt, press the trigger.

Vapensmia NM149S (Norway)

mandatory. The stock is of laminated beech and the butt is adjustable for length and may be fitted with a cheek-piece. A bipod and a sound suppressor are also available for this rifle.

This was developed as a sniper rifle for the Norwegian Army and police forces and is also available commercially as a target or hunting rifle. The action is that of the Mauser Gew. 98, using the standard Mauser three-lug bolt. The barrel is exceptionally heavy, and it is normally issued with a 6 x 42 telescope sight; there are emergency iron sights fitted, but optical sights are virtually

SPECIFICATION & OPERATION

CARTRIDGE
7.62 x 51mm NATO

DIMENSIONS
Length o/a: 1120mm (44,0in)
Weight: 5.60kg (12lb 6oz)
Barrel: 600mm (23.6in)
Rifling: 4 grooves, rh
Magazine capacity: 5 rounds

IN PRODUCTION 1990-

MARKINGS
NM149 on left side of action. Serial on right side.

SAFETY
Manual safety catch on rear end of bolt. Turn to the right for safe, to the left to fire.

UNLOADING
Magazine catch behind the magazine. Remove magazine and empty it of ammunition. Open the bolt to extract any round in the chamber. Examine the chamber and feedway, close the bolt, pull the trigger, replace the empty magazine.

Mosin-Nagant rifles (Russia)

This design originated in 1891 with a long rifle which remained in service until World War Two. It was generally superseded by the short 1938 carbine and the 1944, carbine which had an attached bayonet. Copies of the 1944 model were also made in China, Hungary and Poland, and Mosin-Nagant rifles were converted to 8mm in Austria and 7.92mm in Germany and Poland during and after World War One. Large numbers of 1891 rifles were made in France and the USA on contract.

SPECIFICATION & OPERATION

CARTRIDGE
7.62 x 54R Russian Service

DIMENSIONS: (Model 1938 Carbine)
Length o/a: 1020mm (40.16in)
Weight: 3.45kg (7lb 10oz)
Barrel: 510mm (20.0in)
Rifling: 4 grooves, rh
Magazine capacity: 5 rounds

IN PRODUCTION 1892-1950

MARKINGS
Arsenal mark, year and serial number on top of chamber.

Serial number on bolt.

SAFETY
Manual safety by pulling back the cocking-piece at the rear of the bolt and rotating it to the left as far as it will go, then releasing it. This turns part of the cocking-piece so that it rests on a solid part of the receiver. The trigger still functions but the striker cannot go forward.

UNLOADING
Open bolt to extract any round remaining in the chamber.

Examine the magazine aperture; if there is ammunition in the magazine, release the magazine floor plate by pressing the catch behind the plate, in front of the trigger guard, and allowing the plate to hinge forward. This will allow the contents of the magazine to fall out. Close the magazine floor plate, check that the chamber and magazine are empty, close the bolt, pull the trigger.

Schmidt-Rubin M1931 carbine (Switzerland)

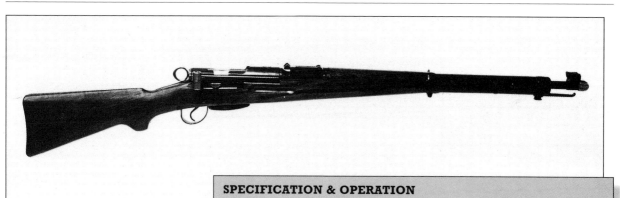

Although called a carbine, this was really a short rifle for use by the entire Swiss Army, and numbers are still in use today. The Schmidt action was completely revised; what had been the bolt sleeve became the bolt, with lugs at the front end locking into the chamber, so that the action body was shortened by almost half from the 1889 pattern. Numbers of these carbines were adapted as sniper rifles in 1942-43, and in the 1930s 100 were supplied to the Papal Guard in the Vatican City.

SPECIFICATION & OPERATION

CARTRIDGE
7.5 x 54mm Swiss Service M1911

DIMENSIONS
Length o/a: 1105mm (43.5in)
Weight: 4.00kg (8lb 13oz)
Barrel: 652mm (25.66in)
Rifling: 4 grooves, rh
Magazine capacity: 6 rounds

IN PRODUCTION 1933-58

MARKINGS
Serial number on left side of the action body and on bolt; Swiss cross on top of the chamber.

SAFETY
Pull back on the ring at the rear of the bolt, turn it to the right and release it. This withdraws the firing pin and locks it, making the rifle safe.

UNLOADING
Magazine catch on right side at top of magazine. Press in and remove magazine. Open bolt, examine chamber and feedway, close bolt. Press trigger.

SIG SSG-2000 (Switzerland)

The SIG 2000 uses an unusual bolt system; hinged wedges just in front of the bolt handle are forced outwards by cam action when the handle is turned down. These lock into recesses in the receiver; the bolt body does not revolve. Once cocked the trigger is pulled to a distinct check to 'set' it; thereafter a slight touch is sufficient to fire. This weapon has been designed as a target rifle and as a law enforcement sniper. There are no iron sights; a telescope is mandatory. In addition to the 7.62mm calibre it is also chambered for the 5.56 x 45mm and 7.5 x 55mm military calibres and the .300 Weatherby Magnum calibre.

SPECIFICATION & OPERATION

CARTRIDGE
7.62 x 51mm NATO and others

DIMENSIONS
Length o/a: 1210mm (47.64in)
Weight: 6.6kg (14lb 9oz) with sight.
Barrel: 510mm (20.0in) without flash hider.
Rifling: 4 grooves, rh
Magazine capacity: 4 rounds

IN PRODUCTION 1989-

MARKINGS
SIG-SAUER SSG 2000 on left side of action. Serial number alongside chamber on right side.

SAFETY
A sliding manual safety catch behind the bolt. When pushed forward, to reveal a red dot, the weapon is ready to fire. Pulled back, the weapon is safe.

UNLOADING
Magazine catch behind the magazine. Remove magazine and empty it of ammunition. Open the bolt to extract any round in the chamber. Examine the chamber and feedway, close the bolt, pull the trigger, replace the empty magazine.

SIG SSG-3000 (Switzerland)

This is a military and police sniping rifle derived from a successful target rifle. It is modular in form; the barrel and receiver are joined by screw clamps, and the trigger and magazine systems form a single unit which fits into the receiver. The stock is of laminated wood and ventilated to counter possible heat warping the heavy barrel. The bolt has six lugs and locks into the barrel. There is a rail under the fore-end to take a bipod or a firing sling. There are no iron sights; a mount for the standard Hensoldt telescope sight is normal, but a NATO STANAG sight mount can also be found.

SPECIFICATION & OPERATION

CARTRIDGE
7.62 x 51mm NATO

DIMENSIONS
Length o/a: 1180mm (45.45i)
Weight: 5.40kg (11lb 14oz)
Barrel: 610mm (24.0in)
Rifling: 4 grooves, rh
Magazine capacity: 5 rounds

IN PRODUCTION 1991-

MARKINGS
SIG-SAUER SSG 3000 on left side of action. Serial number alongside chamber on right side.

SAFETY
A sliding manual safety catch above the trigger, inside the trigger guard. When pushed forward the weapon is ready to fire. Pulled back, the weapon is safe.

UNLOADING
Magazine catch behind the magazine. Remove magazine and empty it of ammunition. Open the bolt to extract any round in the chamber. Examine the chamber and feedway, close the bolt, pull the trigger, replace the empty magazine.

Enfield Rifle No 2 (Pattern '14) (UK)

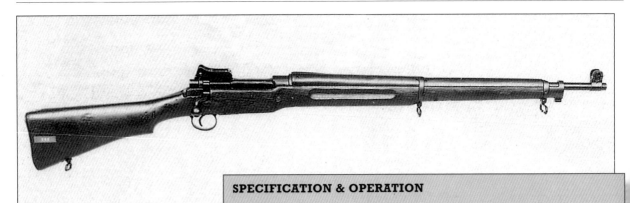

This was developed in 1912-14 as a potential replacement for the Lee-Enfield and uses a Mauser-type action. The design was in .276 calibre, firing a very powerful cartridge, and proved to be a ballistic disaster. On the outbreak of war in 1914 the project was abandoned, but to satisfy the enormous demand for rifles it was re-designed to fire the .303 cartridge and manufactured in the USA under contract by Remington and Winchester. The rifles remained in store during 1919-40 and were then brought out again and issued to the Home Guard and to some home defence units. Thousands were sold after 1945 for target rifles.

SPECIFICATION & OPERATION

CARTRIDGE
.303 British

DIMENSIONS
Length o/a: 1176mm (46.3in)
Weight: 4.14kg (9lb 2oz)
Barrel: 660mm (25.98in)
Rifling: 5 grooves, lh
Magazine capacity: 5 rounds

IN PRODUCTION 1915-17

MARKINGS
Maker's mark and serial number on top of chamber.

SAFETY
Manual safety catch on right side of action, behind the bolt handle. Forward for fire, rearward for safe.

UNLOADING
Place safety catch in the 'fire' position. Open bolt to extract any round in the chamber. Inspect magazine; if it contains ammunition continue working the bolt until all rounds have been loaded and ejected. Depress the magazine platform to allow the bolt to go forward, close the bolt, pull the trigger.

Lee-Enfield, Rifle, Short, Magazine, MkIII (UK)

The SMLE comes in one or two sub-varieties, with minor differences, but the Mark III is the one which matters; over three million were made in Britain, India and Australia and it served in both world wars. Indeed, many British soldiers in 1939-1945 went to great lengths to acquire one instead of the wartime replacement, the Rifle No 4 (below); there was nothing wrong with the No 4 but the SMLE was a legend in its own time. Utterly reliable and with the smoothest bolt-action ever made, the SMLE was sneered at by the purists for not being a Mauser, but it silenced all its critics in 1914: German units on the receiving end thought they were under machine-gun fire.

SPECIFICATION & OPERATION

CARTRIDGE
.303 British Service

DIMENSIONS
Length o/a: 1132mm (44.56in)
Weight: 3.96kg (8lb 12oz)
Barrel: 640mm (25.2in)
Rifling: 5 grooves, lh
Magazine capacity: 10 rounds

IN PRODUCTION 1907-43.

MARKINGS
Maker, date and 'SHT L.E.' on right side of the stock band beneath the bolt. Serial number on right side of chamber.

SAFETY
Manual safety catch on left side of action. Press forward to fire, rearward for safe.

UNLOADING
Press up on magazine catch inside the trigger guard to release the magazine, which should be removed, with its contents, and emptied. Open the bolt to extract any cartridge in the chamber. Pull out the magazine cut-off by pressing down the round catch on the right side of the action and pulling it out. Examine the chamber and feedway, close the bolt, pull the trigger, replace the empty magazine and push the cut-off back in.

Enfield US service rifle M1917 (Pattern '17) (UK)

This is the same rifle as the British Pattern '14. When the USA entered the war in 1917 it, too, needed rifles, the British contract had just ended, so the Americans re-designed it to take the standard US .30 rimless cartridge and went on to make almost two million before the end of the war. They were extensively used by US troops and after the war went into store. About 119,000 were sent to Britain in 1940 and issued to the Home Guard where they had to be marked with a red band on stock and fore-end to distinguish them from the .303 Pattern 14 rifles. After 1946 most were sold off to target shooters and as hunting rifles.

SPECIFICATION & OPERATION

CARTRIDGE
.30-06 US Service

DIMENSIONS
Length o/a: 1175mm (46.26in)
Weight: 4.08kg (9lb 0oz)
Barrel: 660mm (25.98in)
Rifling: 5 grooves, rh
Magazine capacity: 5 rounds

IN PRODUCTION 1917-18

MARKINGS
'U.S.RIFLE M1917' over chamber. Serial number on right side of action.

SAFETY
Manual safety catch on right side of action, behind the bolt handle. Forward to fire, rearward for safe.

UNLOADING
Place safety catch in the 'fire' position. Open bolt to extract any round in the chamber. Inspect magazine; if it contains ammunition continue working the bolt until all rounds have been loaded and ejected. Depress the magazine platform to allow the bolt to go forward, close the bolt, pull the trigger.

Lee-Enfield; Rifle No 4 (UK)

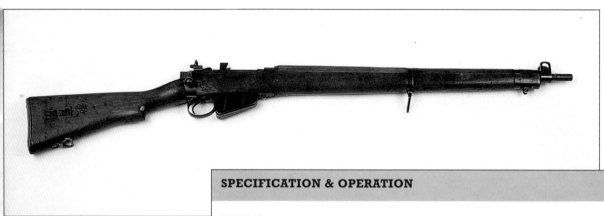

This was the replacement for the SMLE Mark III; it was virtually the same rifle but simplified in order to make wartime mass-production easier. The nosecap was changed and a spike bayonet replaced the old sword, and the sights changed to a tangent aperture pattern on the rear of the receiver instead of a U-notch tangent halfway along the rifle. It made teaching recruits easier but expert shots felt they had better control with the older pattern. About four million were made in Britain, the USA, Canada, India and Australia, and about 40,000 American-made rifles were also supplied to China.

SPECIFICATION & OPERATION

CARTRIDGE
.303 British Service

DIMENSIONS
Length o/a: 1128mm (44.40in)
Weight: 4.11kg (9lb 1o\)
Barrel: 640mm (25.2in)
Rifling: 5 grooves, lh
Magazine capacity: 10 rounds

IN PRODUCTION 1940-45

MARKINGS
Maker and year on right of stock band beneath bolt handle. Serial number on right side of chamber. Rifles manufactured in the USA may have `UNITED STATES PROPERTY' on the left side of the receiver; those made in Canada may have `LONG BRANCH' in the same place.

SAFETY
Manual safety catch on left side of action. Press forward to fire, rearward for safe.

UNLOADING
Press up on magazine catch inside the trigger guard to release the magazine, which should be removed, with its contents, and emptied. Open the bolt to extract any cartridge in the chamber. Examine the chamber and feedway, close the bolt, pull the trigger, replace the empty magazine.

Lee-Enfield: Rifle No 5 (UK)

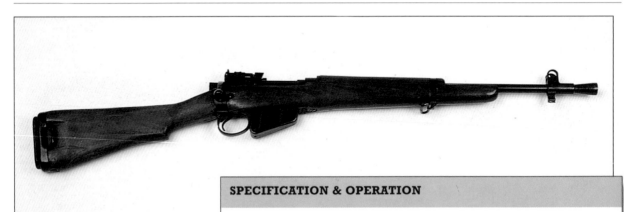

This is the familiar Lee-Enfield action attached to a short-barrelled compact rifle intended for jungle warfare. A handsome weapon, it never lived up to its appearance; blast and recoil were unpleasant due to the short barrel and powerful cartridge, and the rifle suffered from a 'wandering zero': zero it today and it would shoot beautifully, but tomorrow it would miss by miles and need re-zeroing. Much time and energy was spent on trying to solve this but in the end the authorities gave up and the rifle was declared obsolete in 1947.

SPECIFICATION & OPERATION

CARTRIDGE
.303 British

DIMENSIONS
Length, stock extended:
875mm (34.45in)
Length, stock retracted:
600mm (23.62in)
Barrel: 300mm (11.81in)
Weight, empty: 2.90kg
(6lb 6oz)
Rifling: 5 grooves, lh
Magazine capacity: 10 rounds

IN PRODUCTION 1943-47

MARKINGS
No 5 Mk1 on left side of action. Serial number, year and manufacturer's mark on left side of butt strap behind trigger.

SAFETY
Manual safety catch on left side of action. Press forward to fire, rearward for safe.

UNLOADING
Magazine catch at rear of magazine. Remove magazine. Place safety catch to 'fire', open bolt to eject any round in the chamber. Inspect chamber, close bolt, press trigger.

Accuracy International L96A1 (UK)

The standard sniping rifle of the British Army, this features an aluminium chassis to support the action and barrel, clothed in a plastic outer casing. It is also sold commercially in various models, the 'Long Range' chambered for 7mm Remington Magnum or .300 Winchester Magnum; the 'Counter-Terrorist' in 7.62mm, the 'Moderated' with an integral silencer, and the 'Infantry' with a non-zoom telescope sight. The Long Range model is a single shot, the rest are magazine rifles.

SPECIFICATION & OPERATION

CARTRIDGE
7.62 x 51mm NATO

DIMENSIONS
Length o/a: 1124mm (44.25in)
Weight: 6.50kg (14lb 5oz)
Barrel: 654mm (25.75in)
Rifling: 4 grooves, rh
Magazine capacity: 10 rounds

IN PRODUCTION 1985 -

MARKINGS
CR 156 GA ACCURACY INTERNATIONAL ENGLAND NATO stock number; serial number (all on left side of action).

SAFETY
Manual safety catch on the left rear of the action. Forward for fire, back for safe. The safety catch locks the bolt, trigger and firing pin; the bolt cannot be closed when the safety is applied, and the safety cannot be applied unless the striker is cocked.

UNLOADING
Magazine catch behind magazine. Remove magazine, empty out any ammunition. Set the safety catch to 'fire'. Open bolt to extract any round remaining in the chamber. Examine chamber and feedway, close bolt, press trigger, replace empty magazine.

De Lisle silent carbine (UK)

This unusual weapon was designed around the standard Lee-Enfield bolt action but barrelled for the US .45 pistol cartridge, and with an integral silencer. Since this cartridge is subsonic, the De Lisle is probably the most silent of all silenced weapons. Two versions were made, with a fixed butt and with a metal folding butt; and the resemblance between the folding butt of the De Lisle and that of the Sterling submachine gun is because both weapons were made by Sterling. A similar weapon, but based on the action of the Remington 700 rifle and chambered for the 7.62 x 51mm NATO round is currently manufactured in England and called the 'De Lisle Mark 4'.

SPECIFICATION & OPERATION

CARTRIDGE
.45 ACP

DIMENSIONS
Length o/a: 960mm (37.80in)
Weight: 3.70kg (8lb 2oz)
Barrel: 210mm (8.27in)
Rifling: 4 grooves, lh
Magazine capacity: 8 rounds

IN PRODUCTION 1942-45

MARKINGS
Serial number on right side of receiver.

SAFETY
Manual safety catch on left side of receiver; forward for fire, back for safe.

UNLOADING
Magazine catch inside trigger guard. Remove magazine. Place safety catch to 'fire', open bolt to extract any round in the breech. Close bolt, press trigger.

Enfield Enforcer (UK)

This was developed by the Royal Small Arms Factory as a result of requests from British police forces for a sniping rifle. It uses the basic Lee-Enfield action, allied to a heavy barrel and a shortened 'sporter' fore-end. It is, in fact, the same rifle as the British Army's L42A1 sniping rifle; the difference is that when issued to the British Army it had a plain sighting telescope, but when sold to the police it was given a more modern zoom telescope sight. A very similar weapon was also sold, without optical sight, in the civil market as the 'Envoy' target rifle.

SPECIFICATION & OPERATION

CARTRIDGE
7.62 x 51mm NATO

DIMENSIONS
Length o/a: 1180mm (46.45in)
Weight: 4.42kg (9lb 12oz)
Barrel: 700mm (27.55in)
Rifling: 4 grooves, rh
Magazine capacity: 10 rounds.

IN PRODUCTION 1970-85

MARKINGS
'ENFIELD' and year of manufacture on the stock band beneath the bolt. Serial number on right side of chamber.

SAFETY
Manual safety catch on left side of action. Forward for fire, back for safe.

UNLOADING
Magazine catch behind the magazine. Remove magazine. Place safety catch to 'fire', open bolt to eject any round in the chamber. Inspect chamber, close bolt, press trigger.

This is a sniping rifle which employs a commercial Mauser 98 bolt action allied to a heavy cold-forged barrel. It was adopted as the military sniping rifle of the Australian, New Zealand and Canadian armies. A version using a shorter butt and a shortened wooden fore-end was adopted by the British Army as the L81A1 Cadet Training Rifle in 1983. These rifles are still in service with the various forces, though Parker-Hale have given up rifle manufacture.

SPECIFICATION & OPERATION

CARTRIDGE
7.62 x 51mm NATO

DIMENSIONS
Length o/a: 1162mm (45.75in)
Weight: 4.80kg (10lb 9oz)
Barrel: 660mm (26.0in)
Rifling: 4 groove, rh
Magazine capacity: 4 rounds

IN PRODUCTION 1982-84

MARKINGS
PARKER-HALE LTD BIRMINGHAM ENGLAND 7.62 NATO on top of barrel. Serial on left of chamber.

SAFETY
A manual safety catch on the rear of the bolt. Turned to the left, the rifle is ready to fire. Turned to the right the rifle is safe.

UNLOADING
Press in the magazine floor plate catch in the front of the trigger guard; the floor plate will hinge forward and the contents of the magazine will fall out. Open the bolt to extract any round remaining in the chamber. Examine the chamber and the magazine space, close the bolt, pull the trigger, close the magazine floor plate.

Parker-Hale 85 (UK)

Parker-Hale designed this weapon as a potential sniping rifle for the British Army, but the Accuracy International L96A1 design was selected. Parker-Hale then gave up the rifle business and sold their designs to the Gibbs Rifle Co in the USA in 1990, and this company now manufactures the M85 under the Parkler-Hale title. The butt is adjustable for length and there is an easily detached bipod under the fore-end. A camouflage-pattern synthetic stock is also available.

SPECIFICATION & OPERATION

CARTRIDGE
7.62 x 51mm NATO

DIMENSIONS
Length o/a: 1150mm (45.27in)
Weight: 5.70kg (12lb 9oz) with sight
Barrel: 700mm (27.55in)
Rifling: 4 grooves, rh
Magazine capacity: 10 rounds

IN PRODUCTION 1986-

MARKINGS
'PARKER HALE M85 GIBBS RIFLE CO MARTINSBURG WV USA' and serial number on right of receiver.

SAFETY
A manual safety catch on the rear of the bolt. Turned to the left, the rifle is ready to fire. Turned to the right the rifle is safe.

UNLOADING
Magazine catch behind magazine. Remove magazine and empty out any ammunition. Open bolt to extract any cartridge remaining in the chamber. Examine chamber and feedway. Close bolt, press trigger, replace empty magazine.

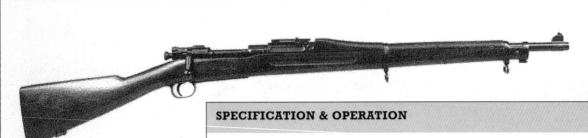

Standard US service rifle from 1903 to the mid-1940s, though it remained in service until the early 1960s as a sniping rifle. The M1903 had a straight stock; the 1903A1 a pistol-grip stock; both had the rear sight ahead of the chamber. The 1903A3 had a straight stock and the sight was just in front of the bolt handle; the 1903A4 is the sniper version of the A3, has no iron sights and has the bolt handle cut away to avoid striking the sighting telescope when opening.

SPECIFICATION & OPERATION

CARTRIDGE
.30-06 (7.62 x 63mm)

DIMENSIONS
Length o/a: 1097mm (43.20in)
Weight: 3.94kg (8lb 11oz)
Barrel: 610mm (24.0in)
Rifling: 4 grooves RH; WWII make may have 2 grooves
Magazine capacity: 5 rounds

IN PRODUCTION 1903-65

MARKINGS
'SPRINGFIELD ARSENAL' above the chamber. 'UNITED STATES PROPERTY' on left side of receiver. Serial number on right side of receiver, bolt handle and magazine cover.

SAFETY
Manual safety catch on the rear end of the bolt: Turn to the RIGHT for safe, when the word 'Safe' will be seen. Turn LEFT for fire, when the word 'Fire' can be seen.

UNLOADING
There is a magazine cut-off which prevents rounds feeding from the magazine to the breech; the control for this is on the left side of the receiver. Press down and the word 'OFF' can be seen, meaning that the magazine contents will NOT load. Lift up until the word 'ON' is visible and the magazine can be loaded and the contents can be fed to the breech. Now lift and pull back bolt handle to eject cartridge in the breech. Close bolt and repeat opening until the magazine is empty. When the cut-off is set 'OFF' the bolt cannot move back far enough to collect a cartridge from the magazine but the rifle can be used as a single-shot weapon, loading each round individually.

Ruger M77 (USA)

The Model 77 has been manufactured in a wide range of styles and calibres over the years and is widely distributed. The bolt action is adapted from the Mauser 98 pattern. The Model 77V, described here, is a 'varmint' rifle, intended for small game, and has a heavy barrel and no iron sights, being invariably used with a telescope sight. As such it has been used by some police forces as a sniping rifle.

SPECIFICATION & OPERATION

CARTRIDGE
7.62 x 51mm NATO and others

DIMENSIONS: (M77V)
Length o/a: 1118mm (44.0in)
Weight: 4.08kg (9lb 0oz)
Barrel: 610mm (24.0in)
Rifling: 4 grooves, rh
Magazine capacity: 5 rounds

IN PRODUCTION 1968-

MARKINGS
'STURM, RUGER INC SOUTHPORT CONN USA' and serial number on receiver.

SAFETY
A manual safety catch on the rear of the bolt. Turned to the left, the rifle is ready to fire. Turned to the right the rifle is safe.

UNLOADING
Press in the magazine floor plate release catch in the front edge of the trigger guard to allow the floor plate to hinge forward and dump the contents of the magazine. Open the bolt to remove any cartridge remaining in the chamber. Examine the chamber and feedway. Close the bolt, press the trigger and close the magazine floor plate.

and no iron sights are fitted, the rifle being issued with a 10x telescope sight. It is currently in service with the US Marine Corps, and the commercial original (the Model 700) has sold in large numbers.

SPECIFICATION & OPERATION

CARTRIDGE
7.62 x 51mm NATO

DIMENSIONS
Length o/a: 1118mm (44.0in)
Weight: 6.57kg (14lb 8oz)
Barrel: 610mm (24.0in)
Rifling: 4 grooves, rh
Magazine capacity: 5 rounds

IN PRODUCTION 1962-

MARKINGS
'US RIFLE M40A1' and serial number over chamber.

SAFETY
Manual safety catch at right rear of receiver. Forward to fire, back for safe.

UNLOADING
Press the release catch at the front edge of the magazine floor plate, so allowing the plate, spring and magazine contents to be removed. Open the bolt to eject any round in the chamber. Examine chamber and feedway, close bolt, press trigger, replace magazine spring and floor plate.

This is a militarised version of the commercial Remington 700 sporting rifle. The bolt is a Remington design, using two lugs locking into the receiver behind the chamber. There is a catch inset into the front of the trigger guard which, when pressed, allows the bolt to be removed from the receiver. The barrel is particularly heavy and rigid,

This rifle, and the following Harris model, were previously known by the name of McMillan; the McMillan Gun Works was acquired by the Harris Gunworks in 1995, and the McMillan models were continued in production under their old model numbers.

The M87 rifle was originally a single shot weapon of conventional bolt-action type. It was then given a magazine and became the M87R. It is half-stocked, without being hollowed out to firm a pistol grip, and has a very heavy barrel with a pepper-pot muzzle brake. A bipod fits on to the front end of the stock, and a telescope mount is provided. No iron sights are fitted. It is also possible to have the rifle with a synthetic stock, the butt of which has facilities for adjustment for length and rake.

SPECIFICATION & OPERATION

CARTRIDGE
50 Browning

DIMENSIONS
Length o/a: 1346mm (53.0in)
Barrel: 737mm (20.0in)
Weight: 9.52kg (21lb)
Rifling: 8 grooves, rh
Magazine capacity: 5 rounds

IN PRODUCTION 1987-

MARKINGS
None

SAFETY
Manual safety lever alongside the bolt cocking-piece.

UNLOADING
Remove magazine. Open bolt to extract any cartridge in the chamber. Examine magazine aperture and chamber to ensure both are empty. Close bolt, pull trigger.

Harris M93 (USA)

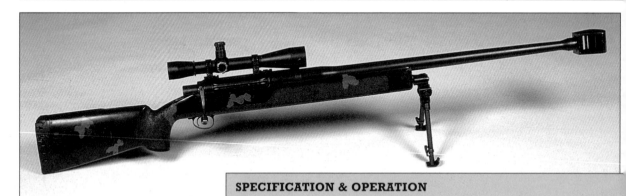

T his is a modified version of the M87R described
above, the principle change being the fitting of a
hinged butt-stock for easier storage and
transportation. The magazine capacity was also
increased. Like the M87R it has been adopted by the
French army and is in wide use in US law
enforcement agencies. In addition to the obvious
counter-sniper role, it is used by a number of
explosive ordnance disposal teams to detonate
explosive devices at a distance. If the shot does not
detonate the device, the impact of the bullet usually
disrupts any firing or switching device so that it
becomes less of a hazard to examine and dispose of.

SPECIFICATION & OPERATION

CARTRIDGE
50 Browning

DIMENSIONS
Length, butt extended:
1346mm (53.0in)
Length, butt folded: 991mm
(39.0in)
Barrel: 737mm (20.0in),
Weight: 9.52kg (21lb)
Rifling: 8 grooves, rh
Magazine capacity: 10 or 20
rounds

IN PRODUCTION 1989-

MARKINGS
None

SAFETY
Manual safety lever alongside
the bolt cocking-piece.

UNLOADING
Remove magazine. Open bolt to
extract any cartridge in the
chamber. Examine magazine
aperture and chamber to ensure
both are empty. Close bolt, pull
trigger.

AUTOMATIC RIFLES

This was developed in the early 1980s for the Argentine Army but financial problems led to slow production and it is probable that only a part of the army received this weapon. It is of local design and uses the usual gas piston, bolt carrier and rotating bolt method of operation. Note that the cocking handle lies on top of the gas cylinder, well forward of the receiver and actually operates on the gas piston, which has the bolt carrier machined as an integral part. The rifle may be encountered with a bipod attached below the gas block, in which case it has a special fore-end with a recess to accept the folded bipod legs. Note also that the twist of rifling allows M193 or NATO ammunition to be fired with equal facility.

SPECIFICATION & OPERATION

CARTRIDGE
5.56 x 45mm

DIMENSIONS
Length, stock extended:
1000mm (39.37in)
Length, stock folded: 745mm
(29.33in)
Weight: 3.95kg (8lb 11oz)
Barrel: 452mm (17.8in)
Rifling: 6 grooves, rh
Magazine capacity: 30 rounds
Rate of fire: 750 rds/min

IN PRODUCTION 1984-90

MARKINGS
'FMAP DOMINGO MATHEU',
year and serial number on top
of receiver.

SAFETY
Manual safety catch inside the trigger guard. Push to the rear for safe, forward to fire. There is a fire selector for either single shots or automatic fire on the right side of the receiver above the trigger.

UNLOADING
Magazine catch behind magazine housing. Remove magazine. Pull back cocking handle to eject any round remaining in the chamber. Inspect chamber and feedway via the ejection slot. Release cocking handle, press trigger.

Steyr-Mannlicher AUG (Austria)

This was designed to an Austrian Army specification and was adopted by them in 1979. It has since been adopted by Ireland, Australia, several Middle Eastern countries, the US Customs service, the Falkland Islands Defence Force, and recently the Netherlands. It is made under licence in Australia as the F88. Modular in design, the barrel can be quickly removed and changed for a longer or shorter one, the firing mechanism can be removed and changed for one giving three-round bursts or semi-

SPECIFICATION & OPERATION

CARTRIDGE
5.56 x 45mm M198 or NATO

DIMENSIONS
Length o/a: 790mm (31.1in)
Weight: 3.85kg (8lb 8oz)
Barrel: 508mm (20.0in)
Rifling: 6 grooves, rh
Magazine capacity: 30 or 42 rounds
Rate of fire: 650 rds/min

IN PRODUCTION 1978-

MARKINGS
`STEYR-DAIMLER-PUCH AG AUSTRIA` or `STEYR-MANNLICHER GmbH AUSTRIA`, and `AUG/A1` moulded into the stock on the right side. Serial number on right side of barrel.

SAFETY
A push-through safety is fitted into the stock behind the trigger. When pushed from left to right, the rifle is safe. Pushed from right to left, the rifle is ready to fire. Selection of fire is performed by the trigger; a light pull gives single shots, a heavier pull gives automatic fire.

UNLOADING
Magazine catch is behind the magazine. Remove magazine. Pull back cocking handle to eject any round remaining in the chamber, inspect chamber and feedway via the ejection slot. Release the cocking handle, pull the trigger.

automatic fire only or any other combination of possibilities; the receiver can be changed to replace the built-in telescope by a mounting platform to which other types of sight can be fitted. It was the first rifle to make extensive use of plastics, not only for the furniture but also for the firing mechanism.

Steyr 15.2mm IWS2000 (Austria)

to be rather like that of a heavy-caliber sporting rifle. The weapon strips into two major groups so that it can be easily carried by a two-man team. There is a bipod and an adjustable monopod under the butt, and a 10x telescope sight is standard.

The current cartridge is a fin stabilised, discarding sabot , tungsten alloy dart weighing 308 grains (20 grammes). Fired at 4757 ft/sec (1450 m/sec) this will completely penetrate 40mm or rolled homogenous steel armour at 1000 metres range, and at this velocity the dart never reaches more than 31 inches (80cm) above the direct line of sight; for all practical purposes this can be considered as a flat trajectory.

This is an anti-nateriel rifle in bullpup form and is semi-automatic in action, operating on the long recoil system. The bolt and barrel recoil together for about 8 inches (200mm); the bolt is then rotated to unlock and is held, while the barrel returns to battery. During this movement the empty case is stripped from the chamber and mechanically ejected, after which the bolt is released and runs forward to chamber the next round and lock.

The barrel is supported in a ring cradle which incorporates a hydro-pneumatic recoil system which, assisted by a high-efficiency muzzle brake, absorbs much of the shock of discharge, making the weapon moderately comfortable to fire; the felt recoil is said

SPECIFICATION & OPERATION

CARTRIDGE
15.2mm APFSDS

DIMENSIONS
Length: 1800mm (70.86in)
Weight: ca 18kg (40lbs)
Barrel: 1200mm (47.24in)
Rifling nil: smoothbore
Magazine: 5 rounds

IN PRODUCTION 1999

MARKINGS
None

SAFETY
Two-position safety catch on left side of receiver above pistol grip.

UNLOADING
The magazine housing and release catch are behind the pistol grip. Remove the magazine. Draw back the cocking handle until it is possible to inspect the chamber and verify that it is empty. Release the cocking handle, pull the trigger.

Development of this rifle actually started in the 1930s but the war caused a halt in the proceedings and it was not until 1949 that it was completed. It was adopted in various calibres by Belgium, Egypt, Argentine, Luxembourg, Venezuela, Brazil and Colombia and was reliable, if somewhat expensive. The locking system used a tilting bolt, gas-operated, and generally formed the prototype for the later and better-known FAL model. The magazine was loaded by chargers, through the top of the open action. The designer, M.Saive, worked with the British in Enfield during the Second World War and the earliest version of this rifle was tested by the British in 7.92mm calibre in 1946/47.

SPECIFICATION & OPERATION

CARTRIDGE
7.92 x 57mm Mauser and others

DIMENSIONS
Length o/a: 1116mm (43,54in)
Weight: 4.31kg (9lb 8oz)
Barrel: 590mm (23.23in)
Rifling: 4 grooves, rh
Magazine capacity: 10 rounds

IN PRODUCTION 1950-58

MARKINGS
FABRIQUE NATIONALE D'ARMES DE GUERRE HERSTAL BELGIQUE on right of action. Serial number on side of chamber and on bolt.

SAFETY
Manual safety catch on the right side of the trigger guard. Press DOWN for safe, which also places the catch in a position to interfere with the finger if an attempt it made to press the trigger. There is no fire selector - this rifle fires only single shots.

UNLOADING
Magazine catch is in front of the magazine and needs to be pressed in by a bullet or some similar pointed tool. Remove the magazine and pull back the cocking handle to eject any round remaining in the chamber. Inspect chamber and feedway through the ejection port. Release the cocking handle, press the trigger.

The FN-FAL is probably the most widely-used rifle in history, adopted by over 90 countries. Many of these have demanded their own minor modifications; many countries have manufactured under license and, again, have incorporated their own modifications. The FN factory recognises four standard models; the fixed-butt rifle 50-00; the folding butt rifle 50-64; a folding-butt carbine 50-63; and a fixed-butt heavy-barrel model with bipod 50-41. Moreover most models were available in either semi-automatic-only or selective-fire form. Permutate all these and there are a huge number of minor variant models possible. Add to that the commercial semi-automatic models and it becomes obvious that a complete book would scarcely scratch the surface of absolute identification of some models. All one can do is identify it as an FN-FAL, decide the nationality from its markings, and leave it at that.

SPECIFICATION & OPERATION

CARTRIDGE
7.62 x 51mm NATO

DIMENSIONS
Length o/a: 1090mm (42.9in)
Weight: 4.45kg (9lb 13oz)
Barrel: 533mm (21.0in)
Rifling: 4 grooves, rh
Magazine capacity: 20 rounds
Rate of fire: 650 rds/min

IN PRODUCTION 1953-

MARKINGS
'FABRIQUE NATIONALE HERSTAL' on Belgian-made weapons. Since this rifle has appeared in numerous variations, has been employed by 90 countries and made under license or copied in many of them, the variety of possible markings is infinite and a full list cannot be given. The origin of the weapon will usually be evident from the markings.

SAFETY
Manual safety catch and fire selector lever on left side of receiver over the trigger. In semi-automatics the weapon is safe with the catch pressed UP, ready to fire when pressed DOWN. The same applies to weapons capable of automatic fire but they also have a third position, pushed down and forward past the single-shot position, which gives full automatic fire.

UNLOADING
Magazine catch is behind the magazine housing. Remove magazine. Pull back cocking handle to eject any round left in the chamber. Examine chamber and feedway through the ejection port. Release cocking handle, press trigger.

FN CAL (Belgium)

The CAL (Carabine, Automatic, Legère) was broadly a scaled-down FAL, using the same sort of gas action but with a rotating bolt instead of a tilting breech-block. It was a reasonable enough weapon, but it was somewhat in advance of its time, since most countries were happy with their 7.62mm weapons and did not regard the 5.56mm cartridge with much enthusiasm, so sales of the CAL were poor. Experience also showed that its reliability was not up to the usual FN standards, and FN realised that a better rifle could be made more cheaply, so the design was closed down and work began on the FNC.

SPECIFICATION & OPERATION

CARTRIDGE
5.56 x 45mm M193

DIMENSIONS
Length o/a: 978mm (38.50in)
Weight: 3.35kg (7lb 6oz)
Barrel: 467mm (18.39in)
Rifling: 6 grooves, rh
Magazine capacity: 20, 25 or 30 rounds
Rate of fire: 650 rds/min

IN PRODUCTIO 1966-75

MARKINGS
'FABRIQUE NATIONALE HERSTAL Mod CAL 5.56mm serial number' on left side of receiver.

SAFETY
A combined safety catch and fire selector lever is on the left side of the receiver above the trigger. Rotated to the rear for safe; DOWN one notch for single shots; forward to the next notch for three-round bursts; fully forward for automatic fire.

UNLOADING
Magazine catch at left rear of magazine housing. Remove magazine. Pull back cocking handle to eject any round remaining in the chamber. Examine chamber and feedway through the ejection slot. Release cocking handle, press trigger.

FN FNC (Belgium)

This succeeded the CAL at a time when the potential customers were taking note of the NATO adoption of a 5.56mm cartridge, and consequently it met with a better reception; it was also cheaper and more reliable than the CAL. Steel, alloy and plastic have been used in the construction and much use has been made of pressings and stampings. The mechanism is similar to that of the CAL, gas operated with a rotating bolt, and the magazine interface is NATO standard and will thus accept M16 and similar types of magazine. A variant model is used by Sweden as the AK5, and it is also made under license in Indonesia.

SPECIFICATION & OPERATION

CARTRIDGE
5.56 x 45mm NATO

DIMENSIONS
Length, stock extended:
997mm (39.25in)
Length, stock folded: 766mm
(30.16in)
Weight: 3.80kg (8lb 6oz)
Barrel: 450mm (17.71in)
Rifling: 6 grooves, rh
Magazine capacity: 30 rounds
Rate of fire: 700 rds/min

IN PRODUCTION 1979-

MARKINGS
'FN' monogram; 'FNC 5.56 serial
number'; all on left side of
receiver.

SAFETY
A combined safety catch and
fire selector lever is on the left
side of the receiver above the
trigger. Rotated to the rear for
safe; DOWN one notch for
single shots; forward to the

next notch for three-round
bursts; fully forward for
automatic fire.

UNLOADING
Magazine catch at left rear of
magazine housing. Remove
magazine. Pull back cocking
handle to eject any round
remaining in the chamber.
Examine chamber and feedway
through the ejection slot.
Release cocking handle, press
trigger.

IMBEL MD2 (Brazil)

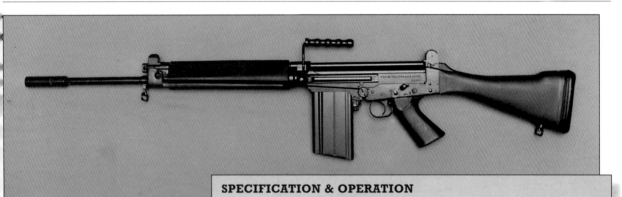

I MBEL (Industrias de Materiel Belico), the government arms manufacturer for Brazil, began making FN FAL rifles under licence in the early 1950s. Using this design as a basis, they have developed their own 5.56mm rifle for supply to the Brazilian Army and also for export. Except for being slightly shorter it is virtually identical with the 7.62mm FAL made by IMBEL apart from using a curved M16-type magazine instead of a straight one. There is also a fixed-butt model (MD1) made for export, and both the MD1 and MD2 can be found with bipods fitted underneath the gas regulator.

SPECIFICATION & OPERATION

CARTRIDGE
5.56 x 45mm NATO or M193

DIMENSIONS
Length, stock extended:
1010mm (39.76in)
Length, stock folded: 764mm (30.1in)
Weight: 4.40kg (9lb 11oz)
Barrel: 453mm (17.83in)
Rifling: 6 grooves, rh
Magazine capacity: 20 or 30 rounds

Rate of fire: 700 rds/min

IN PRODUCTION 1990 -

MARKINGS
`FABRICA DE ITAJUBA - BRASIL MD2 5.56mm` and serial number left side of receiver.

SAFETY
Manual safety catch and fire selector lever on left side of receiver above the trigger. Back

for safe, central for single shots, forward for automatic fire.

UNLOADING
Magazine release behind magazine housing, beneath the receiver. Remove magazine. Pull back cocking handle to eject any round in the chamber. Inspect chamber and feedway via the ejection slot. Release cocking handle, pull trigger.

Chinese Type 56 carbine (China)

SPECIFICATION & OPERATION

The Type 56 is simply a Chinese copy of the Soviet Simonov SKS rifle; any differences between this weapon and its Soviet ancestor are minimal matters of manufacturing convenience. Later versions have a folding spike bayonet in place of the normal folding sword bayonet. It has been retired from military service, except for occasional appearances in ceremonials, for some years, but is still widely sold commercially as a hunting rifle. Without the bayonet, of course.

CARTRIDGE
7.62 x 39mm Soviet M1943

DIMENSIONS
Length o/a: 1025mm (40.35in)
Weight: 3.85kg (8lb 8oz)
Barrel: 521mm (2-.5in)
Rifling: 4 grooves, rh
Magazine capacity: 10 rounds

IN PRODUCTION 1956-

MARKINGS
Chinese factory mark and serial number on left front of receiver.

SAFETY
Manual safety catch on the rear of the trigger guard is pushed forward and UP to make the weapon safe, when it obstructs the trigger finger and movement of the trigger.

UNLOADING
Magazine catch at the rear of the magazine, under the receiver. Press in and the magazine swings open, allowing the contents to be removed. Pull back the cocking handle, inspect the chamber and feedway, release the cocking handle, press the trigger. Close the empty magazine.

Chinese Type 56 assault rifle (China)

SPECIFICATION & OPERATION

CARTRIDGE
7.62 x 39mm Soviet M1943

DIMENSIONS
Length o/a: 874mm (34.40in)
Weight: 3.80kg (8lb 6oz)
Barrel: 414mm (16.30in)
Rifling: 4 grooves, rh
Magazine capacity: 30 rounds
Rate of fire: 600 rds/min

IN PRODUCTION 1958-

MARKINGS
Chinese markings for factory, year and serial number on left side of receiver. There may also be Chinese symbols on the safety lever on early production models.

SAFETY
Combined safety catch and fire selector lever on the right rear side of the receiver. When pressed all the way UP it is in the safe position and obstructs the movement of the cocking handle and bolt; moved DOWN one notch to the first mark or the letter 'L' gives full automatic fire, and moved to the bottom position, or the letter 'D', produces single shots.

UNLOADING
Magazine catch at rear of magazine housing. Remove the magazine. Pull back the cocking handle to extract any round which may be in the chamber. Inspect the chamber via the ejection port. Release the cocking handle, pull the trigger.

The Type 56 is, quite obviously, the Chinese copy of the Kalashnikov, and it well illustrates the dangers of terminology; this is the Type 56 rifle, it is 874mm long; the Type 56 carbine (above) is 1025mm long; yet carbines are always supposed to be shorter than rifles. There are three variants; the Type 56 has a fixed butt and folding bayonet; the 56-1 has a folding stock which passes over the receiver, and the 56-2 has a folding stock which folds sideways to lie along the right side of the receiver. Neither the 56-1 or 56-2 have folding bayonets. All these models are commercially available in semi-automatic form.

Chinese Type 68 rifle (China)

This is a purely Chinese design which has adapted the best features of various rifles of which the Chinese have had experience. Although it resembles the Type 58 carbine the mechanism is based upon that of the AK47 Kalashnikov rifles. It has the usual type of folding bayonet beneath the fore-end. The standard magazine is a 15-round box, but it is possible to use the 30-round AK47 magazine if the hold-open stop for the bolt is removed or ground down; so that it may be found with either type. In current use with the Chinese forces, it is also available for export.

SPECIFICATION & OPERATION

CARTRIDGE
7.62 x 39mm Soviet M1943

DIMENSIONS
Length o/a: 1029mm (40.5in)
Weight: 3.49kg (7lb 11oz)
Barrel: 521mm (20.5in)
Rifling: 4 groove, rh
Magazine capacity: 15 or 30 rounds
Rate of fire: 750 rds/min

IN PRODUCTION 1970-

MARKINGS
Chinese symbols for factory identification and year, and serial number on left side of receiver.

SAFETY
Combined safety catch and selector lever in front of the trigger on the right side. Pulled to the rear, to the mark `0', the weapon is safe; the trigger is locked but the bolt can be opened. Moved to the vertical

position, to the mark `1', gives single shots, and moved fully forward to the mark `2' gives automatic fire.

UNLOADING
Magazine catch beneath the receiver, behind the magazine. Remove the magazine. Pull back the cocking handle to eject any round left in the chamber. Inspect the chamber and feedway via the ejection port. Release the cocking handle, pull the trigger.

CZ52 (Czechoslovakia)

The CZ52 was developed in Czechoslovakia in the short time between the end of WWII and the country's absorption into the Communist Bloc. It was an unusual design, gas-operated with a gas piston in the form of a sleeve surrounding part of the barrel and acting on the bolt carrier, and it fired a unique cartridge. When the country came under Soviet domination, it was required to conform to Soviet standards and the rifle was therefore redesigned to fire the 7.62 x 39 Soviet cartridge. Such models are known as the 'vz.52/57' and are so marked. They are not as accurate or reliable as the original 7.62 x 45mm models. Note that there is a permanently-attached folding sword bayonet on both models of this rifle.

SPECIFICATION & OPERATION

CARTRIDGE
7.62 x 45mm M52 or 7.62 x 39mm Soviet M1943

DIMENSIONS
Length o/a: 1003mm (39.5in)
Weight: 4.10kg (9lb 1oz)
Barrel: 523mm (20.55in)
Rifling: 4 grooves, rh
Magazine capacity: 10 rounds

IN PRODUCTION 1952-59

MARKINGS
Factory identifier and serial number on right side of receiver. The later model 52/57 will be so marked at the right front of the receiver.

SAFETY
A manual safety catch is fitted in the forward edge of the trigger guard. Pulled back, so that it protrudes into the trigger-guard space, the weapon is safe. Push forward to fire.

UNLOADING
Magazine catch behind magazine. Remove magazine. Pull back cocking handle to extract any round remaining in the chamber. Examine chamber and feedway via the ejection port. Release cocking handle, pull trigger.

CZ58 (Czechoslovakia)

Although this may resemble the Kalashnikov, it is an entirely different weapon, of Czech design although, due to Warsaw Pact standardisation, chambered for the standard Soviet cartridge. It is gas operated and the bolt is locked to the receiver by a vertically-moving block similar to that of the Walther P38 pistol. Gas pressure on a piston drives a bolt carrier back, this lifts the lock and the bolt then opens. The original design used a fixed stock of plastic material; later versions used a folding metal stock. Either may be fitted with a flash hider on the muzzle and a bipod attached to the barrel.

SPECIFICATION & OPERATION

CARTRIDGE
7.62 x 39mm Soviet M1943

DIMENSIONS
Length, stock extended:
820mm (32.28in)
Length, stock folded: 635mm
(25.0in)
Weight: 3.14kg (6lb 15oz)
Barrel: 401mm (15.8in)
Rifling: 4 grooves, rh
Magazine capacity: 30 rounds
Rate of fire: 800 rds/min

IN PRODUCTION 1959-80

MARKINGS
Factory identifier and serial number on rear top of receiver.

SAFETY
Combined manual safety catch and fire selector on right side of receiver above trigger. Rotate to the vertical position for safe; this locks the trigger but permits the bolt to be opened. Turn the selector forward for automatic fire, rearward for single shots.

UNLOADING
Magazine catch between magazine and trigger guard. Remove magazine. Pull back the cocking handle to extract any round remaining in the chamber. Inspect chamber and feedway via the ejection port. Release cocking handle, press trigger.

This is simply the Finnish version of the Kalashnikov AK rifle and the differences are largely those which the Finns regard as being necessary to withstand their permanently Arctic conditions. The first model was the M60, which had a plastic fore-end and tubular steel butt; some were without trigger-guards for use with Arctic mittens. Then came the M62, with a machined steel receiver and some changes to the sights and furniture. Then came the M71 which adopted a stamped steel receiver, but this proved less strong and was dropped for a return to the M62 but with a new folding butt. Finally came the M76 with a stronger sheet steel receiver and a variety of fixed or folding steel, plastic or wooden butts. As well as being used by the Finns, these rifles have also been bought by Qatar and Indonesia and have also been sold in semi-automatic form on the commercial market.

SPECIFICATION & OPERATION

CARTRIDGE
7.62 x 39mm Soviet M1943

DIMENSIONS
Length, stock extended: 950mm (37.40in)
Length, stock folded: 710mm (29.13in)
Weight: 3.60kg (7lb 15oz)
Barrel: 418mm (16.46in)
Rifling: 4 grooves, rh
Magazine capacity: 15, 20 or 30 rounds
Rate of fire: 700 rds/min

IN PRODUCTION 1976-86

MARKINGS
'VALMET Jyvaskyla' and serial number on right side of receiver.

SAFETY
Combined safety catch and fire selector lever on the right rear side of the receiver. When pressed all the way UP it is in the safe position and obstructs the movement of the cocking handle and bolt; moved DOWN one notch to the first mark (three dots) gives full automatic fire, and moved to the bottom position, a single dot, produces single shots.

UNLOADING
Magazine catch at rear of magazine housing. Remove the magazine. Pull back the cocking handle to extract any round which may be in the chamber. Inspect the chamber via the ejection port. Release the cocking handle, pull the trigger.

Valmet M78 (Finland)

The M78 is essentially a heavy-barrelled model of the M76 intended as a light squad support weapon. The longer and heavier barrel extends the effective range from the 400m or so of the rifle to 600/700 metres. It appears to have been taken into service in small numbers by the Finnish Army, but other sales are not known. It was also offered in 5.56 x 45mm calibre with selective fire and in 7.62 x 51mm in semi-automatic form as a long range rifle.

SPECIFICATION & OPERATION

CARTRIDGE
7.62 x 39mm Soviet M1943 and others

DIMENSIONS
Length o/a: 1060mm (41.73in)
Weight: 4.70kg (10lb 6oz)
Barrel: 480mm (18.9in)
Rifling: 4 grooves, rh
Magazine capacity: 15 or 30 rounds
Rate of fire: 650 rds/min

IN PRODUCTION 1978-86

MARKINGS
'VALMET Jyvaskyla M78' and serial number on right side of receiver.

SAFETY
Combined safety catch and fire selector lever on the right rear side of the receiver. When pressed all the way UP it is in the safe position and obstructs the movement of the cocking handle and bolt; moved DOWN one notch to the first mark (three dots) gives full automatic fire, and moved to the bottom position (single dot), produces single shots.

UNLOADING
Magazine catch at rear of magazine housing. Remove the magazine. Pull back the cocking handle to extract any round which may be in the chamber. Inspect the chamber via the ejection port. Release the cocking handle, pull the trigger.

Sako M90 (Finland)

The Sako M90 is the successor to the Valmet M62/M76 series of Finnish service rifles, Sako having absorbed Valmet in the late 1980s. The original Valmet designs were based upon Kalashnikov AK 47s obtained from Russia in the 1950s; they followed the Kalashnikov pattern but had a few small changes due to Finnish preferences. There was no wood, the fore-end and pistol grip both being steel with a plastic coating; the butt was a large-diameter tube with a cross-member welded on at the end, and there was a prominent pronged flash hider. The M90 merely streamlined and improved the design, adopting a new side-folding butt, new sights with night-firing aids, and a new flash hider which also functions as a grenade launcher. It is probably the best Kalashnikov clone ever made.

SPECIFICATION & OPERATION

CARTRIDGE
7.62 x 39mm Soviet M1943 or 5.56 x 45mm NATO

DIMENSIONS: (7.62mm version)
Length, stock extended: 930mm (36.6in)
Length, stock folded: 675mm (26.58in)
Weight: 3.85kg (8lb 8oz)
Barrel: 416mm (16.38in)
Rifling: 4 grooves, rh
Magazine capacity: 30 rounds
Rate of fire: 700 rds/min
IN PRODUCTION 1991-

MARKINGS
'M90' and serial number on left side of receiver.

SAFETY
Combined safety catch and fire selector lever on the right rear side of the receiver. When pressed all the way UP it is in the safe position and obstructs the movement of the cocking handle and bolt; moved DOWN one notch to the first mark gives full automatic fire, and moved to the bottom position produces single shots.

UNLOADING
Magazine catch at rear of magazine housing. Remove the magazine. Pull back the cocking handle to extract any round which may be in the chamber. Inspect the chamber via the ejection port. Release the cocking handle, pull the trigger.

MAS-49 (France)

This was adopted somewhat hurriedly in 1949 when the French Army was anxious to equip with a modern rifle instead of the collection of oddments which had survived the war.

Gas-operated, it uses direct gas blast to blow the bolt carrier backwards, instead of the more usual piston. . It remained the standard French rifle until the arrival of the FAMAS in 1980, and large numbers were handed over to former colonies, who later disposed of them. A very small number were converted to 7.62 x 51mm calibre for use by French Gendarmeries, which suggests that such conversions could also be done by others, since the French 7.5mm ammunition is not now in common supply.

SPECIFICATION & OPERATION

CARTRIDGE
7.5 x 54mm French Service

DIMENSIONS
Length o/a: 1100mm (43.3in)
Weight: 4.70kg (10lb 6oz)
Barrel: 580mm (22.83in)
Rifling: 4 grooves, lh
Magazine capacity: 10 rounds

IN PRODUCTION 1951-65

MARKINGS
'MAS 49', year and serial number on left side of receiver. May have script 'St Etienne' marking in the same area.

SAFETY
Manual safety catch is on the right side of the receiver, above the front end of the trigger guard. Turn DOWN to make safe, UP to fire.

UNLOADING
Magazine catch is on the right side of the magazine housing; press in the lower end with the thumb to remove the magazine. Pull back the cocking handle to eject any round remaining in the chamber. Examine the chamber and feedway, release the cocking handle, pull the trigger.

SPECIFICATION & OPERATION

CARTRIDGE
5.56 x 45mm Type France

DIMENSIONS
Length o/a: 757mm (29.80in)
Weight: 3.61kg (7lb 15oz)
Barrel: 488mm (19.2in)
Rifling: 6 grooves, rh
Magazine capacity: 25 rounds
Rate of fire: 950 rds/min

IN PRODUCTION 1975-

MARKINGS
FA MAS 5.56 F1 and serial on right side of magazine housing. Serial repeated on bolt.

SAFETY
A rotary switch inside the front of the trigger guard acts as safety catch and fire selector. When parallel with the bore it is set safe; when switched to the right it gives single shots, and when to the left, automatic fire. With the switch in the automatic position, operation of a burst-limiting button, beneath the buttstock and behind the magazine, brings in a three-round burst limiter.

UNLOADING
Magazine catch in front of magazine. Remove magazine. Pull back cocking handle (between the receiver and the carrying handle) to eject any round left in the chamber. Inspect chamber via the ejection port. Release cocking handle, pull trigger.

This odd-looking weapon is the standard French Army rifle and was the first 'bullpup' design to enter military service. It uses a two-part bolt in a delayed blowback system and has the chamber fluted to avoid difficult extraction, so that cartridges from this weapon are easily recognised by their longitudinal marks. It handles well and shoots accurately, and can also launch grenades. There is also a .22 rimfire training version which looks exactly like the service weapon. In 1994 a new model, the F2, appeared with a full-sized handguard instead of a small trigger guard and a NATO-standard magazine housing to accept M16 type magazines. Note that all 5.56mm ammunition will chamber in this weapon but optimum performance is only achieved with the French service ammunition.

MP 44 (Germany)

This is the father of all assault rifles, developed in Germany in 1941-42 and using a new short cartridge. Originally known as the MP (Machine Pistol) 44 for Nazi political reasons, it was renamed the 'Sturmgewehr 44' after its successful introduction into battle on the Eastern Front. It introduced the concept of using a short cartridge with limited range in order to permit controllable automatic fire and a compact weapon, and because experience

SPECIFICATION & OPERATION

CARTRIDGE
7.92 x 33mm 'Kurz'

DIMENSIONS
Length o/a: 940mm (37.0in)
Weight: 5.22kg (11lb 8oz)
Barrel: 419mm (16.45in)
Rifling: 4 grooves, rh
Magazine capacity: 30 rounds
Rate of fire: 500 rds/min

IN PRODUCTION 1943-45

MARKINGS
'MP44'; factory mark - 'fxo' (Haenel & Co) or 'ayf' (Ermawerke); year; serial number. All on top of receiver, and serial number often repeated on the left side of the magazine housing.

SAFETY
Manual safety catch on the left of the receiver, above the pistol grip. Press UP for safe, DOWN to fire. There is also a push-button, just behind and above the safety catch, which selects single shots or automatic fire.

UNLOADING
The magazine release is a push-button on the left side of the magazine housing. Remove the magazine. Pull back the cocking handle to eject any round left in the chamber. Inspect the chamber and feedway via the ejection port. Release the cocking handle, pull the trigger.

showed that most rifle fire was conducted at ranges under 400 metres. After the war it was examined and dissected by almost every major gunmaking nation and led, in one way and another, to the present-day 5.56mm assault rifles. In postwar years it was used by East German Border Guards and many found their way into central Africa.

Heckler & Koch G3 (Germany)

The heart of the G3, as with almost every other Heckler & Koch weapon, is the roller-delayed blowback breech system, which has a long and curious history. It was designed by Mauser in 1944–45; taken to Spain and developed further by CETME, taken to Holland to manufacture, then given to Heckler & Koch to perfect. Which they did to very good effect. The G3 has armed the German Army for many years and is made under license in Mexico, Portugal, Greece, Turkey, Pakistan, Norway, Greece and Saudi Arabia as well as being employed by some 60 armies. There are variant models with short barrels, fixed or folding butts, and there are also variations in the licence-produced models of some countries, but these are generally minor.

SPECIFICATION & OPERATION

CARTRIDGE
7.62 x 51mm NATO

DIMENSIONS
Length o/a: 1025mm (40.35in) (fixed butt)
Weight: 4.40kg (9lb 11oz)
Barrel: 450mm (17.71in)
Rifling: 4 grooves, rh
Magazine capacity: 20 rounds
Rate of fire: 550 rds/min

IN PRODUCTION 1964–

MARKINGS
'G3 HK serial number month/year of manufacture' on left side of magazine housing. Weapons which have been refurbished will have 'HK' and the month/year stamped into the right side of the magazine housing.

SAFETY
A combined safety catch and fire selector is on the left side, above the trigger. In the topmost position (marked '0' or 'S') the weapon is safe; fully down ('F' or '20') gives full automatic fire, while the mid-position ('E' or '1') gives single shots.

UNLOADING
Magazine catch at rear of magazine housing. Remove magazine. Pull back cocking handle to eject any round remaining in the chamber. Examine chamber and feedway through the ejection slot. Release cocking handle, press trigger.

Heckler & Koch PSG1 (Germany)

The PSG1 is a high-precision sniping rifle using the standard H&K roller-locked delayed blowback breech system with a special long and heavy barrel. The trigger unit can be removed from the pistol grip, and can be adjusted for pull. The stock is fully adjustable in all directions so that every individual can fit the weapon to his own stance. No iron sights are fitted; a NATO-standard mounting is built into the receiver top and the rifle is always issued with a 6 x 42 telescope with illuminated graticule. The accuracy is outstanding; it will put 50 rounds of match ammunition inside an 80mm circle at 300 metres range.

SPECIFICATION & OPERATION

CARTRIDGE
7.62 x 51mm NATO

DIMENSIONS
Length o/a: 1208mm (47.55in)
Weight: 8.10kg (17lb 13oz)
Barrel: 650mm (25.6in)
Rifling: 4 grooves, rh
Magazine capacity: 5 or 20 rounds

IN PRODUCTION 1975 -

MARKINGS
`PSG1 HK Kal 7.62x51 serial number'; all on left side of magazine housing.

SAFETY
Manual safety catch on left side of receiver, above trigger. UP for safe, DOWN to fire.

UNLOADING
Magazine catch on right side behind magazine housing.

Remove magazine. Pull back cocking handle to eject any round remaining in the chamber. Examine chamber and feedway through the ejection slot. Holding the cocking handle, press the trigger and allow the cocking handle to go forward under control. Push on the bolt-closing catch on the right side of the receiver to firmly close the bolt.

Heckler & Koch MSG90 (Germany)

This is intended as a military sniping rifle and is really a lighter and less expensive version of the PSG1. The barrel is lighter, cold-forged and tempered; the trigger mechanism is pre-adjusted to a 1.5kg pull and the trigger has an adjustable shoe which gives better control. There is usually a bipod fitted to a rail in the fore-end, and the standard sight is a 10x telescope with range settings to 1200 metres. The sight mount is to NATO standard and thus any compatible day or night sight can be fitted. The butt can be adjusted in most directions to obtain an individual fit.

SPECIFICATION & OPERATION

CARTRIDGE
7.62 x 51mm NATO

DIMENSIONS
Length o/a: 1165mm (45.87in)
Weight: 6.40kg (14lb 2oz)
Barrel: 600mm (23.62in)
Rifling: 4 grooves, rh
Magazine capacity: 5 or 20 rounds

IN PRODUCTION 1987-

MARKINGS
'HK MSG90 7.62 x 51 serial number'; all on left side of magazine housing.

SAFETY
Manual safety catch on left side of receiver, above trigger. UP for safe, DOWN to fire.

UNLOADING
Magazine catch at rear of magazine housing. Remove magazine. Pull back cocking handle to eject any round remaining in the chamber. Examine chamber and feedway through the ejection slot. Release cocking handle, press trigger.

Heckler & Koch HK33E (Germany)

This is more or less the standard G3 reduced to 5.56mm calibre; its mechanical operation is exactly the same, as is its outline; several parts are common, but interchanging parts is not to be recommended; some are not common, though they may look and fit in apparently the same way in both weapons. There is a fixed butt model and also a short-barrelled carbine version known as the HK33K E. There was also an HK33SG1 sniper version, with special sight mount and telescope sight, and the fixed butt model can be found with a bipod. It has been used by Chile, Brazil, Malaysia and Thailand and various other forces in SE Asia and South America.

SPECIFICATION & OPERATION

CARTRIDGE
5.56 x 45mm NATO or M193

DIMENSIONS
Length, stock extended: 940mm (37.0in)
Length, stock folded: 735mm (28.94in)
Weight: 3.65kg (8lb 1oz)
Barrel: 390mm (15.35in)
Rifling: 6 grooves, rh
Magazine capacity: 25 rounds
Rate of fire: 750 rds/min

IN PRODUCTION 1968-
MARKINGS
`HK 33E 5.56mm serial number`; all on left side of magazine housing.

SAFETY
A combined safety catch and fire selector is on the left side, above the trigger. In the topmost position (marked `0` or `S`) the weapon is safe; fully down (`F` or `20`) gives full automatic fire, while the mid-position (`E` or `1`) gives single shots.

UNLOADING
Magazine catch at rear of magazine housing. Remove magazine. Pull back cocking handle to eject any round remaining in the chamber. Examine chamber and feedway through the ejection slot. Release cocking handle, press trigger.

Heckler & Koch G11 (Germany)

This revolutionary weapon was destined to become the German Army's standard in 1990 but politics got in the way and only a limited number were issued to Special Forces. A similar weapon was tested in the USA as the 'Advanced Combat Rifle'. It uses entirely different principles to any other firearm and fires a special caseless cartridge which is simply a block of explosive with a bullet buried inside it. The mechanism moves back and forth in recoil inside the outer plastic casing, the amount of recoil varying with the type of fire selected. Although of

SPECIFICATION & OPERATION

CARTRIDGE
4.7 x 33mm caseless

DIMENSIONS
Length o/a: 750mm (29.52in)
Weight: 3.65kg (8lb 1oz)
Barrel: 540mm (21.26in)
Rifling: 6 grooves rh
Magazine capacity: 50 rounds
Rate of fire: 600 rds/min

IN PRODUCTION 1989 -1990

MARKINGS
'HK G11K3 4.7 x 33 serial number'. On left of body.

SAFETY
Manual safety catch on left side, above trigger. Rear ('S') position is safe; forward one notch ('1') single shots; forward two notches ('3') three-round burst; fully forward ('50') full automatic.

UNLOADING
Magazine catch beneath the front end of the carrying handle/sight. Remove magazine by sliding it out forwards. Unfold the rotary key on the left side of the body and turn it counterclockwise until it stops. Point the gun in a safe direction and pull the trigger. Repeat. The weapon is now empty.

peculiar appearance it is comfortable to use and shoots well; it delivers its three-round burst at a rate of 2000 rds/min and puts them all into the target.

Heckler & Koch HK36 (Germany)

In the early 1970s, when small calibres were all the rage, Heckler & Koch developed this rifle to go with a 4.6mm 'Loffelspitz' ("spoon point") bullet, The low bullet weight and straight-line layout gave a very reduced recoil impulse, and the velocity was such as to give it a virtually flat trajectory out to 300 metres, which was about the limit of its effect. This was the rifle which introduced the three-round burst concept to improve the chance of a first round hit. Another unusual feature was the magazine, permanently mounted on the rifle and reloaded by pulling down the magazine platform and sliding a pre-packed box of cartridges into the open rear of the magazine. The rifle operated on Heckler & Koch's usual delayed blowback system. The design was never accepted for military service but gave the design team some useful ideas for the future.

SPECIFICATION & OPERATION

CARTRIDGE
4.6 x 36mm 'Loffelspitz'

DIMENSIONS
Length: 890mm (35.0 in), stock extended
Barrel: 400mm (15.75in)
Weight: 2.85kg (6.28lbs) lbs
Rifling: 6 grooves, rh
Magazine capacity: 30

IN PRODUCTION: NO. TRIALS 1970-73

MARKINGS
HK36 and serial number on magazine housing.

SAFETY
Manual safety/selector lever on left side of frame giving Safe, Single, Three-round and full automatic fire.

UNLOADING
Pull down on the button at the base of the magazine to relieve pressure on the magazine spring and remove the ammunition pack through the rear of the magazine body. Pull back the cocking handle (left side of fore-end) to open the bolt and eject any round left in the chamber. Examine the feedway and chamber via the ejection port. Release the cocking handle, pull the trigger.

Heckler & Koch G41 (Germany)

This was designed as an improved HK33 specifically for the NATO-standard 5.56mm cartridge. It incorporates the low-noise bolt closing device first used on the PSG1 sniping rifle, has a dust-cover on the ejection port, has a hold-open device that keeps the bolt open when the magazine is emptied, uses the NATO-standard magazine interface, accepting M16 and similar magazines, has a NATO-standard sight mount for day or night optical sights, and may be fitted with a bipod. There is also a folding-butt model.

SPECIFICATION & OPERATION

CARTRIDGE
5.56 x 45mm NATO

DIMENSIONS
Length o/a: 997mm (39.25in)
Weight: 4.10kg (9lb 1oz)
Barrel: 450mm (17.71in)
Rifling: 6 grooves, rh
Magazine capacity: 30 rounds
Rate of fire: 850 rds/min

IN PRODUCTION 1983-

MARKINGS
'HK G41 5.56mm serial number', all on left side of magazine housing.

SAFETY
A combined safety catch and fire selector is on the left side, above the trigger. In the topmost position (marked by a white bullet and cross) the weapon is safe; one notch down (single red bullet) gives single shots; two notches down (three red bullets) gives a three-round burst, and fully down (7 red bullets) gives full automatic fire.

UNLOADING
Magazine catch at rear of magazine housing. Remove magazine. Pull back cocking handle to eject any round remaining in the chamber. Examine chamber and feedway through the ejection slot. Release cocking handle, press trigger.

sight. The cocking handle is underneath the carrying handle and also acts as a bolt-closing assist if needed.

The G36 was adopted by the German army in 1996. An export version, the G36E is also available; this differs only in the optical sight, the G36E having a 1.5x telescope. A short-barrelled version, the G36K, is issued to German special forces; it differs in having a prong-type flash hider.

When the G11 program collapsed the German Army was left without a 5.56mm rifle to conform to NATO standard, and after a rapid comparative trial selected this as their new standard rifle. In this design H&K abandoned their well-tried roller-locked delayed blowback system and adopted a gas-operated rotating bolt solution. The layout is conventional, with the gas cylinder beneath the barrel, a pistol grip, box magazine, and folding tubular butt. A raised sight block at the rear of the receiver carries a 3x optical sight, and the integral carrying handle runs from this block to the front end of the receiver, with an aperture for the line of

SPECIFICATION & OPERATION

CARTRIDGE
5.56 x 45mm NATO

DIMENSIONS (G36)
Length, butt extended: 998mm (39.29in)
Length, butt folded: 758mm (29.84in)
Weight: 3.43kg (7lb 9oz)
Barrel: 480mm (18.89in)
Rifling: 6 grooves, rh
Magazine capacity: 30 rounds
Rate of fire: 750 rds/min

DIMENSIONS (G36K)
Length, butt extended: 858mm (33.78in);
Length, butt folded: 613mm (24.13in)
Weight: 3.13kg (6lb 14oz)
Barrel: 320mm (12.60in),
Rifling: 6 grooves, rh
Magazine: 30 rounds
Rate of fire: 750 rds/min

IN PRODUCTION 1995-

SAFETY
Combined safety catch and fire selector switch on both sides of the receiver, behind and above the trigger.

UNLOADING
Magazine catch on magazine housing. Remove magazine. Pull back cocking handle (beneath carrying handle) and examine the feedway and chamber via the ejection port, ensuring both are empty. Return cocking handle and bolt to the forward position, pull trigger.

12.7mm Gepard M2, M2A1 (Hungary)

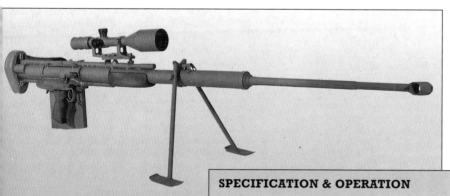

the barrel jacket, and a telescope sight is standard.

The M2A1 is simply a short-barrelled version of the M2 intended for use by airborne and special forces who require a more compact weapon.

The Gepard M2 is a similar to the M1 previously described but is a semi-automatic rifle operating on the long recoil system. The barrel recoils inside a cylindrical jacket and receiver, and uses a rotating bolt to lock the breech. On firing the barrel and bolt recoil for about six inches; the bolt is then unlocked and held, while the barrel runs forward again. During this movement the cartridge case is extracted. As the barrel stops, it trips a catch to release the bolt, which then runs forward, chambering a cartridge. The magazine is oddly placed on the left-side of the pistol grip, making it impossible to fire left-handed. A bipod is attached to

SPECIFICATION & OPERATION

CARTRIDGE
12.7 x 107mm Soviet

DIMENSIONS (M2)
Length o/a: 1530mm (60.23in)
Barrel: 1100mm (43.31in)
Weight: 12.0kg (26lbs 7oz)
Rifling: 8 grooves, rh
Magazine: 5 or 10 rounds

DIMENSIONS (M2A1)
Length o/a: 1260mm (49.60in)
Weight: 10.0kg (22lbs 1oz)

Barrel: 830mm (32.68in),
Rifling: 8 grooves, rh
Magazine: 5 or 10 rounds

IN PRODUCTION 1994-

MARKINGS
None

SAFETY
Manual safety catch on left side of receiver.

UNLOADING
Magazine release is located on the magazine housing, left side of the pistol grip. Remove magazine. Pull back cocking handle and examine feedway and chamber through the ejection port. Release cocking handle, pull trigger.

14.5mm Gepard M3 (Hungary)

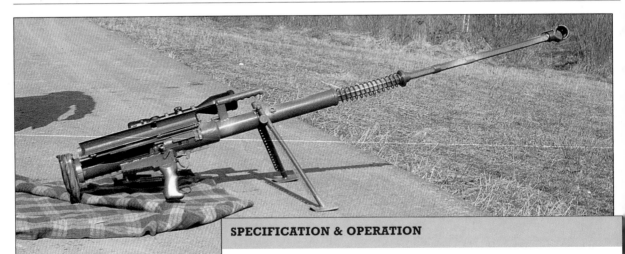

SPECIFICATION & OPERATION

This is more or less an enlarged version of the Gepard M2, with the addition of a hydro-pneumatic recoil system and a more effective muzzle brake to absorb some of the firing shock . Firing the powerful 14.5mm AP bullet, with a muzzle velocity of 3280 ft/sec (1000 m/sec) it can penetrate 25mm of homogenous armour plate at 600 metres range and has a maximum range well in excess of 1000 yards.

CARTRIDGE
14.5 x 114mm Soviet

DIMENSIONS
Length o/a: 1880mm (74.0in)
Barrel: 1480mm (58.27in)
Weight: 20.0kg (44lbs 1oz)
Rifling: 8 grooves, rh
Magazine: 5 or 10 rounds

IN PRODUCTION 1995-

MARKINGS
None

SAFETY
Manual safety catch on left side of receiver.

UNLOADING
Magazine release is located on the magazine housing, left aide of the pistol grip. Remove magazine. Pull back cocking handle and examine feedway and chamber through the ejection port. Release cocking handle, pull trigger.

5.56mm INSAS assault rifle (INSAS - Indian Small Arms System)

butt-plate so as to provide a trap for the cleaning material and oil bottle. The rifle uses the well-tried operating system of a gas piston driving a bolt carrier and rotating bolt, and the magazine housing has been standardised on the M16 dimensions. The fire selector permits single shots or three-round bursts, but there is no provision for automatic fire. The assault rifle is made in fixed and folding butt versions, and there is also a heavy-barrelled version for use in the squad automatic role.

Developed in the middle 1980s, this is a gas-operated selective-fire assault rifle which is an interesting mixture of features taken from other designs. The receiver and pistol grip show Kalashnikov influence, the fore-end resembles that of the M16, and the forward cocking handle is based on the Heckler & Koch rifles. Nevertheless, these various features have been well combined to produce a well-balanced and attractive weapon. An unusual feature is the use of the old Lee-Enfield

SPECIFICATION & OPERATION

CARTRIDGE
5.56 x 45mm

DIMENSIONS
Length fixed butt: 945mm (37.20in)
Length, butt folded: 750mm (29.52in)
Length, butt extended: 960mm (37.80in)
Weight: 3.20kg (7lbs 1oz)
Barrel: 464mm (18.27in)
Rifling: 6 grooves, rh

Magazine capacity: 22 rounds
Cyclic rate: 650 rds/min

IN PRODUCTION 1999

MARKINGS

SAFETY
Large thumb-operated safety catch and fire selector lever on left side of receiver above the pistol grip. Up for safe, down in two steps for single shots and

automatic fire.

UNLOADING
Magazine release is behind magazine housing, in front of trigger guard. Remove magazine. Pull back cocking handle to open bolt and remove any round from chamber. Examine chamber and feedway, ensuring both are empty. Release cocking handle, pull trigger.

Galil (Israel)

The Galil was the result of careful Israeli
examination of practically every rifle they could
find, and in the end they settled for a modified
version of the Kalashnikov rotating bolt system;
indeed, the first rifles were built up from Finnish
M62 rifle bodies. It was originally developed in
5.56mm calibre, but later a 7.62 x 51mm model
was also produced, though this was never as
popular as the 5.56mm version. It is, of course, used
by the Israeli Defence Force and has also been
adopted by several Central and South American and
African armies.

SPECIFICATION & OPERATION

CARTRIDGE
5.56 x 45mm M193

DIMENSIONS
Length, stock extended:
979mm (38.54in)
Length, stock folded: 742mm
(29,2in)
Weight: 3.95kg (8lb 11oz)
Barrel: 460mm (18.1in)
Rifling: 6 grooves, rh
Magazine capacity: 35 or 50
rounds
Rate of fire: 550 rds/min

IN PRODUCTION 1971-

MARKINGS
Hebrew markings on left side of
receiver, including serial
number.

SAFETY
A combined safety catch and
fire selector is on the left side,
at the top of the pistol grip.
Forward is safe; fully rearward
gives single shots, the central
position gives automatic fire.

UNLOADING
Magazine catch at rear of
magazine housing. Remove
magazine. Pull back cocking
handle to eject any round
remaining in the chamber.
Examine chamber and feedway
through the ejection slot.
Release cocking handle, press
trigger.

Beretta BM59 (Italy)

In the late 1940s the Beretta company began making the US Rifle M1 under license for the Italian Army, and they later made more for Denmark and Indonesia. In 1959 they set about redesigning the Garand, giving it the capability for automatic fire, fitting it with a larger magazine and adapting the barrel to grenade launching. Apart from these points it is much the same as any US M1 Garand. Various models were produced, with bipods, folding butts, folding bayonets, removable grenade launching adapters, or shorter barrels, but the mechanism remains the same. If it looks like a Garand but has a removable magazine it is either a US M14 or an Italian BM59.

SPECIFICATION & OPERATION

CARTRIDGE
7.62 x 51mm NATO

DIMENSIONS
Length o/a: 1095mm (43.1in)
Weight: 4.60kg (10lb 2oz)
Barrel: 490mm (19.3in)
Rifling: 4 grooves, rh
Magazine capacity: 20 rounds
Rate of fire: 750 rds/min

IN PRODUCTION 1961-66

MARKINGS
`P BERETTA BM59 serial number';
on top rear end of receiver.

SAFETY
Manual safety catch in the front edge of the trigger guard; push forward to fire, rearward for safe. A fire selector is mounted on the left side of the receiver alongside the chamber, marked 'A' for automatic fire and 'S' for single shots. It may

be permanently locked in the single-shot position in some rifles.

UNLOADING
Magazine catch is behind the magazine. Remove magazine. Pull back cocking handle to open bolt and extract any round left in the chamber. Examine the chamber and feedway, release the bolt, press the trigger.

Beretta AR 70/.223 (Italy)

This was Beretta's first 5.56mm rifle, using gas actuation and a two-lug bolt. It was adopted by Italian Special forces and sold to some other countries but it failed to attract much of a market and experience showed it to have a few minor defects, notably a lack of rigidity in the receiver. It appeared with some variations; a solid butt model was standard but there was also a folding butt model with long and short barrels. The muzzle is adapted for grenade firing, and a hinged tap on the gas block has to be raised to allow a grenade to be loaded; this also shuts off the gas supply to the cylinder, ensuring that all the gas from the launching cartridge goes to propel the grenade.

SPECIFICATION & OPERATION

CARTRIDGE
5.56 x 45mm (M109)

DIMENSIONS
Length o/a: 955mm (37.60in)
Weight: 3.80kg (8lb 6oz)
Barrel: 450mm (17.71in)
Rifling: 4 grooves, rh
Magazine capacity: 30 rounds
Rate of fire: 650 rds/min

IN PRODUCTION 1972-80

MARKINGS
'P BERETTA AR 70/223 MADE IN ITALY serial number', on left side of receiver.

SAFETY
Manual safety catch and fire selector on left side of receiver above pistol grip. Turned DOWN for safe, UP for automatic fire, midway for single shots.

UNLOADING
Magazine catch is behind the magazine. Remove the magazine. Pull back the cocking handle to eject any round left in the chamber. Inspect the chamber via the ejection port. Release the cocking handle, pull the trigger.

This is the squad automatic version of the 5.56mm AR70-90 assault rifle. It uses the same gas-operated rotating bolt system as the rifle but fires from an open bolt, and has a heavy barrel which cannot be quick-changed. The butt is cut away to provide a firm grip and has an over-shoulder strap, and there is a long, perforated barrel jacket. The bipod is articulated and can be adjusted for height. A carrying handle is fitted and, like that of the rifle, it can be easily removed to expose a mount for optical sights. The AR70-90 has been extensively tested by the Italian Army but as yet no decision has been taken about adopting a 5.56mm machine gun in their service.

SPECIFICATION & OPERATION

CARTRIDGE
5.56 x 45mm NATO

DIMENSIONS
Length: 1000mm (39.37in)
Weight: 5.34kg (11lb 12oz)
Barrel: 465mm (18.30in)
Rifling: 6 grooves, rh
Magazine capacity: 30 rounds
Cyclic rate: 800 rds/min

IN PRODUCTION 1995 -

SAFETY
Manual three-position safety catch and change lever on both sides of the receiver, giving safe, single shot and automatic fire.

UNLOADING
Magazine release catches on both sides of the receiver, above the magazine. Remove magazine. Pull back bolt until held by the sear. Examine chamber and feedway through the ejection opening and ensure both are empty. Grasp cocking handle, press trigger and allow the bolt to go forward under control.

Japan Type 64 (Japan)

This rifle was developed in Japan and made by the Howa Machinery Company. It uses a gas-piston operating system driving a tilting bolt. The principal concern was to provide a rifle suited to the smaller stature of the Japanese soldier, and this weapon fires a special reduced-load cartridge as standard and uses a muzzle brake to further reduce the recoil force. The gas regulator is adjustable and can be set to a position permitting the use of full-power NATO cartridges if required. The rifle can also launch grenades.

SPECIFICATION & OPERATION

CARTRIDGE
7.62 x 51mm Japanese Service

DIMENSIONS
Length o/a: 990mm (39.00in)
Weight: 4.40kg (9lb 11oz)
Barrel: 450mm (17.71in)
Rifling: 4 grooves, rh
Magazine capacity: 20 rounds
Rate of fire: 500 rds/min

IN PRODUCTION 1964-90

MARKINGS
Ideographs 64 and 7.62mm with serial number and year in western form and arsenal mark all on left side of receiver.

SAFETY
Manual safety catch and fire selector on right side of receiver, above trigger. Rearward for safe, forward for single shots, fully upward for automatic.

UNLOADING
Magazine catch behind magazine housing. Remove magazine. Pull back cocking handle to remove any round in the chamber. Examine chamber and feedway through the ejection port. Release cocking handle, press trigger.

This rifle was designed by the Japanese Defence Agency and is replacing the Type 64 as the standard Japanese service rifle. Gas-operated, with a rotating bolt, it uses a somewhat unusual gas system which ensures a lower initial impulse on the gas piston, so giving a lower felt recoil and prolonging the life of the weapon. There is a fixed-butt version as well as the folding butt type, and both models are equipped with a bipod. Another unusual feature is the fitting of an entirely separate three-round burst mechanism, so that if anything should go wrong with it, the single-shot and automatic functions are not impaired.

SPECIFICATION & OPERATION

CARTRIDGE
5.56 x 45mm NATO

DIMENSIONS
Length, stock extended:
916mm (36.0in)
Length, stock folded: 570mm
(22.44in)
Weight: 3.50kg (7lb 12oz)
Barrel: 420mm (16.54in)
Rifling: 6 grooves, rh
Magazine capacity: 20 or 30
rounds
Rate of fire: 750 rds/min

IN PRODUCTION 1990-

MARKINGS
Ideographs 89 and 5.56mm with serial number and year in western form and arsenal mark all on left side of receiver.

SAFETY
Manual safety catch and fire selector on right side of receiver above trigger. UP for safe, DOWN one notch for single shots, DOWN and fully forward for automatic fire. Set at automatic, operate the other catch behind trigger for 3-round burst.

UNLOADING
Magazine catch is in the right side of the magazine housing. Remove magazine. Pull back cocking handle to eject any round remaining in the chamber. Inspect chamber and feedway. Release cocking handle, pull trigger.

Daewoo K2 (South Korea)

A gas operated, selective-fire rifle with a folding plastic butt, the weapon can fire single shots, three-round bursts or fully automatic. The barrel is fitted with a muzzle brake and compensator that also doubles as a grenade-launcher. The three-round burst mechanism is unusual in that it does not re-set to zero if a part-burst is fired; thus, if only two shots of a burst are fired, the next pull of the trigger will fire a single shot.

SPECIFICATION & OPERATION

CARTRIDGE
5.56mm x 45

DIMENSIONS
Length, butt extended: 38.98in (990mm); butt folded 28.74in (730mm)
Weight unloaded: 7lb 3oz (3.26kg)
Barrel: 18.30in (465mm), 6 grooves, right-hand twist
Magazine: 30-round detachable box
Cyclic rate: 650 rds/min

Muzzle velocity: 3018 ft/sec (920m/s)

IN PRODUCTION: 1987-

MARKINGS
DAEWOO PRECISION INDUSTRIES LTD on receiver top. 5.56MM K2 and serial number on left side of magazine housing.

SAFETY
Three position switch on left side of receiver; turned so that the pointer is forward – SAFE; vertical – single shots; to the rear – automatic or three round burst.

UNLOADING
Magazine catch on left side of magazine housing. Remove magazine. Pull back cocking handle and inspect chamber to ensure it is empty. Release cocking handle. Press trigger.

The various Kalashnikov models, variants, clones and copies would fill a book on their own; indeed have done. But no matter how they vary, the basic structure remains the same and is always recognisable. The basic AK47 turned into the AKM by virtue of improved production design and into the AK74 by changing calibre to 5.45mm. The various versions turned out by other countries are usually distinguished by personal preference - handgrips, different styles of butt, grenade launching attachments and so forth, but the basic Kalashnikov can always be seen in the receiver and the safety lever. Larger differences may appear when the principle is applied to a 'new' design, e.g. the Galil, R4 and Finnish models. Once seen as being a Kalashnikov in origin, the nationality can then be determined by the markings.

SPECIFICATION & OPERATION

CARTRIDGE
7.62 x 39mm Soviet M1943

DIMENSIONS
Length, stock extended:
869mm (34.21in)
Length, stock folded: 699mm (27.52in)
Weight: 4.30kg (9lb 8oz)
Barrel: 414mm (16.3in)
Rifling: 4 grooves, rh
Magazine capacity: 30 rounds
Rate of fire: 600 rds/min

IN PRODUCTION 1947-

MARKINGS
Model number, factory identifier and serial number on top of rear end of receiver.

SAFETY
Combined safety catch and fire selector lever on the right rear side of the receiver. When pressed all the way UP it is in the safe position and obstructs the movement of the cocking handle and bolt; moved DOWN one notch to the first mark or the letters `AB' gives full automatic fire, and moved to the bottom position, or the letter `O', produces single shots.

UNLOADING
Magazine catch at rear of magazine housing. Remove the magazine. Pull back the cocking handle to extract any round which may be in the chamber. Inspect the chamber via the ejection port. Release the cocking handle, pull the trigger.

Kalashnikov AK47 and variants (Russia)

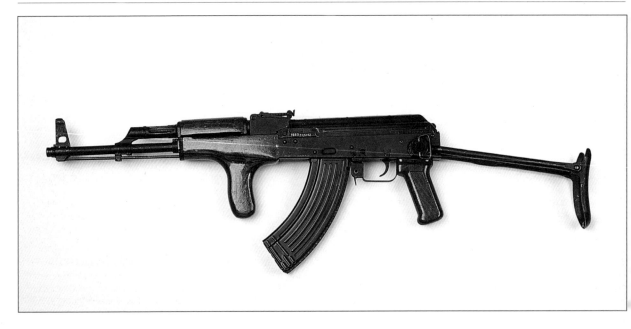

Above: The AKM can be distinguished from the original AK47 by the small indentation above the magazine. On the AK47 this is longer, running the full width of the magazine housing.

The East German MPi KM is distinguishable by its stippled plastic furniture. Note the addition of a compensator.

Kalashnikov 1974 (AK-74) (Russia)

level and keeping the weapon steady during automatic fire. The AKS74 version has a folding steel butt which swings to lie along the left side of the receiver.

The AK74 is a small-calibre version of the AKM, and it uses the same receiver, furniture and system of operation. The 5.45mm round is almost the same length as the 7.62 x 39mm round and the magazine thus fits into the same opening in the receiver. A noticeable feature of this rifle is the laminated plastic and steel magazine, the design of which has subtly changed since its introduction as stiffening fillets have been added. Another feature is the muzzle brake and compensator, designed to reduce the recoil and compensate for the upward climb always present in automatic weapons. It is highly efficient, reducing the felt recoil to a low

SPECIFICATION & OPERATION

CARTRIDGE
5.45 x 39.5mm

DIMENSIONS
Length: 36.53in (928mm); (AKS stock folded: 27.2in (690mm))
Weight unloaded: 8lb 8oz (3.86kg)
Barrel: 15.75in (400mm) 4 grooves, right-hand twist
Magazine: 30-round detachable plastic box
Cyclic rate: 650 rds/min
Muzzle velocity: 2952 ft/sec (900 m/sec)
IN SERVICE: 1975 –

MARKINGS
Model number, factory identifier and serial number on top of receiver.

SAFETY
Standard Kalashnikov combined safety and selector lever on left side of receiver. When pressed all the way UP it is in the SAFE position and obstructs the movement of the cocking handle and bolt. Moved down one notch, for automatic fire. Moved all the way down for single shots.

UNLOADING
Magazine catch at rear of magazine housing. Remove magazine. Pull back cocking handle to extract any round in the chamber, and examine the chamber through the ejection port to ensure that it is empty. Release the cocking handle, pull the trigger.

Dragunov (Russia)

Although similar to the Kalashnikov in principle, this rifle differs in using a short-stroke piston to operate the bolt carrier; the AK series uses a long-stroke piston, which would be inappropriate in this case, since this is a sniping rifle and the shift of balance during a long-stroke piston's movement can degrade the accuracy. The rifle is normally provided with the PSO-1 telescope sight, though the image-intensifying night sight NSPU-3 is also an item of issue with this rifle. It is claimed to have an effective range of 1000 metres and is now on open sale.

SPECIFICATION & OPERATION

CARTRIDGE
7.62 x 54R Soviet

DIMENSIONS
Length o/a: 1225mm (48.22in)
Weight: 4.31kg (9lb 8oz)
Barrel: 610mm (24.0in)
Rifling: 4 grooves, rh
Magazine capacity: 10 rounds

IN PRODUCTION 1963-

MARKINGS
Factory identification, year and serial number on left side of receiver.

SAFETY
This uses a similar safety lever to the Kalashnikov rifles, mounted on the left rear of the receiver. Pressed UP it makes the weapon safe; pressed DOWN it permits single shots.

UNLOADING
Magazine catch behind the magazine. Remove magazine. Pull back the cocking handle to extract any cartridge remaining in the chamber. Inspect chamber and feedway via the ejection port. Release cocking handle, press trigger.

Simonov SKS (Russia)

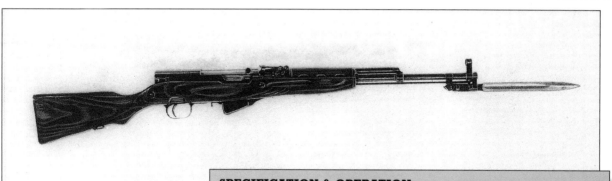

Simonov survived the SVT fiasco and set about designing a new carbine, but this was abandoned when the German invasion took place in 1941. He returned to it when the Soviets captured their first MP44s from the Germans and developed their own 7.62 short cartridge. Changing the design to suit this new cartridge , experimental models were in the hands of troops in combat in 1944, modifications were made, and in1946 mass-production of the first Soviet weapon to fire the 7.62 x 39mm cartridge began. It was thereafter widely issued, and also supplied to several Communist bloc countries, being copied in China, North Korea, East Germany and Yugoslavia. It is estimated that perhaps 15 million have been made.

SPECIFICATION & OPERATION

CARTRIDGE
7.62 x 39mm Soviet M1943

DIMENSIONS
Length o/a: 1122mm (44.17in)
Weight: 3.86kg (8lb 8oz)
Barrel: 620mm (24.4in)
Rifling: 4 grooves, rh
Magazine capacity: 10 rounds

IN PRODUCTION 1946-

MARKINGS
Serial number on left side receiver and on bolt.

SAFETY
Manual safety catch on the rear of the trigger guard is pushed forward and UP to make the weapon safe, when it obstructs the trigger finger and movement of the trigger.

UNLOADING
Magazine catch at the rear of the magazine, under the receiver. Press in and the magazine swings open, allowing the contents to be removed. Pull back the cocking handle, inspect the chamber and feedway, release the cocking handle, press the trigger. Close the empty magazine.

turning up in the wrong hands. It is claimed that the special cartridge will defeat all levels of body armour protection out to ranges of 400 metres or more; as with all Russian weapons, such claims should be treated with reserve until confirmed independently.

SPECIFICATION & OPERATION

CARTRIDGE
9 x 39mm special

DIMENSIONS
Length, stock extended: 875mm (34.45in)
Length, stock folded: 615mm (24.21in)
Weight: 2.50kg (5lb 8oz)
Barrel: Not known.
Rifling: not known
Magazine capacity: 20 rounds
Rate of fire: not known
IN PRODUCTION 1993-

MARKINGS
Factory identifier and serial number on right side of receiver.

SAFETY
Manual safety catch behind trigger, press upper portion in for safe, press lower portion in for fire.

UNLOADING
Magazine catch behind magazine on front end of trigger guard. Remove magazine, pull back cocking handle to eject any round in the chamber. Inspect chamber and feedway via the ejection slot. Release cocking handle, press trigger.

This weapon was only revealed in 1994 and full examination has not yet been possible. It is a silent semi-automatic rifle firing a heavy 9mm bullet at subsonic velocity, and, in view of the current accessibility of Russian small arms, it is likely to attract attention from various quarters, eventually

Singapore SR88 (Singapore)

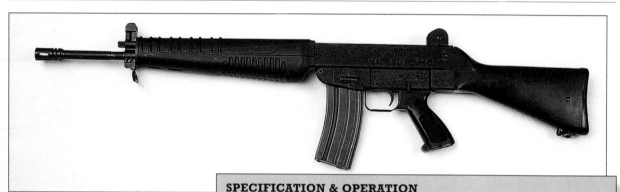

Chartered Industries of Singapore began by making the M16 under license from Colt. They then had Sterling of Britain design an automatic rifle for them which they produced as the SAR-80. The SR88 is an improved version and became the standard rifle of the Singapore armed forces. It has also been sold elsewhere in the Far East. The mechanism is different to that of the M16, using a gas piston to drive the bolt carrier back and operate a rotating bolt. The gas cylinder is chromed to reduce fouling and corrosion, the butt, fore-end and pistol grip are of glass-reinforced nylon, and the US M203 grenade launcher can be fitted beneath the barrel.

SPECIFICATION & OPERATION

CARTRIDGE
5.56 x 45mm M198

DIMENSIONS
Length o/a: 912mm (35.9in)
Weight: 3.66kg (8lb 1oz)
Barrel: 460mm (18.1in)
Rifling: 6 grooves, rh
Magazine capacity: 20 or 30 rounds
Rate of fire: 750 rds/min

IN PRODUCTION 1988-

MARKINGS
Serial Number; 'CAL 5.56 SR 88' on right side of magazine housing.

SAFETY
Manual safety catch and fire selector on left side of receiver, over the trigger. Rearward position for safe, forward in two steps, first for single shots, second for automatic fire.

UNLOADING
Magazine catch is a push-button on the right rear side of the magazine housing. Remove magazine. Pull back cocking handle to eject any round left in the chamber. Inspect chamber and feedway via the ejection port, release the cocking handle, pull trigger.

Singapore SR88A (Singapore)

An improved version of the SR88; mechanically it is the same but there are significant differences in construction. The lower receiver is now an aluminium alloy casting, and the upper receiver a steel pressing. Stock, fore-end and pistol grip are of fibre-glass reinforced nylon, and the fixed stock model has part of the stock cut away for lightness and strength. The barrel is fitted to the receiver by a locknut and locating lug system which considerably simplifies barrel replacement in the field. The barrel is hammer-forged and has a chromed chamber. There is also a carbine version with shorter barrel, intended for use by paratroops or others requiring a compact rifle.

SPECIFICATION & OPERATION

CARTRIDGE
5.56 x 45mm NATO

DIMENSIONS
Length, stock extended:
960mm (37.8in)
Length, stock folded: 810mm
(31.9in)
Weight: 3.68kg (8lb 2oz)
Barrel: 460mm (18.1in)
Rifling: 6 grooves, rh
Magazine capacity: 30 rounds
Rate of fire: 800 rds/min

IN PRODUCTION 1990-

MARKINGS
Serial Number 'SR88A CAL 5.56'
on right side of magazine
housing.

SAFETY
Manual safety catch and fire
selector on left side of receiver,
over the trigger. Rearward
position for safe, forward in
two steps, first for single shots,

second for automatic fire.

UNLOADING
Magazine catch is a push-
button on the right rear side of
the magazine housing. Remove
magazine. Pull back cocking
handle to eject any round left
in the chamber. Inspect
chamber and feedway via the
ejection port, release the
cocking handle, pull trigger.

SPECIFICATION & OPERATION

CARTRIDGE
5.56 x 45mm NATO

DIMENSIONS
Length, stock extended:
930mm (36.6in)
Length, stock folded:
675mm (26.58in)
Weight: 3.85kg (8lb 8oz)
Barrel: 416mm (16.38in)
Rifling: 6 grooves, rh
Magazine capacity: 10 or 30
rounds
Rate of fire: 650 rds/min

IN PRODUCTION 1984-

MARKINGS
'CETME 5.56 (.223)' on left
side of magazine housing.
Serial number on left side of
receiver above trigger.

SAFETY
Manual safety catch and fire
selector lever on left side of
receiver above the pistol grip.
With the catch pushed UP to
the letter 'S' the rifle is safe;

one notch DOWN to 'T' gives
single shots; two notches
DOWN to 'R' for automatic
fire. Some weapons will have
a fourth notch, though the
lever will not move into it;
this is because the design
originally had a three-round
burst setting but this was not
adopted by the Spanish Army.
However the receivers are
made with the notch since
the three-round burst
mechanism can be fitted as

an option for other
customers.

UNLOADING
Magazine catch behind
magazine housing on the
right side. Press in and
remove magazine. Pull back
cocking handle to eject any
round left in the chamber.
Inspect chamber and
feedway via the ejection
port. Release the cocking
handle, press trigger.

CETME (Centre for Technical Studies of Military
Equipment) is a Spanish design agency; the weapons
are actually made by the Empresa Nacional Santa Barbara
at Oviedo arsenal. CETME began designing rifles shortly
after WWII and were responsible for the design which
eventually became the German G3. The CETME rifles all
use the same roller-locked delayed blowback system that
is used by the G3; they began with a 7.92mm weapon,
then 7.62mm NATO and with the Model L moved into the
5.56mm field. There is also a short-barrel carbine with
folding butt known as the Model LC.

This is the South African standard rifle and is a slightly modified Israeli Galil; the modifications consisted of changing the butt and fore-end to synthetic materials rather than steel, in consideration of the bush temperatures common in Africa, and lengthening the butt since the average South African was rather larger than the average Israeli. Other components were strengthened, a bipod with wire-cutting ability was provided. There is also a carbine version, the R5, with a 332mm barrel, and a compact version, the R6, with a 280mm barrel. Semi-automatic versions of all three weapons are produced for use by police and para-military forces and for export.

SPECIFICATION & OPERATION

CARTRIDGE
5.56 x 45mm M193

DIMENSIONS
Length, stock extended:
1005mm (39.57in)
Length, stock folded: 740mm (29.13in)
Weight: 4.30kg (9lb 8oz)
Barrel: 460mm (18.1in)
Rifling: 6 grooves, rh
Magazine capacity: 35 rounds
Rate of fire: 700 rds/min

IN PRODUCTION 1982-

MARKINGS
Vektor badge (V in circle) on right of receiver in front of ejection port. Serial number on left.

SAFETY
Combined safety catch and fire selector lever on the right rear side of the receiver. When pressed all the way UP it is in the safe position (letter 'S') and obstructs the movement of the cocking handle and bolt; moved DOWN one notch to the first mark or the letter 'A' gives full automatic fire, and moved to the bottom position, or the letter 'R', produces single shots.

UNLOADING
Remove the magazine. Pull back the cocking handle to extract any round which may be in the chamber. Inspect the chamber via the ejection port. Release the cocking handle, pull the trigger.

Bofors AK5 (Sweden)

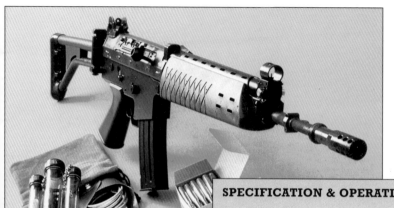

This is actually a variant of the Belgian FN-FNC rifle, extensively modified to meet Swedish requirements after a comprehensive series of trials in the mid-1980s. Changes were made to the butt, sights, cocking handle, bolt, selector switch, trigger guard and sling swivels, largely in order to better withstand extreme cold conditions and be more easily operated by gloved hands. The three-round burst option was removed. The metal is finished in a deep green enamel, making the rifle very easily recognisable.

SPECIFICATION & OPERATION

CARTRIDGE
5.56 x 45mm NATO

DIMENSIONS
Length, stock extended:
1008mm (39.70in)
Length, stock folded: 753mm (29.65in)
Weight: 3.90kg (8lb 10oz)
Barrel: 450mm (17.71in)
Rifling: 6 grooves, rh
Magazine capacity: 30 rounds

Rate of fire: 650 rds/min
IN PRODUCTION 1984-

MARKINGS
Month/year of manufacture at bottom right of receiver. Serial number and month/year of manufacture on left side.

SAFETY
Manual safety catch and selector lever on left side of receiver, above the trigger. Turn to the letter 'S' for safe, '1' for single shots, '30' for full automatic fire.

UNLOADING
Remove magazine. Pull back cocking handle. Inspect the chamber via the ejection port. Release cocking handle, press trigger.

Ljungman AG42 (Sweden)

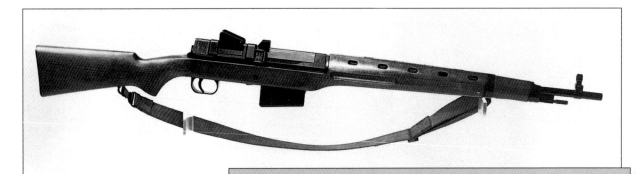

This appeared in Sweden in 1942 and uses a direct gas impingement system acting on the bolt carrier. Used by the Swedish Army until the 1970s, it was also used by the Danish Army in 7.92mm Mauser calibre from 1945 to the 1960s. In 1954 the Swedish tooling was bought by Egypt and the rifle produced there as the 'Hakim', also in 7.92mm Mauser calibre In 1959-60 a somewhat modified design, chambered for the 7.62 x 39mm Soviet cartridge was produced in Egypt as the 'Rashid' in small numbers.

SPECIFICATION & OPERATION

CARTRIDGE
6.5 x 55mm Swedish service

DIMENSIONS
Length o/a: 1214mm (47.8in)
Weight: 4.71kg (10lb 6oz)
Barrel: 622mm (24.5in)
Rifling: 6 grooves, rh
Magazine capacity: 10 rounds

IN PRODUCTION 1942-62

MARKINGS
MADSEN and serial number on left side of chamber.

SAFETY
Lever at end of receiver: move right for safe.

UNLOADING
There are two types of rifle, one with the magazine fixed and the other removable. In the case of the fixed model the only way to unload is to operate the cocking handle back and forth until the magazine is empty. Then check the chamber and feedway, release the cocking handle and pull the trigger. Where there is a magazine catch behind the magazine, remove the magazine, pull back the cocking handle to eject any round in the chamber, inspect chamber and feedway, release the cocking handle and pull the trigger.

SIG SG510-4 (Stgw 57) (Switzerland)

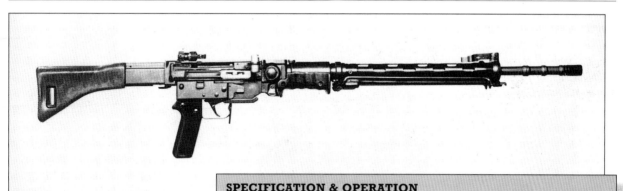

This Swiss service rifle is related to the German G3 and Spanish CETME Model L rifles insofar as they are all based on the roller-locked delayed-blowback system first designed by Mauser in Germany for the abortive Sturmgewehr 45. Somewhat heavy, it is a superbly accurate and comfortable-to-shoot rifle and is noted for its reliability in harsh climatic conditions. The commercial version, semi-automatic only, is the SIG 510-4, chambered for the 7.62mm cartridge; the two can be best told apart by the Stgw 57 having a rubber-covered butt which is virtually straight behind the receiver, while the 510-4 has a wooden butt with a distinct drop.

SPECIFICATION & OPERATION

CARTRIDGE
7.5 x 55mm Swiss Service or 7.62 x 51mm NATO

DIMENSIONS
Length o/a: L1016mm (40.0in)
Weight: 4.25kg (9lb 6oz)
Barrel: 505mm (19.88in)
Rifling: 4 grooves, rh
Magazine capacity: 20 rounds
Rate of fire: 600 rds/min

IN PRODUCTION 1957-83

MARKINGS
Serial number on left rear of receiver.

SAFETY
A combined safety catch and fire selector is on the left side of the receiver, above the trigger. Vertical for safe, slanting forward for single shots, horizontal for automatic fire.

UNLOADING
Magazine catch in rear of magazine housing. Remove magazine. Pull back cocking handle to eject any round left in the chamber. Inspect chamber and feedway via the ejection port. Release cocking handle, press trigger.

SIG SG540 (SG542) series (Switzerland)

This family - the SG540 in 5.56mm with long barrel, SG542 in 7.62mm with long barrel, and SG543 in 5.56mm with short barrel - was designed by SIG of Switzerland and forthwith licensed to Manurhin of France for manufacture; Swiss arms export laws making it impossible for SIG to supply weapons to most countries. Manurhin made about 20,000 for the French Army who used them while FAMAS rifle production got up to speed, and they were supplied to Chile, Bolivia, Paraguay, Ecuador and Nicaragua. In 1988 the license was relinquished and passed to INDEP of Portugal,. who re-assigned it to Chile, who currently make the 540 and 542.

SPECIFICATION & OPERATION

CARTRIDGE
5.56 x 45mm or 7.62 x 51mm

DIMENSIONS: (SG542)
Length o/a: 1000mm (39.37in)
Weight: 3.55kg (7lb 13oz)
Barrel: 465mm (18.31in)
Rifling: 4 grooves, rh
Magazine capacity: 20 or 30 rounds
Rate of fire: 800 rds/min

IN PRODUCTION 1977-

MARKINGS
`MANURHIN FRANCE SG54X`
and serial number on right side of receiver. May also have national army markings, e.g. `EJERCITO DE CHILE`.

SAFETY
A four-position safety catch and fire selector on the left side of the receiver, above the pistol grip. The upper position is safe; rotated DOWN and forward there are positions for single shots, three-round burst, and full automatic fire.

UNLOADING
Magazine catch in rear of magazine housing. Remove magazine. Pull back cocking handle to eject any round left in the chamber. Inspect chamber and feedway via the ejection port. Release cocking handle, press trigger.

SIG SG 550/551 (Stgw 90) (Switzerland)

This is an improved SG540 developed in competition to meet a Swiss Army requirement in 1984. The SIG design was selected and became the Sturmgewehr 90 and will eventually replace the Stgw 57 as the official Swiss rifle. It is also made in a civilian version, without automatic fire. An interesting feature of this rifle is the provision of studs and slots on the plastic magazines so that two or three magazines can be clipped together side-by-side; one can then be inserted into the magazine housing, and when the last shot is fired, changing to a full magazine can be done by pulling the assembly out, shifting it sideways and pushing in one of the loaded magazines.

SPECIFICATION & OPERATION

CARTRIDGE
5.56 x 45mm NATO

DIMENSIONS: (SG550)
Length, stock extended: 998mm (39,30in)
Length, stock folded: 772mm (30.4in)
Weight: 4.10kg (9lb 1oz)
Rifling: 6 grooves, rh
Magazine capacity: 20 or 30 rounds
Rate of fire: 700 rds/min

IN PRODUCTION 1986-

MARKINGS
'SG 550' and serial number on left side of receiver.

SAFETY
A four-position safety catch and fire selector on the left side of the receiver, above the pistol grip. The rear position is safe; rotated UP and forward there are positions for single shots, three-round burst, and full automatic fire.

UNLOADING
Magazine catch in rear of magazine housing. Remove magazine. Pull back cocking handle to eject any round left in the chamber. Inspect chamber and feedway via the ejection port. Release cocking handle, press trigger.

SSG550 Sniper (Switzerland)

they eye when the firer's face is against the cheek-piece. An anti-reflective screen can be drawn over the top of the rifle, which also prevents air disturbance due to barrel heat interfering with the sight line. Altogether, just about everything for the sniper's convenience has been considered and catered for in this rifle

The SSG550 was developed from the standard SG550 rifle by fitting it with a heavy hammer-forged barrel and altering the mechanism for semi-automatic fire only. The trigger is a two-stage type, adjustable to the firer's personal preference, and the butt is adjustable for length and has an adjustable cheek-piece. The pistol grip is also adjustable for rake and carries a hand-rest which can be positioned as required. A bipod is fitted, and the telescope can be varied in its position so as to fall naturally to

SPECIFICATION & OPERATION

CARTRIDGE
5.56 x 45mm

DIMENSIONS
Length butt extended: 1130mm (44.49in)
Length, butt folded: 905mm (35.63in)
Barrel: 650mm (25.60in)
Weight: 7.3kg (16lb 1oz)
Rifling: 6 grooves, rh
Magazine capacity: 20 or 30 rounds

MARKINGS
'SSG 550' and serial number on left side of receiver.

SAFETY
A two-position safety catch is on the right and left sides of the receiver, above the pistol grip. With the thumb-piece up and to the rear, the weapon is SAFE. Pressing the thumb-piece down and forward takes it to FIRE.

UNLOADING
Magazine release is behind the magazine housing and in front of the trigger-guard. Remove the magazine. Pull back the cocking handle, opening the breech and withdrawing any round from the chamber. Examine the chamber and feedway through the ejection port, ensuring both are empty. Release the bolt. Press the trigger.

Taiwan Type 65 (Taiwan)

This rifle was developed and manufactured by the Taiwanese Hsing Hua arsenal and is broadly based upon the M16. The general shape of the receiver is similar to that of the M16, though only prototypes were made with the carrying handle, the production rifle having a flat top. The fore-end is longer than that used with the M16, and a bipod may be fitted, though it is not a standard fitment. A later model of this rifle has a three-round burst facility in addition to full automatic fire.

SPECIFICATION & OPERATION

CARTRIDGE
5.56 x 45mm M193 or NATO

DIMENSIONS
Length o/a: 990mm (39.0in)
Weight: 3.17kg (7lb 0oz)
Barrel: 508mm (20.0in)
Rifling: 4 grooves, rh
Magazine capacity: 20 or 30 rounds
Rate of fire: 750 rds/min

IN PRODUCTION 1976-

MARKINGS
5.56m Type 65 on left of magazine housing.

SAFETY
Combined safety catch and fire selector on left side of receiver above the trigger. With the catch pulled back so that the pointer is directed to 'SAFE' the weapon is safe. With the catch pressed DOWN and forward to the vertical, the weapon fires single shots. With the catch pressed forward so that the pointer is to the rear against 'AUTO' automatic fire is available.

UNLOADING
Magazine catch is a push-button on the right side of the receiver above the trigger. Remove magazine. Pull back cocking handle (T-shaped 'wings' behind the carrying handle) to eject any round remaining in the chamber. Inspect chamber and feedway via the ejection port. Release cocking handle, pull trigger.

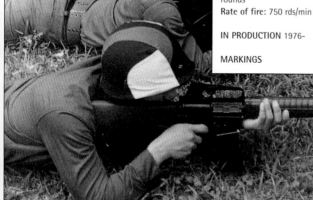

Enfield L85A1 (UK)

The Enfield L85A1 (also called the SA80) was developed by the Royal Small Arms Factory, originally in 4.85mm calibre. The designers were astute enough to realise that this calibre had little chance of being adopted as NATO standard, and thus when the standard was eventually defined as 5.56mm, the re-design was relatively easy. Unfortunately, the transition from hand-built prototypes to mass-produced service weapons was less easy and the initial issues had many

SPECIFICATION & OPERATION

CARTRIDGE
5.56 x 45mm NATO

DIMENSIONS
Length o/a: 785mm (30.90in)
Weight: 3.80kg (8lb 6oz)
Barrel: 518mm (20.4in)
Rifling: 6 grooves, rh
Magazine capacity: 30 rounds
Rate of fire: 700 rds/min

IN PRODUCTION 1985-94

MARKINGS
RIFLE 5.56MM L85A1 and NATO stock number impressed into right side of handguard.

SAFETY
A push-through bolt above the trigger, pushed from the left to the right for safe. On the left side of the stock is a fire selector: up for single shots and down for fully automatic.

UNLOADING
Magazine catch on left side of receiver above magazine housing. Remove magazine. Pull back cocking handle to eject any round remaining in the chamber. Inspect chamber and feedway via the ejection port. Release cocking handle, pull trigger.

serious defects. After the privatisation of the RSAF, an entirely new factory was erected in Nottingham, contractor's standards were tightened and eventually the various defects were eliminated. It may be found fitted with the optical SUSAT sight, or with iron sights, the latter being standard issue for non-infantry troops. There is also a carbine version, which is not yet adopted by the British Army, and a single-shot cadet training version.

US M1 Rifle (Garand) (USA)

SPECIFICATION & OPERATION

CARTRIDGE
7.62 x 63mm (US .30-06)

DIMENSIONS
Length o/a: 1106mm (43.6in)
Weight: 4.30kg (9lb 8oz)
Barrel: 610mm (24.0in)
Rifling: 4 grooves, rh
Magazine capacity: 8 rounds

IN PRODUCTION 1936-59

MARKINGS
`U.S RIFLE .30 M1 SPRINGFIELD ARSENAL` and serial number on upper rear of receiver. Other manufacturer's names are: `WINCHESTER`; `INTERNATIONAL HARVESTER`; `HARRINGTON & RICHARDSON`. May also be found with `BERETTA` and with Indonesian markings.

SAFETY
Manual safety catch in the front of the trigger guard. Pulled back toward the trigger, the rifle is safe; push forward to fire.

UNLOADING
Ensure the safety catch is forward. Pull back the cocking handle to eject any round in the chamber, and hold it to the rear. Inspect the chamber and magazine. If there is ammunition in the magazine, grasp the rifle with the left hand in front of the trigger guard and, without releasing the cocking handle, reach across the action with the right thumb and press the clip latch on the left side of the receiver. The clip, with any remaining ammunition in front of the trigger guard will be ejected from the magazine into the right hand. Remove the clip and ammunition, check chamber and magazine area again, release the cocking handle, press the trigger.

The first automatic rifle to achieve the status of being the regulation sidearm for a major army, the Garand served well and was popular for its reliability and power. If it had a defect, it was the clip loading system which prevented `topping up' the magazine during a lull in the firing; it was a full clip or nothing. There was also the embarrassment of the empty clip being ejected after the last round and advertising the fact if it fell on a hard surface. But these were minor faults, and with over six million rifles made and distributed to many countries after 1945, they will continue to appear for many years to come.

SPECIFICATION & OPERATION

CARTRIDGE
7.62 x 33mm (.30 Carbine)

DIMENSIONS: (M1)
Length o/a: 904mm (35.6in)
Weight: 2.36kg (5lb 3oz)
Barrel: 458mm (18.0in)
Rifling: 4 grooves, rh
Magazine capacity: 15 or 30 rounds
Rate of fire: (M2/M3) 750 rds/min

IN PRODUCTION 1942-

MARKINGS
'U.S.CARBINE CAL .30 M1'

across the top of the chamber. Serial number and maker's mark on the rear of the receiver. Various maker's marks and initials may be found on the receiver and barrel.

SAFETY
Manual safety catch on the right front edge of the trigger guard. Push DOWN for fire, UP for safe. Original models had a push-through cross-bolt but this was later changed and almost all were modified. The M2 and M3 models have a selector switch on the front left side of the receiver, alongside the chamber; push forward for automatic fire, rearward for single shots.

UNLOADING
Magazine release is a push-button on the right side of the receiver, behind the magazine. Remove magazine. Pull back cocking handle to eject any round remaining in the chamber. Inspect chamber and feedway, release cocking handle, pull trigger.

One of the most appealing of weapons, light, handy, easy to shoot and totally useless at ranges over 200 yards, since it fired a pistol bullet. It was intended simply to replace the pistol with something having more range, but it found itself being used as a light rifle more often than not. Over six million were made in various forms; the M1 was the original semi-automatic; the M1A1 had a folding steel butt, for use by paratroops; the M2 added automatic fire; and the M3 was an M2 with special fittings for mounting infra-red sights. After the war several companies began making them for the commercial market and still do.

Stoner SR-25 (USA)

This remarkable weapon is actually an M16 modified to fire the 7.62mm NATO cartridge. Its purpose in life is suggested as a support weapon for sniper teams, the second man using it for local defence but having sufficient accuracy to stand in for the sniper should some accident befall him or his weapon. It is certainly designed for accuracy, with a very heavy free-floating barrel and with the bipod attached to the fore-end and the fore-end attached only to the receiver so as not to place any strain on the barrel. The receiver is a flat top design to which the user can apply various options, from a carrying handle to the most sophisticated night vision sights. Tests show that this rifle can consistently put all the shots of a group into a 19mm circle at 100m range.

SPECIFICATION & OPERATION

CARTRIDGE
7.62 x 51mm NATO

DIMENSIONS
Length o/a: 1175mm (46.25in)
Weight: 4.88kg (10lb 12oz)
Barrel: 508mm (20.0in)
Rifling: 4 grooves, rh
Magazine capacity: 10 or 20 rounds

IN PRODUCTION 1992-

MARKINGS
`KNIGHT'S ARMAMENT CO SR25 serial number' on left side of magazine housing.

SAFETY
Manual safety catch on the left side of the receiver, above the trigger. Rear for safe, forward for fire.

UNLOADING
Magazine catch in rear of magazine housing. Remove magazine. Pull back cocking handle (`wings' above the rear of the receiver) to eject any round in the chamber. Release the cocking handle, pull the trigger.

M14 Rifle (USA)

When the US needed a new 7.62mm rifle to meet NATO standardisation requirements, it seemed good sense to give the Garand a few tweaks; give it a detachable magazine instead of the clip feed and rebarrel it. Job done. Or it would have been, if somebody hadn't said 'Let's make it automatic'. Provision of automatic fire with a cartridge as heavy as the 7.62 meant strengthening everything, and the result was a clumsy weapon. Most were converted by locking the system at semi-automatic, and with some modifications the weapon was reasonably serviceable. Early models had wooden furniture, then with a glass-fibre handguard, finally with all-synthetic furniture.

SPECIFICATION & OPERATION

CARTRIDGE
7.62 x 51mm NATO

DIMENSIONS
Length o/a: 1120mm (44.1in)
Weight: 5.10kg (11lb 4oz)
Barrel: 559mm (22.0in)
Rifling: 4 grooves, rh
Magazine capacity: 20 rounds
Rate of fire: 750 rds/min

IN PRODUCTION 1957-63

MARKINGS
'US RIFLE 7.62MM M14'; Maker's name (e.g. 'WINCHESTER'; 'SPRINGFIELD ARMORY') and serial number on top rear of receiver.

SAFETY
Manual safety catch in the front of the trigger guard. Pulled back toward the trigger, the rifle is safe; push forward to fire. Fire selection is by a rotary catch in the right side of the receiver above the trigger. Press in and turn to point DOWN for single shots, UP for automatic fire.

UNLOADING
Magazine catch behind the magazine housing beneath the receiver. Remove magazine. Pull back cocking handle to eject any round remaining in the chamber. Inspect chamber and feedway, release cocking handle, pull the trigger.

Colt M16A2 (USA)

SPECIFICATION & OPERATION

CARTRIDGE
5.56 x 45mm NATO

DIMENSIONS
Length: 1000mm (39.37in)
Weight: unloaded: 5.78kg (12lb 12oz)
Barrel: 510mm (20.0in)
Rifling: 6 grooves, rh
Magazine capacity: 30 rounds
Cyclic rate: 700 rds/min

IN PRODUCTION 1991 -

MARKINGS
COLT M16A2 PROPERTY OF U.S.GOVT CAL 5.56MM serial number on left side of magazine housing. COLT FIREARMS DIVISION COLT INDUSTRIES HARTFORD CONN USA on left side of receiver.

SAFETY
The normal M16-type three-position safety catch and fire selector switch on the left side of the receiver above the pistol grip. Thumb-piece to the rear for safe, vertical for single shots, to the front for automatic fire.

UNLOADING
Magazine catch on the side of the receiver above the magazine housing. Remove magazine. Pull back cocking handle until the bolt is held by the sear. Inspect the chamber and feedway through the ejection port, ensuring both are empty. Grasp cocking handle, press trigger, and allow the bolt to go forward under control.

Developed in collaboration with Diemaco of Canada, this is based upon the M16A2 rifle. It has a heavier barrel, larger and stronger for-end and handguard with carrying handle, an attached folding bipod and a forward assault hand grip. The basic mechanism remains that of the Stoner rotating bolt, driven by gas impingement. The standard 30-round magazine is used, but there are a number of proprietary large-capacity magazines available in the USA which will also fit the magazine housing.

The M16A2 machine gun has been adopted by the US Marines and also by Brazil, El Salvador and other countries.

US M4 Carbine (USA)

This is a true carbine, being simply a short-barrelled version of the M16A2 rifle and with a collapsible stock; it can be thought of as an intermediate between the full sized rifle and the ultra-short Commando. All mechanical components are interchangeable with those of the M16A2, and it will accept any M16 or NATO STANAG 4179 magazines. As well as being used by US forces it is in service with the Canadian Army as their C8 rifle and with a number of Central and South American forces.

SPECIFICATION & OPERATION

CARTRIDGE
5.56 x 45mm NATO

DIMENSIONS
Length, stock extended: 840mm (33.07in)
Length, stock folded: 760mm (29.92in)
Weight: 2.54kg (5lb 10oz)
Barrel: 368mm (14.5in)
Rifling: 6 grooves, rh
Magazine capacity: 20 or 30 rounds

Rate of fire: 700 - 1000 rds/min

IN PRODUCTION 1984-

MARKINGS
'COLT FIREARMS DIVISION COLT INDUSTRIES HARTFORD CONN USA' on left side of receiver. 'COLT M4 CAL 5.56mm serial number' on left side of magazine housing.

SAFETY
Combined safety catch and fire selector on left side of receiver above the trigger. With the catch pulled back so that the pointer is directed to 'SAFE' the weapon is safe. With the catch pressed DOWN and forward to the vertical, the weapon fire single shots. And with the catch pressed forward so that the pointer is to the rear against 'AUTO' automatic fire is available.

UNLOADING
Magazine catch is a push-button on the right side of the receiver above the trigger. Remove magazine. Pull back cocking handle (T-shaped 'wings' behind the carrying handle) to eject any round remaining in the chamber. Inspect chamber and feedway via the ejection port. Release cocking handle, pull trigger.

Armalite AR-18

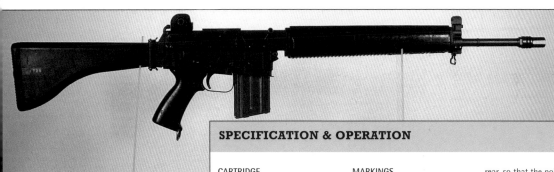

The AR-18 was intended to be the poor man's M16, a simplified weapon capable of being made in countries with limited manufacturing capability. But it was still cheaper to buy M16s than to set up a factory to make AR-18s. ArmaLite sold the rights to Howa Machinery of Japan in the early 1960s, but the Japanese government forbade them to make war weapons. Then Sterling Armaments of England bought the rights in 1974 and began manufacturing, but they found few takers before they went out of business in the 1980s.

SPECIFICATION & OPERATION

CARTRIDGE
5.56 x 45mm M109

DIMENSIONS
Length, stock extended:
940mm (37.00in)
Length, stock folded: 738mm
(29.00in)
Weight: 3.17kg (7lb 0oz)
Barrel: 464mm (18.25in)
Rifling: 6 grooves, rh
Magazine capacity: 20, 30 or
40 rounds
Rate of fire: 800 rds/min

IN PRODUCTION ca 1966-79

MARKINGS
`AR 18 ARMALITE' moulded into the pistol grips. `ARMALITE AR-18 PATENTS PENDING' on left side of magazine housing. Serial number on top rear of receiver, or on left of receiver or on magazine housing. May be found with `MADE BY STERLING ARMAMENTS' on left side of receiver.

SAFETY
A combined manual safety catch and fire selector switch is on the left side, above the pistol grip. The switch is turned to the rear, so that the pointer points forward, to make the rifle safe. With the switch vertical the weapon is set for single shots, and with the switch forward and the pointer to the rear, the weapon fires full-automatic.

UNLOADING
Magazine catch on right side of magazine housing. Remove magazine. Pull back cocking handle on right side, inspect chamber through the ejection port. Release cocking handle, pull trigger.

Barrett 'Light Fifty' M82A1 (USA)

One of the first heavy sniping rifles to achieve success, the Barrett has been adopted by several military and police forces as an anti-material sniping weapon and also for detonating explosive devices at a safe distance. Originally there was little danger of confusing it with anything else, but in the late 1980s a number of competing designs appeared and the Barrett is no longer quite so individual.

SPECIFICATION & OPERATION

CARTRIDGE
12.7 x 99 (.50 Browning)

DIMENSIONS
Length o/a: 1549mm (61.0in)
Weight: 13.40kg (25lb 9oz)
Barrel: 737mm (29.0in)
Rifling: 12 grooves, rh
Magazine capacity: 11 rounds
Rate of fire: semi-automatic only

IN PRODUCTION 1983-92

MARKINGS
'BARRETT FIREARMS MANUFACTURING INC MURFREESBORO, TN, USA. CAL .50' and serial number on left side of receiver.

SAFETY
Thumb-operated manual safety on left side of receiver, above the pistol grip. Turned to the horizontal position, the weapon is safe; to the vertical position for fire.

UNLOADING
Magazine catch behind magazine. Remove magazine and empty out any ammunition. Pull back cocking handle, examine chamber via the ejection slot. Release cocking handle, press trigger, replace empty magazine.

SPECIFICATION & OPERATION

CARTRIDGE
12.7 x 99mm (.50 Browning)

DIMENSIONS
Length o/a: 1409mm (55.5in)
Weight: 12.24kg (27lb 0oz)
Barrel: 737mm (29.0in)
Rifling: 12 grooves, rh
Magazine capacity: 11 rounds
Rate of fire: semi-automatic only

IN PRODUCTION 1990 -

MARKINGS
`BARRETT FIREARMS MANUFACTURING INC MURFREESBORO, TN, USA. CAL .50' and serial number on left side of receiver.

SAFETY
Thumb-operated manual safety on left side of receiver, above the pistol grip. Turned to the horizontal position, the weapon is safe; to the vertical position

for fire.

UNLOADING
Magazine catch behind magazine. Remove magazine and empty out any ammunition. Pull back cocking handle, examine chamber via the ejection slot. Release cocking handle, press trigger, replace empty magazine.

This was developed in order to make the heavy sniping rifle a little less cumbersome. The change is simply to a 'bullpup' layout, in which the action and barrel are placed further back in the stock so as to retain the same length of barrel but in a lesser overall length. This places the receiver and action alongside the firer's face and the magazine now lies behind the pistol grip and trigger.

La France M16K (USA)

there is a better chance of a first-round hit with this weapon than with most submachine guns firing from open bolts. The fore-end and handguard are cylindrical, surrounding the barrel, and there is a short pronged flash-hider on the muzzle.

SPECIFICATION & OPERATION

CARTRIDGE
.45 ACP

DIMENSIONS
Length o/a: 676mm (26.61in)
Barrel: 184mm (7.24in)
Weight: 3.86kg (8lb 8oz)
Rifling: 6 grooves rh
Magazine: 30 rounds
Rate of Fire: 625 rds/min

IN PRODUCTION 1994-

MARKINGS
Las France Specialties San Diego CA USA M16K .45ACP and serial number on right side of magazine housing.

SAFETY
The safety catch/selector switch system of the M16 is retained, a three-position switch on the left side of the receiver, above the pistol grip. Turned to the rear is SAFE. Pushed forward to the vertical for single shots, push fully forward for automatic.

UNLOADING
Magazine catch on left side, behind magazine housing. Remove magazine. Pull back cocking handle examine chamber through ejection aperture to ensure it is empty. Release cocking handle, press trigger.

Designed for use by special forces and similar units, the M16K utilises the butt and other parts of the M16 rifle, and allies them to a blowback system of operation, firing from a closed bolt. This, combined with the straight-line layout, means that

Ruger Mini-Thirty (USA)

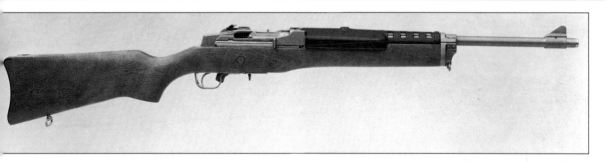

This came about as a variation of the Mini-14 Ranch Rifle, being chambered for the Soviet 7.62 39mm cartridge since this allowed a compact rifle with a cartridge superior to the .223 Remington for medium game shooting. However, it also offers an excellent para-military semi-automatic weapon in a calibre which is widely used throughout the world. It is a robust weapon and uses Ruger's patented optical sight mount, with which, it is claimed, accuracy superior to any other rifle in this calibre can be achieved.

SPECIFICATION & OPERATION

CARTRIDGE
7.62 x 39mm Soviet M1943

DIMENSIONS
Length o/a: 948mm (37.25in)
Weight: 3.26kg (7lb 3oz)
Barrel: 470mm (18.5in)
Rifling: 6 grooves, rh
Magazine capacity: 5 rounds

IN PRODUCTION 1987-

MARKINGS
`STURM, RUGER & Co Inc SOUTHPORT CONN USA' on left rear of receiver. Serial number on left of receiver alongside chamber. `RUGER MINI-30 Cal 7.62' on rear top of receiver.

SAFETY
Manual safety catch in front edge of trigger-guard. Push back into the guard for safe, forward for fire.

UNLOADING
Magazine catch beneath receiver. Remove magazine. Pull back cocking handle to eject any round left in the chamber. Inspect chamber and feedway. Release cocking handle, pull trigger.

Ruger Mini-14 (USA)

The Mini-14 is based on the same gas piston and rotating bolt mechanism as used by the US M1 and M14 rifles, but the use of modern high tensile alloy steels has allowed considerable weight and bulk to be saved, making this a light and handy weapon firing a now-common cartridge. Although intended as a hunting rifle it was gladly adopted by many para-military and police forces throughout the world. A militarised version, the K Mini/14-20GB has a bayonet lug, flash suppressor and heat resistant glass-fibre handguard and is also available with a folding stock. The AC-556 is also militarised and provided with selective fire, giving automatic fire at about 750 rds/min; a folding stock version is also available.

SPECIFICATION & OPERATION

CARTRIDGE
5.56 x 45mm M193 or NATO

DIMENSIONS
Length o/a: 946mm (37.25in)
Weight: 2.90kg (6lb 6oz)
Barrel: 470mm (18.5in)
Rifling: 6 grooves, rh
Magazine capacity: 5, 20 or 30 rounds

IN PRODUCTION 1973-

MARKINGS
`STURM, RUGER & Co Inc SOUTHPORT CONN USA' on left rear of receiver. Serial number on left of receiver alongside chamber. `RUGER MINI-14 Cal .223' on rear top of receiver.

SAFETY
Manual safety catch in front edge of trigger-guard. Push back into the guard for safe, forward for fire.

UNLOADING
Magazine catch beneath receiver. Remove magazine. Pull back cocking handle to eject any round left in the chamber. Inspect chamber and feedway. Release cocking handle, pull trigger.

Zastava M59/66 (Yugoslavia)

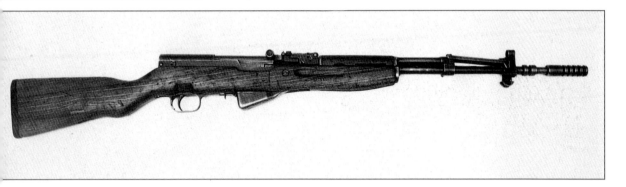

Yugoslavia adopted the Simonov SVS in the 1950s as their M59, but after some experience decided to modify it better to suit their requirements. The barrel was lengthened and provided with a 22mm grenade-launching sleeve, the gas cylinder connection to the barrel was altered and a new foresight unit, which includes a night sight and a grenade sight, was attached to the extended barrel. The fore-end was shortened, but the hinged sword bayonet was retained, making several generations of Yugoslav conscripts very wary about where they put their fingers. They were widely exported before the end of Yugoslavia.

SPECIFICATION & OPERATION

CARTRIDGE
7.62 x 39mm Soviet M1943

DIMENSIONS
Length o/a: 1120mm (44.1in)
Weight: 4.10kg (9lb 1oz)
Barrel: 620mm (24.4in)
Rifling: 4 grooves, rh
Magazine capacity: 10 rounds

IN PRODUCTION 1966-72

MARKINGS
Factory identifier and serial number on right side of receiver.

SAFETY
Thumb-operated safety catch at the right rear of the receiver. Forward to fire, back for safe.

UNLOADING
Magazine catch behind magazine, beneath receiver. Remove magazine. Pull back cocking handle to eject any round remaining in the chamber. Inspect chamber and feedway. Release cocking handle, pull trigger.

Zastava M70B1 (Yugoslavia)

This is generally based on the AK47 Kalashnikov which the Yugoslavs obtained from the USSR and adopted as their M60. As with the Simonov, they felt that there were a few alterations that needed doing, and the M70 is the result. While the general layout remains the same, there is a folding grenade sight behind the foresight which, when raised, shuts off the gas supply to the gas actuating cylinder. There is no grenade launching fitment on the rifle but one can be quickly fitted, a groove around the muzzle acting as anchor for a snap ring. Both fixed and folding stock models were made and it remains the standard Yugoslavian service rifle.

SPECIFICATION & OPERATION

CARTRIDGE
7.62 x 39mm Soviet M1943

DIMENSIONS
Length, stock extended: 900mm (35.43in)
Length, stock folded: 640mm (25.20)
Weight: 3.70kg (8lb 3oz)
Rifling: 4 grooves, rh
Magazine capacity: 30 rounds
Rate of fire: 650 rds/min

IN PRODUCTION 1974-

MARKINGS
Model number, factory identifier and serial number on top of rear end of receiver.

SAFETY
Combined safety catch and fire selector lever on the right rear side of the receiver. When pressed all the way UP it is in the safe position and obstructs the movement of the cocking handle and bolt; moved DOWN one notch to the first mark or the letter 'R' gives full automatic fire, and moved to the bottom position, or the letter 'J', produces single shots.

UNLOADING
Magazine catch at rear of magazine housing. Remove the magazine. Pull back the cocking handle to extract any round which may be in the chamber. Inspect the chamber via the ejection port. Release the cocking handle, pull the trigger.

Zastava M76 (Yugoslavia)

This is based on the action of the M70 rifle but chambered for a much more powerful cartridge and with a longer and heavier barrel as befits a sniping rifle. The sight bracket can be adapted to almost any type of optical or electro-optical sight. The rifle was taken into service by Yugoslavian forces and was also offered for export chambered for the 7.62 x 51mm NATO and the 7.62 x 54R Soviet cartridges, but details of any sales have never been made public.

SPECIFICATION & OPERATION

CARTRIDGE
7.92 x 57mm Mauser and others

DIMENSIONS
Length o/a: 1135mm (44.70in)
Weight: 4.20kg (9lb 4oz)
Barrel: 550mm (21.65in)
Rifling: 4 grooves, rh
Magazine capacity: 10 rounds

IN PRODUCTION 1975-

MARKINGS
Model number, factory identifier and serial number on top of rear end of receiver.

SAFETY
Manual safety catch on the right rear side of the receiver. When pressed all the way UP it is in the safe position and obstructs the movement of the cocking handle and bolt; moved

DOWN to the lower notch, the rifle is ready to fire.

UNLOADING
Magazine catch at rear of magazine housing. Remove the magazine. Pull back the cocking handle to extract any round which may be in the chamber. Inspect the chamber via the ejection port. Release the cocking handle, pull the trigger.

Zastava M80 (Yugoslavia)

This rifle, and its folding-stock companion the M80A, was designed in order to provide the export market with a Kalashnikov pattern rifle in 5.56mm calibre. The gas regulator has been redesigned in order to cope with the different energy levels possible with various makes of 5.56mm ammunition, and there is a grenade launching spigot and sight provided with every rifle which can be attached when required. How far this particular export venture had got when the present war broke out is not known, but the possibility of these rifles appearing anywhere in the world cannot be overlooked.

SPECIFICATION & OPERATION

CARTRIDGE
5.56 x 45mm M193 or NATO

DIMENSIONS
Length o/a: 990mm (39.0in)
Weight: 3.50kg (7lb 11oz)
Barrel: 460mm (18.1in)
Rifling: 6 grooves, rh
Magazine capacity: 30 rounds
Rate of fire: 750 rds/min

IN PRODUCTION 1985-

MARKINGS
Model number, factory identifier and serial number on top of rear end of receiver.

SAFETY
Combined safety catch and fire selector lever on the right rear side of the receiver. When pressed all the way UP it is in the safe position and obstructs the movement of the cocking handle and bolt; moved DOWN one notch to the first mark gives full automatic fire, and moved to the bottom position produces single shots.

UNLOADING
Magazine catch at rear of magazine housing. Remove the magazine. Pull back the cocking handle to extract any round which may be in the chamber. Inspect the chamber via the ejection port. Release the cocking handle, pull the trigger.

MACHINE GUNS

Steyr AUG/HB (Austria)

This is basically the AUG rifle (described in the 'Automatic Rifles' section), but fitted with a heavy barrel and a bipod to act in the light automatic role. The barrel is supplied in either 178mm, 228mm or 305mm pitch of rifling, and a muzzle attachment acts as a flash hider and reduces recoil and muzzle climb during automatic firing.

There are two different versions, the HBAR and HBAR/T: the former has the carrying handle with built-in optical sight as on the AUG rifle; the latter has a mounting bar on which any sighting telescope or night vision sight can be fitted. Both the HBAR

SPECIFICATION & OPERATION

CARTRIDGE
5.56 x 45mm NATO or M193

DIMENSIONS
Length o/a: 900mm (35.43in)
Weight: 4.90kg (10lb 12oz)
Barrel: 621mm (24.45in),
Rifling: 6 grooves, rh
Magazine capacity: 30 or 42 rounds
Rate of Fire: 680 rds/min

IN PRODUCTION 1980-

MARKINGS
STEYR-DAIMLER-PUCH AG AUSTRIA or STEYR-MANNLICHER GmbH AUSTRIA and AUG/HB moulded into the left rear of the buttstock. Serial number on right side of barrel.

SAFETY
Push-through cross-bolt safety catch above the trigger. Pushed to the right for Safe, to the left to fire. Selecting of single shots

or automatic fire is done by the trigger, a light pull for a single shot, a heavier pull for automatic fire.

UNLOADING
Magazine release catch is behind the magazine, under the butt. Remove magazine. Pull back cocking handle to eject any round in the chamber; inspect chamber, release cocking handle, pull trigger.

and the HBAR/ T can, if required, be further modified to fire from an open bolt; a new hammer assembly is inserted into the butt and a new cocking piece is fitted to the bolt assembly. This modification can be made retrospectively to weapons already issued. Changing to open-bolt firing does not change any of the firing characteristics.

FN BAR Type D (Belgium)

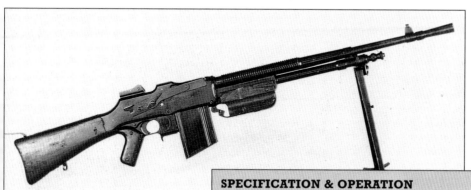

and can be encountered in Central Africa and the Middle East. Calibre may be 6.5mm Swedish Mauser, 7mm Spanish Mauser, 7.5mm Belgian Mauser or 7.92 x 57mm Mauser.

This is the Browning Automatic Rifle as improved by Fabrique Nationale of Belgium. As with most of Browning's designs, they held a license to manufacture and to modify it as they saw fit, and in line with European thought of the 1920s they soon did so. By fitting it with a quick-change barrel, modifying it so as to fire from belt or magazine as required, giving it a pistol grip, changing the system of dismantling to make it easier, and redesigning the gas regulator. Belt-fed versions failed to appeal, but the magazine-fed version was adopted by Belgium, Poland, Egypt and various other countries in the pre-1939 period. Well-made, many have survived

SPECIFICATION & OPERATION

CARTRIDGE
Various - see below

DIMENSIONS
Length o/a: 1145mm (45,0in)
Weight: 9.20kg (20lb 5oz)
Barrel: 500mm (19.7in)
Rifling: 4 grooves, rh
Feed system: 20-round magazine
Rate of fire: 450 or 650 rds/min

IN PRODUCTION 1923-39

MARKINGS
FN monogram, BROWNING PATENTED (year) and serial number on top of receiver above magazine. FABRIQUE NATIONALE D'ARMES DE GUERRE HERSTAL-BELGIQUE on left above magazine.

SAFETY
Combined safety catch and rate regulator on the left side above the trigger. Set to 'S' for safe, to 'F' for slow rate automatic fire and to 'M' for fast rate automatic fire.

UNLOADING
Magazine release is below the trigger guard. Remove magazine. Pull back cocking handle to eject any round remaining in the chamber. Inspect chamber and feedway. Release cocking handle, pull trigger

FN MAG (Belgium)

This was the Belgian entry into the 'general purpose' machine gun stakes, and it became extremely popular, being adopted by at least 80 countries and license-made in the USA, UK, Argentina, Egypt, India and Singapore. Well-made and reliable, it uses a similar gas system to that of the Browning Automatic Rifle, but inverted so that the bolt locks into the bottom of the receiver. This allows the top of the bolt to carry a lug which drives the feed system, which is adapted from that of the German MG42. There are a number of minor variations of the MAG to suit firing it from vehicles or helicopters.

SPECIFICATION & OPERATION

CARTRIDGE
7.62 x 51mm NATO

DIMENSIONS
Length o/a: 1250mm (49.2in)
Weight: 10.15kg (22lb 6oz)
Barrel: 546mm (21.45in)
Rifling: 4 grooves, rh
Feed system: belt
Rate of fire: 850 rds/min

IN PRODUCTION 1955-

MARKINGS
'Fabrique Nationale d'Armes de Guerre Herstal Belgium' on right side receiver. Weapons produced by other countries will have their own markings; e.g. British 'L7A1'.

SAFETY
The safety catch is a push-button above the trigger. Push from left side to right to make safe; from right side to left to fire.

UNLOADING
Press the cover catch, in front of the rear sight, and open the cover. Lift out the belt if present, inspect the feedway, close the cover. Pull the cocking handle back to eject any round in the chamber, and while holding it back press the trigger and then ease the cocking handle forward.

FN Minimi (Belgium)

SPECIFICATION & OPERATION

CARTRIDGE
5.56 x 45mm NATO

DIMENSIONS
Length o/a: 1040mm (41.0in)
Weight: 6.85kg (15lb 2oz)
Barrel: 466mm (18.35in)
Rifling: 6 grooves, rh
Feed system: 30-round
magazine or 200-round belt
Rate of fire: 700-1000 rds/min

IN PRODUCTION 1982-

MARKINGS
'FN MINIMI 5.56' on left side
receiver.

SAFETY
Push-through safety catch on
left of receiver: push from right
to left to fire. Left to right for
safe.

UNLOADING
Press in the two spring catches
at top rear of receiver and lift
cover. Remove belt or magazine.
Pull back cocking handle,
examine chamber and feedway,
release cocking handle, press
trigger.

The Minimi was designed to extract the utmost
performance from the 5.56mm cartridge and has
acquired a reputation for reliability. It is gas
operated, using a simple rotating bolt system, but is
unusual in being able to fire from an M16-type
magazine or a belt without any modification having
to be made. A special cover plate closes the belt
aperture when a magazine is loaded, or closes the
magazine aperture when a belt is in place, so that
there is no danger of trying to double-feed. There is
a light, short-barrelled paratroop version with a
collapsible butt, and a slightly modified version of
the standard model is produced for the US Army as
the M249 machine gun.

FN-BRG-15 heavy machine gun (Belgium)

ammunition, such as discarding sabot armour-defeating rounds. The belts used disintegrating links and feed into the weapon from the top. The weapon was cocked by pulling on a cocking handle at the rear which was connected by a flexible cable to the bolt carrier. Unfortunately, just as the design had been perfected, FN ran into organizational and financial problems, and in 1991 the decision was taken to shelve the BRG-15 and concentrate upon perfecting and marketing the P-90 personal defence weapon.

This machine gun was first announced in October 1983 and was a new design intended to replace the Browning .50 HB heavy machine gun. The weapon was gas-operated, the piston acting on a bolt carrier holding a rotating bolt which locked by four lugs into the barrel extension. The weapon had dual feed, an ammunition belt entering each side of the receiver, and a selector lever at the rear permitted the gunner to select which belt he required. There was also a single-shot selector which was intended for use with specialized types of

SPECIFICATION & OPERATION

CARTRIDGE
15.5 x 106mm

DIMENSIONS
Length: 86.65in (2.15m)
Weight unloaded: 132lb 4oz (60.0kg)
Barrel: 59.05in (1.50m)
Magazine: Dual, disintegrating link belts
Cyclic rate: 600 rds/min
Muzzle velocity: 3460 ft/sec (1055 m/sec)

IN PRODUCTION: NO

MARKINGS
Not determined

SAFETY
Four safety devices are incorporated: a manual bolt lock in the rotary feed selector; a neutral position of the feed selector which throws both belts out of engagement; a safety catch under the bolt carrier which automatically functions if the working parts fail to recoil completely to the rear; and a mechanism which

prevents the firing pin from striking the cartridge unless the bolt was fully closed and locked.

UNLOADING
Move the selector lever to one side, so freeing one belt, and remove the belt. Move the lever to the other side and remove the other belt. Draw back the bolt by means of the cable and handle behind the receiver. Examine chamber via the ejection slot. Release bolt and press trigger.

Type 77 (China)

outwards and lock into recesses in the receiver walls. The weapon is fed by belt, from a box carried on the left side. An optical anti-aircraft sight is standard and there is also a somewhat complex tripod air defence mount.

This first appeared in the late 1980s and was designed primarily for air defence purposes, though it is also capable of operating as a ground gun. It uses a direct gas system, most unusual for a weapon of this calibre, with a gas tube running from the barrel take-off and regulator at the front of the receiver and delivering the gas directly to the lower portion of the bolt carrier. Breech locking is a modified form of the Kjellman flap, the two flaps being operated by the bolt carrier so as to move

SPECIFICATION & OPERATION

CARTRIDGE
12.7 x 107mm Soviet

DIMENSIONS
Length: 84.65in (2150mm)
Weight: 123lb 11oz (56.10kg)
with tripod
Barrel: 40.0in (1016mm), 8
grooves, right-hand twist.
Magazine: 60-round metal belt
Cyclic rate: 700 rds/min
Muzzle velocity: 2625 ft/sec
(800 m/sec)

IN PRODUCTION:
1980-

MARKINGS
Unknown

SAFETY
Unknown

UNLOADING
Unknown

VZ-26 (Czechoslovakia)

from the Bren or Vickers-Berthier by the finned barrel and by the long gas cylinder beneath the barrel, extending almost to the muzzle.

The vz26 (vz = vzor = model) was designed by the Zbrojovka Brno (Brno Arms Factory) in Czechoslovakia in the early 1920s and was one of those rare occasions when everything came together first time. It was an immediate success and was adopted by over 25 countries around the world. A slightly modified version became the ZGB33, the modification being to suit it to the British .303 cartridge, and this, in turn, became the famous Bren light machine gun. The German Army used it as the vz26, so that the same gun was being used on both sides in 1939-45. ZB continued to offer the gun in their catalogues after 1946, but none were ever made after the war. The vz26 can be distinguished

SPECIFICATION & OPERATION

CARTRIDGE
7.92 x 57mm Mauser and others

DIMENSIONS
Length o/a: 1161mm (45.70on)
Weight: 9.60kg (21lb 3oz)
Barrel: 672mm (26.45in)
Rifling: 4 grooves, rh
Feed system: 30-round box magazine
Rate of fire: 500 rds/min

IN PRODUCTION 1928-45

MARKINGS
'VZ 26' and serial number top rear receiver. 'BRNO' and factory marks on left side of receiver, 'LEHKY KULOMET ZB VZ 26' on right side of receiver.

SAFETY
A combined safety catch and fire selector on the right side, above the trigger. Turn forward for automatic fire, midway for safe, rearward for single shots.

UNLOADING
Magazine catch is behind magazine. Remove magazine. Pull back cocking handle, examine chamber and feedway through the magazine opening. Release the cocking handle, pull the trigger.

VZ-37 (Czechoslovakia)

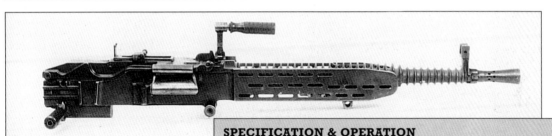

The vz37 was another Zbrojovka Brno product from Czechoslovakia, intended to accompany the vz26 as the heavy support weapon. It was belt fed and could be adjusted to two rates of fire. An odd feature, repeated in some other Czech designs, is the use of the pistol grip and trigger unit as the cocking handle. To cock the gun, push the pistol grip forward until it engages with the bolt system, then pull back. Another oddity is that it is recoil operated and the cartridge is fired while the barrel and bolt are still moving forwards on the return stroke; this means that the recoil force must first stop the moving parts before driving them back, and this additional load soaks up quite a lot of the recoil energy. The gun was widely adopted in Europe in 1938/9 and was licensed by the British, who used it as the Besa gun on armoured vehicles.

SPECIFICATION & OPERATION

CARTRIDGE
7.92 x 57mm Mauser

DIMENSIONS
Length o/a: 1104mm (43.46in)
Weight: 18.60kg (41lb 0oz)
Barrel: 635mm (25.0in)
Rifling: 4 grooves, rh
Feed system: 100-round belt
Rate of fire: 500 or 700 rds/min

IN PRODUCTION 1937-45

MARKINGS
'VZ37' and serial number on rear top of receiver. 'BRNO' on left side of receiver.

SAFETY
A combined safety catch and fire selector is on the right side of the receiver, behind the grips. When in its central position the gun is safe. Turned left it provides single shots, turned right automatic fire. There is also a rate of fire selector on the left side of the receiver just in front of the grip. UP and forward gives slow rate, DOWN and back gives fast rate.

UNLOADING
Set the safety catch to safe. Pull out the cover pin, at the right rear corner of the receiver, press and hold back the cover catch on the left side of the cover, and lift the cover open as far as it will go. Inspect to see that no rounds remain in the feedway. Close the cover, pressing the cover catch until it closes and then inserting the pin. Hold the grips and press up the trigger mechanism catch at the rear bottom of the receiver, and ease the grips, bolt and trigger unit forward. Pull out on the grips and swing them up against the receiver.

CZ Model 52/57 (Czechoslovakia)

Although classed as a light machine gun, this obviously leans toward the 'general purpose' concept, being capable of using magazines or belts without need for modification. It was originally designed to fire the Czech 7.62 x 45mm cartridge, as the CZ52, but was then modified to fire the 7.62 x 39mm Soviet round when Warsaw Pact countries standardised on Soviet calibres. Either model may be encountered, though the earlier version is less common. They were supplied to Communist bloc countries in some numbers and have turned up in central Africa and the Far East at various times.

SPECIFICATION & OPERATION

CARTRIDGE
7.62 x 45mm Czech; 7.62 x 39mm Soviet M1943

DIMENSIONS
Length o/a: 1041mm (41.0in)
Weight: 7.96kg (17lb 9oz)
Barrel: 686mm (27.0in)
Rifling: 4 grooves, rh
Feed system: 25-round box or 100-round belt
Rate of fire: 900 rds/min (magazine) or 1150 rds/min (belt)
IN PRODUCTION 1952-

MARKINGS
Serial number on top behind magazine housing, with 'egf' or 'tgf' factory mark.

SAFETY
Manual safety catch above the pistol grip on the left side. Press UP for safe, DOWN for fire. Fire selection is done by the trigger; press the upper portion (marked 1) for single shots, and the lower portion (marked D) for automatic fire.

UNLOADING
Magazine catch in rear of magazine housing. Press in and remove the magazine if the weapon is being magazine fed; if it is being belt fed, press in so that the magazine feed cover swings open, then lift the side feed cover lever (on the right side, alongside the magazine housing) UP and forward until the side feed cover opens. Lift and remove the belt if one is present. Inspect to see that no ammunition remains in the feedways, close all covers. Grasp the pistol grip, press the pushbutton in the left side of the grip and allow the grip to run forward under control. Then push UP the safety catch to lock the weapon.

Madsen (Denmark)

It has been said that the remarkable thing about the Madsen is not that it works well, but that it works at all. The mechanism is practically a mechanised version of the Martini breech-block, swinging up and down by the action of a cam driven by the barrel recoil. Since there is no bolt to push the cartridge into the chamber it has a separate rammer. The cartridge actually travels in a curve during loading, which is theoretically almost impossible. However it was certainly the first practical light machine gun, pioneered the overhead magazine among other things, was adopted by the

SPECIFICATION & OPERATION

CARTRIDGE
Various, from 6.5 to 8mm

DIMENSIONS
Length o/a: 1143mm (45.0in)
Weight: 9.07kg (20lb 0oz)
Barrel: 584mm (23.0in)
Rifling: 4 grooves, rh
Feed system: 25, 30 or 40-round box magazine
Rate of fire: 450 rds/min

IN PRODUCTION 1897-55
MARKINGS
'Madsen Model' (year) and serial number, right side receiver.

SAFETY
Safety catch on left above trigger. Move UP for SAFE when gun is cocked.

UNLOADING
Press in catch behind magazine and remove magazine. Pull back operating handle, inspect chamber and release. Pull trigger.

Danish Marines in the 1890s, and first saw action with Russia in the Russo-Japanese war in 1904. After that the same model, with very minor modifications, stayed in production for fifty years and was used all over the world in tanks and aircraft as well as on the ground, yet it never became the official weapon of any major army.

Madsen-Saetter (Denmark)

This was the last Madsen military weapon before they left the arms business. It was designed as a general purpose machine gun, to be used on a tripod for sustained fire support or on a bipod as the squad light automatic weapon. It was designed so that by simply changing the barrel and bolt it could accommodate any calibre from 6.5mm to 8mm, and construction was largely of pressings and sheet metal. Gas operated, the bolt is locked by lugs entering recesses in the receiver sides and the rate of fire was adjustable between wide limits. It was adopted by Indonesia, who built it under licence, but no other army was interested and Madsen decided they could find better things to do.

SPECIFICATION & OPERATION

CARTRIDGE
7.62 x 51mm NATO

DIMENSIONS
Length o/a: 1165mm (45.87in)
Weight: 10.65kg (23lb 8oz)
Barrel: 565mm (22.25in)
Rifling: 4 grooves, rh
Feed system: belt
Rate of fire: 650 to 1000 rds/min

IN PRODUCTION 1952-60

MARKINGS
MADSEN-SAETTER and serial on front left of receiver beneath the sight.

SAFETY
There is no safety on this weapon.

UNLOADING
Open the feed cover by pressing the catch at its rear end. Remove the belt. Pull back the cocking handle, examine the feedway and chamber. Release the cocking handle, pull the trigger.

Chatellerault M1924/29 (France)

SPECIFICATION & OPERATION

CARTRIDGE
7.5 x 54mm French Service

DIMENSIONS
Length o/a: 1082mm (42,6in)
Weight: 9.24kg (20lb 6oz)
Barrel: 500mm (19.68in)
Rifling: 4 grooves, rh
Feed system: 25-round box
magazine
Rate of fire: 500 rds/min

IN PRODUCTION 1930-40

MARKINGS
'Mle 1924M29" and serial
number on right side of receiver.

SAFETY
Manual safety catch behind the
rear trigger. Turn DOWN for
safe, UP for fire.

UNLOADING
Magazine catch behind the
magazine housing. Push the
safety catch DOWN, remove the
magazine, pull the cocking
handle to the rear. Inspect the
feedway and chamber through
the magazine opening. Push the
safety catch UP and holding the
cocking handle, press one of the
triggers and ease the cocking
handle forward. Close the
magazine dust cover and
ejection port dust cover. Press
the safety catch down and pull
back the magazine catch until it
locks.

Having had some unsatisfactory weapons during
WWI the French considered a new machine gun
to be imperative, and wisely began by developing a
new rimless cartridge in 7.5mm calibre. After some
modification the combination worked successfully
and as the M1924/29 the light machine gun became
standard in the French Army and remained in use
until the 1950s. Numbers were also seized by the
Germans in 1940 and used by them, so that
specimens with German markings can appear from
time to time. Numbers were handed over to the
armies of former French colonies when they became
independent, and when replaced they then found
their way into all sorts of places.

Hotchkiss M1922/26 (France)

This was Hotchkiss' post-WWI design, put on the market in 1922. It used gas operation, locking the breech by a tilting plate, and also had a rate of fire regulator in a housing in front of the trigger. Feed was either by a top-mounted magazine or by the usual type of side-feeding Hotchkiss trip, including the three-cartridge-per-link strip belt devised for the M1914 gun. Business was slow in the 1920s, however, and apart from some 5000 to Greece, 1000 to Czechoslovakia, and unknown quantities to the Dominican Republic and Brazil, which were supplied variously as the M1922, M1924 or M1926 model, there were scarcely sufficient sales to keep Hotchkiss in business.

SPECIFICATION & OPERATION

CARTRIDGE
Various calibres

DIMENSIONS
Length o/a: 1215mm (47.83in)
Weight: 9.52kg (21lv 0oz)
Barrel: 577mm (22.72in)
Rifling: 4 grooves, rh
Feed system: 25 or 30-round metal strip
Rate of fire: 500 rds/min

IN PRODUCTION 1922-39

MARKINGS
`HOTCHKISS 1922 Brevete' on right of receiver. Serial number on top rear of receiver.

SAFETY
Grip safety in front of pistol grip

UNLOADING
Magazine catch is behind magazine. Remove magazine, pull back cocking handle, inspect chamber. Release cocking handle and pull trigger.

AAT-F1 (France)

SPECIFICATION & OPERATION

CARTRIDGE
7.5 x 54 French Service; 7.62 x
51mm NATO

DIMENSIONS
Length o/a: 990mm (38.9in)
Weight: 9.88kg (21lb 13oz)
Barrel: 488mm (19.2in)
Rifling: 4 grooves, rh
Feed system: 50-round belt
Rate of fire: 700 rds/min

IN PRODUCTION 1952-

MARKINGS
'AA F1 MAT' and serial number
on left side of receiver (or AA
52 as applicable).

SAFETY
A cross-bolt safety catch in the
top of the pistol grip. Push
through from right to left to
make safe, from left to right to
fire.

UNLOADING
Pull the cocking handle back and
then push it fully forward and
press the safety catch to the left.
Press the cover latch (on top of
the receiver) and open the feed
cover. Lift out the belt if present.
Inspect the feedway, close the
cover. Push the safety catch to
the right, pull the cocking
handle back and, while holding
it, press the trigger and ease the
handle forward.

Known variously as the AAT-52, MAS-52 or F1,
this is the standard French Army general purpose
machine gun. Operation is by delayed blowback,
using a two-piece bolt similar to that of the FA-MAS
rifle, in which the light forward part of the bolt has
to overcome the inertia of the heavy rear section
before the breech can be opened. The chamber is
fluted so as to float the case on a layer of gas to
ease extraction, but the result is somewhat on the
borders of absolute safety, and the extraction is
violent. Nevertheless, the gun is reliable and
efficient and has been put into service by several
former French colonies.

Maxim MG'08 (Germany)

This is the classic Maxim recoil-operated machine gun and is essentially the same as every other Maxim of the period; heavy, water-cooled, and in the case of the '08 model, mounted on a unique four-legged 'sledge' mounting which folded up to allow the crew to drag the gun across the ground. Mounted on this, the total weight became 62kg. The gun uses a toggle system of breech-locking; barrel and toggle recoil together, until a spur on the toggle strikes a lug on the receiver wall. This causes the toggle to fold and withdraw the breech-block. A spring then folds the toggle forward again to load a fresh cartridge and fire. A very reliable weapon, during World War I MG '08s proved able to fire for hours on end provided they had cooling water and ammunition. It remained in the postwar German Army and one or two were actually taken to war in 1939, though they were soon discarded in favour of more modern and lighter designs.

SPECIFICATION & OPERATION

CARTRIDGE
7.92 x 57mm Mauser

DIMENSIONS
Length o/a: 1175mm (46.25in)
Weight: 26.44kg (58lb 5oz)
Barrel: 719mm (28.30in)
Rifling: 4 grooves, rh
Feed system: 250-round cloth belt
Rate of fire: 450 rds/min
In production: 1908-18

MARKINGS
'Deutsche Waffen und Munitionsfabriken BERLIN' (Year) on left receiver.'8mm MASCH GEWEHR 1908' and serial number top rear of receiver.

SAFETY
Safety latch between spade grips. It has to be lifted by the fingers to allow trigger to be pressed.

UNLOADING
Press pawl depressor on right of feedway to remove belt. Pull back and release cocking handle twice. With a pencil or similar tool, check ejection hole under barrel for possible live cartridge. Press trigger.

Maxim '08/15 (Germany)

The '08/15 was an attempt to provide the German infantry with something rather more portable than the standard '08 on its sledge mount. It was given a small bipod, a shoulder stock and a pistol grip, and the receiver was re-designed in order to try and save weight. Feed was still by a cloth belt, but a special short belt was used which could be coiled on a reel and carried in a container clamped to the side of the gun. In fixed positions the standard 250-round belt could be used. There was also an aircraft version of this gun which has a perforated barrel jacket instead of the water jacket, relying upon the airstream to cool the barrel.

SPECIFICATION & OPERATION

CARTRIDGE
7.92 x 57mm Mauser

DIMENSIONS
Length o/a: 1448mm (57.0in)
Weight: 14.06kg (31lb 0oz)
Barrel: 719mm (23.30in)
Rifling: 4 grooves, rh
Feed system: 50-round cloth belt
Rate of fire: 500 rds/min

IN PRODUCTION 1915-18

MARKINGS
'LMG 08/15 SPANDAU' (year) on top of receiver; or 'MG 08/15 SPANDAU (year) GEWEHRFABRIK' on lock spring cover at left rear side of receiver. Serial number on left side of receiver.

SAFETY
Safety latch between spade grips. It has to be lifted by the fingers to allow trigger to be pressed.

UNLOADING
Press pawl depressor on right of feedway to remove belt. Pull back and release cocking handle twice. With a pencil or similar tool, check ejection hole under barrel for possible live cartridge. Press trigger.

MG34 (Germany)

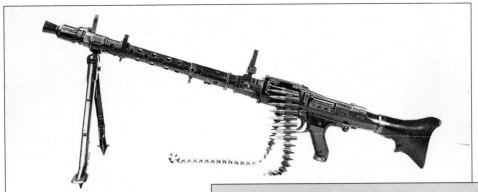

line layout which reduced the tendency to lift the muzzle in firing, and the ability to use it on a bipod as the rifle squad automatic weapon or on a tripod for sustained support fire; it was the original 'general purpose' machine gun.

This began as the Solothurn Model 30, developed in Switzerland in the 1920s. The company was then bought by Rheinmetall, after which Solothurn became their development engineering and production plant, since this work was outlawed in Germany by the Versailles Treaty. Rheinmetall then went to work on the MG30 and modified it into the MG34 which was introduced into the German Army in 1936 and became their standard weapon until superseded by the MG42, although it continued in production until the end of the war. The notable features of this design include the method of stripping by simply twisting the butt; the straight-

SPECIFICATION & OPERATION

CARTRIDGE
7.92 x 57mm Mauser

DIMENSIONS
Length o/a: 1219mm (48.0in)
Weight: 12.10kg (26lb 11oz)
Barrel: 627mm (24.7in)
Rifling: 4 grooves, rh
Feed system: 50-round belt or 75-round saddle drum
Rate of fire: 900 rds/min

IN PRODUCTION 1934 - 1945

MARKINGS
'MG34' serial number, top rear receiver.

SAFETY
Manual safety catch on the left side above the trigger. Press in and UP for fire, press in and DOWN for safe.

UNLOADING
Cover latch at rear of receiver. Press in and allow the cover to open. Remove the belt if one is present, check that no cartridge remains in the feed tray. Pull the cocking handle to the rear and inspect the chamber and feedway. Push the feed slide to the left and close the cover. Press the trigger.

MG42 (Germany)

Good as the MG34 was, it suffered from being complex and expensive to make, and in 1941 the German Army asked for something which retained all the advantages of the MG34 but was easier to mass-produce. Experts in metal stamping were called in to assist the Mauser company in the redesign, and the result was the MG42. It used a new system of locking the breech, a highly efficient method of changing the barrel, and it was highly resistant to dust and dirt. In the 1950s, when the Federal German Army was established, they simply put the MG42 back into production since they could see no other weapon which was as good, and as the MG1, and later MG3, it is still in use. As the

SPECIFICATION & OPERATION

CARTRIDGE
7.92 x 57mm Mauser

DIMENSIONS
Length o/a: 1219mm (48.0in)
Weight: 11.50kh (25lb 6oz)
Barrel: 533mm (21.0in)
Rifling: 4 grooves, rh
Feed system: 50-round belt
Rate of fire: 1200 rds/min

IN PRODUCTION 1938-45

MARKINGS
'MG42', serial number and factory identifier on left side of receiver.

SAFETY
Push-button safety catch in the top of the pistol grip. Push through from right to left for safe, from left to right to fire.

UNLOADING
Pull the cocking handle to the rear, push the safety catch to the left. Press the cover latch at the rear of the receiver and lift the cover. Lift the belt from the feed tray. Push forward the barrel cover lock (right side of receiver) until the barrel swings out and the chamber can be inspected. Pull back on the lock and replace the barrel, check that no cartridge is in the feed tray or receiver and close the cover. Press the safety catch to the right, grasp the cocking handle, press the trigger and ease the cocking handle forward.

MG42/59 it is used by the Austrian and Italian armies, and as the 'Sarac' it was manufactured in Yugoslavia.

Heckler & Koch HK13 (Germany)

This was developed to accompany the HK33 5.56mm rifle and was among the earliest 5.56mm calibre machine guns; it is generally similar to the rifle but has a heavier barrel which can quickly be removed and exchanged during sustained fire. The action is that of the rifle, a delay blowback using a roller-locked delay system, and the magazines are interchangeable with those of the HK33 rifle. The HK13 was somewhat early in the 5.56mm era, and consequently its initial sales were largely to South-East Asian countries. It has since been improved into the HK33E mode, which incorporates a three-round burst setting in the selector lever and which can be changed to belt feed by replacing the magazine housing and bolt.

SPECIFICATION & OPERATION

CARTRIDGE
5.56 x 45mm M193 or NATO

DIMENSIONS
Length o/a: 980mm (38.6in)
Weight: 6.03kg (13lb 5oz)
Barrel: 450mm (17.71in)
Rifling: 6 grooves, rh
Feed system: 20 or 40 round magazine
Rate of fire: 750 rds/min

IN PRODUCTION 1972-

MARKINGS
'HK 13 5.56 x 45' and serial number on left side of magazine housing.

SAFETY
A combined safety catch and fire selector is on the left side of the receiver, above the pistol grip. UP for safe, midway for single shots (marked 'E') and fully DOWN for automatic fire (marked 'A').

UNLOADING
Magazine catch behind magazine housing, beneath the receiver. Remove magazine. Pull back cocking handle to eject any round in the chamber. Inspect chamber and feedway via the ejection port. Release the cocking handle, press the trigger.

Heckler & Koch HK21 (Germany)

The HK21 was designed as a general-purpose machine gun, capable of being used on a bipod or tripod, to accompany the G3 rifle. It is much the same as the rifle but with a heavier barrel which can quickly be changed and is belt-fed. However, it is possible to remove the belt-feed mechanism and replace it with a magazine adapter, using the G3

SPECIFICATION & OPERATION

CARTRIDGE
7.62 x 51mm NATO

DIMENSIONS
Length o/a: 1021mm (40.2in)
Weight: 7.92kg (17lb 7oz)
Barrel: 450mm (17.71in)
Rifling: 4 grooves, rh
Feed system: belt
Rate of fire: 900 rds/min

IN PRODUCTION 1970-

MARKINGS
Serial number on rib of receiver top.

SAFETY
A combined safety catch and fire selector is on the left side of the receiver, above the pistol grip. UP for safe, midway for single shots (marked `E') and fully DOWN for automatic fire (marked `A').

UNLOADING
Press the serrated catch beneath the rear end of the belt slot and allow the belt feed to hinge down and forward. Pull back the cocking handle to eject any round in the chamber. Inspect the chamber and feedway via the ejection port. Release the cocking handle, press the trigger, close the belt feed assembly by hinging it up until the catch engages.

rifle magazine. It could also be converted to 5.56 x 45mm or 7.62 x 39mm calibres by changing the barrel, belt feed plate and bolt, making it a very versatile design. It was adopted by Portugal and some African and South-East Asian countries in the 1970s and many are still in use. It was replaced in production by the HK21A1, an improved model, and then by the present HK21E which has a three-round burst facility and various other improvements.

HK MG36 (Germany)

SPECIFICATION & OPERATION

This is derived from the G36 rifle, and like that weapon breaks with the H&K delayed blowback tradition by being gas operated. It has a somewhat heavier barrel, and is fitted with a bipod, but apart from these features it is precisely the same as the rifle. A variant mode, the MG36E, is offered for export; it differs from the German service G36 only in the optical sight, which is of 1.5x magnification instead of 3x.

CARTRIDGE
5.56 x 45mm

DIMENSIONS
Length: 998mm (39.29in)
Weight: unloaded: 3.58kg
(7lb 14oz)
Barrel: 480mm (18.90in)
Rifling: 6 grooves, rh
Magazine capacity: 30 rounds
Rate of fire: 750 rds/min

IN PRODUCTION 1995 -

MARKINGS

SAFETY
Combined safety catch and fire selector switch on both sides of the receiver, behind and above the trigger.

UNLOADING
Magazine catch on magazine housing. Remove magazine. Pull back cocking handle (beneath carrying handle) and examine the feedway and chamber via the ejection port, ensuring both are empty. Return cocking handle and bolt to the forward position, pull trigger.

INSAS (India)

bayonet can be fitted. The bipod is instantly recognisable as that produced in the Indian factories for the Bren and Vickers-Berthier machine guns during World War Two. The Indians obviously see no point in re-inventing the wheel.

At the time of writing the INSAS LMG has been approved for service with the Indian Army, but, like the rifle, issue has been held up until the ammunition production has been organised.

This is the heavy-barrelled version of the INSAS (Indian Small Arms System) assault rifle, described elsewhere. It is gas-operated, using a rotating bolt, and can deliver single shots or automatic fire. The barrel is heavier than that of the rifle, is chromed internally, and has a different rifling contour to develop better long-range ballistic performance. The weapon is sighted up to 1000 meters. The muzzle is formed to the NATO-standard 22mm diameter for grenade launching, and a

SPECIFICATION & OPERATION

CARTRIDGE
5.56 x 45mm

DIMENSIONS
Length: 1050mm (41.34in)
Weight: unloaded: 6.23kg
(13lb 11oz)
Barrel: 535mm (21.06in),
Rifling: 4 grooves, rh
Magazine capacity: 30 rounds
Rate of fire: 650 rds/min

IN PRODUCTION

MARKINGS

SAFETY
Large thumb-operated safety catch and fire selector lever on left side of receiver above the pistol grip. Up for safe, down in two steps for single shots and automatic fire.

UNLOADING
Magazine release is behind magazine housing, in front of trigger guard. Remove magazine. Pull back cocking handle to open bolt and remove any round from chamber. Examine chamber and feedway, ensuring both are empty. Release cocking handle, pull trigger.

Negev (Israel)

The Negev is a multi-purpose weapon which can feed from standard belts, drums or box magazines and can be fired from a bipod, tripod or vehicle mounts. The standard barrel is rifled for SS109 ammunition; an alternative barrel is rifled for US M193 ammunition. The weapon is gas operated with a rotating bolt which locks into the barrel extension, and fires from an open bolt. The gas regulator has three positions, allowing the rate of fire to be changed from 650-800 rds/min to 800-

SPECIFICATION & OPERATION

CARTRIDGE
5.56 x 45mm NATO or M193

DIMENSIONS
Length, butt extended:
1020mm (40.16in)
Length, butt folded: 780mm
(30.71in)
Weight: unloaded: 7.50kg
(16lb 8oz)
Barrel: 460mm (18.11in)
Rifling: 6 grooves, rh
Feed system: 30- or 35-round
box, link belt or drum
Cyclic rate: 800 rds/min

IN PRODUCTION 1988-

MARKINGS

SAFETY
Manual safety and fire selector switch at the top of the left side of the pistol grip. The button moves in an arc at the extreme rear position it is set for automatic fire, at the central position, bottom of the arc, safe; at the forward position single shots.

UNLOADING
Magazine release catch is at the rear of the magazine housing, in front of the trigger guard. Remove magazine if fitted. Press in catch at rear of feed cover and lift cover to remove any belt. Leaving this cover open, pull back the bolt until the feedway and chamber can be inspected. When satisfied that they are both clear, close the cover, release the bolt and pull the trigger.

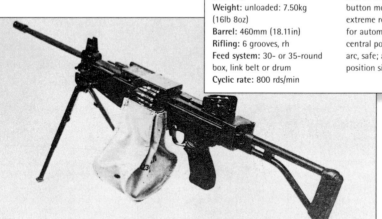

950 rds/min or the gas supply cut off to permit launching grenades from the muzzle. The weapon will fire in semi- or full-automatic modes, and by removing the bipod and attaching a normal fore-end and short barrel it can be used as an assault rifle. The Negev was introduced in 1988 and has been adopted by the Israel Defence Force.

Ameli (Spain)

Although this looks like a scaled-down MG42 it is entirely different in its operation, using the same roller-locked delayed blowback mechanism as the CETME Model L rifle or the Heckler & Koch rifles and machine guns. Several of the parts are interchangeable with the Model L rifle. It can be used on its bipod for squad support or on a tripod for sustained fire, having a quick-change barrel. It

SPECIFICATION & OPERATION

CARTRIDGE
5.56 x 45mm NATO

DIMENSIONS
Length o/a: 970mm (38.2in)
Weight: 6.35kg (14lb 0oz)
Barrel: 400mm (15.75in)
Rifling: 6 grooves, rh
Feed system: belt
Rate of fire: 850 or 1200 rds/min

IN PRODUCTION 1982-

MARKINGS
'CETME AMELI 5.56' and serial number; or 'AMELI 5.56 9.223' and Santa Barbara monogram and serial number. All on left side of receiver.

SAFETY
A manual safety catch on the right side of the pistol grip. Turn forward for safe, back for fire.

UNLOADING
Slide forward the cover catch at the front edge of the butt and open the cover. Lift the cartridge belt from the feedway and lift the belt box from its attachment to the side of the gun. Pull back the cocking handle. Inspect the feedway and chamber. Close the cover, press the trigger.

has been adopted by the Spanish Army and it will probably find acceptance elsewhere, as it is certainly one of the best 5.56mm light machine guns currently on offer.

Breda Model 30 (Italy)

anything goes wrong with the one magazine, the gun is useless, and the slow method of loading reduces the effective rate of fire to a very low figure. Another oddity is that the barrel can be quickly changed but there is no handle, so getting the hot barrel off must have been an interesting exercise.

This was another of the idiosyncratic machine guns which the Italians were so expert at in the 1930s. In this case, the oddity lay in the feed system; the magazine is a box on the right side of the receiver which can be unlatched and hinged forward. In this position the gunner's mate loaded it from rifle chargers; he then swung the box back and latched it, whereupon the moving bolt could feed the rounds one by one. The advantage is that the whole magazine can be very well made, and the lips carefully machined, so that there is less likelihood of a stoppage than there is from sheet-steel magazines which get knocked about. On the debit side, if

SPECIFICATION & OPERATION

CARTRIDGE
6.5 x 52mm Carcano

DIMENSIONS
Length o/a: 1230mm (48.4in)
Weight: 10.20kg (22lb 7oz)
Barrel: 520mm (20.5in)
Rifling: 4 grooves, rh
Feed system: 20-round box magazine
Rate of fire: 475 rds/min

IN PRODUCTION 1930-37

MARKINGS
'Mtr Legg Mod 30, serial number, BREDA ROMA' on top of receiver.

SAFETY
Spring-loaded catch alongside cocking handle. Having pulled cocking handle to rear, press catch to lock in cocked position. To release: pull back slightly on cocking handle.

UNLOADING
Press magazine release catch behind magazine and hinge magazine forward. Pull back cocking handle, inspect chamber and feedway. Release handle and pull trigger.

Breda Model 37 (Italy)

fact remained that the overworked gunner had to remove all the empties from the strip before he could reload it. In spite of this it was well liked, principally for its reliability.

Standard heavy machine gun of the Italian Army from 1937 to 1945, this had some peculiarities. The ammunition had to be oiled before it was loaded, to prevent the cases sticking in the chamber after firing, which was a feature of some other machine guns, but the Breda was fed by metallic strips into which cartridges were clipped. The gun took the cartridge from the strip, fired it, and then put the empty case neatly back into the strip before loading the next round. No reasonable explanation for this has ever appeared; it sounded good, but the

SPECIFICATION & OPERATION

CARTRIDGE
8 x 59mm Breda

DIMENSIONS
Length o/a: 1270mm (50.0in)
Weight: 19.50kg (43lb 0oz)
Barrel: 679mm (26.75in)
Rifling: 4 grooves, rh
Feed system: 20-round strip
Rate of fire: 450 rds/min

IN PRODUCTION 1936-43

MARKINGS
MITRAGLIATRICE BREDA MOD 37, serial number, ROMA and year on left side of receiver.

SAFETY
Manual safety between grips: push right to lock trigger.

UNLOADING
Push in pawl depressor on left side under feedway and remove feed strip. Pull back cocking handle to eject any round in chamber. Release cocking handle, pull back a second time, examine feedway and chamber. Release cocking handle and pull trigger.

Japanese Type 99 (Japan)

manufacturing tolerances were held to a fine limit. There was more than one item of the design which suggested that a good look had been taken at the Czech vz26 gun, several of which had been captured from the Chinese in the middle 1930s.

When the Japanese Army decided to adopt a 7.7mm rimless cartridge instead of the 6.5mm round, this gun was developed to fire it. To save development time the Type 96 was taken as the basis, but the 99 was a considerable improvement. The 7.7mm cartridge did not need to be oiled, the extraction system was designed so as to give a slow unseating movement before a more rapid extraction, so curing all the ruptured case problems, the quick-change barrel was far easier to use, and

SPECIFICATION & OPERATION

CARTRIDGE
7.7 x 58mm Arisaka

DIMENSIONS
Length o/a: 1181mm (46.46in)
Weight: 10.43kg (23lb 0oz)
Barrel: 545mm (21.46in)
Rifling: 4 grooves, rh
Feed system: 30-round box magazine
Rate of fire: 850 rds/min

IN PRODUCTION 1939-45

MARKINGS
Model and serial number on top of the receiver

SAFETY
Safety catch in front of trigger guard on right side: push down and forward to fire, up and back for safe.

UNLOADING
Magazine catch behind magazine. Remove magazine and pull back cocking handle. Inspect chamber and feedway, release cocking handle and pull trigger.

Daewoo K3 (South Korea)

The K3 is a lightweight, gas-operated, full-automatic machine gun which appears to have drawn a good deal of its inspiration from the FN Minimi. It uses a similar system of belt or magazine feed and is fitted with a bipod for the squad automatic rifle, though it can also be tripod

SPECIFICATION & OPERATION

CARTRIDGE
5.56 x 45mm NATO or M193

DIMENSIONS
Length: 1030mm (40.55in)
Weight: unloaded: 6.85kg (15lb 21oz)
Barrel: 533mm (21.0in)
Rifling: 6 grooves, rh
Feed system: 30 round box or 250-round metal belt
Cyclic rate: 700rds/min (belt), 1000 rds/min (magazine)

IN PRODUCTION 1987-

MARKINGS
5.56mm K3 (serial number) pn left side of magazine housing. DAEWOO PROCISION INDUSTRIES LTD on right side of upper receiver housing.

SAFETY
M16-pattern three-position safety catch and selector switch on left side of receiver above the pistol grip. Turned fully clockwise to SAFE. Turned vertical for single shots, fully anti-clockwise for automatic fire.

UNLOADING
Magazine catch on left side of receiver behind magazine housing. Remover magazine if fitted. Press in the two spring buttons at the top rear of the receiver and lift the top cover to remove any belt which may be in the feedway, Leaving the top cover open, pull back cocking handle and hold to the rear while examining the chamber and feedway. When satisfied that both are clear, close the top cover, let the bolt forward and press the trigger.

mounted for use in the sustained fire support role. The rear sight is adjustable for elevation and windage, and the foresight can be adjusted in elevation for purposes of zeroing. The barrel is fitted with a carrying handle and can be quickly changed in action so as to permit sustained fire; as the barrel also carries the foresight it follows that each can be individually zeroed. The action is gas piston driven, using the usual rotating bolt in a bolt carrier.

SPECIFICATION & OPERATION

Mendoza has been producing machine guns for the Mexican Army since 1933 and all have been noted for their lightness and cheap construction without sacrificing reliability. They use a gas cylinder system which delivers a short impulse to the piston, and the bolt is similar to that of the Lewis gun, rotating and driven by two cams engaged with the piston rod. The RM2 is the most recent model and adds a simplified method of stripping; by simply removing a lock pin, the stock and rear of the receiver can be folded down to allow the bolt and piston to be withdrawn backwards.

CARTRIDGE
.30-06 US Service

DIMENSIONS
Length o/a: 1092mm (43.0in)
Weight: 6.30kg (13lb 14oz)
Barrel: 609mm (24.0in)
Rifling: 4 grooves, rh
Feed system: 20-round box magazine
Rate of fire: 600 rds/min

IN PRODUCTION c. 1965 -

MARKINGS
`Fusil Ametrallador Mendoza/ Hecho en Mexico/ Caliber 30-06/ Modeleo RM2' (year) all on left side of receiver.

SAFETY
Left side above trigger: forward for SAFE, up for single shot and to the rear for automatic fire.

UNLOADING
Magazine catch behind magazine. Remove magazine, pull back cocking handle, inspect chamber, release cocking handle and pull trigger.

Vektor SS77 (South Africa)

The SS-77 is gas operated and uses a breech-block which swings sideways into a recess in the receiver wall to lock, a method very similar to that used by the Soviet Goryunov. After firing, gas drives the piston back and a post on the piston extension rides in a cam groove in the block and swings it out of engagement, then withdraws it to extract the empty case. During this movement a post on top of the block engages with a belt feed arm in the top cover, and this moves the ammunition belt a half-step inwards. On the return stroke the belt is moved

SPECIFICATION & OPERATION

CARTRIDGE
7.62 x 51mm

DIMENSIONS
Length, butt extended: 45.47in (1155mm); butt folded: 37.0in (940mm)
Weight unloaded: 21lb 3oz (9.60kg)
Barrel: 21.65in (550mm), 4 grooves, right-hand twist
Magazine: disintegrating or non-disintegrating metal link

belt
Cyclic rate: 800 rds/min
Muzzle velocity: c.2756 ft/sec (840 m/sec)

IN PROPDUCTION: 1986 –

MARKINGS
Model number, serial number and factory identifier on top of receiver

SAFETY

UNLOADING
Press release catch and lift feed cover, remove belt. Pull back cocking handle, examine chamber to ensure it is empty. Release cocking handle press trigger, close cover.

a further half-step and the block strips out the fresh cartridge and chambers it. The final forward movement of the piston forces the block back into engagement with the receiver recess; the piston post then strikes the firing pin to fire the next round. The barrel has a quick-change facility and is externally fluted to save weight and also increase the cooling surface. The gas regulator is adjustable and also has a position which closes the exhaust to give minimal emission of gas, allowing the gun to be safely fired in enclosed spaces. There is an adjustable bipod and a carrying handle.

Maxim 1910 (Russia)

weighs 45.22kg with its small steel shield, though this was usually removed since it was too small to be of much use. The gun remained in use until the 1960s, after which it was given away freely to various other countries and numbers can be expected to be available, particularly in the Far East, for some years to come.

This is much the same weapon as the German '08, since they were both built from the same licensee. The Russians adopted the Maxim in 1905, using a bronze water jacket; they changed this in 1910 to the cheaper and easier corrugated type of jacket as used by the British Vickers gun, after which no change was made until 1942, when the jacket was fitted with an over-sized water filler which allowed handfuls of snow to be dumped into it quickly when necessary. The most usual mounting is the 'Sokolov' which is wheeled and had the gun on a small turntable. It

SPECIFICATION & OPERATION

CARTRIDGE
7.62 x 54R Soviet

DIMENSIONS
Length o/a: 1107mm (43.6in)
Weight: 23.80kg (52lb 8oz)
Barrel: 721mm (28.4in)
Rifling: 4 grooves, rh
Feed system: 250-round cloth belt
Rate of fire: 550 rds/min

IN PRODUCTION 1910-50

MARKINGS
Factory identifier, year and serial number on spring cover, left or top of receiver.

SAFETY
Latch above between spade grips. Lift to fire.

UNLOADING
Press pawl depressor on right of feedway to remove belt. Pull back and release cocking handle twice. With a pencil or similar tool, check ejection hole under barrel for possible live cartridge. Press trigger.

Degtyarev DP (Russia)

Adopted by the Soviet Army in 1928 after two years of trials, the DP became the standard infantry squad machine gun. It remained in service until the 1950s in the Warsaw Pact and was widely distributed to sympathisers around the world. It fires only at automatic, and uses the old rimmed 7.62mm round. The thin flat pan magazine is somewhat susceptible to damage, and the piston return spring, beneath the barrel, tends to lose its spring after being subjected to barrel heat for long periods. The

SPECIFICATION & OPERATION

CARTRIDGE
7.62 x 54R Soviet

DIMENSIONS
Length o/a: 1290mm
Weight: 9.12kg
Barrel: 605mm
Rifling: 4 grooves, rh
Feed system: 47-round drum
Rate of fire: 550 rds/min

IN PRODUCTION 1928-41

MARKINGS
Factory identifier and serial number on top of receiver.

SAFETY
This weapon has an automatic grip safety device behind the trigger guard; when the butt is gripped in order to position the hand on the trigger, the safety is pressed in and the weapon can be fired. As soon as the butt is released the weapon is made safe.

UNLOADING
The magazine release is also the rear sight guard. Pull back, and lift the drum magazine upwards off the receiver. Pull back the cocking handle, inspect the feedway and chamber to ensure no cartridge is present, release the cocking handle, pull the trigger.

bipod was too weak for its job and frequently bent. All these defects came to light during 1941, when the gun was first put to the test of war, which led to the development of the DPM (below).

Degtyarev DPM (Russia)

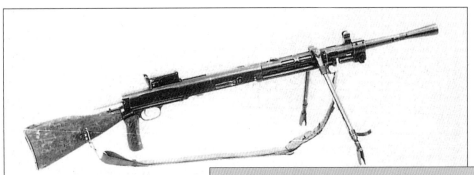

The DPM appeared in 1942 and was a modification of the DP to get over the two principal defects. The return spring was removed from around the gas piston and put behind the bolt, necessitating a tubular extension behind the receiver; this meant that it could no longer be gripped around the butt and a pistol grip had to be added. The bipod was strengthened and attached to the barrel casing, raising the roll centre and making the weapon easier to hold upright. It almost completely replaced the DP and was widely distributed to various Communist-backed forces after the war.

SPECIFICATION & OPERATION

CARTRIDGE
7.62 x 54R Soviet

DIMENSIONS
Length o/a: 1265mm (49.8in)
Weight: 12.20kg (26lb 14oz)
Barrel: 605mm (23.8in)
Rifling: 4 grooves, rh
Feed system: 47-round drum
Rate of fire: 550 rds/min

IN PRODUCTION 1941-50

MARKINGS
Factory identifier and serial number on top of receiver.

SAFETY
A manual safety catch above the right side of the trigger. Turn forward for safe, DOWN and to the rear to fire.

UNLOADING
The magazine release is also the rear sight guard. Pull back, and lift the drum magazine upwards off the receiver. Pull back the cocking handle, inspect the feedway and chamber to ensure no cartridge is present, release the cocking handle, pull the trigger.

Degtyarev DT and DTM (Russia)

The DT was more or less the same weapon as the DP, described above, but intended for fitting into tanks and other armoured vehicles. It had a heavier barrel and a two-layer magazine, and was fitted with a telescoping metal butt and pistol grip. To allow it to be used outside the vehicle a bipod and front sight were carried, to be fitted when required. Like the DP it suffered from the return spring beneath the barrel weakening from heat, and like the DP it was modified into the DTM in 1942, the same solution being applied: the return spring was put into a tubular receiver extension behind the bolt. After being cast from tank employment many were given to other countries as infantry light machine guns.

SPECIFICATION & OPERATION

CARTRIDGE
7.62 x 54R Soviet

DIMENSIONS: (DTM)
Length o/a: 1181mm (46.5in)
Weight: 12.90kg (28lb 7oz)
Barrel: 597mm (23.5in
Rifling: 4 grooves, rh
Feed system: 60-round drum
Rate of fire: 600 rds/min

IN PRODUCTION 1929-45

MARKINGS
Factory identifier and serial number on top of receiver.

SAFETY
A manual safety catch above the right side of the trigger. Turn forward for safe, DOWN and to the rear to fire.

UNLOADING
Magazine release may be in front of, or behind, the rear sight. Press it to the side or to the rear and remove the drum magazine. Pull back the cocking handle, inspect the chamber and feedway, release the cocking handle and press the trigger.

Goryunov SG43 (Russia)

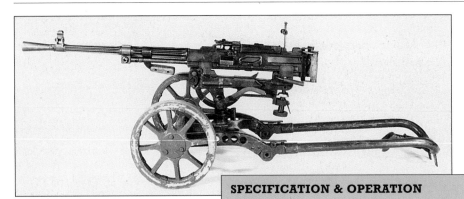

The SG43 became the standard Soviet medium machine gun during World War II, replacing the Maxim 1910 as the latter were lost in action or wore out. Gas-operated, the mechanism is rather complex since the feed has to pull the cartridge out of the belt backwards, lower it into the feed way and then chamber it. The locking system is similar to that of the Bren machine gun, but instead of tilting the bolt, it is swung sideways to lock into one wall of the receiver. Original models were smooth-barrelled; later versions have a grooved barrel to aid cooling. The design was copied in Hungary and China; the Chinese version is almost identical; the Hungarian sometimes has a pistol grip, butt and bipod.

SPECIFICATION & OPERATION

CARTRIDGE
7.62 x 54R Soviet

DIMENSIONS
Length o/a: 1120mm (44.1in)
Weight: 13.60kg (30lb 0oz)
Barrel: 720mm (28.35in)
Rifling: 4 grooves, rh
Feed system: 250-round cloth belt
Rate of fire: 650 rds/min

IN PRODUCTION 1943-55

MARKINGS
Factory identifier and serial number on top of receiver.

SAFETY
There is a safety device on the firing button between the spade grips which prevents the button being pushed in. The safety flap must be lifted with the thumb to permit the firing button to be pressed.

UNLOADING
The cover latch is on the left rear side of the cover. Press forward and open the cover. Lift the belt off the feed pawls and remove it. Lift the lower feed cover and remove any cartridge which may be in the feed. Pull the cocking handle to the rear, examine the interior of the receiver, press the trigger and ease the cocking handle forward. Close both covers.

DShK (Russia)

shuttle feed, so that the receiver cover became flat once more. Copies of these models have been made at various times in China, Pakistan and Romania and can be identified by their national markings.

This has been the premier heavy machine gun of the Soviet and Warsaw Pact armies since 1946 and is still in wide use, though now being replaced by the NSV (above). It has also been widely distributed to sympathisers around the world and will undoubtedly be used for many more years. It was originally produced in 1934 in limited numbers, revised in 1938 (the DShK-38), used during WWII and then revised once more in 1946 (the DShK38/46). The 1938 revision gave it a rotary feed, and thus a characteristic rounded cover to the receiver. The 1946 change reverted to a form of flat

SPECIFICATION & OPERATION

CARTRIDGE
12.7 x 107mm Soviet

DIMENSIONS
Length o/a: 1588mm (62.50in)
Weight: 35.70kh (78lb 12oz)
Barrel: 1070mm (42.12in)
Rifling: 4 grooves, rh
Feed system: 50 round belt
Rate of fire: 550 rds/min

IN PRODUCTION 1938-80

MARKINGS
Factory mark (arrow), year and serial number on top rear of the receiver, above the grips.

SAFETY
Manual safety catch on the lower left edge of the receiver. Turn forward for safe, backward to fire.

UNLOADING
Cover latch in front of the rear sight. Press in and lift the cover. Remove any belt, lift the feed drum and check that no cartridges remain in it. Inspect to see that no rounds remain in the feedway or chamber. Close all covers, turn the safety catch to the rear, pull back the cocking handle, press the trigger.

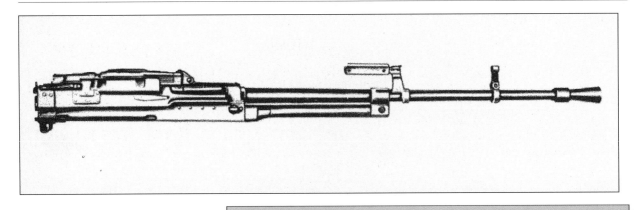

This weapon appeared in the late 1970s on tank turrets as a commander's machine gun; it was later seen on a tripod for heavy support use by infantry, and then on an air defence mounting. The gun is gas operated, using a piston to drive a bolt carrier, and can be set up during manufacture to feed from the left or from the right as required. In addition to being made in Russia, it has been licensed to Poland, Bulgaria and Yugoslavia, all of whom have offered it on the export market for some years. It appears to have been developed as a replacement for the DShK model, but there seems to be little advance in performance over the earlier weapon.

SPECIFICATION & OPERATION

CARTRIDGE
12.7 x 107mm Soviet

DIMENSIONS
Length o/a: 1560mm (61.4in)
Weight: 25.00kg (55lb 2oz)
Barrel: 1070mm (42.12in)
Rifling: 8 grooves, rh
Feed system: belt
Rate of fire: 750 rds/min

IN PRODUCTION ca 1980-

MARKINGS
Serial number on the top of the receiver.

SAFETY
There is no safety device on this weapon

UNLOADING
Press catch in front of the sight and lift cover. Remove the belt. Pull back the cocking handle, examine chamber and feedway. Release cocking handle, press trigger and close cover.

PK (Russia)

SPECIFICATION & OPERATION

CARTRIDGE
7.62 x 54R Soviet

DIMENSIONS
Length o/a: 1193mm (47.0in)
Weight: 8.90kh (19lb 10oz)
Barrel: 660mm (26.0in)
Rifling: 4 grooves, rh
Feed system: belt
Rate of fire: 650 rds/min

IN PRODUCTION 1964-

MARKINGS
Serial number and year on top of feed cover.

SAFETY
Manual safety catch above the trigger. Turn forward to fire, rearward for safe.

UNLOADING
Cover latch is at the rear of the receiver. Press in and allow the cover to open. Lift out the belt, if one is present, and check that no cartridge remains in the cartridge gripper. Pull back the cocking handle, inspect the chamber and feedway. Close the cover. Press the trigger.

The PK was the first general purpose machine gun to go into Soviet service; it replaced the RP46 but, surprisingly, retained the old rimmed cartridge, presumably because of its better long-range performance when compared to the M1943 rimless round. The design is a combination of Kalashnikov breech mechanism and a new feed system; it is light in weight and the quality of manufacture is high. There are a number of variant models: the PK is the basic company gun; the PKS is the tripod-mounted battalion support weapon; the PKT is the version for use in tanks, with no pistol grip or butt. As with other Soviet designs, the PK family can be found in all the former Warsaw Pact countries.

SPECIFICATION & OPERATION

CARTRIDGE
7.62 x 39mm Soviet M1943

DIMENSIONS
Length o/a: 1035mm (40.75in)
Weight: 4.76kh (10lb 8oz)
Barrel: 590mm (23.23in)
Rifling: 4 grooves, rh
Feed system: 30- or 40-round box or 75-round drum magazine
Rate of fire: 660 rds/min

IN PRODUCTION 1955-

MARKINGS
Serial and factory mark on left of receiver.

SAFETY
Combined safety catch and fire selector on the left side of the receiver. Lifted to its upper position the weapon is safe; one notch DOWN gives single shots, all the way DOWN gives automatic fire.

UNLOADING
Magazine catch behind magazine housing. Remove magazine. Pull back cocking handle to eject any round in the chamber, inspect chamber via the ejection slot, release the cocking handle and pull the trigger.

The RPK replaced the RPD as the standard squad automatic for Soviet infantry and then went on to arm the Warsaw Pact armies and be distributed to sympathisers across the world. It is simply a heavy-barrelled version of the standard AK47 rifle and it will accept AK magazines, which makes resupply in the field relatively easy. Like the rifle, the barrel is fixed, so that sustained fire is not entirely practical, though the bore and chamber are chromium-plated in an endeavour to keep the wear rate down as far as possible.

RP-46 (Russia)

The RP46 was a modernisation of the DPM, intended for use as a company support gun. The basic layout of the DPM was retained, the principal addition being that of a belt feed so that sustained fire could be delivered. However, the original 47 round DP drum can still be used if required, so the RP46 could still be used in the squad automatic role. The barrel has been made heavier, again something demanded by the sustained fire role. It was replaced in Soviet service by the RPD, which was a further modification of the original DP design, and almost all the RP46 were shipped off to sympathisers overseas; they turn up in Africa and the Middle East quite regularly.

SPECIFICATION & OPERATION

CARTRIDGE
7.62 x 54R Soviet

DIMENSIONS
Length o/a: 1283mm (50.5in)
Weight: 13.00kg (28lb 11oz)
Barrel: 607mm (23.9in)
Rifling: 4 grooves, rh
Feed system: 250-round cloth belt
Rate of fire: 600 rds/min

IN PRODUCTION: 1946-54
MARKINGS
Factory identifier and serial number on top rear of receiver.

SAFETY
A manual safety catch above the trigger on the right side. Turn forward for safe, rearward to fire.

UNLOADING
Belt cover catch is behind the rear sight. Press the catch backwards and the cover will open. Lift out the belt if one is present. Pull the cocking handle to the rear and inspect the chamber and feedway. Press the trigger and ease the operating handle forward. Close the cover.

7.62mm RPD (Russia)

The RPD was for some years the standard light machine-gun of the Soviet Army, having been introduced in the 1950s as the complementary squad weapon to the AK rifle. It was the logical development of the earlier DP and DPM , and it was progressively improved during its life. It was a gas-operated weapon and the modifications were principally to the gas piston system to improve stability and

SPECIFICATION & OPERATION

CARTRIDGE
7.62 X 39mm

DIMENSIONS
Length: 41.00in (1041mm)
Weight unloaded: 15lb 7oz (7.00kg)
Barrel: 20.50in (520mm), 4 grooves, right-hand twist
Magazine: 100-round belt
Cyclic rate: 700 rds/min
Muzzle velocity: c.2410 ft/sec (734 m/sec)

IN PRODUCTION: 1962 –

MARKINGS
Model number, factory identifier and serial number on top of receiver.

SAFETY
Thumb switch of right side of receiver above trigger. Rotate forward for SAFE, to the rear to fire.

UNLOADING.
Pull back the cocking handle and rotate the safety catch to the front, push forward the cover latch and lift the receiver cover. Draw the belt to the left and feed it back into the drum. Check to see that the feedway and chamber are empty. Close the cover. Turn the drum lock (rear of drum, beneath receiver body) and slide the drum off to the rear. Rotate the safety to the rear, grasp the bolt handle, pull the trigger and allow the bolt to go forward under control.

provide sufficient power to lift the belt under adverse conditions. The replaceable barrel of the DP was abandoned in this fresh design, and it became a matter of drill and training for the gunner to avoid firing more than 100 rounds in one minute to prevent overheating the barrel. The remainder of the mechanism was similar to the DP, suitably scaled down for the smaller ammunition, and, like its predecessor the DP, the RPD was capable of automatic fire only.

RPK-74 (Russia)

mount on the left side of the receiver for an electronic night sight; and the RPKS-N3 is the folding stock model with night sight mount.

The RPK-74 bears the same relationship to the AK-74 rifle as the RPK does to the AK-47 rifle; in other words it is the heavy-barrel squad automatic in 5.45mm calibre. Once the Soviets adopted the 5.45mm cartridge it was simply a matter of time before they produced the light automatic weapon to go with it, but it was not until 1980 that the first details reached the western world. It seems likely that the Soviets, too, had found problems in developing a small-calibre machine gun that didn't shoot the rifling out of its barrel within 5000 rounds. There are four variant models; the RPK-74 is the basic weapon; the RPKS-74 has a folding butt; the RPK-N3 is the standard weapon with a special

SPECIFICATION & OPERATION

CARTRIDGE
5.45 x 39mm Soviet

DIMENSIONS
Length o/a: 1060mm (41.75in)
Weight: 4.60kg (10lb 2oz)
Barrel: 616mm (24.25in)
Rifling: 4 grooves, rh
Feed system: 30, 40 or 45-round magazines
Rate of fire: 650 rds/min

IN PRODUCTION 1977-

MARKINGS
Factory identifier and serial number on top rear of receiver.

SAFETY
Combined safety catch and fire selector lever on the right rear side of the receiver. When pressed all the way UP it is in the safe position and obstructs the movement of the cocking handle and bolt; moved DOWN one notch to the first mark or

the letters `AB' gives full automatic fire, and moved to the bottom position, or the letter `O', produces single shots.

UNLOADING
Magazine catch at front end of trigger guard. Remove magazine. Pull back cocking handle, inspect chamber and feedway via the ejection port. Release cocking handle, pull trigger.

Ultimax (Singapore)

The Ultimax was developed by Chartered Industries of Singapore as the partner to their SAR-80 5.56mm rifle; unfortunately their timing was out, and it appeared some time after the FN Minimi, with the result that several armed forces which would probably have chosen the Ultimax had already committed themselves to the Minimi. The Ultimax is an excellent weapon and is particularly comfortable to fire, using a long-stroke bolt and buffer system which keeps the recoil impulse to a very low level. It can be fed from a drum or a box magazine and uses the now-common bolt carrier and rotating bolt driven by a gas piston. It is currently used by the Singapore armed forces and has been favourably evaluated by several armies. It has also been seen in the current civil war in Bosnia.

SPECIFICATION & OPERATION

CARTRIDGE
5.56 x 45mm M193 or NATO

DIMENSIONS
Length o/a: 1030mm (40.55in)
Weight: 4.79kg (10lb 9oz)
Barrel: 506mm (19.92in)
Rifling: 6 grooves, rh
Feed system: 30-round box or 100-round drum
Rate of fire: 550 rds/min

IN PRODUCTION 1982-

MARKINGS
`ULTIMAX Mk III Mfd by Singapore Chartered Industries 5.56´ and serial number on left side of receiver.

SAFETY
Manual safety catch on left side above trigger. Forward for automatic fire, rearward for safe.

UNLOADING
Remove magazine. Pull back cocking handle to eject any round in the chamber. Inspect chamber and feedway via the ejection port. Release cocking handle, pull trigger.

CIS 50MG (Singapore)

The CIS .50 is modular in construction, with five basic groups. It is gas operated and fires from the open bolt position. The locking system is the now-familiar bolt carrier and rotating bolt, the firing pin being part of the carrier assembly and driven on to the cap by the final forward movement of the gas piston; there are actually two gas pistons and cylinders,

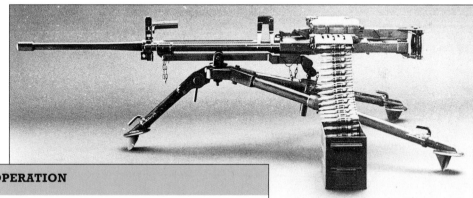

SPECIFICATION & OPERATION

CARTRIDGE
.50 Browning MG

DIMENSIONS
Length: 70.0in (1778mm)
Weight unloaded: 66lb 2oz (30.0kg)
Barrel: 45.0in (1143mm), 8 grooves, right-hand twist
Magazine: dual disintegrating link belt
Cyclic rate: 600 rds/min

Muzzle velocity: c.2920 ft/sec (890 m/sec)

IN PRODUCTION: 1988-

MARKINGS
CIS 50 MFG BY CHARTERED INDUSTRIES OF SINGAPORE PTE LTD on left side of receiver.

SAFETY
Two position switch above trigger; SAFE and automatic fire.

UNLOADING
Release catch and lift feed cover. Remove belt (note that this weapon can be adjusted to feed the belt from either side). Pull back bolt until it locks. Examine chamber and feedway to ensure they are empty. Holding the cocking handle, press trigger and ease the bolt forward. Close cover.

disposed below the barrel so as to obviate any torque twisting. The barrel is a quick-change pattern and is fitted with an efficient muzzle brake. Feed is by two belts, entering one on each side of the receiver, and the gunner can select either belt as required. The gun can be provided with either a tripod mount or a pintle mount for fitting into APCs.

Bren (UK)

Britain adopted this from Czechoslovakia, where it was known as the vz26, under which name it appears elsewhere. The Bren version differs because the British .303 cartridge was rimmed, whereas the vz26 was designed around the 7.92mm Mauser, a rimless round. This is the reason for the characteristic curved magazine and some less visible minor internal changes. Very reliable, accurate, slow-firing, the Bren was probably the best light machine gun of the WWII period and, changed to 7.62mm

SPECIFICATION & OPERATION

CARTRIDGE
.303 British Service; 7.62 x 51mm NATO

DIMENSIONS
Length o/a: 1150mm (45.27in)
Weight: 10.15kg (22lb 6oz)
Barrel: 635mm (25.0in)
Rifling: 6 grooves, rh
Feed system: 30-round box magazine
Rate of fire: 500 rds/min

IN PRODUCTION 1936-

MARKINGS
'BREN Mk XX' on right side.

SAFETY
A combined safety catch and selector lever is on the left side above the trigger. Forward position for automatic fire, central for safe, rearward for single shots.

UNLOADING
Magazine catch behind magazine housing. Press in and remove magazine. Pull cocking handle to the rear, examine the chamber through the magazine opening. Hold the cocking handle and press the trigger, easing the cocking handle forward. Close the magazine cover by sliding it back, close the ejection port cover (beneath the gun) by sliding it back.

NATO calibre, is still in use today. There are a number of variant models, differing in the sights, barrel length, bipod and general degree of refinement, but all operate in the same way.

Vickers (UK)

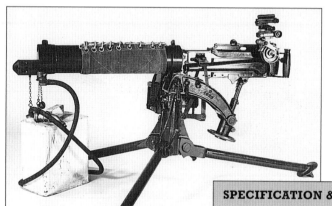

during WWI, was adopted as the standard synchronised aircraft gun, armed the earliest armoured cars and tanks and was, of course, also adopted by the various armies of the British Empire and Commonwealth, some of whom continued using it into the 1970s. It was also made in .50 calibre for aircraft and tank use, and a number were made by Colt in the USA in .30 calibre for the US Army in 1915. Vickers also sold the gun commercially in the 1920-38 period, principally to South American countries.

Like many others, the British started with the Maxim gun and then sought something lighter. Vickers developed their answer, reducing the weight by use of high quality steel and aluminium and better stress analysis, and inverting the Maxim toggle system for compactness. The resulting 'Mark 1' Vickers gun entered service in 1912 and stayed unchanged until made obsolete in 1968. Utterly reliable, it set up world records for non-stop firing

SPECIFICATION & OPERATION

CARTRIDGE
.303 British and others

DIMENSIONS
Length o/a: 1155mm (45.47in)
Weight: 18.10kg (39lb 14oz)
Barrel: 723mm (28.46in)
Rifling: 4 grooves, rh
Feed system: 250 round cloth belt
Rate of fire: 450 rds/min

IN PRODUCTION 1912-45

MARKINGS
Serial number on top rear of water jacket.

SAFETY
Safety catch above trigger, between spade grips. Lift with the fingers to allow trigger to be pressed.

UNLOADING
Pawl depressor on right side under feedway. Press in and remove belt. Pull back cocking handle, examine feedway and chamber. Release cocking handle and press trigger.

Enfield L86 (UK)

trigger mechanism so that when set to automatic it stops firing with the breech held open, while when set for single shots it stops with the breech closed and a fresh round loaded. At single shot it is exceptionally accurate, a function of the longer and heavier barrel, and in 1995 a single-shot-only version was being promoted as a sniper weapon.

This should really be classed as a 'machine rifle', since it lacks that vital feature of a light machine gun, a quick-change barrel, and it also uses a low-capacity rifle magazine. It is, nevertheless, the British 5.56mm squad automatic weapon or 'Light Support Weapon' as the current phrase has it. It uses some 80 percent of the components of the L85 rifle, has a heavier and longer barrel, some changes in the

SPECIFICATION & OPERATION

CARTRIDGE
5.56 x 45mm NATO

DIMENSIONS
Length o/a: 900mm (35.43in)
Weight: 5.40kg (11lb 14oz)
Barrel: 646mm (25.4in)
Rifling: 6 grooves, rh
Feed system: 30-round box magazine
Rate of fire: 700 rds/min

IN PRODUCTION 1985-

MARKINGS
MG 5.56mm LIGHT SUPPORT L86 ENFIELD on right of receiver. Serial above magazine housing.

SAFETY
Push-through bolt above trigger: push from left to right for safe. Selector on left UP for single shots, DOWN for automatic.

UNLOADING
Remove magazine. Pull back cocking handle to eject any round in the chamber. Inspect chamber and feedway via ejection port. Release cocking handle and pull trigger.

Browning M1917 (USA)

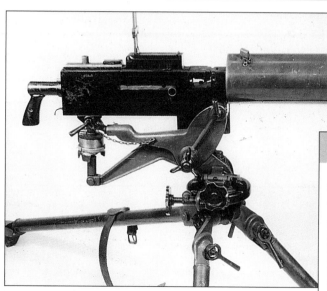

The M1917 was Browning's original recoil-operated military machine gun, upon which all the later models (except the BAR) were based. As was the accepted form in those days, it was a heavy water-cooled gun mounted on a tripod, reliable and long-wearing. It survived through WWII in the same form and well into the 1950s before it was finally ousted by the air-cooled models, largely because it was there and still worked well.

SPECIFICATION & OPERATION

CARTRIDGE
.30-06 US Service

DIMENSIONS
Length o/a: 978mm (38.5in)
Weight: 14.97kg (32lb 0oz)
Barrel: 610mm (24.0in)
Rifling: 4 grooves, rh
Feed system: 250-round cloth belt
Rate of fire: 500 rds/min

IN PRODUCTION 1917-45
MARKINGS
US INSP BROWNING MACHINE GUN
US CAL 30 MODEL OF 1917 MFD BY
(manufacturer's name).

SAFETY
There is no safety device on this machine gun.

UNLOADING
Pull back the milled knob on the top cover (behind the rear sight) to release the cover; lift it open. Remove any belt. Pull back the operating handle and inspect the front face of the bolt, pushing out any cartridge which may have been extracted. Examine the chamber of the gun. Close the cover, release the cocking handle, pull the trigger.

Browning M1919 A4 (USA)

This is an air-cooled version of the M1917, developed in 1918-19 to arm American tanks. The barrel was shortened to 457mm and placed in a perforated jacket, and a small tripod was provided so that it could be used outside the tank. This proved that air-cooled guns could work as well as water-cooled and the gun was adopted by the US Cavalry in the early 1920s. Various modifications were made and eventually the M1919A4 appeared, having reverted to the same barrel length as the M1917. It

SPECIFICATION & OPERATION

CARTRIDGE
.30-06 US Service

DIMENSIONS
Length o/a: 1041mm (41.0in)
Weight: 14.05kg (31lb 0oz)
Barrel: 610mm (24.0in)
Rifling: 4 grooves, rh
Feed system: 250-round cloth belt
Rate of fire: 500 rds/min

IN PRODUCTION 1934-

MARKINGS
'BROWNING M1919A4 US Cal .30' (Maker's name) (year) (serial number) on left side of receiver.

SAFETY
There is no safety device on this machine gun.

UNLOADING
Pull back the milled knob on the top cover (in front of the rear sight) to release the cover; lift it open. Remove any belt. Pull back the operating handle and inspect the front face of the bolt, pushing out any cartridge which may have been extracted. Examine the chamber of the gun. Close the cover, release the cocking handle, pull the trigger.

was adopted as the standard ground gun for all arms in the late 1930s and remained so until replaced by the M60 in the 1960s. Many are still in use in various parts of the world, some modified to 7.62mm NATO and other calibres, and they will undoubtedly be around for many years to come.

Browning M1919 A6 (USA)

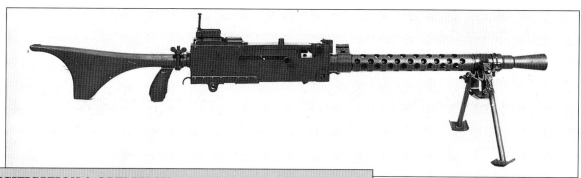

SPECIFICATION & OPERATION

CARTRIDGE
.30-06 US Service

DIMENSIONS
Length o/a: 1346mm (53.0in)
Weight: 14.73kg (32lb 8oz)
Barrel: 610mm (24.0in)
Rifling: 4 grooves, rh
Feed system: 250-round cloth belt
Rate of fire: 500 rds/min

IN PRODUCTION 1943-54

MARKINGS
US INSP BROWNING MACHINE GUN US CAL 30 MFD BY (manufacturer's name).

SAFETY
There is no safety device on this machine gun.

UNLOADING
Pull back the milled knob on the top cover (in front of the rear sight) to release the cover; lift it open. Remove any belt. Pull back the operating handle and inspect the front face of the bolt, pushing out any cartridge which may have been extracted. Examine the chamber of the gun. Close the cover, release the cocking handle, pull the trigger.

The M1919A6 was developed during WWII and adopted in 1943 to be the squad light machine gun in place of the BAR. As the figures above show, it was far from light, since it was no more than the M1919A4 with the addition of a shoulder stock, muzzle flash hider and a bipod. It was heavy, cumbersome and heartily disliked by all who encountered it; most of them appear to have had the shoulder stock and bipod removed so as to bring them back to M1919A4 standard and then put on tripods, the BAR being retained as long as possible as the squad automatic. The arrival of the M60 machine gun enabled the remaining A6's to be got rid of; some were unloaded on to other, unsuspecting, armies and may turn up from time to time, particularly in Central America.

Browning Automatic Rifle (BAR) (USA)

SPECIFICATION & OPERATION

CARTRIDGE
.30-06 US Service

DIMENSIONS
Length o/a: 1219mm (48.0in)
Weight: 7.28kg (16lb 1oz)
Barrel: 610mm (24.0in)
Rifling: 4 grooves, rh
Feed system: 20-round box magazine
Rate of fire: 500 rds/min

IN PRODUCTION 1917-45

MARKINGS
BROWNING BAR M1918 CAL 30 MFD BY (manufacturer's name).

SAFETY
There is a combined safety catch and fire selector lever above the trigger on the left side. In the rear position the rifle is safe; pushed forward to the central position the rifle fires at the slow automatic rate; pushed fully forward the rifle fires at the fast automatic rate.

UNLOADING
Press in the magazine release button in the front of the trigger guard and remove the magazine. Pull back the cocking handle, on the left side of the receiver, to eject any round in the chamber. Inspect the chamber through the ejection port. Push the cocking handle back to its forward position, pull the trigger.

This is a gas-operated, magazine-fed weapon, entirely different to the other Browning machine guns. Designed as a light machine gun for World War I, the BAR became the US Army's squad automatic weapon, remaining in service until the Korean war. It was finally replaced by the M249 Minimi in the 1980s. Numbers were also issued to the British Home Guard in 1940-45. With a fixed barrel and a limited-capacity magazine the BAR was never really a serious light machine gun; too much sustained fire and the fore-end burst into smoke and flames. It was too heavy to be a serious automatic rifle either, but since there was nothing better, it survived. It was also sold commercially by Colt as the 'Monitor' for police use, in semi-automatic form.

Browning M2HB .50 (USA)

In 1918 the Germans developed a 13mm anti-tank machine gun; the US Army in France demanded something similar. The Winchester company developed a .50 inch cartridge, and Browning scaled-up his M1917 machine gun to fire it. It originally appeared as a water-cooled anti-aircraft machine gun, but in the 1930s the M2 air-cooled version was developed for use on tanks. Since it used a very thick barrel to

SPECIFICATION & OPERATION

CARTRIDGE
12.7 x 99mm (.50 Browning)

DIMENSIONS
Length o/a: 1653mm (65,0in)
Weight: 38.22kg (84lb 4oz)
Barrel: 1143mm (45.0in)
Rifling: 8 grooves, rh
Feed system: belt
Rate of fire: 500 rds/min

IN PRODUCTION 1933-

MARKINGS
US serial number BROWNING MACHINE GUN CAL 50 M2 MFD BY (manufacturer's name).

SAFETY
There is no safety catch as such, but a bolt latch release, in the centre of the thumb trigger, will lock the bolt to the rear. This must be pressed DOWN before pressing the trigger.

UNLOADING
Press down the bolt latch release. Turn the catch on the top cover and open the cover. Remove any belt in the gun. Pull back the operating handle on the right side of the gun until the bolt locks back. Examine the front of the bolt, knocking free any cartridge which may have been extracted from the chamber, and check that the chamber is empty. Press down the extractor at the front of the bolt, close the cover, press the bolt latch release and allow the bolt to go forward, press the trigger.

dissipate the heat generated by firing, it became the `HB' for Heavy Barrel. Some three million have been made by different companies, they have been used by virtually every armed force outside the Communist bloc, they never wear out, and there are a lot of them about. In the 1980s quick-change barrel versions became common; these do away with the need for a ticklish adjustment when changing barrels or re-assembling the weapon after cleaning.

Armalite AR-10 (USA/Holland)

SPECIFICATION & OPERATION

CARTRIDGE
7.62 x 51mm NATO

DIMENSIONS
Length o/a: 1029mm (40.5in)
Weight: 4.10kg (9lb 1oz)
Barrel: 608mm (23.9in)
Rifling: 4 grooves, rh
Feed system: 20 round magazine
Rate of fire: 700 rds/min

IN PRODUCTION 1958-61

MARKINGS
`ArmaLite AR10 Manufactured by Al Nederland' on left side of magazine housing. `CAL 7.62 NATO' and serial number on left side of receiver.

SAFETY
Combined safety catch and selector switch on left side, above trigger. Vertical for safe; forward for single shots, rearward for automatic fire.

UNLOADING
Magazine catch is a serrated plate on the left side of the receiver behind the magazine. Remove magazine. Pull back cocking handle (inside carrying handle) to eject any round in the chamber, inspect chamber through the ejection slot, release cocking handle, pull trigger.

Developed by the ArmaLite Division of the Fairchild Aircraft Company, manufacture of this weapon was licensed to Artillerie Inrichtingen of Holland since ArmaLite had no production facilities. Small numbers were sold to Nicaragua, Burma and the Sudan, and others were purchased by various countries for trial, but large orders eluded the company and production stopped in 1961. Shortly after that ArmaLite began the development which was to result in the AR15/M16 rifle, and it is not hard to see the family resemblance between the AR10 and the M16.

GAU 19/A (USA)

This was originally developed by General Electric and called the 'GECAL 50', gaining its more formal nomenclature after adoption by the US Army. It is a three-barrelled Gatling-type weapon requiring an external source of power such as vehicle batteries. Although it produces a much higher volume of fire than a standard M2HB gun, it is only slightly heavier and delivers lesser recoil force to its mounting. It can be adjusted to give two rates of fire.

The mechanism is based upon the Gatling gun

SPECIFICATION & OPERATION

CARTRIDGE
.50 Browning

DIMENSIONS
Length o/a: 1181mm (46.50in)
Weight: unloaded: 33.60kg
(74lb 1oz)
Barrel: 914mm (36.0in)
Rifling: 8 grooves, rh
Feed system: linkless feed
Cyclic rate: Selectable 1000 or
2000 rds/min

IN PRODUCTION 1986-

MARKINGS
Usually found with am identification plate riveted to the receiver, bearing the serial number, sotck number, designation and ROCK ISLAND ARSENAL.

SAFETY
Safety in this weapon is controlled by simply cutting off the power supply to the breech rotor, and is a function on the

control box rather than a mechanism on the gun.

UNLOADING
Unloading should not be necessary since the operating system will stop the ammunition supply and empty the gun when the trigger or firing button is released. The gun is therefore always unloaded except when actually firing.

system with the three barrels rotating in front of a receiver unit in which cam tracks control the movement of the three bolts. The gun will fire any type of .50 Browning ammunition, including SLAP discarding sabot rounds. A de-linking feed system accepts standard machine gun belts and removes the rounds from the belt prior to feeding into the linkless supply chutes.

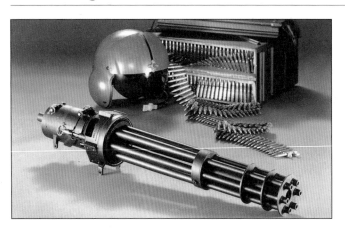

This multiple-barrel 'Gatling-type' machine-gun is based on the 20mm Vulcan development, and was specifically designed for use in helicopters in Vietnam. Due to its demands for power and ammunition, its application is limited to helicopters or vehicle mounts which provide the necessary space. The six barrels are revolved by an electric motor; they are normally parallel but can be clamped into various degrees of convergence if required. The action body, behind the barrels, carries six bolts in a rotating unit; these bolts lock into the barrels by rotation of their heads. The ammunition is belt-fed into the action body, the rounds are stripped out and located in front of the bolts, and as the bolt unit revolves so each round is chambered; at the uppermost position the firing pin is released and the round fired, after which the empty case is extracted and the bolt makes a complete circuit to pick up another round. When the trigger is released, the ammunition feed is isolated so that there is no danger of a cook-off during the short time the barrel and bolt assembly is coming to rest.

SPECIFICATION & OPERATION

CARTRIDGE
7.62 x 51mm NATO

DIMENSIONS
Length: 800mm (31.50in)
Weight: unloaded: 15.90kg (35lb 0oz)
Weight: w/ power supply 26.8kg (59lb 0oz)
Barrels: 559mm (22.00in)
Rifling: 4 grooves, rh
Feed system: 4000-round linked belt
Cyclic rate: c.6000 rds/min

IN PRODUCTION 1963 -

MARKINGS
An identification plate bearing the nomenclature, serial number, stock number and date of manufacture, together with either GENERAL ELECTRIC CO or ROCK ISLAND ARSENAL will be found riveted to the receiver body.

SAFETY
Safety in this weapon is controlled by simply cutting off the power supply to the breech rotor, and is a function on the control box rather than a mechanism on the gun.

UNLOADING
Unloading should not be necessary since the operating system will stop the ammunition supply and empty the gun when the trigger or firing button is released. The gun is therefore always unloaded except when actually firing.

is particularly well suited to tank installation since case ejection is forward, under control, and the relatively long bolt closure dwell time reduces the amount of fumes released into the vehicle. The Hughes Chain Gun is one of the few new operating principles which have appeared in recent years, and is in use in 25mm calibre in the US M2 Bradley MICV and in 7.62mm calibre on the British 'Warrior' MICV, being manufactured under license in Britain as the L94A1.

The Chain Gun derives its name from the use of a conventional roller chain in an endless loop which drives the bolt. The chain is driven by an electric motor, and a shoe on the chain engages in the bolt, carries it forward to chamber a round, holds it closed, then retracts it to extract the spent case. Cams rotate the bolt head to lock into the barrel and also actuate the firing pin as the bolt locks. A dynamic brake on the motor ensures that when the trigger is released the bolt stops in the open position, so that there is no danger of cook-off. The belt feed is also driven by the motor, independently of the bolt mechanism, so that there is ample power to handle long belts, particularly in a vehicle bounding over rough country. The Chain Gun

SPECIFICATION & OPERATION

CARTRIDGE
7.62 x 51mm NATO

DIMENSIONS
Length o/a: 1250mm (49.21in)
Weight: 17.86kg (39lb 6oz)
Barrel: 703mm (27.68in)
Rifling: 6 grooves, rh
Feed system: disintegrating link belt
Rate of Fire: 520 rds/min

IN PRODUCTION 1980 -

SAFETY
There are two independent safety devices; a mechanical safety catch in the form of a knob on the right front of the receiver, with Safe and Fire markings, and the electrical Master Switch on the control panel. The mechanical safety locks the sear and positively prevents the striker from reaching the firing pin. The Master Switch controls the supply of power to the gun. Note that if the Master Switch

is on and the mechanical safety is at safe, it is possible to operate the gun and cycle unfired rounds through it.

UNLOADING
A dynamic brake ensures that the gun always stops in the unloaded position with the chamber empty. The ammunition belt can be removed from the feed rotor by opening the feed cover.

gun up in the air while the barrel was changed.

The later M60E1 had a simpler barrel with the gas cylinder and bipod fixed to the gun, and it also had a handle for barrel changing. There were other less important changes which brought the M60E1 more into line with current practice, and gave it improved reliability. A feature of both models was the Stellite lining to the barrels which prolonged their lives beyond that normally experienced with unprotected steel, and both models had a constant-energy gas system to work the piston.

The M60, with its modified successor the M60E1, is the standard squad general purpose machine-gun of the United States Army. It was designed during the last years of the 1950s and has been in service since the early 1960s. The M60 is interesting in that it uses the feed system of the German MG42 and the bolt and locking system of the FG42, but in spite of these illustrious forebears, the original M60 had some serious drawbacks, the most noticeable of which was in the barrel change. Each barrel had its own gas cylinder and bipod attached to it - but no handle. It was, therefore, not only an expensive item but also unnecessarily heavy and dangerous to handle when hot. An asbestos glove formed part of the gun's equipment, and since the bipod vanished with the barrel, the poor gunner had to hold the

SPECIFICATION & OPERATION

CARTRIDGE
7.62 x 51mm NATO

DIMENSIONS
Length: 1100mm (43.5in)
Weight: 10.51kg (23lb 3oz)
Barrel: 560mm (22.04in)
Rifling: 4 grooves, rh
Feed system: Disintegrating link belt
Cyclic rate: 550 rds/min

IN PRODUCTION 1960 -

MARKINGS
MACHINE GUN 7.62 MM M60
SACO DEFENSE DIVISION
MAREMONT CORP USA or
SACO-LOWELL SHOPS USA or
other manufacturer, on top of
the feed cover.

SAFETY
A two-position safety catch is
on the left side of the receiver
above the pistol grip. There is
no fire selector - this weapon
fires only in the automatic
mode. Note that the safety

catch must be in the Fire
position to allow the gun to be
cocked.

UNLOADING
Pull back the cocking handle
until the bolt engages behind
the sear. Unlock and open the
top cover by lifting the latch at
the rear right of the receiver,
remove the ammunition belt.
Check that no rounds remain in
the feedway or chamber. Close
the cover, pull the trigger.

US Machine Gun M60E3 (USA)

This was the further development of the M60 design, intended to produce a more handy weapon, with a forward handgrip. The barrel may be a short, assault, barrel or a longer and heavier one for sustained fire missions. The feed cover has been modified to permit it being closed whether the bolt is forward or back, and the bipod is attached to the receiver. A winter trigger guard allows firing when wearing heavy gloves. The M60E3 was taken into use by the US Navy and Marine Corps and sold to several other countries.

SPECIFICATION & OPERATION

CARTRIDGE
7.62 x 51mm NATO

DIMENSIONS
Length: 1077mm (42.40in)
Weight: 8.80kg (19lb 6oz)
Barrel: 558mm (22.0in)
Rifling: 4 grooves, rh
Feed system: disintegrating link belt
Cyclic rate: 600 rds/min

IN PRODUCTION 1994 -

MARKINGS
MACHINE GUN 7.62MM M60E3 SACO DEFENSE INC on feed cover.

SAFETY
A two-position safety catch is on the left side of the receiver above the pistol grip. There is no fire selector - this weapon fires only in the automatic mode.

UNLOADING
Unlock and open the top cover by lifting the latch at the rear right of the receiver, remove the ammunition belt. Check that no rounds remain in the feedway. Pull back the cocking handle to eject any round in the chamber, inspect the chamber and feedway. Close the cover, release the bolt, pull the trigger.

M249 SAW (Squad Automatic Weapon) (USA)

As a result the US Army had to purchase 1000 Minimi guns rather rapidly in 1992 when the Gulf Live-Firing Exercise took place.

The changes were largely to suit US manufacturing methods and were relatively small, though nonetheless important; the principal exterior difference is the presence of a heat shield above the barrel. All other characteristics of the Minimi are unchanged.

The M249 is the FN Minimi with sundry small changes to meet the US Army's requirements for a light machine gun. It was approved in 1982 but did not enter production until the early 1990s due to a long drawn-out period of testing and modification before the requirements were satisfied.

SPECIFICATION & OPERATION

CARTRIDGE
5.56 x 45mm NATO

DIMENSIONS
Length: 1040mm (40.95in)
Weight: 6.85kg (15lb 2oz)
Barrel: 523mm (20.60in)
Rifling: 6 grooves, rh
Feed system: 30-round detachable box or 200-round metal belt
Cyclic rate: 750 rds/min

IN PRODUCTION 1992-

MARKINGS
FABRIQUE NATIONALE HERSTAL M249 5.56mm and serial number on left side of receiver.

SAFETY
Push-through safety catch on left side of receiver. Push from right to left to fire, left to right to make safe.

UNLOADING
Press in the two spring catches at the top rear of the receiver and lift the feed cover. Remove belt or magazine. Pull back cocking handle, examine chamber and feedway, release cocking handle, press trigger.

MANUFACTURERS

This lists the 'short title' used in the list of Brand Names, or the common title of the company which is used as an identifying name for their products. Against this is the full title and location of the company; a brief history is given where the firm has changed hands or titles or other distinctive features during its life, since this can often assist in approximately dating a weapon. Where there were no changes the period of the company's activity is indicated if known. Note also that the addresses are those relevant to the period, and, particularly in central Europe, place-names can change over the years. Thus 'Zella St Blasii' changed into 'Zella Mehlis', 'Bohemia' into 'Czechoslovakia' into 'Czech Republic'.

There are, of course, many omissions from this list; every country has numerous small provincial gunmakers whose name is unknown beyond a fifty-mile radius, and every country has a host of 'gunmakers' who purchase guns from major manufacturers and engrave their own names on them. These are difficult to discover and tabulate, so their absence must be excused. There are also custom gunmakers who built expensive rifles, shotguns and free-style target pistols to order, and obviously their products defy listing.

A

Accuracy Int	Accuracy International, Portsmouth, England
Acha	Originated as Acha Hermanos y Cia in Ermua, Spain, ca 1915, and ca 1920 became Domingo Acha y Cia, then Fabrica de Acha Hermanos. Closed ca 1935.
Adams	Adams Patent Small Arms Co, London. (1864-1893)
Adler	Adler Waffenwerke Max Hermsdorff, Zella St Blasii, Germany. Active 1905-1907
Adolph	Frederick Adolph, Genoa, NY, USA. (ca 1900-1924)
Advantage	Advantage Arms, St Paul, Minn., USA
Aetna	Aetna Arms Co, NY, USA. (1876-1890)
Agner	Agner-Saxhoj Products, Denmark
Aguirre	Aguirre y Cia, Eibar, Spain. Also operated as Aguirre, Zamacolas y Cia. 1915-30.
Alkartasuna	Soc. Anon. Alkartasuna Fabrica de Armas, Guernica, Spain. Began operating in 1915 as contractors to Gabilondo; factory burned down 1920, company liquidated 1922.
Allen	Allen & Wheelock, Worcester, Mass, USA to 1865. Ethan Allen & Co, Worcester, Mass, USA (1865-71)
All Right	All Right Firearms Co, Lawrence, Mass, USA (1876-1885)
Alpha	Alpha Arms Co, Flower Mound, Texas, USA (1983 - 1987)
AMAC	American Military Arms Corp, Jacksonville, Arkansas, USA. Bought the remains of Iver Johnson (qv) in 1987. Closed 1990.
American Arms (1)	The American Arms Co, Boston Mass., and Milwaukee Wis., USA. Founded 1882 in Boston, moved to Milwaukee 1897, closed down 1904.
American Arms (2)	American Arms Co, Garden Grove, Calif., USA. (1984-1985)
American Derringer	American Derringer Corp, Waco, Texas, USA. 1980-
American Firearms	American Firearms Mfg Co Inc, San Antonio, Texas, USA (1972 - 1974)
American Industries	American Industries. Cleveland, Ohio, USA. Ca. 1980; later re-organized to become the Calico Corp (qv).
American Standard	American Standard Tool Co, Newark, New Jersy, USA. Ca 1870; successor to the Manhattan Firearms Co.
Alsop	C.R.Alsop, Middletown, Conn., USA. (Ca 1870-1880)
Ames	Ames Sword Co, Chicopee Falls, Mass., USA. Not a firearms company but spent 1897-1910 making the Turbiaux repeating pistol as contractor.
Ancion-Marx	L. Ancion-Marx, Liege, Belgium. (1860-1914)
Anschutz	J.G.Anschutz, Zella St Blasii / Zella Mehlis, Germany (1886-1945) J.G.Anschutz GmbH, Ulm/Donau, Germany. (1950-)
Apaolozo Hermanos	Apaolozo Hermanos, Zumorraga, Spain. (1917-1935)
Arcadia	Arcadia Machine & Tool Co., Covina, Calif., USA
Arizaga	Gaspar Arizaga, Eibar, Spain. (1812-1936)
Arizmendi	Began as Arizmendi y Goenaga, Eibar, Spain, in 1886. In 1914 re-organised as Francisco Arizmendi and

MANUFACTURERS

Arizmendi, Zulaica	remained in business until 1936. Arizmendi, Zulaica y Cia, Eibar, Spain. relationship with Francisco Arizmendi not known; in business 1916-1925.
ArmaLite	ArmaLite Div of Fairchild Engine & Airplane Co, Costa Mesa, Calif., USA (1954 - 1983)
Armas de Fuego	Manufactura Arnas de Fuego, Guernica, Spain. Operated about 1920-25 and appears to have been the Alkartasuna company revived.
Armero Especialistas	Armeros Especialistas Reunidas, Eibar, Spain. A worker's cooperative which made pistols 1920-25 and thereafter became a sales agency for other makers until 1936.
Armigas	Armigas-Comega Costruzioni Mecchaniche Gardonesi Attilio Zanoletti, Gardone Val Trompia, Brescia, Italy. (1961-)
Armi-Jager	Armi-Jager di Armando Piscetti, Milan, Ittaly.
Arminex	Arminex Inc, Scottsdale, Arizona, USA (1979-1988)
Armitage	Armitage International Ltd, Seneca, South Carolina, USA
Arostegui	Eulogio Arostegui, Eibar, Spain. (1924-1936)
Arrieta	Arrieta y Cia, Elgoibar, Span
Arrizabalaga	Hijos de Calixto Arrizabalaga, Eibar, Spain. (1915-1936)
Ascaso	Francisco Ascaso, Tarassa, Cataluna, Spain. Small factory which made copies of the government-issue Astra 400 for the Republicans in the Spanish Civil War.
ASP	Armament Systems & Procedures, Appleton, Wisconsin, USA.
A-Square	A-Square Co, Inc, Madison, Indiana, USA
A.S.T.	see American Standard.
Astra-Unceta	Astra-Unceta y Cia SA, Apartado 3, Guernica (Vizcaya), Spain. Began in 1907 as Pedro Unceta y Juan Esperanza, Eibar; moved to Guernica in 1913 and became Esperanza y Unceta, adopted 'Astra' as their

	principal trade-name in 1914, became Unceta y Cia in 1926 , Astra-Unceta in 1955 and Astra Gernika SA in 1994.
ATCSA	Armas de Tiro y Casa, Barcelona, Spain (1931-1936)
Atkin	Atkin, Grant & Lang, London, England (1960-)
Automag	The Automag pistol has been made by various companies, listed here for convenience:-Sanford Arms Co, Pasadena, Calif., USA. Designers and initial development only. (1963 - 1970) Auto-Mag Corp, Pasadena, Calif.; Initial production (1970 - 1972) TDE Corp, North Hollywood, Calif. (1973 - 1977). During this period marketing was done by the High Standard Company) Sanford Arms, Pasadena, Calif. (1977 - 1980) Arcadia Machine & Tool Corporation, Covina, Calif (1980-85)
Auto-Ordnance	Auto-Ordnance, West Hurley, NY, USA
Azanza y Arrizabalaga	Azanza y Arrizabalaga, Eibar, Spain. (1915-1919)

B

Bacon	Bacon Manufacturing Co, Norwich,. Conn., USA. Then became Bacon Arms Co 1862-1891, when it failed and the remains were bought to form the basis of the Crescent Firearms Co (qv).
Baford	Baford Arms, Bristol, Tenn., USA
Baker	Baker Gun & Forging Co, Batavia, NY, USA
Ballard	C.H.Ballard & Co, Worcester, Mass., USA
Barrett	Barrett Firearms Mfg Co, Murfreesboro, Tenn., USA
Bar-Sto	Bar-Sto Precision Machine Co, Burbank, Calif, USA (1972-1975)
Barthelmes	Fritz Barthelmes KG, Heidenheim-Oggenhause, Germany (1948-)
Bascaran	Martin A.Bascaran, Eibar, Spain. (1915-1931)

Bauer	Bauer Firearms Corp., Fraser, Mich., USA. (1976-1984)
Bayonne	Manufacture d'Armes de Bayonne, Bayonne, France. (1921-1988)
Beaumont	Frans Beaumont, Maastricht, The Netherlands. Patentee and manufacturer of Dutch service revolvers and rifles (1873-1905)
Becker	Becker & Hollander, Suhl, Germany. ca (1885-1945)
Beistegui	Beistegui Hermanos, Eibar, Spain. (1915-1936)
Benelli	Benelli Armi SpA, Urbino, Italy. (ca 1850-)
Beretta	Pietro Beretta SpA, Gardone Val Trompia, Italy. (1680-)
Bergeron	L.Bergeron, St Etienne, France
Bergmann	Th. Bergmann Waffenfabrik, Suhl, Germany (1885-1918)
	Bergmann's Industriewerke, Gaggenau, Germany (1918-1945)
Bern	Eidgenossische Waffenfabrik Bern, Bern, Switzerland. Government arsenal since 1875. Name changed in 1993 to 'w + f Bern'
Bernadon-Martin	Bernadon-Martin, St Etienne, France. (1906-1912)
Bernardelli	Vincenzo Bernardelli SpA, Gardone Val Trompia, (Brescia), Italy. (1865 -)
Bernedo	Vincenzo Bernedo y Cia, Eibar, Spain. (1875-1914)
Bersa	Fabricas de Armas Bersa SA, Ramos Mejia, Argentina
Bertrand	Manufacture Generale d'Armes et Munitions Jules Bertrand, Liege. (ca 1885 - 1914)
Bertuzzi	Bertuzzi, Brescia, Italy
Bighorn	Bighorn Rifle Co, Orem, Utah, USA
	Bighorn Rifle Co, American Fork, Utah, USA
Bighorn Arms	Bighorn Arms Co, Watertown, South Dakota, USA.
Billings	Billings & Spencer, Hartford, Conn., USA (ca 1865)
Bingham	Bingham Ltd, Norcross, Georgia, USA. (1976 - 1985) Makers of .22RF calibre imitations of the Kalashnikov rifle, Soviet PPSh submachine gun and similar weapons.
Blake	J.H.Blake, New York, NY, USA (1890 - 1912)
Bland	Thomas Bland, London, England. Gunmaker; name found on revolvers, rifles and shotguns of his own make and on other makes sold by him. (1876 -)
Blaser	Blaser-Jagdwaffen GmbH, Isny/Allgau, Switzerland (1978 -)
Bliss	Franklin D. Bliss, New Haven, Conn., USA. (ca 1870)
Bock	Otto Bock, Berlin, Germany (ca 1900-1915)
Bolumburu	Gregorio Bolumburu, Eibar, Spain. (1908-1936)
Boss	Boss & Co, London, England (1832 -)
Boswell	Charles Boswell, London, England. (1884 -)
Braendlin	Braendlin Armoury, Birmingham, England (1871 - 1889)
Brenneke	Wilhelm Brenneke, Leipzig and Berlin, Germany. (ca 1920-1945)
	W.Brenneke GmbH, Berlin, Germany (ca 1950 -)
Britarms	This name has passed between several companies; it appears to have originated with the Berdan Group of Aylesbury, Bucks, England in about 1973 and thereafter went through various hands before ending with Westlake Engineering of Bordon, Hants, England in the middle 1980s.
Brixia	Metallurgica Bresciana Tempini, Brescia, Italy. (1908-1915)
Brooklyn Arms	Brooklyn Arms Co., Brooklyn, NY, USA. (ca 1865)
Brown	Brown Precision Inc, Los Molinos, Calif., USA
Browning	Browning Arms Co, Morgan, Utah, USA
Bruchet	P.Bruchet, St Etienne, France. Began manufacturing shotguns on the Darne system in 1982.
Bryco	Bryco Firearms, Carson City, Nevada, USA
BSA	Birmingham Small Arms Co Ltd (1861-1875)
	Birmingham Small Arms & Metal Co Ltd (1875-1919)
	BSA Guns Ltd (1919 - 1986)
Bullard	Bullard Repeating Arms Co, Springfield, Mass., USA . (1883 - 1890)
Burgsmuller	Hugo Burgsmuller & Sohn, Kreiensen, Germany. (ca 1880-1914)

MANUFACTURERS

C

Cadillac Gage	Cadillac Gage Corp, Warren, Mich., USA
Century	Century Arms, Evansville, Indiana, USA. (1976-85)
	Century Mfg Corp, Greenfield, Indiana, USA (1986-)
Century Int'l	Century International Arms, St Albans, Vermont, USA
Champlin	Champlin-Haskins Firearms Co, Enid, Oklahoma, USA (1966 - 1970)
	Champlin Firearms Inc, Enid, Oklahoma, USA (1971 -)
Charlier	Fabrique d'Armes Charlier et Cie, Liege, Belgium (pre-1914)
Charter Arms	Charter Arms Corp, Bridgeport, Conn., USA (1964-82); then at Stratford, Conn., 1982-
Chipmunk	Chipmunk Mfg Corp, Medford, Oregon, USA
Christ	Albert Christ, California, Ohio, USA
Churchill	E.J.Churchill Ltd, London, England (1892 -)
Classic	Classic Rifle Co., Charleroi, Penna., USA
Classic Arms	A division of Navy Arms (qv)
Clement	Charles Clement, Liege, Belgium. (1900-1914)
Cobray	Cobray Industries, Atlanta, Georgia, USA. Made semi-automatic copies of the Ingram M10 submachine gun
Cogswell	Cogswell & Harrison, London, England (1863-)
Colt	Colt's Patent Firearms Manufacturing Co, Hartford, Conn,, USA. (1847-1947)
	Colt's Manufacturing Co (1947-1955)
	Colt's Patent Firearms Manufacturing Co (1955-1964)
	Firearms Division of Colt Industries (1964 - 1989)
	Colt Manufacturing Corp (1990 -
Columbia	Columbia Armory, Columbia, Tenn., USA. A fictitious company invented for sales purposes by Maltby, Henley & Co of New York in the 1885-1900 period and marked on pistols made by the Norwich Falls Pistol Co.
Competition	Competition Arms, Tucson, Arizona, USA
Conn Arms	Connecticut Arms Co, Norwich, Conn., USA
Conn Mfg	(ca 1855-70) Connecticut Arms & Manufacturing Co, Naubuc, Conn., USA.
Coonan	Coonan Arms, St Paul, Minn., USA
Copeland	T.Copeland, Worcester, Mass.. USA
Cowles	Cowles & Son, Chicopee, Mass, USA
Cranston	Cranston Arms Co, Providence, Rhode Island, USA. A 'paper company' formed by Universal Windings Co of Providence to manufacture the Johnson automatic rifle in 1941 - 1942 since at that time the Johnson Automatics Co had no manufacturing capability. The factory was located in Cranston, a suburb of Providence.
Crescent Firearms	Crescent Firearms Co., Norwich, Conn., USA. (1892-?)
Crucelegui	Crucelegui Hermanos, Eibar, Spain (1900-1925)
Cummings	O.S.Cummings, Lowell, Mass., USA (ca 1866-1875)
	Cummings & Wheeler, Lowell, Mass., (ca 1875 - 1885)
CZ	Ceska Zbrojovka a.s., Prague, Czechoslovakia (1921-)

D

Daewoo	Daewoo Precision Industries, Pusan, South Korea
Daffini	Libero Daffini, Montini, Brescia, Italy
Daisy	Daisy Mfg Co., Rogers, Arkansas, USA
Dakin	Dakin Gun Co, San Francisco, Calif., USA. (1960s) Shotguns
Dakota	Dakota Arms Inc, Sturgis, SD, USA (1987 -)
Dan Wesson	Dan Wesson Arms, Monson, Mass., USA. (1968-
Dardick	Dardick Corp, Hamden, Conn., USA (1950-62)
Darne	Darne SA, St Etienne, France. (1881 - 1979)
Davenport	Davenport Firearms Co, Norwich, Conn., USA. (1880 - 1910)
Davis	Davis Industries, Chino, Calif., USA (1986-
Davis-Warner	Davis-Warner Corp, Assonet, Mass., USA (1917-1919)
Decker	Wilhelm Decker, Zella St Blasii, Germany (1910-1914)
Deringer	Deringer Rifle & Pistol Works, Philadelphia, Penna.,

	USA.
	Deringer Revolver & Pistol Co, Philadelphia, Penna., USA
Detonics	Detonics Associates, Seattle, Washington, USA (ca 1972 - 1988)
	Detonics Inc, Bellevue, Washington, USA (1988-
Deutsche Werke	Deutsche Werke AG, Erfurt, Germany. Manufactured the Ortgies pistol 1921-39.
Diana	Mayer & Grammelspacher, Rastatt, Germany. (1890-
Dickinson	E.L. & J. Dickinson, Springfield, Mass. USA (ca 1860-1885)
Dickson	John Dickson & Sons, Edinburgh, Scotland
Dornaus	Dornaus & Dixon, Huntingdon Beach, Calif., USA (1980-86)
Dornheim	G.C.Dornheim, Suhl, Germany. Marketed pistols made by other firms, also made an automatic pistol and rifles under their own name. Bought out by Albrecht Kind in 1940.
Doumoulin	Doumoulin et Fils, Liege, Belgium
Drulov	Dilo Svratouch, Litomysl, Czechoslovakia
DuBiel	DuBiel Arms Co, Sherman, Texas, USA (1975- 1990)
Dumoulin	Dumoulin Freres & Cie, Liege, Belgium
Dusek	Frantisek Dusek, Opocno, Czechoslovakia. From about 1926 until absorbed by CZ in about 1947.
DWM	Deutsche Waffen und Munitionsfabrik, Berlin (1897-1945)

E

Echave y Arizmendi	Echave y Arizmendi y Compania SA, Eibar, Spain. (1911-1979)
Echeverria	Bonifacio Echeverriia y Cia, Eibar, Spain. (1908-
Eiler	Eiler, Pecs, Hungary.
Em-Ge	Em-Ge Sportgerate GmbH & Co KG, Gerstenberger & Eberwein, Gerstetten-Gussenstadt, Germany (Formerly

	known as Moritz & Gerstenberger, from which came the Em-Ge trademark)
Encom	Encom-America Inc, Atlanta, Georgia, USA
Enfield	Royal Small Arms Factory, Enfield Lock, England 1854-1988, after which the operation was purchased by British Aerospace (Royal Ordnance) and transferred to the Royal Ordnance Factory, Nottingham, England.
Erma	Erma-Werke, B Giepel GmbH, Erfurt, Germany. (1919 - 1945)
	Erma-Werke GmbH, Munchen-Dachau, Germany (1949-)
Erquiaga	Erquiaga y Cia, Eibar, Spain (1915-19), then Erquiaga, Muguruzu y Cia, Eibar until ca 1935
Errasti	Antonio Errasti, Eibar, Spain (1904-1936)
Escodin	Manoel Escodin, Eibar, Spain. (ca 1920-1933)
Esprin	Esprin Hermanos, Eibar, Spain (1906 - 1917)
Evans	Evans Rifle Mfg Co, Mechanic Falls, Maine, USA (1871 - 1880)

F

Fabarm	Fabricca di Armi Brescia, Brescia, Italy
Fajen	Reinhart Fajen Mfg Co, Warsaw, Missouri, USA
Falcon	Falcon Firearms Mfg Corp, Granada Hills, Calif., USA. Made left-handed versions of the Colt M1911 pistol. (1986 -1989)
FAMAE	Fabrica de Material de Ejercito, Santiago, Chile. Previously known as Fabrica de Material de Guerra.
Farrow	Farrow Arms Co, Holyoke, Mass., USA. (1885 - 1900)
FAS	Fabbrica Armi Sportive Srl, Settimo Milanese, Italy. Took over the business of IGI (qv) in 1973.
FAVS	Fabbrica Armi Valle Susa, Vilaforchado, Turin, italy
Feather	Feather Industries Inc, Boulder, CO, USA. (1986 -)
Federal	Federal Engineering Corp, Chicago, Illinois, USA (1984 -)

MANUFACTURERS

Federal Ordnance	Federal Ordnance Inc, South El Monte, Calif., USA. (ca 1985 -)
FEG	see Fegyver, below
Fegyver	Fegyver es Gepgyar Reszvenytarsasag, Budapest, Hungary from ca 1880 to 1945; then became Femaru es Szersazamgepgyar NV until ca 1985 when it became the FEG Arms & Gas Appliances Factory.
Feinwerkbau	Feinwerkbau Westinger & Altenburger GmbH & Co KG, Oberndorf/Neckar, Germany. (1948-
Fiala	Fiala Arms & Equipment Co, New Haven, Conn., USA (1920 - 1923)
Firearms	Firearms Co, Ltd, Bridgewater. England
Firearms Int'l	Firearms International Corp, Washington, DC, USA (ca 1962-1974)
FN	Fabrique National de Armes de Guerre, Herstal, Liege, Belgium (1889-1945)
	Fabrique National SA , Herstal, Liege, Belgium. (1949-1990)
	It was then purchased by Giat (qv) and became FN Nouvelle Herstal SA, Liege, Belgium (1990-96). Giat got into financial difficulties and FN was repurchased by the Walloon local authorities, and became FN Herstal SA, Liege, Belgium (1996-)
Foehl & Weeks	Foehl & Weeks Firearms Mfg Co, Philadelphia, Penna., USA. Pistol manufacturer, 1890-1894.
Forehand	Forehand & Wadsworth, Worcester, Mass., USA (1871-1890)
	Forehand Arms Co, Worcester, Mass., USA (1890-1902 in which year the company was taken over by Hopkins & Allen)
Fox	Fox Gun Co, Philadelphia, Penna., USA. (1903 - 1930) when acquired by the Savage company, who continued making shotguns with the Fox name until 1942.)
Franchi	Luigi Franchi SpA, Fornaci, Brescia, Italy.
Francotte	August Francotte & Cie, Herstal, Belgium (1805-)
Franklin	C.W.Franklin, Liege, Belgium. (ca 1885 - 1914)
Franconia	Waffen-Franconia, Wurzburg, Germany
Fraser	Daniel Fraser & Co, Edinburgh, Scotland (ca 1871 - 1914)
Freedom	Freedom Arms, Freedom, Wyo, USA
Fyrberg	Andrew Fyrberg, Hopkinton, Mass., USA. Fl. 1880-1910, principally as a patentee of various firearms items which he licensed to other makers. He entered the pistol business under his own name between 1903 and 1910 producing the Fyrberg revolver.

G

Gabbett-Fairfax	Hugh Gabbett-Fairfax, Leamington Spa, England. Patentee of the 'Mars' automatic pistol 1895-1904
Gabilondo	Founded at Eibar, Spain, in 1904 as Gabilondos y Urresti; one of the Gabilondo brothers left in 1909 and it then became Gabilondo y Urresti until 1920 when the firm moved to Elgoeibar and became Gabilondo y Cia. In 1936 it changed its name to Llama-Gabilondo y Cia, and in 1940 moved to Vitoria.
Galand	Charles Francoise Galand, Liege Belgium. Ca. (1870-1914)
Galesi	Industria Armi Galesi, Collebeato, Brescia, Italy. Also known, at various times, as Armi Galesi; Rino Galesi; Soc Italiana Fili Galesi
Garate	Garate Hermanos, Eibar, Spain. ca (1910-1927)
Garate Anitua	Garate, Anitua y Cia, Eibar, Spain. (1900-1936)
Gasser	Leopold Gasser, Vienna, Austria. (1880-1914)
Gatling	Gatling |Arms & Ammunition Co, Birmingham, England. Formed in 1888 to market the Gatling machine gun in Europe and manufactured the Dimancea revolver until liquidated in 1890.
Gavage	Fabrique d'Armes de Guerre de Haute Precision

	Armand Gavage, Liege, Belgium (ca 1934-44)
Gaztanaga	Isidro Gaztanaga, Eibar, Spain 1904-1936, during which period he also traded as 'Gaztanaga, Trocaoloa y Ibarzabal' making and selling pistols.
Gehmann	Walter Gehmann, Karlsruhe, Germany
Genschow	Gustav Genschow AG, Hamburg, Germany. Primarily an ammunition company (Geco) now part of Dynamit Nobel, but prior to 1914 marketed pistols under the Geco name.
GIAT	Groupement Industriel des Armamentes Terrestres, Saint-Cloud, France. (1950-1990). During this period it was a government agency coordinating the activities of all French munition factories. In 1990 it was 'privatised' and became GIAT Industries, at the same address and doing the same job, but as a private industry it was able to purchase a number of munitions companies (eg FN, Matra, Manurhin) which would otherwise have gone to the wall.
Gibbs	George Gibbs, Bristol, England (ca 1900-1940)
Gibbs	Gibbs Rifle Co. Inc., Martinsburg, West Virginia, USA (1992- This company, a subsidiary of Navy Arms Co, acquired the rights to the Parker-Hale rifle designs and manufactures them under the Parker-Hale name.
Gibbs	Gibbs Guns Inc, Greenback, Tenn, USA. Made a semi-automatic copy of the Thomson submachine gun 1985-88.
Glaser	W. Glaser, Zurich, Switzerland (ca 1925 - 1950)
Glock	Glock GmbH, Deutsch-Wagram, Austria. (Began making pistols in 1982, but had been a manufacturer of knives and edged tools for several years prior.)
Golden Eagle	Golden Eagle Rifles Inc, Houston, Texas, USA. Marketed rifles under this name made by Nikko of Japan, 1976-1982.
Golden State	Golden State Arms Corp, Pasadena Calif., USA (1960s)
Goncz	Goncz Co., North Hollywood, Calif., USA (1985-90)
Grabner	Georg Grabner, Rehberg, Austria. Manufactured the Kolibri pistol 1914-1927
Grand Precision	Fabrique d'Armes de Guerre de Grand Precision, Eibar, Spain. A trading name registered by Extezagarra y Abitua, gunmakers of Eibar, as a sales agency for pistols of their own make and those made by other small concerns in Eibar, in the period 1918-36.
Great Western	Great Western Gun Works, Pittsburgh, Penna., USA
Green	Edwinson C Green, Cheltenham, England. Maker of pistols and sporting guns 1880-1982
Greener	W.W.Greener, Birmingham, England (1864 -)
Greifelt	Greifelt & Co, Suhl;, Germany
Grendel	Grendel Inc, Rockledge,. Florida, USA.
Griffin & Howe	Griffin & Howe, New York, NY, USA
Grunel	Grunig & Elmiger, Malters, Switzerland
Guide Lamp	Guide Lamp Division of General Motors, Detroit, Mich., USA. Made the Liberator single-shot pistol for three months in 1942.
Gunworks	Gunworks Ltd, Buffalo, NY, USA. Made a two-barrel Derringer pistol in 1985-86.

H

Haenel	C.G.Haenel Gewehr & Fahrradfabrik, Suhl, Germany. (1840-1945, after which it became one of the ~ founders of VEB)
Hafdasa	Hispano-Argentine Fabrica de Automobiles SA, Buenos Aires, Argentina.
Halger	Halbe & Gerlich (Halger-Waffenwerke) Kiel and Berlin, Germany. (ca 1923-1939)
Hammerli	Hammerli AG, Lenzburg, Switzerland (1863-)
Harrington & Richardson	Harrington & Richardson , Worcester, Mass., USA (1874-1975)
	Harrington & Richardson Inc, Gardner, Mass., USA

MANUFACTURERS

	(1975-1984)
Harris	Harris Gun Works, Phoenix, Ariz. USA. Took over the McMillan company in 1993 and continues to make the McMillan .50 heavy rifles under the Harris nane.
Hartford Arms	Hartford Arms & Equipment Co, Hartford, Conn., USA. Made a .22RF automatic pistol from 1929 to 1932, when they were liquidated and the remains taken over by the High Standard Company. Note that there was no connection between this firm and the earlier revolvers bearing the sales name Hartford Arms and made by the Norwich Pistol Company in the 1880s.
HDH	Henrion, Dassy & Heuschen, Liege, Belgim. (ca 1880 - 1914)
Hebsacker	Hege, Schwabisch Hall, Germany (1960-80)
Heckler & Koch	Heckler & Koch GmbH, Oberndorf/Neckar, Germany 1949- Purchased by British Aerospace in 1992
Heinzelmann	C.E.Heinzelmann, Plochingen, Germany (1930-1939)
Henry	Alexander Henry & Co, Edinburgh, Scotland
Heym	Friedrich Wilh. Heym GmbH & Co KG, Munnerstadt, Germany Founded 1865; located in Suhl until 1945.
Higgins	J.C.Higgins, Chicago, Illinois, USA. A fictitious company used as a sales name by Sears, Roebuck 1946 - 1952. The weapons (shotguns, rifles and revolvers) were made by various companies and were usually cheaper versions of their standard products.
High Standard	High Standard Inc, Hartford, Conn., USA. (1926-1985). Originally barrel-makers, they bought the remains of the Hartford Arms Co in 1932 and used their pistol design as a basis for their own developments.
Holland	Holland & Holland, London, England (1877-)
Holmes	Holmes Firearms, Wheeler, AR, USA Made semi-automatic pistol styled as submachine guns 1985 - 1986.

Hood	Hood Firearms Co, Norwich, Conn., USA (1873-1882)
Hopkins & Allen	Hopkins & Allen, Norwich, Conn., USA (1868-1917) when absorbed into the Marlin-Rockwell Corporation. A second company of this name,owing nothing to its forebearers, was formed in Hawthorne, New Jersey, in the early 1960s to make replica percussion pistols which it sold through the Numrich Arms Corporation, though there is some doubt whether 'Hopkins & Allen' actually made them.
Hourat	Hourat et Vie, Pau, France (1920-40)
Howa	Howa Industries, Aichi, Japan
Hunter (1)	Hunter Arms Co, Syracuse, NY, USA. Re-organised name for what had been the L.C.Smith Gun Co. (1890 - 1948 when it became a division of Marlin.)
Hunter (2)	Hy Hunter Firearms Mfg Co, Hollywood, Calif., USA. Actually an importer and wholesaler, dealing in the cheaper European pistols such as Rigarmi, Reck and Pyrenees, and having the Hunter name on them.
Husqvarna	Husqvarna Wapenfabrik, Huskvarna, Sweden

I

IGI	Italguns International, Zingone de Tressano, Italy. (1972-1985); acted as a sales agency for Fabbricca Armi Sportive, Settimo Milanese, Italy.
IMBEL	Industrias de Materials Belico do Brasil, Sao Paulo, Brazil
IMI	Israel Military Industries, Ramat Hasharon, Israel (1950-93, 1996-). It became Ta'as Israel Industries in 1993-96, but then reverted to the original name.
Inglis	John Inglis & Co, Toronto, Canada. Made the Browning High-Power pistol for China and Canada in 1944 - 1945.
Interarms	Interarms, Alexandria, Virginia, USA. ca 1965 -
Interdynamics	Interdynamics of America, Miami, FL, USA. Made semi-

automatic pistols styled as submachine guns 1981 - 1985. It had links with a company of the same name set up in Sweden in the late 1970s to promote an assault rifle firing a high-powered rimfire cartridge, and it is probable that the weapon designs sold in the USA originated in Sweden.

Intratec	Intratec Inc, Miami, FL, USA. Assumed the business of Interdynamics (above) 1985 - 1990.
Irving	William Irving, New York, NY, USA. (1863-70)
Ithaca	W.H.Baker & Co, Ithaca, NY, USA (1883 - 1889)
	Ithaca Gun Co, Ithaca, NY, (1889 - 1988)
	Ithaca Gun Co, Kingferry, NY. (1988 -)
ITM	Industrial Technology & Machines AG, Solothurn, Switzerland. 1984-1989 and then absorbed into Sphinx Engineering and its products known under the Sphinx name thereafter.

J

Jacquemart	Jules Jacquemart, Liege, Belgium. (1912 - 1914)
Jager	F.Jager & Co, Suhl, Germany (1907-1945)
Jager Armi	Jager-Armi di Armando Piscetta, Milan, Italy
Iver Johnson	Iver Johnson & Co, Worcester, Mass., USA 1883-1891;
	Iver Johnson Arms & Tool Co , Fitchburg, Mass., USA 1891-1982.
	Iver Johnson Arms Inc, Jacksonville, Ark., USA 1982-1986
	Became a division of American Arms Corp in 1987.
Jeffrey	W.J.Jeffrey, London, England (1888-1889)
	Jeffrey & Davis, London, England (1889 - 1891)
	W.J.Jeffrey & Co, London, England (1891-)
Jennings	Jennings Firearms Inc, Stateline, Nevada, USA (1981-
Johnson	Johnson Automatics Mfg Co, Cranston, Rhode Island, USA (1936 - 1944)
Johnson, Bye	Johnson, Bye & Co, Worcester, Mass., USA. Founded

1871 to manufacture cheap revolvers; in 1883 Bye sold his holding to Johnson who then re-organised the firm as Iver Johnson & Co (qv).

K

Kassnar	Kassnar Imports, Harrisburg, Penna., USA Distributes rifles made by Sabatti (qv).
Keberst	Keberst International, Paris, Kentucky, USA. (1987 - 1988)
Kessler	F.W.Kessler, Suhl, Germany. (pre-1914)
Kessler	Kessler Arms Corp, Silver Creek, NY,. USA. Shotguns, (1951 - 1953)
Kettner	Edward Kettner, Suhl, Germany. Made combination rifle/shotguns 1920 - 1939.
Kimball	Kimball Arms Co, Detroit, Mich., USA (1955-58)
Kimber	Kimber of Oregon Inc, Clackamas, Oregon, USA
Kind	Albrecht Kind AG, Nuremberg, Germany (1920-1945)
	Albrecht Kind AG, Hunstig, Germany (1950-)
Kodiak	Kodiak Mfg Co., North Haven, Conn., USA (ca 1959-1974)
Kohout	Kohout & Spolecnost, Kdyne, Czechoslovakia. (1927-1939)
Kolb	Henry M. Kolb, Philadephia, Penna., USA. (1892-1930)
Kommer	Theodor Kommer Waffenfabrik, Zella Mehlis, Germany. (1920-1939)
Korriphila	Korriphila Prazisionsmechanik GmbH, Ulm/Donau, Germany
Korth	Waffenfabrik W. Korth, Ratzeburg/Holstein, Germany
Kragujevac	Yugoslavian military arsenal set up by Fabrique National of Belgium in the early 1900s. Became known as Voini Techniki Zavod (Army Technical Factory) in the 1920s. More or less destroyed 1939-45, it was reconstituted as Crvena Zastava, and in 1990 changed its name to Zastava Arms.

MANUFACTURERS

Krauser — Alfred Krauser, Zella Mehlis, Germany (1920-31)

Krico — Krico GmbH, Stuttgart, Germany

Krieghoff — Heinrich Krieghoff Waffenfabrik, Suhl, Germany (pre-1945)
H. Krieghoff GmbH, Ulm/Donau, Germany (post-1945)

Kynoch — The Kynoch Gun Factory, Birmingham, England 1888-1890.
(The name is more usually associated with ammunition, but George Kynoch set up this pistol factory independently of his ammunition business in order to manufacture a pistol of his own design. He unfortunately died two years later and the factory was closed down.)

L

Lancaster — Charles Lancaster, London, England. Actually a trading name for Henry Thorn who had been Lancaster's apprentice, and under which name he produced various sporting weapons and pistols in the 1880-1900 period

Langenhan — Friedrich Langenhan, Zella Mehlis, Germany (1842 - 1936)

Laurona — Laurona SA, Eibar, Spain

LAR — LAR Manufacturing Inc, Jordan, Utah, USA

Lebeau — Lebeau-Courally, Liege, Belgium. (1910-)

Lecocq — Lecocq et Hoffmann, Liege, Belgium (? - 1940; 1955-70)

Lee Arms — Lee Arms Co, Wilkes Barre, Penna., USA (ca 1865-85)

Lefever — Lefever Arms Co, Syracuse, NY, USA. (1884 -1916, when acquired by Ithaca, who continued to make shotguns with the Lefever name until 1948.) The founder was forced out by a board-room revolution in 1901 and set up a separate firm D.M.Lefever, Sons & Co, also making shotguns, until his death in 1906, when the company folded.

Leigoise — Manufacture Liegoise d'Armes de Feu SA, Liege, Belgium

LePage — Manufacture d'Armes LePage SA, Liege, Belgium (ca 1780 - 1940)

Lignose — Lignose Pulverfabrik AG, Germany. Bought the Bergmann factory in 1921 and made Bergmann and other pistols under the Lignose name until 1939.

Ljutic — Ljutic Industries, Yakima, Washington, USA (1980-88)

Llama — Llama-Gabilondo y Cia SA, Vitoria, Spain (1936-. For earlier history see under 'Gabilondo)

Loewe — Ludwig Loewe & Co, Berlin, Germany. Founded in the 1850s as an engineering firm, began making rifles on contract, then licensed Smith & Wesson pistols for Russia and backed Borchardt and Luger in their automatic pistol designing. Amalgamated with a cartridge company in 1896 to become DWM (qv)

Lorcin — Lorcin Engineeering Co, Riverside, Calif., USA (1988-)

Lowell (1) — Lowell Arms Co, Lowell, Mass., USA. (Formerly the Rollin White company, formed 1864, closed 1868)

Lowell (2) — Lowell Arms Co, Lowell, Mass., USA. Marked on Phoenix pistols made by Robar and imported into the USA ca 1925 - 1933. May have been an import agency, or even a fictitious name. It is unlikely that it had any connection with Lowell (1)

Lower — John P.Lower, Philadelphia, Penna., USA. (Ca 1865-70)

M

Maadi — Maadi Military & Civil Industries Co, Cairo, Egypt

MAB — Manufacture d'Armes de Bayonne, Bayonne, France. (1921-1988.) A private company manufacturing automatic pistols.

MAC — Miitary Armaments Corp, Atlanta, Georgia, USA. Made

	the Ingram submachine gun ca 1976 - 1982
M.A.C.	Manufacture d'Armes Chatellerault, Chatellerault, France. State arms factory, particularly noted for machine guns.
McMillan	McMillan Gun Works Inc, Phoenix, Arizona, USA. Was taken over in 1993 and became the Harris Gun Works.
Madsen	Dansk Industrie Syndikat AS 'Madsen', Copenhagen, Denmark. Now known as DISA Systems, and no longer in the firearms business.
M.A.S.	Manufacture d'Armes de Ste Etienne, St. Etienne, France. State arms factory; rifles, submachine guns, pistols.
Manhattan	Manhattan Firearms Co, New York, NY, USA. (1850-65)
Mann	Fritz Mann Werkzeugfabrik, Suhl, Germany. (1919 - 1929)
Manufrance	Manufacture Francaise d'Armes et Cycles de Saint Etienne, St Etienne, France. Later (post-1945) adopted the name Manufrance SA
Manurhin	Manufacture de Machines du Haut-Rhin, Mulhouse-Bourtzwiler, France. Began firearms manufacture in the early 1950s. Later changed its name to 'Manurhin' and later to 'Manurhin Defense' until taken over by GIAT in 1990. It still retains its own identity within the GIAT organisation and markets arms under the Manurhin name. Also a major producer of ammunition-making machinery.
Marathon	Marathon Products, Weathersfield, Conn., USA (1984-88)
Marble	Marble Manufacturing Co, Gladstone, Mich., USA. Made the 'Marble Game Getter' a combination rifle/shotgun from about 1907 to 1929.
Marlin	John M.Marlin, New Haven, Conn., USA (1865-1881) Marlin Firearms Co, New Haven, Conn., USA. (1881- 1969) Marlin Firearms Co, North Haven, Conn., USA (1969 -)
Marston	W.W.Marston & Co, New York, NY, USA. (1850 - 1874)
Marston & Knox	Fictitious sales name used by W.W.Marston
Mateba	Macchine Termo Ballistiche, Pavia, Italy. (ca 1980-1987). Manufactured the Mateba revolver.
Mauser	Gebruder Mauser, Oberndorf/Neckar, Germany (1872-74) Gebruder Mauser & Co (1874-1884) Waffenfabrik Mauser (1884-1922) Mauserwerke AG (1922-45) Mauserwerke Oberndorf AG (1950-
Maverick	Maverick Arms Co, Eagle Pass, Texas, USA. (1989 -)
Mayor	E & F Mayor, Lausanne, Switzerland
MBA	MB Associates, San Ramon, Calif., USA. 1960-70. Made the 'Gyrojet' pistol/rifle rocket launchers,
Menz	Waffenfabrik August Menz, Suhl, Germany. 1914-1937
Meriden	Meriden Firearms Co, Meriden, Conn., USA 1895-1915. Sold revolvers under their own name and also supplied them to Sears, Roebuck.
Merkel	Gebruder Merkel & Co, Suhl, Germany (1781-1945) It was then, like all East German gunsmiths, absorbed into the state-run VEB organisation but continued to produce guns for export under the Merkel name.
Merrill	The Merrill Co, Fullerton, Calif., USA.
Merwin, Hulbert	Merwin and Bray, New York, NY, USA (1853-64) Merwin, Taylor & Simson, New York (1864-1868) Merwin, Hulbert & Co, New York (1868-1892) Hulbert Brothers, New York (1892-1896) This company acted as an agency for various revolver makers, notably Hopkins & Allen, and owned a number of patents which were worked by various firms. Hopkins & Allen produced revolvers bearing the Merwin, Hulbert name.
Miroku	Miroku Firearms Co KK, Kochi City, Shikoku, Japan 1965-
Mitchell	Mitchell Arms Inc, Santa Ana, Calif., USA
MKEK	Makina ve Kimya Endustrisi Kurumu, Ankara, Turkey.

MANUFACTURERS

Makers of the Kirrikale pistol and various licensed
Heckler & Koch weapons.

MOA	MOA Corp., Dayton, Ohio,USA
Mondial	MM-Mondial, Modesto Molgora, Milan, Italy.
Moore	Moore's Patent Firearms Co, Brooklyn, NY, USA. 1860-1865, when taken over by the National Arms Co.
Morini	Morini Competition, Lamone, Switzerland
Moritz	Heinrich Moritz, Zella-Mehlis, Germany (1920s)
Mossberg	O.F.Mossberg & Sons, New Haven, Conn., USA
Muller	Muller & Greiss, Munich, Germany. (? - 1914)
Musgrave	Musgrave (Pty), Bloemfontein, South Africa. Originally an independent company founded by Musgrave, after his death it became part of the Armscor organisation. Manufactures hunting rifles; ammunition bearing their name is made by PMP.

N

Nagant	Emile Nagant, Liege, Belgium (?-1910) Fabrique d'Armes Leon Nagant, Liege, Belgium (?-1910) Fabrique d'Armes et Automobiles Nagant Freres, Liege, Belgium (1910-1914)
National	National Arms Co, Brooklyn, NY, USA. 1865-1870, when bought out by Colt.
Navy Arms	Navy Arms Co, Ridgefield, New Jersey, USA. (1957-)
New England	New England Firearms Co, Gardner, Mass., USA. Founded 1988 out of the remains of Harrington & Richardson.
Newton	Newton Arms Co, Buffalo, NY, USA (1914-18) Charles Newton Rifle Corp, Buffalo, NY. (1921-22) Buffalo-Newton Rifle Co, Buffalo, NY (1923-24) Buffalo-Newton Rifle Co, Springfield, Mass, (1924-1929) Lever-Bolt Rifle Co, New Haven, CT (1929-32)
Nikko	Nikko Firearms Mfg Co, Tochigi, Japan

Noble	Noble Firearms Co, Haydenville, Mass., USA (1950 - 1971)
Norarmco	North Armament Co, Mount Clemens, Mich., USA. (1972-1977)
Norinco	Noth China Industries Corporation, Pekin, China. Sales organisation for the Chinese national munitions factories.
North American (1)	North American Arms Co, Quebec, Canada (1917-20). Set up for wartime production of various weapoins, notable for producing a small number of Colt .45 auto pistols on contract.
North American (2)	North American Arms Corp, Toronto, Canada (1948-52) (There is no connection between these two companies) This firm appears to have been set up solely to promote the 'Brigadier' pistol, an enlarged Browning 1935 chambered for a special .45 NAACO cartridge. It failed.
North American (3)	North American Arms, Spanish Fork, Utah, USA. (1975 -)
Norton	Norton Arms Co, Mount Clemens, Mich., USA. Manufactured the Budischowsky pistol 1977 - 1979.
Norwich Falls	Norwich Pistol Co, Norwich, Conn.,USA (1875-1881); Norwich Falls Pistol Co, Norwich Falls, Conn., USA (1881-1887)

O

O.D.I.	O.D.Inc, Midland Park, New Jersey, USA. (1981 - 1982)
Ojanguren	Ojanguren y Marcaido, Eibar, Spain. 1895-1930, when it was liquidated and revived as Ojanguren y Vidosa, surviving until 1936.
Olympic	Olympic Arms Inc, Olympia, Washington, USA
Omega	Omega Firearms Co, Flower Mound, Texas, USA (1968 - 1975)
Orbea	Orbea Hermanos, Eibar, Spain. (ca 1860-1936)

Ortgies	Heinrich Ortgies & Co, Erfurt, Germany. (1919-21, when he was bought out by Deutsche Werke.)
Osgood	Osgood Gun Works, Norwich, Conn., USA. (ca 1878-1882)
Osterreich	Osterreichische Werke Anstalt, Vienna, Austria (1920-25)

P

PAF	Pretoria Arms Factory, Pretoria, South Africa. (1960-70)
Page-Lewis	Page-Lewis Arms Co, Chicopee Falls, Mass., USA. (1920 - 1926 when bought out by Stevens Arms Co)
Para-Ordnance	Para-Ordnance Mfg. Inc, Scarborough, Ontario, Canada. Makes conversions and kits for M1911 type pistols. (1989 -)
Pardini	Fiocchi SpA, Lecco, Italy
Parker	Parker Bros, Meriden, Conn., USA. Shotguns. (1868 - 1934, when bought out by Remington)
Parker-Hale	Parker Hale Ltd, Birmingham, England. (1880-1992) In 1992 the rights and patents to Parker-Hale rifles were sold to the Gibbs Rifle Co (qv) who then began making rifles under the Parker-Hale name.
Pedersen	Pederson Custom Guns, North Haven, Conn., USA. This was a division of Mossberg which produced higher-quality versions of Mossberg shotguns from 1975 to 1977.
Pedersoli	Armi D.Pedersoli, Gardone Val Trompia, Brescia, Italy.
Perrazi	Perazzi, Brescia, Italy. Shotguns
Perugini	Perugini-Visoli & Co, Nuovolera, Brescia, Italy. Shotguns
Peters-Stahl	PSW Vertriebsgesellschaft mbH, Aachen, Germany
Pfannl	F. Pfannl, Krems, Austria (1912-1936)
Phelps	E.F.Phelps Mfg Co, Evansville, Indiana, USA
Phoenix	Phoenix Arms Co; fictitious sales name used by W.W.Marston

Pickert	Friedrich Pickert Arminius Waffenwerk, Zella Mehlis, Germany (1900-1939)
Pieper	Henri & Nicolas Pieper, Herstal, Belgium 1866-1905. Then became Ancien Etablissments Pieper until about 1955.
Pietta	Fabricca d'Armi Filli Pietta di Giuseppe & Co, Gussago, Italy
Pilsen	Zbrojovka Plzen, Plzen, Czechoslovakia. An offshoot of the Skoda company, set up in the 1920s to manufacture pistols and probably closed down in 1938.
Pirandelli	Pirandelli & Gasparini, Brescia, Italy. Shotguns
Plainfield (1)	Plainfield Machine Co, Dunellen, New Jersey, USA. Made reproduction M1 carbines ca 1963 until 1975 when bought out by Iver Johnson.
Plainfield (2)	Plainfield Ordnance Co, Middlesex, New Jersey, USA. Made .22 and .25 pistols in the 1970-80 period, Their relationship to Plainfield (1) is unclear.
Pond	Lucius W. Pond, Worcester, Mass., USA
Powell	William Powell & Son, Birmingham, England (1822 -)
Praga	Praga Zbojovka, Prague, Czechoslovakia. (1918-1926)
Prescott	E.A.Prescott, Worcester, Mass., USA. (1860s)
Pretoria	Pretoria Small Arms Factory, Pretoria, South Africa. (ca 1955-1960)
Protector	Protector Arms Co, Philadelphia, Penna.,USA. An off-shoot of the Rupertus company in the 1870s.
Providence	Providence Tool Co, Providence, Rhode Island, USA
PSMG	P.S.M.G. Gun Co, Arlington, Mass., USA. (1988 -)
Purdey	James Purdey & Sons Ltd, London, England
Pyrenees	Manufacture d'Armes des Pyrenees Francaise, Hendaye, France. (1923-) Principally known for the 'Unique' range of pistols.

Q

Quackenbush	O. Quackenbush, Herkimer, NY, USA. (ca1880 - 1910)

MANUFACTURERS

R

Radom	Fabrika Brony w Radomu, Radom, Poland.
Rahn	Rahn Gun Works, Grand Rapids, Mich., USA
Raick	Raick Freres, Liege, Belgium.
Raven	Raven Arms, Industry, Calif., USA (ca 1976 -)
Reck	Reck Division, Umarex-Sportwaffen GmbH & Co KG, Arnsberg i Neheim-Husten, Germany.
Reid	James Reid, New York, NY, USA. Rimfire revolvers ca 1862 - 1890)
Reising	Reising Arms Co, Hartford, Conn., USA. (1916 - 1924) Made a .22 pistol. Note that there is no connection between this firm and the Reising automatic weapons made during World War Two other than the name; Reising designed these weapons but they were made by Harrington & Richardson.
Remington	Eli Remington & Son, Ilion, NY, USA. (1816-1886) Remington Arms Co, Bridgeport, Conn., USA (1886-)
Renato Gamba	Armi Renato Gamba SA, Gardone Val Trompia, Italy Re-organised in the late 1980s and became SAB (qv)
Retolaza	Retolaza Hermanos, Eibar, Spain. (1895-1936)
Reunies	Soc. Anonyme des Fabriques d'Armes Reunies, Liege, Belgium. (1909-1918) Fabrique d'Armes Unies, Liege, Belgium (1918-1931)
Reynolds	Reynoilds, Plant & Hotchkiss, New Haven, Conn., USA (ca 1863-1870)
Rheinmetall	Rheinische Metallwaren und Maschinenfabrik, Sommerda, Germany. Began as an engineering firm in 1889, purchased the Waffenfabrik von Dreyse in 1901 and thereafter used the Dreyse name on pistols and machine guns. Amalgamated with Borsig AG in 1936 to become Rheinmetall-Borsig, re-organised after 1945 to become Rheinmetall AG. Still extant but not in the small arms business.
Rhode Island	Rhode Island Arms Co, Hope Valley, Rhode Island, USA. Shotguns, 1949 - 1953.
Richland	Richland Arms, Blissfield, Mich., USA. American importer and distributor of Spanish shotguns of various makes.
Rigarmi	Rigarmi di Rino Galesi, Brescia, Italy. (1951-)
Rigby	John Rigby & Co, London, England (1867-)
Robar	Robar & DeKerkhove, Liege, Belgium (ca 1890 - 1927) L Robar & Cie Liege (1927-1948) Manufacture Leigoise d'Armes a Feu Robar et Cie, Liege 1948-1958)
Rocky Mountain	Rocky Mountain Arms Corp, Salt Lake City, Utah, USA
Rohm	Rohm GmbH, Sontheim a.d. Brenz, Germany.
Rome	Rome Revolver & Novelty Works, Rome, NY, USA.
Romer	Romerwerke AG, Suhl, Germany. 1924-1927
Ronge	J.B.Ronge et Fils, Liege, Belgium. 1880-1914
Roper	Roper Repeating Rifle Co, Amherst, Mass., USA. (ca 1870)
Ross	Ross Rifle Co, Quebec, Canada (ca 1900 - 1917)
Rossi	Amadeo Rossi SA, Sao Leopoldo, Brazil (1881-
RPM	R & R Sporting Arms, La Brea, Calif., USA
Ruby	Ruby Arms Co, Eibar, Spain. Fictitious company, marked on Ruby pistols made by Gabilondo.
Ruger	Sturm, Ruger & Co Inc, Southport, Conn., USA (1949-)
Rupertus	Rupertus Patent Pistol Mfg Co, Philadelphia, Penna., USA.
Ryan	Thomas E.Ryan, Norwich, Conn., USA

S

SAB	Societe Armi Bresciana, Gardone Val Trompia, Italy
Sabatti	Fab. d'Armi Sabatti SpA, Gardone Val Trompia, Italy
SACM	Societe Alsacienne de Constructions Mecaniques, Cholet, France (1930-40)
Safari	Safari Arms, Phoenix, Arizona, USA. Pistols. (1978 - 1987, when bought out by Olympic Arms.)
S.A.G.E.M.	Societe d'Applications Generales Electriques et

	Mecaniques, Mulhouse (?) France (ca 1930-1940)
St Etienne	Manufacture Nationale d'Armes de Saint Etienne, St Etienne, France.
St Etienne Automatique	Manufacture d'Armes Automatiques, St Etienne, France
St Louis	St Louis Arms Co. Fictitious name adopted by American importer of Belgian shotguns . (ca 1895 - 1910)
Sako	Oy Sako AB, Riihimaki, Finland
San Marco	Armi San Marco di Ruffoli, Brescia, Italy
San Paolo	Armi San Paolo, San Paolo, Italy
Santa Barbara	Empresa Nacional de Industrias Militares 'Santa Barbara', La Coruna and Madrid, Spain. Spanish government arsenal which also makes sporting rifle actions and barrels
Sarasqueta	Victor Sarasquete, Eibar, Spain. Shotguns.
Sauer	J.P.Sauer & Sohn GmbH, Suhl, Germany (1733-1945) J.P.Sauer & Sohn GmbH, Eckernforde, Germany (1945-)
Savage	Savage Repeating Arms Co, Utica, NY, USA (1893-1970) Savage Arms Corp, Westfield, Mass., USA (1970-)
Schilling	V.Chr. Schilling, Suhl, Germany. (ca 1860-1934)
Schmidt	Herbert Schmidt, Ostheim-a-d-Rhon, Germany. (1955-)
Schmidt & H	Schmidt & Habermann, Suhl, Germany.
Schuler	Waffenfabrik August Schuler, Suhl, Germany. (? - 1939)
Schutz	Schutz & Larsen, Otterup, Denmark. Sporting rifles. Were active in developing taper-bore weapons in the 1930s.
Schwarzlose	Andreas W.Schwarzlose GmbH, Berlin, Germany (1893-1919)
S.E.A.M.	Fabrica d'Armes de Sociedade Espanol de Armas y Municiones, Eibar, Spain. (ca 1910-1936). Principally a marketing organisation for Urizar and other makers.
Sears	Sears, Roebuck Co. American mail order store; sold all types of firearms under various brand names and also

	had a revolver factory in Meriden, Conn., USA until some time in the 1930s.
Security	Security Industries, Little Ferry, New Jersey, USA. (1973 - 1978)
Sedgley	R.F.Sedgley Inc, Philadephia, Penna., USA. Successors to H.M.Kolb. (1930 - 1938)
Seecamp	L.W.Seecamp Inc, New Haven, Conn., USA (1980-)
Semmerling	Semmerling Corp, Newton, Mass., USA
Sempert	Sempert & Krieghoff, Suhl, Germany. (? - 1924, when merged with Krieghoff)
Sharps	Christian Sharps & Co, Philadelphia, Penna., USA (1850-1874)
	Sharps Rifle Mfg Co, Hartford, Conn., USA (1874 -)
Shattuck	C.S.Shattuck, Hatfield, Mass., USA. (1880 - ca 1892)
Sheridan	Sheridan Products, Racine, Wisconsin, USA. Principally air and pneumatic guns, but made a .22 SS pistol 1953 - 1960
Shilen	Shilen Arms, Ennis, Texas, USA. (1961-)
Shiloh	Shiloh Products, Farmingdale, NY, USA. (1976-83)
	Shiloh Rifle Mfg Co, Big Timber, Montana, USA. (1983-)
Shin Chuo Kogyo	Shin Chuo Kogyo K.K., Tokyo, Japan. (1956-)
SIG	Schweizerische Industrie Gesellschaft, Neuhausen/Rheinfalls, Switzerland. (1853-)
Simson	Waffenfabrik Simson & Co, Suhl, Germany (ca 1860 - 1945)
Sirkis	Sirkis Industries, Ramat Gan, Israel.
S.J & D	Simonis, Janssen et Doumoulin, Liege. (1880-1900)
SKB	S.K.B. Arms, Tokyo, Japan. Manufacturers of shotguns since ca 1885, and produce shotguns for various companies which claim to manufacture them. They also sell under their own name, but their products for others are hard to identify.
Slough	John Slough of London, Hereford, England (1975 -)
Smith (1)	Otis A Smith, Rock Falls, Conn., USA (1873-1898)
Smith (2)	L.C.Smith Gun Co, Syracuse, NY, USA. (1877 - 1890,

MANUFACTURERS

	when it became the Hunter Gun Co.) Major US shotgun maker, but equally famous for typewriters..
Smith & Wesson	Smith & Wesson, Springfield, Mass., USA. (1852-)
Soc. Franc. d'Armes	Societe Francaise d'Armes Automatiques de St Etienne
Sodia	Franz Sodia, Ferlach, Austria
Sokolovsky	Sokolovsky Corp, Sunnyvale, Calif., USA. (1984-89)
Spirlet	A. Spirlet, Liege, Belgium (ca 1865-1900. Spirlet was principally a designer and patentee who licensed his ideas to other makers)
Sporting	Sporting Arms Mfg Co, Little Field, Texas, USA.
Sprague	Sprague and Marston; fictitious sales name used by W.W.Marston.
Springfield	Springfield Armory Inc, Genesee, Illinois,USA (1975-1994)
	Springfield Inc, Genesee, Illinois,USA (1994-)
Squibman	Squires Bingham Mfg Co Inc, Manila, Philippine Rep
Stafford	T.J.Stafford, New Haven, Conn., USA (ca 1875-90)
Standard	Standard Arms Co, Wilmington, Delaware, USA (1906 - 1912)
Starr	Starr Arms Co, Yonkers, NY, USA (1860-1875)
Steel City	Steel City Arms Inc., Pittsburg, Penna., USA (1984 -)
Stenda	Stendawerke Waffenfabrik GmbH, Suhl, Germany (ca 1910-1926)
Sterling (UK)	Sterling Armaments Co, Dagenham England (1940-1988)
Sterling (USA)	Sterling Arms Corp, Gasport, NY, USA (1953-64)
	Sterling Arms Corp, Lockport, NY, USA (1964 - 1986)
Stevens Tool	J.Stevens & Co, Chicopee Falls, Mass., USA (1854-1888)
	J. Stevens Arms & Tool Co, Chicopee Falls, Mass. (1888-1920, when taken over by the Savage Arms Co.)
Steyr	Josef Werndl, Steyr, Austria (1863-69)
	Osterreichische Waffenfabrik Gesellschaft GmbH, Steyr, Austria (1869-1919)
	Steyr-Werke AG (1919-1934)
	Steyr-Daimler-Puch, Steyr, Austria (1934-1990)
	Steyr-Mannnlicher GmbH, Steyr, Austria (1990-)

	(A subsidiary company, Steyr-Solothurn AG, existed 1934-45 as a marketing organisation for military weapons made by Steyr, Rheinmetall and Solothurn AG)
Stiga	Stiga AB, Tranas, Sweden
Stock	Franz Stock Maschinen und Werkbaufabrik, Berlin, Germany.(1915-1938)
Stoeger	Stoeger Arms Corp, South Hackensack, New Jersey, USA (1920-76)
	Stoeger Industries, South Hackensack, New Jersey, USA (1976-86)
Sundance	Sundance Industries Inc, North Hollywood, Calif., USA.
Super Six	Super Six Industries, Elkhorn, Wisconsin, USA
Swift	Swift Rifle Co, London, England
Swing	Swing Target Rifles, Newcastleton, Roxburgh, Scotland.

T

Ta'as	Israel Military Industries, Ramat Hasharon, Israel (1950-93) became Ta'as Israel Industries in 1993-96, after which it reverted to the original name.
Tanfoglio	Sabotti & Tanfoglio, Gardone Val Trompia, Brescia, Italy (1935- 1958)
	Fabbrica d'Armi Giuseppe Tanfoglio, Gardone Val Brescia, Italy. (1958-)
Trompia,	
Tanner	Andre Tanner, Fulenbach, Switzerland. (1955-)
Taurus	Forjas Taurus SA, Porto Alegre, Brazil
Taylor	L.B.Taylor & Co, Chicopee, Mass., USA (1860 - 1875)
Texas	Texas Longhorn Arms Inc, Richmond, Texas, USA (1984 -)
Thames	Thames Arms Co, Norwich, Conn., USA (ca 1870 - 1910. May have been a marketing subsidiary of the Meriden Arms Corp.)
Thayer	Thayer, Robertson & Cary, Norwich, Conn., USA (1890-1914)
Thieme & Edeler	Thieme & Edeler, Eibar, Spain (1914-16)

Thompson/Center	Thompson/Center Arms, Rochester, NH, USA (1962-)
Tipping & Lawden	Caleb & Thomas Tipping Lawden, Birmingham, England (ca 1845-1877, when sold to P.Webley & Son)
Tikka	Oy Tikkakoski AB, Tikkakoski, Finland (1893-
Tomas de Urizar	Tomas de Urizar y Cia, Eibar, Spain. (1903-1921. Appear to have been absorbed by Garate Anitua y Cia.)
Tomiska	Alois Tomiska, Pilsen, Bohemia (1902-1919)
Triple-S	Triple-S Development Co Inc, Wickliffe, Ohio,USA (1976-1981)
Trocaola	Trocaoloa, Aranzabal y Cia, Eibar, Spain (1903-1936)
Tulskii	Tulskii Oruzhenyi Zavod, Tula, Russia

U

Uberti	Aldo Uberti, Ponte Zanano, (Brescia), Italy. (1959-)
Ultra-Light	Ultra-Light Arms Inc, Granville, West Virginia,USA
Unceta	see 'Astra-Unceta'
Union	Union Firearms Co, Toledo, Ohio,USA. ca 1900-1919
Union Arms	Union Arms Co, New York, NY, USA (ca1863-70) Possibly a sales name used by W.W.Marston
Union, Eibar	Union des Fabricants d'Armes, Eibar, Spain (fl 1911-14)
United States	United States Arms. Ficitious company name used by Otis A. Smith on a .44 revolver in the 1870s
Universal	Universal Sporting Goods, Hialeah, FL, USA. Made reproduction M1 carbines from 1962 to 1983, when taken over by Iver Johnson.
U.S.Arms (1)	U.S.Arms Co, New York, NY, USA. (ca 1870-90)
U.S.Arms (2)	U.S.Arms Co, Riverhead, NY, USA. (1976 - 1983)

V

Valmet	Valmet AB, Jyvaskyla, Finland. Taken over by Sako in 1992.
Varner	Varner Sporting Arms, Marietta, Georgia, USA
VEB	VEB Fahrzeug- und Jagdwaffenfabrik Ernst Thalmann,

	Suhl, (East) Germany. (1945-1989).
Venus	Venus Waffenwerke Oskar Will, Zella Mehlis, Germany. Ca 1900-1918
Verney-Carron	Manufacture d'Armes Verney-Carron et Cie, St Etienne, France
Vickers	Vickers Ltd, Crayford, Kent, England. (1919-39)
Victory	Victory Arms, Northampton, England. (1988- 1992)
Voere	Voetter & Co, Schwarzwald, Germany. (1950 - 1977) Tiroler Jagd- und Sport-waffenfabrik, Kufstein, Austria (1978-1987) Mauserwerke, Oberndorf/Neckar, Germany (1988-) who now make the Voere rifles under the Mauser name.
Voetter	Voetter & Co, Vohrenbach, Germany
Voini Techniki Zavod	see Kragujevac
Vom Hofe	Vom Hofe & Scheinemann,. Berlin, Germany (1927-1945) The name was adopted by Gehmann of Karlsruhe (qv) in 1955

W

Wahl	Albin Wahl, Zella Mehlis, Thuringia, Germany (Pre 1914)
Walther	Carl Walther Waffenfabrik, Zella Mehlis, Germany (1886-1945). Then re-organised in Ulm.a.d.Donau in 1950 and now known as Carl Walther Waffenfabrik, Postfach 4325, D-7900 Ulm/Donau, Germany.
Warnant	L & J Warnant Freres, Hognee, Belgium. 1870-1914
Warner	Warner Arms Corp, Brooklyn NY and Norwich Mass., USA Set up in 1912, merged to become the Davis-Warner Corp in 1917, liquidated 1919. Marketed the Schwarzlose 1908 automatic in the USA under their own name, then manufactured pistols for a short time.
Washington	Washington Arms Co; fictitious sales name used by W.W.Marston
Weatherby	Weatherby Inc, South Gate, Calif., USA (1949 -)
Weaver	Weaver Arms, Escondido, Calif., USA (1983 - 1990)

MANUFACTURERS

Webley Originated as Philip Webley in 1845; became P Webley & Son (1860-1897); The Webley & Scott Revolver & Arms Company (1897-1906) and finally Webley & Scott Ltd (1906 -.) all of Birmingham, England. In 1958 the company was acquired by R.H.Windsor Ltd; in 1959 the Windsor group was taken over by Arusha Industries, who later became General & Engineering Industries Ltd. In 1965 this company acquired W.W.Greener, and in 1973 sold Greener and Webley & Scott to the Harris & Sheldon Group. In 1980 firearms production ceased; the shotgun business was re-established as W&C Scott, and subsequently sold to Holland & Holland, and the revolver designs and tooling were sold to Pakistan in 1983. The Harris & Sheldon group still manufacture air rifles and pistols under the Webley name.

Weihrauch Herman Weihrauch Waffenfabrik, Mellrichstadt, Germany Founded in 1899 in Zella St Blasii, dissolved in 1945 and re-constituted in Mellrichstadt, West Germany in 1948 making airguns. It adopted the 'Arminius' trade-name formerly associated with Pickert (qv) and began making firearms again in the 1960s.

Wesson Frank Wesson, Worcester, Mass., USA. (1854 - 1865) Frank Wesson, Springfield, Mass., USA (1865 - 1875) Co-existed with Wesson & Harrington but specialised in rifles and single-shot and double-barrelled pistols, while W&H made revolvers.

Wesson & Harrington Wesson & Harrington, Worcester, Mass., USA (ca 1868-1875)

Western Arms Western Arms Co; fictitious sales name used by W.W.Marston.

Western Field Sales name used by the Montgomery Ward mail-order company in the USA for rifles and shotguns made by various manufacturers on contract.

Westley Richards Westley Richards & Co, London, England. (1850 -)

White Rollin White, Lowell, Mass., USA. (ca 1860 - 1864, when the name changed to Lowell Arms)

Whitney Whitney Firearms Co Inc, New Haven, Conn., USA. (1954-1965)

Whitneyville Whitney Arms Co, Whitneyville, Conn., USA. ca 1840-1888, when bought out by Winchester.

Wichita Wichita Arms, Wichita, Kansas, USA (1977 -)

Wiener Wiener Waffenfabrik, Vienna, Austria. Made the 'Little Tom' pistol 1919 - 1925, having purchased the patents of Tomiska.

Wildey Wildey Firearms Co Inc, PO Box 447, Cheshire, Conn., USA. 1972-

Wilkinson (1) Wilkinson Sword Co, London, England. Had revolvers made for them by Webley, 1885-1914.

Wilkinson (2) Wilkinson Arms, Parma, Indiana, USA

Wilkinson Arms US importer's sales name for Belgian-made shotguns

Winchester Winchester Arms Co, New Haven, Conn., USA. (1866-1977) US Repeating Arms Co, New Haven, Conn., USA (1978-

Winkler Benedikt Winkler, Ferlach, Austria

Winslow Winslow Arms Co, Camden, SC, USA (1962-1989)

Wurflein William Wurflein, Phiadelphia, Penna., USA. (ca 1852-1884)

Wurthrich W.Wurthrich, Lutzelfluh, Switzerland

Z

Zanotti Fabio Zanotti, Brescia, Italy. Shotguns

Zastava Arms Post 1990 name for Kragujevac arsenal and its successors; see under 'Kragujevac'.

Zbrojovka Brno Ceskoslovenska Zbrojovka, Brno, Czech Republic. (1919-)

Zehner E. Zehner Waffenfabrik, Suhl, Germany. (ca1921-1927)

Zoli Antonio Zoli SpA, Gardone Val Trompia, Brescia, Italy

Zulaica M. Zulaica y Cia, Eibar, Spain. (1902-1936)

BRAND NAMES

Explanatory Notes:

Scope: This covers as many brand names as can be discovered from the beginning of the metallic cartridge era. Percussion pistols and peculiar cartridge weapons are not considered here, since we are primarily concerned with weapons which are likely to be used today, and for which ammunition is available. Age does not come into this: a .22 pistol made in 1870 can be as effective a weapon as a .22 pistol made in 1995.

Name: Brand names given here are those actually marked on weapons; names identifying catalogue variations or purely for factory record purposes are not given. Weapons named for their maker will be identified from the List of Manufacturers

Type: Rev - revolver; Pistol - semi-automatic pistol; RP - repeating pistol or multi-barrelled pistol; MP - machine (automatic) pistol; MG - machine gun; SMG - submachine gun; SS - single shot pistol; Shotg - shotgun

Calibre: Most are obvious. Oblique strokes indicate alternative calibres. Suffixes:- RF rimfire; P Parabellum; S Short; B-B Bergmann-Bayard. `Various' indicates the full range of calibres usually to be found in that class, eg 10,12,16,20,28 bore for shotguns.

Maker: This is the 'short title'; the full name, location and other information will be found in the List of Manufacturers.
Where the maker is not positively known, the country of origin or probable maker is shown in [square brackets]

Name	Type	Calibre	Maker
AAA	Pistol	6.35/7.65	Aldazabal
ABILENE	Rev	357	Mossberg
ABILENE	Rev	357/44	US Arms (2)
ACE	Pistol	22	Colt
ACME ARMS	Rev	22/32	J. Stevens
ACME HAMMERLESS	Rev	32	Hopkins & Allen
ACRA	Rifle	Various	R. Fajen
ACTION	Pistol	6.35/7.65	Modesto Santos
ADLER	Pistol	7.65	Engelbrecht & Wolff
AETNA	Rev	22/32	Harrington & Richardson
AG	Pistol	7.65	Gavage
AJAX ARMY	Rev	44RF	Meacham
AKAH	Rifle`	Various	Kind
ALAMO	Rev	22	Stoeger
ALASKA	Rev	22	Hood
ALASKAN	Rifle	Various	Skinner's
ALASKAN MARK X	Rifle	Various	Zastava
ALERT	Rev	22	Hood
ALEXIA	Rev	32/38/41RF	Hopkins & Allen
ALEXIS	Rev	22	Hood
ALFA	Rev	38	Armero Especialistas
ALFA	All types	Various	Adolf Frank
ALKAR	Pistol	6.357.65	Alkartasuna
ALLEN	Rev	22	Hopkins & Allen
ALLEN	Shotgun	Various	McKeown
ALLIES	Pistol	6.35/7.65	Bersaluze
ALPINE	Rifle	Various	Firearms
AMERICA	Rev	22	Bliss & Goodyear
AMERICA	Rev	32RF	Norwich Falls
AMERICAN, THE	Rev	38	Hopkins & Allen
AMERICAN BARLOCK WONDER	Shotgun	Various	Crescent Firearms
AMERICAN BOY	Rev	22	Bliss & Goodyear
AMERICAN BULLDOG	Rev	Various	Johnson, Bye
AMERICAN CHAMPION	Shotgun	12	?
AMERICAN EAGLE	Rev	22/32	Hopkins & Allen
AMERICAN EAGLE 380	Pistol	9S	American Arms

Name	Type	Calibre	Maker	Name	Type	Calibre	Maker
AMERICAN GUN Co	Rev/Shotgun	Various	Crescent Firearms	BACKUP	Pistol	9S	AMT
AMERICUS	Rev	22	Hopkins & Allen	BAIKAL	Shotg/Rifle	Various	Russian State
APACHE	Rev	38	Garantizada	BANG-UP	Rev	32RF	Bacon Arms
APACHE	Pistol	6.35	Ojanguren y Vidosa	BARRACUDA	Rev	9P	FN Herstal
				BASCULANT	Pistol	6.35	Aguirre Zamacolas
ARICO	Pistol	6.35	Pieper	BASQUE	Pistol	7.65	Echave & Arizmendi
ARISTOCRAT	Rev	22/32RF	Hopkins & Allen	BATAVIA	Rifle/Shotg	22/Various	Baker
ARISTOCRAT	Shotgun	Various	Stevens	BANG-UP	Rev	22	Hopkins & Allen
ARMINIUS (pre-19450	Rev	Various	F Pickert	BANTAM	Pistol	6.35	Beretta
ARMINIUS (Post-1945)	Rev	Various	Weirauch	BAYARD	All types	Various	Pieper
ARMSCOR 38	Rev	38	Squires, Bingham	BEHOLLA	Pistol	7.65	Becker & Hollander
ARVA	Pistol	6.35	[Spain; pre 1914]	BELLMORE	Shotgun	Various	Crescent Arms
ASIATIC	Pistol	6.35/7.65	[Spain, 1920s]	BENEMERITA	Pistol	6.35/7.65	Aldazabal
ASTRA	Pistols	Various	Astra-Unceta	BENGAL NO 1	Rev	22	Iver Johnson
ATLAS	Pistol	6.35	Domingo Acha	BERSA	Pistol	22/38	Ange
AUBREY	Rev	32/38	Meriden Arms/Sears	B.H.	Rev	38	Beistegui Hermanos
AUDAX	Pistol	6.35/7.65	Pyrenees [Spain]	BICYCLE	Rev	22/32	Harrington & Richardson
AURORA	Pistol	6.35	[Spain]				
AUTOGARDE	Rev	7.65	SFM	BIG BONANZA	Rev	22	Bacon Arms
AUTO-MAG	Pistol	.44	Automag	BIG HORN	SS	22	Big Horn Arms Co
AUTOMASTER	Pistol	45	Sokolovsky	BIJOU	Rev	Various	Debouxtay
AUTOMATIC	Rev	32/38	Hopkins & Allen	BIJOU	Pistol	6.35	Menz
AUTOMATIC HAMMERLESS	Rev	32/38	Iver Johnson	BISLEY	Rev	Various	Colt
AUTOMATIC LESTON	Pistol	6.35	Unceta	BISLEY	Rev	357	Ruger
AUTOMATIC POLICE	Rev	32	Forehand & Wadsworth	BISON	Rev	22	Herbert Schmidt
				BLACKHAWK	Rev	357	Ruger
AUTOMATIQUE FRANCAISE	Pistol	6.35	Soc. Franc. d'Armes	BLOODHOUND	Rev	22	Hopkins & Allen
				BLUE JACKET	Rev	22/32RF	Hopkins & Allen
AUTO-POINTER	Shotgun	12	Yamamoto	BLUE WHISTLER	Rev	32RF	Hopkins & Allen
AUTOSHOT	SS	.410	Stevens	BOCK-FITZKOW	SS	22	Buchel
AUTOSTAND	SS	22	Manufrance	BOIX	Pistol	7.65	[Spain}
AVION	Pistol	6.35	Azpiri	BOLTUN	Pistol	7.65	Francisco Arizmendi
AYA	Shotgun	Various	Aguirre y Aranzabal	BONANZA	Rev	22	Bacon Arms
AZUL	Pistol	Various	Arostegui	BOOM	Rev	22	Shattuck
				BORCHARDT	Pistol	7.65	Loewe/DWM
BABY	Pistol	6.35	FN	BOSTON BULLDOG	Rev	Various	Iver Johnson
BABY BULLDOG	Rev	22	[USA; ca 1885]	BOY'S CHOICE	Rev	22	Hood
BABY RUSSIAN	Rev	38	American Arms Co	BREN TEN	Pistol	10mm	Dornaus & Dixon
				BRIGADIER	Pistol	9P	Beretta
				BRIGADIER	Pistol	.45	North American

Name	Type	Calibre	Maker	Name	Type	Calibre	Maker
			Arms				Arrizabalaga
BRISTOL	Pistol	7.65	Bolumburu	CAMPER	Pistol	22/6.35	Astra-Unceta
BRITISH BULLDOG	Rev	Various	Forehand &	CANTABRIA	Pistol/Rev	Various	Garate Hermanos
			Wadsworth	CAPITAN	Pistol	7.65	Pyrenees
BRITISH BULLDOG	Rev	Various	Johnson, Bye	CAPTAIN JACK	Rev	22	Hopkins & Allen
BRNO	Rifle/shotgun	Various	Zbrojovka Brno	CAROLINE ARMS	Shotgun	Various	Crescent Firearms
BROMPETIER	Rev	6.35/7.65	Retolaza	CA-SI	Pistol	7.65	Grand Precision
BRONCHO	Pistol	6.35/7.65	Errasti	CASULL	Rev	454	Freedom Arms
BRONCO	Pistol	6.35/7.65	Echave y Arizmendi	CATTLEMAN	Rev	357/44	Uberti
BRON-GRAND	Rev	6/6.35/7.65	Fernando Ormachea	CAVALIER	Rifle	Various	Zastava
BRONG-PETIT	Rev	6.35	Crucelegui	C.D.M.	Rev	22	[USA ca1980]
BRON-SPORT	Rev	6.35/7.65/8	Crucelegui	CEBRA	Pistol	6.35	Arizmendi Zulaica
BROW	Rev	6.35/7.65/38	Ojanguren &	CELTA	Pistol	6.35	Urizar
			Marcaido	CENTAUR	Pistol	6.35	Reunies
BROWNIE	RP	22	Mossberg	CENTENNIAL 1876	Rev	32/38RF	Derringer
BROWREDUIT	Rev	6.35/7.65	Salvator Arostegui	CENTRAL	Shotgun	Various	Stevens
BRUNSWIG	Pistol	7.65	Esperanza & Unceta	CENTRAL ARMS CO	Shotgun	Various	Crescent Firearms
BRUTUS	Rev	22	Hood	CENTURION	Pistol	9P	Beretta
BUCCANEER	Pistol	7.65	Pyrenees	CENTURION MODEL 100	Rifle	Various	Golden State
BUCKHORN	Rev	357	Uberti	CESAR	Pistol	7.65	Pyrenees
BUDISCHOWSKY	Pistol	22/25	Korriphila	J.CESAR	Pistol	6.35	Tomas de Urizar
BUFALO	Pistol	6.35/7.65	Gabilondo	C.H.	Rev	38	Crucelegui
BUFFALO STAND	SS	22	Manufrance				Hermanos
BULL DOZER	Rev	Various	Norwich Pistol	CHALLENGE	Rev	32RF	Bliss & Goodyear
BULL DOZER	SS	22RF	Conn Mfg	CHAMPION	Pistol	22	Manufrance
BULLDOG	Rev	Various	Forehand &	CHANTECLER	Pistol	7.65	Pyrenees
			Wadsworth	CHANTICLER	Pistol	6.35	Isidor Charola
BULLDOG	Rev	44	Charter Arms	CHARLES LANCASTER	Rifle	Various	Atkin
BULLDOG TRACKER	Rev	357	Charter Arms	CHAROLA Y ANITUA	Pistol	5/7mm	Garate Anitua
BULLFIGHTER	Rev	.300	[Belgium]	CHEROKEE ARMS CO	Shotgun	Various	Crescent Firearms
BULLSEYE	Rev	22	[USA; ca 1885]	CHESAPEAKE GUN CO	Shotgun	Various	Crescent Firearms
BULWARK	Pistol	6.35/7.65	Beistegui	CHEYENNE SCOUT	Rev	22	Herbert Schmidt
BURGHAM SUPERIOR	Pistol	7.65	Pyrenees	CHICAGO ARMS CO	Rev	32/38	Meriden
BURGO	Rev	22	Rohm	CHICAGO CUB	Rev	22	Reck
BUSHMASTER	Pistol/Rifle	223	Gwinn Arms	CHICAGO PROTECTOR	RP	32	Ames Sword Co
				CHICHESTER	Rev	38RF	Hopkins & Allen
CADET	Rev	22	Maltby, Curtis	CHIEFTAIN	Rev	32RF	Norwich Pistol
CADIX	Rev	22/32/38	Astra-Unceta	CHIMERE RENOIR	Pistol	7.65	Pyrenees
CAMINAL	Pistol	7.65	[Spain]	CHORERT	Rev	8mm	[Belgium]
CAMPEON	Pistol	6.35/7.65	Hijos de C	CHURCHILL	Rifles	Various	Kassnar

Name	Type	Calibre	Maker
CHYLEWSKI	Pistol	6.35	SIG
CILINDRO LADEABLE	Rev	32	Ojanguren & Matiade
CLEMENT	Rev	38	Clement, Neumann
CLEMENT	Pistol	5/6.35	Charles Clement
CLEMENT-FULGOR	Pistol	7.65	Charles Clement
CLIMAS	Shotgun	12	Stevens
COBOLD	Rev	9.4mm	HDH
COBOLT	Rev	Various	Ancion Marx
COBRA	Pistol	7.65	[Spain]
COLON	Pistol	6.35	Azpiri
COLON	Rev	32-20	Orbea Hermanos
COLONIAL	Pistol	7.65	Pyrenees
COLONIAL	Pistol	6.35/7.65	Grand Precision
COLUMBIAN	Rev	38	Crescent Firearms
COLUMBIAN AUTOMATIC	Rev	32/38	Foehl & Weeks
COMANCHE	Rev	357	Gabilondo
COMMANDER	Pistol	45	Colt
COMMANDO ARMS	S/A Carbine	Various	Volunteer
COMBAT COMMANDER	Pistol	9P/45	Colt
COMPEER	Shotgun	Various	Crescent Firearms
CONSTABLE	Pistol	7.65	Astra-Unceta
CONSTABULARY	Rev	7.5mm	Ancion Marx
CONSTABULARY	Rev	32/38/45	Robar
CONQUEROR	Rev	22/32RF	Bacon Arms
CONTINENTAL	Pistol	6.35	Bertrand
CONTINENTAL	Pistol	6.35/7.65	RWS
CONTINENTAL	Rifle/Shotgun	Various	Stevens
CONTINENTAL	Rev	22/32RF	Great Western
CONTINENTAL	Rev	22/32RF	Hood
CONTINENTAL	Pistol	6.35	Tomas de Urizar
CORLA	Pistol	22	Zaragoza
CORRIENTES	Pistol	6.35	Modesto Santos
COSMI	Shotgun	Various	Abercrombie & Fitch
COSMOPOLITE OSCILLATORY	Rev	38	Garate Anitua
COUGAR	Pistol	7.65/9	Beretta
COW-BOY	Pistol	6.35	Fabrique Francaise
COWBOY RANGER	Rev	Various	Liege United Arms
CRESCENT	Rev	32RF	Norwich Falls
CREEDMORE	Rev	22	Hopkins & Allen
CRIOLLA	Pistol	22	Hafdasa
CROWN JEWEL	Rev	32RF	Norwich Falls
CRUCERO	Pistol/Rev	7.65/32	Ojanguren & Vidosa
CRUSO	Rifle/Shotgun	Various	Stevens
CUB	Pistol	22/6.35	Astra-Unceta
CUMBERLAND ARMS CO	Shotgun	Various	Crescent Firearms
CZ	All	Various	Ceskoslovenska
CZAR	Rev	22	Hood
CZAR	Rev	22/32RF	Hopkins & Allen
DAISY	Rev	22	Bacon Arms
DAKOTA	Rev	38/45	Uberti
DANTON	Pistol	6.35/7.65	Gabilondo
DEAD SHOT	Rev	22	Pond
DEFENSE	Pistol	6.35	[Spain]
DEFENDER	Rev	22/32RF	Johnson, Bye
DEFENDER	Pistol	6.35	Javier Echaniz
DEFENDER 89	Rev	22	Iver Johnson
DEFENSE	Pistol	6.35	[Spain; 1920s]
DEFIANCE	Rev	22	Norwich Falls
DEK-DU	Rev	5.5/6.35	Tomas de Urizar
DELPHIAN	Shotgun	Various	Stevens
DELTA	Pistol	6.35	[Spain]
DELTA ELITE	Pistol	10mm	Colt
DE LUXE	Pistol	6.35	Bolumburu
DEMON	Pistol	7.65	Pyrenees
DEMON	Pistol	7.65	[Spain]
DEMON MARINE	Pistol	7.65	Pyrenees
DEPREZ	Rev	11mm	[Belgium]
DEPUTY ADJUSTER	Rev	38	Herbert Schmidt
DEPUTY MAGNUM	Rev	357	Herbert Schmidt
DEPUTY MARSHAL	Rev	38	Herbert Schmidt
DESERT EAGLE	Pistol	Various	Taas Israel Industries
DESPATCH	Rev	22	Hopkins & Allen
DESTROYER	Pistol	6.35/7.65	Gaztanaga
DESTRUCTOR	Pistol	6.35/7.65	Salaverria

Name	Type	Calibre	Maker
DETECTIVE	Rev	32	Garate Anitua
DETECTIVE SPECIAL	Rev	38	Colt
DEWAF MODEL IV	Pistol	6.35	[Spain; 1920s]
DIAMOND	Shotgun	Various	Stevens
DIAMONDBACK	Rev	22/38	Colt
DIANA	Pistol	6.35	[Spain]
DIANE	Pistol	6.35	Wilkinson
DIANE	Pistol	6.35	Erquiaga, Muguruzu
DICKSON BULLDOG	Rev	22	Weirauch
DICKSON SPECIAL AGENT	Pistol	7.65	Echave & Arizmendi
DICTATOR	Pistol	6.35	Reunies
DICTATOR	Rev	22/32RF	Hopkins & Allen
DIPLOMAT	Pistol	9S	Bernardelli
DOMINO	Pistol	22	Italguns
DOUBLE DEUCE	Pistol	22	Steel City
DOUBLE NINE	Rev	22	High Standard
DOUGLAS	Pistol	6.35	Lasagabaster
DREADNOUGHT	Rev	38	Errasti
DREADNOUGHT	Rev	22/32RF	Hopkins & Allen
DREUX	Pistol	6.35	[France]
DREYSE	Pistol	Various	Rheinmetall
DRULOV	SS	22	Lidove Drusztvo
DUAN	Pistol	6.35	Ormachea
DUC	Pistol	6.35	[France?]
DUCO	Rev	7.5mm	Dumoulin
DUO	Pistol	6.35	Dusek
DUPLEX	Rev	22/32RF	Osgood Gun Works
DURABEL	Pistol	6.35	Warnant
DURA-MATIC	Pistol	22	High Standard
DURANGO	Rev	22	High Standard
E.A.	Pistol	6.35	Echave y Arizmendi
E.A.	Pistol	6.35	Arostegui
EAGLE 1	Rev	45	Phelps
EAGLE 380	Pistol	9S	American Arms (2)
EAGLE ARMS CO	Rev	Various	Johnson, Bye
EARL HOOD	Rev	32RF	Dickinson
EARTHQUAKE	Rev	32RF	Dickinson
EASTERN	Shotgun	Various	Stevens
EASTERN ARMS CO	Rev	32/38	Meriden/Sears

Name	Type	Calibre	Maker
E.B.A.C.	Pistol	6.35	Pyrenees
ECHASA	Pistol	22/6.35/7.65	Echave y Arizmendi
ECIA	Pistol	7.65	Esperanza y Cia
ECLIPSE	SS	22/25/32RF	Johnson, Bye
EICHEL	Rifle	Various	Kind
EIG	Rev	22	Rohm
EL BLANCO	Rev	22	Ojanguren & Matiade
EL CANO	Rev	32	Arana y Cia
EL CID	Pistol	6.35	Casimir Santos
ELECTOR	Rev	22/32RF	Hopkins & Allen
ELECTRIC	Rev	32RF	Forehand & Wadsworth
ELES	Pistol	6.35	[Spain]
ELEY	Pistol	6.35	[Spain]
ELGIN ARMS CO	Shotgun	Various	Crescent Firearms
ELITE	Pistol	7.65	Pyrenees
EL LUNAR LEBEL RAPIDE	Rev	8mm	Garate Anitua
EL PERRO	Pistol	6.35	Lascuraren & Olasolo
EM-GE	Rev	22	Gerstenberger
EMPIRE	Rev	22/38/41RF	Rupertus
EMPIRE	Rifle	22	Vickers
EMPIRE ARMS	Rev	32/38	Meriden
EMPIRE ARMS CO	Shotgun	Various	Crescent Firearms
EMPIRE STATE	Rev	32/38	Meriden
EMPRESS	Rev	32RF	Rupertus
ENCORE	Rev	22/32/38RF	Johnson, Bye
ENDERS OAKLEAF	Shotgun	Various	Crescent Firearms
ENDERS ROYAL SERVICE	Shotgun	Various	Crescent Firearms
ENFORCER	Pistol	45	Safari Arms
ERIKA	Pistol	4.25	Pfannl
ERMA	All	Various	Ermawerke
ERMUA 1924	Pistol	6.35	Acha
ERMUA 1925	Pistol	6.35	Ormachea
E.S.A.	Pistol	6.35/7.65	{Spain; 1920s]
ESCORT	Pistol	22	Echeverria
ESPECIAL	Pistol	6.35	Arrizabalaga
ESPINGARDA	Rev	38	Machado
ESSEX	Shotgun	Various	Crescent Firearms

Name	Type	Calibre	Maker
ESSEX	Rifle/Shotgun	Various	Stevens
ESTRELA	Pistol	6.35/7.65	Echeverria
ETAI	Pistol	6.35	[Spain]
ETNA	Pistol	6.35	Salaberrin
EUREKA	Rev	22	Johnson, Bye
EUSKARO	Rev	38/44	Esprin Hermanos
EUSTA	Pistol	7.65/9S	[West Germany]
EXCELSIOR	Rev	32RF	Norwich Pistol
EXCELSIOR	Rev	9.1mm	S.J & D
EXPRESS	Rev	22	Bacon Arms
EXPRESS	Pistol	6.35/7.65	Urizar
EXTRACTEUR	Rev	7.5mm	Ancion Marx
F.A.	Rev	32	Francisco Arizmendi
F.A.G.	Rev	7.62/8	Arizmendi & Goenaga
FALCON	Pistol	7.65	Astra-Unceta
FAST	Pistol	Various	Echave y Arizmendi
FAULTLESS	Shotguns	Various	Crescent
FAVORIT	Pistol	6.35	[Spain]
FAVORIT	Rifle	Various	Frankonia
FAVORIT SAFARI	Rifle	Various	Frankonia
FAVORITE	Rev	22/32/38/41RF	Johnson, Bye
FAVORITE NAVY	Rev	44RF	Johnson, Bye
FEDERAL ARMS	Rev	32/38	Meriden
F.E.G.	Pistol	Various	Femaru
FIEL	Pistol	6.35/7.65	Erquiaga, Muguruzu
FIELD KING	Pistol	22	High Standard
FINNISH LION	Rifle	22	Valmet
FIREBALL	SS	221	Remington
FIREBIRD	Pistol	9P	Femaru
FLITE-KING	Pistol	22	High Standard
FLORIA	Pistol	6.35	[Spain]
FME	Pistol	6.35	FAMAE
FORBES	Shotgun	Various	Crescent
FOREHAND 1901	Rev	32	Hopkins & Allen
FORTUNA	Pistol	7.65	Unceta
FORTY-NINER	Rev	22	Harrington & Richardson
FOUR ACES	Rev	22	Svendsen

Name	Type	Calibre	Maker
FOUR ACES	RP	22	ESFAC
FOX	Pistol	6.35	Tomiska
FRANCAISE	Pistol	6.35	Societe Francaise
FRANCO	Pistol	6.35	Manufrance
FREEHAND	Rev	38	[Germany?]
FRONTIER	Rev	32RF	Norwich Falls
FRONTIER ARMY	Rev	44	Ronge
FURIA	Pistol	7.65	Ojanguren & Vidosa
FUROR	Pistol	7.65	Pyrenees
MFG CO	Rev	32-20	Garate Anitua
GALEF	Pistol	7.65	[Spain]
GALEF STALLION	Rev	22/357	[Italy]
GALLIA	Pistol	7.65	Pyrenees
GALLUS	Pistol	6.35	Retolaza
GAME GETTER	Rifle/Shotg	.22/410	Marble
GARRISON	Rev	22	Hopkins & Allen
GARRUCHA	DB Pistol	22	Amadeo Rossi
GAUCHO	Pistol	22	[Argentine]
GAULOIS	Rep Pist	8	Manufrance
G & E	Rev	22	Gerstenberger
GECADO	Pistol	6.35	Dornheim
GECO	Rev	6.35/7.65	Genschow
GECO	Shotgun	12	Genschow
GEM	Rev	22	Bacon Arms
GEM	SS	22/30RF	Stevens Tool
GERMAN BULLDOG	Rev	32/38	Genschow
G.H.	Rev	38	Guisasola Hermanos
GIBRALTAR	Rrev	32/38	Meriden
GIRALDA	Pistol	7.65	Bolumburu
GLENFIELD	Rifle	30-30	Marlin
GLORIA	Pistol	6.35/7.65	Bolumburu
G.M.C.	Pistol	22	Garb, Moretti & Co
GOLDEN BISON	Rev	.45-70	Super Six
GOLDEN EAGLE	Rifle	Various	Nikko
GOLIAT	Rev	32	Antonio Errasti
GOOSE GUN	Shotgun	Various	Stevens

Name	Type	Calibre	Maker
GOVERNOR	Rev	22	Bacon Arms
GP-100	Rev	357	Ruger
GRAND	Rev	357/38	Zbrojovka Brno
GRIZZLY	Pistol	Various	LAR
GRUENEL	Rifle	Various	Gruenig & Elmiger
G.S.M.	Pistl	7.65	[Hungary]
GUARDIAN	Rev	22/32RF	Bacon Arms
GUEURE	Pistol	6.35	Arizmendi
GYROJET	Pistol	13mm	MBA
HAKIM	Rifle	7.92	Maadi
HALF-BREED	Rev	32RF	Hopkins & Allen
HAMADA	Pistol	7.65	Japan Gun Co
HANDY MODEL 1917	Pistol	9S	[Spain]
HARDBALLER	Pistol	45	AMT
HARD PAN	Rev	22/32RF	Hood
HARTFORD ARMS CO	Rev	32RF	Norwich Falls
HARTFORD ARMS CO	Shotgun	Various	Crescent Firearms
HARVARD	Shotgun	Various	Crescent Firearms
HAWES WESTERN MARSHAL	Rev	Various	Sauer
HAWES SILVER CITY	Rev	22	Sauer
HAWES CHIEF MARSHAL	Rev	Various	Sauer
H&D	Rev	Various	Henrion & Dassy
HEGE	Pistol/Combo	Various	Hebsacker
HEIM	Pistol	6.35	Heinzelmann
HELFRICHT	Pistol	6.35	Krauser
HELKRA	Pistol	6.35	Krauser
HELVICE (or HELVECE)	Pistol	6.35	Grand Precision
HE-MO	Pistol	7.65	Moritz
HERCULES	Shotgun	Various	Stevens
HERITAGE 1	Rev	45	Phelps
HERMAN	Pistol	6.35	[Belgium]
HERMETIC	Pistol	7.65`	Bernadon-Martin
HERMITAGE	Shotgun	Various	Stevens
HERMITAGE ARMS CO	Shotgun	Various	Crescent Firearms
HERMITAGE GUN CO	Shotgun	Various	Crescent Firearms
HERO	Rev	22/32/38/41RF	Rupertus
HEROLD	Rifle	22	Jager
HERTER	Rev	357	[Germany]
HEYM	Rev	22	[Germany]

Name	Type	Calibre	Maker
HIGHLANDER	Rifle	Various	Kassnar
HIGH SIERRA	Rev	22	High Standard
HIJO	Pistol	6.35/7.65	Galesi
HIJO QUICK-BREAK	Rev	22/32/38	Iver Johnson
HOPKINS, C.W.	Rev	32/38RF	Bacon Mfg Co
HORSE DESTROYER	Rev	38	Gaztanaga
HOWARD ARMS	Rev	32/38	Meriden
HOWARD ARMS	Shotgun	Various	Crescent Firearms
H.R.	SS	22	Haidurov
H.S.	Rev	22	Herbert Schmidt
			[Spain]
HUDSON	Pistol	6.35	Wichita Arms
HUNTER	SS	Various	Stevens
HUNTER'S PET	SS	22/25/32RF	Hourat
H.V.	Pistol	6.35	Rohm
HY HUNTER	Rev	22	Rohm
HY-SCORE	Rev	22	
I.A.G.	Pistol	7.65	Galesi
IDEAL	SS	22	Buchel
IDEAL	Pistol	6.35	Dusek
ILLINOIS ARMS CO	Rev	6.35	Pickert
IMPERATO	Pistol	6.35/7.65	Heckler & Koch
IMPERIAL	Pistol	6.35	Tomas de Urizar
IMPERIAL	Rev	22/32RF	{USA}
IMPERIAL ARMS	Rev	32/38RF	Hopkins & Allen
INDIAN	Pistol	7.65	Gaztanaga
INDISPENSABLE	Rev	5.5mm	[Belgium]
INFALLIBLE	Pistol	7.65	Davis-Warner
INGRAM	SMG	9/45	MAC
INSPECTOR	Rev	38	Uberti
INTERNATIONAL	Rev	22/32Rf	Hood
INTERNATIONAL	SS	Various	Wichita Arms
INTERSTATE ARMS CO	Shotgun	Various	Crescent Firearms
INVICTA	Pistol	7.65	Salaberrin
IRIQUOIS	Rev	22	Remington
IRIS	Rev	32-20	Ojanguren
ISARD	Pistol	9B-B	[Spain]
IXOR	Pistol	7.65	Pyrenees
IZARRA	Pistol	7.65	Echeverria

Name	Type	Calibre	Maker	Name	Type	Calibre	Maker
JACKRABBIT	Rifle/Shotgun	Various	Continental Arms	KOLIBRI	Pistol	3mm	Grabner
JACKSON ARMS CO	Shotgun	Various	Crescent Firearms	KOLIBRI	Pistol	6.35	Arizaga
JAGA	Pistol	6.35	Dusek	KRAUSER	Pistol	22	Manurhin
J.CESAR	Pistol	6.35	Urizar				
JENKINS SPECIAL	Pistol	6.35	[Spain]	LA BASQUE	Pistol	6.35	[Spain]
JERICHO	Pistol	9P	Ta'as	LA's DEPUTY	Rev	22	Herbert Schmidt
JETFIRE	Pistol	6.35	Beretta	LADYSMITH	Rev	32,38	Smith & Wesson
JEWEL	Rev	22	Hood	LA FURY	Pistol	6.35	Reck
J.G.A.	Rev	7.65	Anschutz	LA INDUSTRIA	Pistol	7.65	Orbea Hermanos
JIEFFECO	Pistol	6.35/7.65	Robar	LA LIRA	Pistol	7.65	Garate Anitua
JOHA	Pistol	6.35/7.65	[Spain]	LAMPO	RP	8mm	Tribuzio
JO-LO-AR	Pistol	7.65	Arrizabalaga	LANCER	Pistol	22	Echeverria
JUBALA	Pistol	6.35	Larranaga & Elartza	LA SALLE	Shotgun	Various	Manufrance
				LAWMAN	Rev	357	Colt
JUBILEE	Rifle	22	Vickers	L.E.	Rev	32	Larranaga y Elartza
JUNIOR	Pistol	6.35	Pretoria Arms Factory	LE AGENT	Rev	8mm	Manufrance
				LE BASQUE	Pistol	7.65	Urizar
JUNIOR	Pistl	22/6.35	Colt	LE BRONG	Rev	5/6.35/7.65	Crucelegui
JUPITER	Pistol	7.65	Grand Precision	LE CAVALIER	Pistol	7.65/9S	Bayonne
JUPITER	Rev	5.5mm	Francotte	LE CHASSEUR	Pistol	11	Bayonne
				L'ECLAIR	Rev	6mm	Garate Anitua
KABA SPEZIAL	Pistol	7.65	Menz	LE COLONIAL	Rev	8mm	Manufrance
KABA SPECIAL	Pistol	6.35/7.65	Arizmendi	LE DRAGON	Pistol	6.35	Urizar
KAPITAIN	Pistol	7.65	Alkartasuna	LE FRANCAIS	Pistol	Various	Manufrance
KAPPORA	Pistol	6.35	[Spain]	LE GENDARME	Pistol	9S	Bayonne
KEBLER	Pistol	7.65	[Spain]	LEGITIMO TANQUE	Rev	38	Ojanguren & Vidosa
KING COBRA	Rev	357	Colt				
KINGLAND SPECIAL	Shotgun	Various	Crescent Firearms	LE MAJESTIC	Pistol	7.65	Pyrenees
KINGLAND 10-STAR	Shotgun	Various	Crescent Firearms	LE MARTINY	Pistol	6.35	[Belgium]
KING NITRO	Rifle/Shotgun	Various	Stevens	LE METEORE	Pistol	6.35	[Belgium]
KIRRIKALE	Pistol	9S	MKEK	LE MILITAIRE	Pistol	9P	Bayonne
KITTEMAUG	Rev	32RF	[USA}	LE MONOBLOC	Pistol	6.35	Jacquemart
KITU	Pistol	6.35	[Spain]	LE NOVO	Rev	6.35	Galand
KLESZEZEWSKI	Pistol	6.35	[Spain]	LE PETIT FORMIDABLE	Rev	6.35	Manufrance
KNICKERBOCKER	Shotgun	Various	Crescent Firearms	LE PROTECTOR	RP	6mm	Turbiaux
KNOCKABOUT	Shotgun	Various	Stevens	LE RAPIDE	Pistol	6.35	Bertrand
KNOCKABOUT	SS	22	Sheridan	LE SANS PARIEL	Pistol	6.35	Pyrenees
KNOXALL	Shotgun	Various	Crescent Firearms	LE SECOURS	Pistol	6.35	Grand Precision
KOBOLD	Rev	Various	Raick Freres	LE SECOURS	Pistol	7.65	Tomas de Urizar
KOBRA	Pistol	6.35	[Germany]	LE STEPH	Pistol	6.35	Bergeron

Name	Type	Calibre	Maker	Name	Type	Calibre	Maker
_E TOUT ACIER	Pistol	6.35/7.65	Pyrenees	LLANERO	Rev	.22	[Argentina]
_EADER	Rev	22/32RF	Hopkins & Allen	LOBO	Pistol	6.35	[Spain]
_EADER GUN CO	Shotgun	Various	Crescent Firearms	LONGHORN	Rev	22	High Standard
_EE SPECIAL	Shotgun	Various	Crescent Firearms	LONGINES	Pistol	7.65	Cooperativa Orbea
_EE'S MUNNER SPECIAL	Shotgun	Various	Crescent Firearms	LONG RANGE WONDER	Shotgun	Various	Sears Roebuck
_EFT WHEELER	Rev	32	HDH	LONG TOM	Shotgun	Various	Stevens
_EGIA	Pistol	6.35	Pieper	LOOKING GLASS	Pistol	6.35/7.65	Acha
_EONHARDT	Pistol	7.65	Gering	LOSADA	Pistol	7.65	[Germany]
_EPCO	Pistol	6.35	[Spain]	LUGER	Pistol	7.65P/9P	Stoeger
_.E.S.	Pistol	9P	Steyr-Mannlicher	LUNA	SS	22	Buchel
_ESTON	Pistol	6.35	Unceta	LUR-PANZER	Pistol	22	Echave y Arizmendi
_.H.	Pistol	6.35	[Germany]	LUSITANIA	Pistoo	7.65	[Spain]
_IBERATOR	SS	.45	Guide Lamp	LUTETIA	Pistol	6.35	[Spain]
_IBERTI	Pistol	7.65	[Spain]	LYNX	Rev	357	[South Africa, ca 1979]
_IBERTY	Rev	22/32RF	Hood				
_IBERTY	Pistol	6.35/7.65	Retolaza				
_IBERTY-11	Rev	22	Herbert Schmidt	M & H	Rev	.44–40	Hopkins & Allen
_IBERTY RG-12	Rev	22	Rohm	MAB	Pistol	Various	Bayonne
_IBERTY CHIEF	Rev	.38	Miroku	MAJESTIC	Pistol	6.35	[Spain]
_IBIA	Pistol	6.35/7.65	Beistegui	MAGMATIC	Pistol	44Mag	Powers
_IEGOISE D'ARMES A FEU	Pistol	6.35/7.65	Robar	MALTBY, HENLEY & Co	Rev	22/32/38	Columbia Armory
_IGHTNING	Pistol	6.35	Echave y Arizmendi	MAMBA	Pistol	9P	Relay Products
_ILIPUT	Pistol	4.25/6.35	Menz	MAMBA	Pistol	9P	Navy Arms
_ILIPUT	Pistol	6.35	Fegyver	MARINA	Pistol	6.35	Bolumburu
_INCOLN	Rev	32	Ancion Marx	MARKE	Pistol	6.35	Bascaran
_INCOLN	Rev	22/32RF	HDH	MARK X	Rifle	Various	Zastava
_INCOLN BOSSU	Rev	5.5/6.35	HDH	MARQUIS OF LORNE	Rev	22/32RF	Hood
_INCOLN BULLDOG	Rev	32	Robar	MARS	Pistol	6.35/7.65	Kohout
_INCOLN HAMMERLESS	Rev	320	Robar	MARS	Pistol	9/45	Webley
_INDA	Pistol	.22	Wilkinson Arms	MARS	Pistol	9BB	Pieper
_ION	Rev	22/32/38/41RF	Johnson, Bye	MARS	Pistol	7.65	Pyrenees
_ITTLE ALL RIGHT	Rev	22	All Right Firearms	MARSHWOOD	Shotgun	Various	Stevens
_ITTLE GIANT	Rev	22	Bacon Arms	MARTE	Pistol	6.35	Erquiaga, Muguruzu
_ITTLE JOHN	Rev	22	Hood	MARTIAL	Rev	357	Gabilondo
_ITTLE JOKER	Rev	22	Marlin, John	MARTIAN	Pistol	6.35/7.65	Martin A Bascaran
_ITTLE PET	Shotgun	Various	Stevens	MARTIGNY	Pistol	6.35	Jorge Bascaran
_ITTLE TOM	Pistol	6.35/7.65	Tomiska	MASSACHUSETTS ARMS	Shotgun	Various	Stevens
_ITTLE TOM	Pistol	6.35	Wiener Waffenfabrik	MAXIM	Pistol	6.35	Galesi
				MAXIMUM	SS	Various	MOA Corp
_LAMA	Pistol	Various	Gabilondo	MELIOR	Pistol	Various	Robar

Name	Type	Calibre	Maker	Name	Type	Calibre	Maker
MENTA	Pistol	6.35/7.65	Menz	MUXI	Pistol	6.35	[Spain]
MERCURY	Pistol/Shotgun	Various	Robar				
MERKE	Pistol	6.35	Ormachea	NALAVA	Pistol	6.35	Eiler
MERKUR	Rifle	Various	Kind	NAPOLEON	Rev	22/32RF	Ryan
MERVEILLEAUX	RP	6mm	[France]	NATIONAL	Rev	32/38RF	Norwich Falls
METEOR	Rifle	22	Stevens	NATIONAL	SS	41RF	Norwich Falls
METROPOLITAN	Shotgun	Various	Crescent Firearms	NATIONAL ARMS CO	Shotgun	Various	Crescent Firearms
METROPOLITAN POLICE	Rev	32RF	Norwich Falls	NERO	Rev	22/32RF	Rupertus
MIDLAND GUN CO	Rifle	Various	Parker-Hale	NERO	Rev	22/32RF	Hopkins & Allen
MIKROS	Pistol	Various	Pyrenees	NEVER MISS	Rev	22/32/41RF	Marlin
MILADY	Rev	7.65	Ancion-Marx	NEW ACE	Pistol	22	Colt
MILADY	Rev	8mm	Jannsen Fils	NEW BABY	Rev	22	Kolb
MILITARY	Pistol	6.35	Retolaza	NEW CHIEFTAIN	Shotgun	Various	Stevens
MILITARY MODEL 1914	Pistol	7.65	Retolaza	NEW JAGUAR	Pistol	22/7.65	Beretta
MILITAR Y POLICIA	Rev	38	Ojanguren &	NEW NAMBU	Rev/Pistol	Various	Shin Chuo Kogyo
			Vidosa	NEW RIVAL	Shotgun	Various	Crescent Firearms
MILITAR Y POLICIAS	Rev	38	Ojanguren &	NEW YORK ARMS CO	Shotgun/Rev	Various	Crescent Firearms
			Matiade	NEW YORK PISTOL CO	Rev	22	Hood
MINERVA	Pistol	6.35	Grand Precision	NEWPORT	Shotgun	Various	Stevens
MINIMA	Pistol	6.35	Boyer	NIGHTHAWK	Pistol	9P	Weaver
MINX	Pistol	6.35	Beretta	NITRO PROOF	Shotgun	Various	Stevens
MISSISSIPPI VALLEY	Shotgun	Various	Crescent Firearms	NIVA	Pistol	6.35	Kohout
MITRAILLEUSE	RP	8mm	St Etienne	NOMAD	Pistol	22	Browning Arms
MITRAILLEUSE	Pistol	6.35	[Spain]	NONPARIEL	Rev	32RF	Norwich Falls
ML	Pistol	6.35/7.65	Robar	NORTHWESTERNER	Rifle/Shotgun	22/Various	Stevens
MOHAWK	Shotgun	Various	Crescent Firearms	NORWICH ARMS CO	Shotgun	Various	Crescent Firearms
MOHEGAN	Rev	32RF	Hood	NORWICH ARMS CO	Rev	22/32RF	Norwich Falls
MONARCH	Rev	22/32/38/41RF	Hopkins & Allen	NOT-NAC MFG CO	Shotgun	Various	Crescent Firearms
MONDIAL	Pistol	6.35	Arrizaga	NOVELTY	RP	32	Mossberg
MONITOR	Shotgun	Various	Stevens	N.Y.PISTOL CO	Rev	22	Hood Arms Co
MONOBLOC	Pistol	6.35	Jacquemart				
M.S.	Pistol	6.35/7.65	Modesto Santos	OAK LEAF	Shotgun	Various	Stevens
MOSSER	Pistol	6.35	[Spain]	OBREGON	Pistol	.45	Fab de Armas
MOUNTAIN EAGLE	Rev	32RF	Hopkins & Allen				Mexico
MUELLER SPECIAL	Rev	6.35	Decker	OCULTO	Rev	32/38	Orueta Hermanos
MUGICA	Pistols	Various	Gabilondo	OFF-DUTY	Rev	38	Charter Arms
MUNICIPAL	Rev	8mm	HDH	O.H.	Rev	22/32/38	Orbea Hermanos
MUSEUM	Pistol	6.35	Echeverria	OICET	Rev	38	Antonio Errasti
MUSTANG	Pistol	9S	Colt	O.K.	SS	22	Marlin
MUSTANG POCKETLITE	Pistol	9S	Colt	OKZET	Pistol	6.35	Menz

Name	Type	Calibre	Maker
OLD TIMER	Shotgun	Various	Stevens
OLYMPIA	Pistol	6.35/7.65	SEAM
OLYMPIC	Shotgun	Various	Stevens
O.M.	Rev	Various	Ojanguren y Matiade
OMEGA	Pistol	6.35/7.65	Armero Especialistas
OMEGA	Pistol	10mm	Springfield
OMEGA	Rev	22	Gerstenberger
OMEGA	Rev	32	Weirauch
OMEGA III	Rifle	Various	Hi-Shear
OMNI	Pistol	45/9P	Gabilondo
ONANDIA	Rev	32	Onandia Hermanos
OREA	Rifle	Various	Orechowsky
ORTGIES	Pistol	Various	Deutsche Werke
OSCILLANT AZUL	Rev	38	Eulogio Arostegui
O.V.	Rev	32	Ojanguren & Vidosa
OWA	Pistol	6.35	Osterreich
OXFORD ARMS	Shotgun	Various	Stevens
OXFORD ARMS CO	Shotgun	Various	Crescent Firearms
OYEZ	Pistol	6.35	[Belgium]
PADRE	Pistol	7.65	Galesi
P.A.F.	Pistol	6.35	Pretoria Arms Factory
PAGE-LEWIS ARMS CO	Shotgun	Various	Stevens
PALMETTO	Shotgun	Various	Stevens
PANTAX	Pistol	22	Woerther
PARAGON	Shotgun	Various	Stevens
PARAMOUNT	Pistol	6.35/7.65	Retolaza
PARKER SAFETY HAMMERLESS	Rev	32	Columbia Armory
PAROLE	Rev	22	Hopkins & Allen
PATENT	Pistol	6.35	[Spain]
PATHFINDER	Rev	22	Charter Arms
PATHFINDER	Pistol	6.35	Echave & Arizmendi
PATRIOT	Rev	32RF	Norwich Falls
PEACEKEEPER	Rev	357	Colt
PEERLESS	Rifle	22	Stevens
PEERLESS	Shotgun	Various	Crescent Firearms
PEERLESS	Rev	32RF	Hood
PENETRATOR	Rev	32RF	Norwich Falls

Name	Type	Calibre	Maker
PERFECT	Rev	38	Foehl & Weeks
PERFECT	Pistol	7.65	Pyrenees
PERFECTION	Shotgun	Various	Crescent
PERFECTION AUTOMATIC	Rev	32	Forehand Arms
PERFECTIONNE	Rev	8mm	Pieper
PERFECTO	Rev	32	Orbea Hermanos
PERLA	Pistol	6.35	Dusek
PETITE	Rev	.22 Short	Iver Johnson
PEUGOT	Pistol	6.35	[France]
PHOENIX	Pistol	6.35	Robar
PHOENIX	Pistol	6.35	Urizar
PHOENIX ARMS CO	Pistol	6.35	Lowell
PICCOLO	Rev	38	Gabilondo
PIEDMONT	Shotgun	Various	Crescent
PILSEN	Pistol	7.65	Zrojovka Plzen
PINAFORE	Rev	22	Norwich Falls
PINKERTON	Pistol	6.35	Gaspar Arizaga
PIONEER	Rev	22/38RF	[USA]
PIONEER	Rifle	22	Stevens
PIONEER ARMS CO	Shotgun	Various	Crescent
PISTOLET AUTOMATIQUE	Pistol	6.35	Arizmendi
PLUS ULTRA	Pistol	7.65	Gabilondo
POLICE BULLDOG	Rev	44	Charter Arms]
POLICE SERVICE SIX	Rev	357	Ruger
POLICE UNDERCOVER	Rev	32/38	Charter Arms
POLICEMAN	Pistol	6.35	Manufrance
PONY	Pistol	9S	Iver Johnson
POPULAIRE	SS	22	Manufrance
PORTSIDER	Pistol	45	Falcon
POSSE	Rev	22	High Standard
POWERMASTER	SS	22	Wamo Mfg Co
PRAGA	Pistol	7.65	SEAM
PRAGA	Pistol	6.35	Novotny
PRAIRIE KING	Rev	22	Norwich Falls
PRATIC	Pistol	6.35	[Spain]
PRECISION	Pistol	6.357.65	Grand Precision
PREMIER	Pistol	6.35/7.65	Urizar
PREMIER	Rifle	22	Stevens
PREMIER	Rev	22/38RF	Ryan

Name	Type	Calibre	Maker	Name	Type	Calibre	Maker
PREMIER TRAIL BLAZER	Rifle	22	Stevens	RAYON	Pistol	6.35	[Spain]
PRICE J.W.	Shotgun	Various	Stevens	R.E.	Pistol	9BB	Republica Espana
PRIMA	Pistol	6.35	Pyrenees	RECKY	Rev	22	Reck
PRINCE	SS	.50RF	Iver Johnson	REDHAWK	Rev	44	Ruger
PRINCEPS	Pistol	7.65	Urizar	RECORD	SS	22	Anschutz
PRINCESS	Rev	22	[USA]	RED CLOUD	Rev	32RF	[USA]
PRINCIPE	Pistol	6.35	Urizar	RED JACKET	Rev	22/32RF	Lee Arms
PROTECTOR	Pistol	6.35	Echave & Arizmendi	REFORM	RP	6.35	Schuler
PROTECTOR	Pistol	6.35	Santiago Salaberrin	REFORM	Pistol	6.35	[Spain]
PROTECTOR	Rev	22/32RF	Norwich Falls	REGENT	Pistol	6.35/7.65	Bolumburu
PROTECTOR	Rev	22	Protector	REGENT	Rev	22	Burgsmuller
PUMA	Pistol	22	Beretta	REGENT	Rifle	Various	Kassnar
PUMA	Pistol	6.35	Urizar	REGINA	Pistol	6.35/7.65	Bolumburu
PUPPET	Pistol	7.65	Ojanguren & Vidosa	REGNUM	RP	6.35	Menz
PUPPET	Rev	6.35	Ojanguren & Vidosa	REID PATENT	Rev	22/32/41RF	Irving
PUPPY	Rev	5mm	Crucelegui Retolaza	REIFGRABER	Pistol	7.65	Union Arms
PUPPY	Rev	5mm	Francisco Arizmendi	REIMS	Pistol	6.35/7.65	Azanza y Arrizabalaga
PUPPY	Rev	5.5mm	Izidro Gaztanaga	REINA	Pistol	7.65	Pyrenees
PUPPY	Rev	22	Ojanguren & Marcaido	RENARD	Pistol	6.35	Echave & Arizmendi
PUPPY	Rev	22	HDH	REPUBLIC	Pistol	7.65	Arrizabalaga
PUPPY	Rev	Various	Colt	RETRIEVER	Rev	32RF	Ryan
PYTHON	Rev	357	Kohout	REV-O-NOC	Shotgun	Various	Crescent Firearms
P.Z.K.	Pistol	6.35		REX	Pistol	6.35/7.65/9S	Bolumburu
QUAIL	Shotgun	Various	Crescent Firearms	RG	Rev	Various	Rohm GmbH
QUAILS FARGO	Shotgun	Various	Dakin	RICKARD ARMS	Shotgun	Various	Crescent Firearms
QUEEN CITY	Shotgun	Various	Crescent Firearms	RIGARMI	Pistol	22/6.35/7.65	Galesi
RADIUM	Pistol	6.35	Gabilondo	RIVAL	pistol	6.35	Union, Eibar
RANGER	Pistol	22	Pyrenees	ROBIN HOOD	Rev	22/32RF	Hood
RANGER	Rev	32RF	Dickinson	ROLAND	Pistol	6.35/7.65	Arizmendi
RANGER	Rifle/Shotgun	Various	Stevens	ROME	Rev	22	Rome
RANGER No 2	Rev	32RF	Dickinson	ROMO	Rev	22	Rohm
RANGER No 2	Rev	22/32RF	Hopkins & Allen	ROWNHNES	Pistol	7.65	[Spain]
RAPID-MAXIMA	Pistol	7.65	Pyrenees	ROYAL	Rev	22/32RF	Hopkins & Allen
RAVEN	Pistol	6.35	Dornheim	ROYAL	Rev	38	[Spain]
				ROYAL	Pistol	Various	Zulaica
				ROYAL NOVELTY	Pistol	6.35/7.65	Zulaica
				RUBI	Pistol	22	Venturini
				RUBY	Pistol	Various	Gabilondo
				RUBY EXTRA	Revolver	Various	Gabilondo

Name	Type	Calibre	Maker
UMMEL	Shotgun	Various	Crescent Firearms
URAL	Rev	32	Garantizada
.A.	Pistol	6.35	Societe d'Armes
& A	Rev	38	Suinaga & Aramperri
ABLE BABY	Rev	22	[Belgium]
.A.C.M.	Pistol	7.65 Longue	SACM
AFETY POLICE	Rev	32	Hopkins & Allen
T HUBERT	Pistol	7.65	Pyrenees
ALSO	Pistol	6.35	Unceta
ALVAJE	Pistol	6.35	Ojanguren & Vidosa
ATA	Pistol	22/6.35	Sabotti & Tanfoglio
ATURN	Rifle	Various	Kind
CARAB SCORPION	Pistol	9P	Armitage
CHMEISSER	Pistol	6.35	Haenel
CHONBERGER	Pistol	8mm	Steyr-Mannlicher
CHOUBOE	Pistol	7.65	Madsen
CHUTZMANN	Rifle	Various	Kind
CORPIO	Rev	38	Gabilondo
COTT ARMS CO	Rev	32RF	Norwich Falls
COTT REVOLVER-RIFLE	Rev-Rifle	38RF	Hopkins & Allen
COUT	Shotgun	Various	Stevens
COUT	Rev	32RF	Hood
ECRET SERVICE SPECIAL	Rev	32/38	Iver Johnson
ECURITAS	Pistol	6.35	St Etienne Automatique
ECURITY SIX	Rev	357	Ruger
ELECTA	Pistol	6.35/7.65	Echave & Arizmendi
ELECTA	Pistol	7.65	Pyrenees
ELF	Pistol	6.35/7.65	[Spain]
ENTINEL	Rev	22/357	High Standard
HARP-SHOOTER	Pistol	6.35/7.65/9S	Arrizabalaga
HERRY	Pistol	.22	Wilkinson
ILESIA	Pistol	6.35	SEAM
ILHOUETTE	SS	Various	Wichita Arms
ILHOUETTE	Pistol	.44	Automag
IMPLEX	Pistol	8mm	Bergmann
INGER	Pistol	6.35/7.65	Arizmendi & Goenaga

Name	Type	Calibre	Maker
SINGER	Pistol	6.35	Dusek
SINGLE SIX	Rev	22	Ruger
SIVISPACEM	Pistol	7.65	SEAM
SIVISPACEM PARABELLUM	Pistol	6.35	Thieme & Edeler
SLAVIA	Pistol	6.35	Vilimec
SLOCUM	Rev	32RF	Brooklyn Arms
S.M.	Pistol	6.35	[Spain]
SMITH AMERICANO	Rec	32/38/44	Antonio Errasti
SMOK	Pistol	6.35	Nakulski
SMOKER	Rev	22/32/38/41RF	Johnson, Bye Sporting
SNAKE CHARMER	Shotg	410	
SOUTHERN ARMS CO	Shotgun	Various	Crescent Firearms
SPEED SIX	Rev	357	Ruger
SPENCER GUN CO	Shotgun	Various	Crescent Firearms
SPENCER SAFETY	Rev	38	Columbia Armory
SPITFIRE	Pistol	9P	Slough
SPORT KING	Pistol	22	High Standard
SPORTSMAN	Shotgun	Various	Stevens
SPORTSMAN	Shotgun	Various	Crescent Firearms
SPORTSMAN BUSH & FIELD	Rifle	Various	Marathon
SPRINGFIELD ARMS	Shotgun	Various	Crescent Firearms
SPRINTER	Pistol	6.35	Bolumburu
SPY	Rev	22	Norwich Falls
SQUARE DEAL	Shotgun	Various	Crescent Firearms
SQUIBMAN	All	Various	Squires., BIngham
STALLION	Rev	Various	Uberti
STAR	Pistol	Various	Echeverria
STARLET	Pistol	6.35	Echeverria
STAR VESTOPKCET	Rev	22/32RF	Johnson, Bye
STATE ARMS CO	Shotgun	Various	Crescent Firearms
STENDA	Pistol	7.65	Stendawerke
STERN	SS	22	Buchel
STERN-PISTOLE	Pistol	6.35	Wahl
STINGRAY	Rev	22	Rohm
STOSEL	Pistol	6.35/7.65	Retolaza
SULLIVAN ARMS CO	Shotgun	Various	Crescent Firearms
SUPER AZUL	MP	7.63	Eulogio Arostegui
SUPER BLACKHAWK	Rev	44	Ruger

Name	Type	Calibre	Maker	Name	Type	Calibre	Maker
SUPER COMANCHE	Rev	357/44	Gabilondo	THE VICTORY	Pistol	6.35	Zulaica
SUPER DESTROYER	Pistol	7.65	Gaztanaga, Trocaola	THOMAS	Pistol	45	James Ordnance
SUPERIOR	Pistol	6.35	[Spain]	THOMPSON	SMG	.45	Auto-Ordnance
SUPER REDHAWK	Rev	44	Ruger	THUNDER	Pistol	6.35	Bascaran
SUPERMATIC	Pistol	22	High Standard	THUNDER CHIEF	Rev	22	Squibman
SURETE	Pistol	7.65	Gaztanaga	TIGER	Shotgun	Various	Crescent Firearms
SWAMP ANGEL	Rev	41RF	Forehand & Wadsworth	TIGER	Rev	32RF	[USA]
SWIFT	Rev	38	Iver Johnson	TIGRE	Pistol	6.35	Garate Anitua
SYMPATHIQUE	Pistol	7.65	Pyrenees	TIKKA	Rifle	Various	Tikkakoski
				TIRO AL BLANCO	Rev	38	Ojanguren & Matiade
T.A.C.	Rev	Various	Trocaola Aranzabal	TISAN	Pistol	6,.35	Salaberrin
TANARMI	Pistol	22	Tanfoglio	TITAN	Pistol	6.35	Armigas
TANKE	Rev	38	Orueta Hermanos	TITAN	Pistol	7.65	Retolaza
TANNE	Rifle	Various	Kind	TITAN	Pistol	6.35	Tanfoglio
TANQUE	Pistol	6.35	Ojanguren & Vidosa	TITANIC	Pistol	6.35/7.65	Retolaza
				TIWA	Pistol	6.35	[Spain]
TARGA	Pistol	Various	Tanfoglio	TOKAGYPT	Pistol	9P	Femaru
TARGET BULLDOG	Rev	357/44	Charter Arms	TOMPKINS	SS	22	Varsity Mfg Co
TARN	Pistol	9P	Swift Rifle Co	TORPILLE	Pistol	7.65	[Spain]
TATRA	Pistol	6.35	Alkartasuna	TOURISTE	Pistol	7.65	Pyrenees
TATRA	Pistol	6.35	SEAM	TOWERS POLICE SAFETY	Rev	38RF	Hopkins & Allen]
TAULER	Pistol	Various	Gabilondo	TOZ	Pistol	6.34	Tulskii
T.E.	Pistol	7.65	Thieme & Edeler	TRAILSMAN	Rev	22	Iver Johnson
TED WILLIAMS	Shotguns	Various	Sears Roebuck	TRAMP'S TERROR	Rev	22	Hopkins & Allen
TELL	SS	22	Buchel	TRIDENT	Rev	38	Renato Gamba
TERRIBLE	Pistol	6.35	Arrizabalaga	TRIFIRE	Pistol	45	Arminex
TERRIER	Rev	22/32/38/41RF	Rupertus	TRIOMPHE	Pistol	6.35	Apaolozo Hermano
TERRIER ONE	Rev	32	[Germany]	TRIOMPHE FRANCAISE	Pistol	7.65	Pyrenees
TERROR	Rev	32RF	Forehand & Wadsworth	TRIPLEX	Pistol	6.35	Domingo Acha
				TRIUMPH	Pistol	7.65	Garate Anitua
TEUF-TEUF	Pistol	6.35	Arizmendi & Goenaga	TROOPER	Rev	22/357	Colt
				TRUE BLUE	Rev	32RF	Norwich Falls
TEUF-TEUF	Pistol	6.35	[Belgium]	TRUST	Pistol	6.35/7.65	Grand Precision
TEXAS LONGHORN	Rev	Various	Texas	TRUST SUPRA	Pistol	6.35	Grand Precision
TEXAS MARSHAL	Rev	45	Sauer	TTIBAR	Pistol	22	S.R.L.
TEXAS RANGER	Rev	38	Unies de Liege	TUE-TUE	Rev	Various	Galand
TEXAS RANGER	Shotgun	12/16	Stevens	TURNER & ROSS	Rev	22	Hood
THALCO	Rev	22	Rohm	TWO-BIT	Pistol	6.35	Steel City
THAMES AUTOMATIC	Rev	22/32/38	Thames	TYCOON	Rev	All RF	Johnson, Bye

Name	Type	Calibre	Maker
A.E.	Pistol	6.35	Union Armera Eibarens
A.Z.	SS	22	Anschutz
C.	Pistol	6.35	Urrejola & Co
M.C.ARMS CO	Rev	32RF	Norwich Falls
JCLE SAM	SS	.50RF	Iver Johnson
NDERCOVER	Rev	38	Charter Arms
NDERCOVERETTE	Rev	32	Charter Arms
NION	Pistol	7.65	Fabrique Francaise
NION	Pistol	6.35/7.65	Seytres
NION	Pistol	6.35/7.65	Unceta
NION	Pistol	6.35	Tomas de Urizar
NION ARMERA	Pistol	6.35	Union Armera Eibarens
NION JACK	Rev	22/32RF	Hood
NION SALES CO	Rev	9RF	[Germany]
NIQUE	Rev/RP	32/38RF	Shattuck
NIQUE	Pistol	Various	Pyrenees
NIQUE CORSAIR	Pistol	22	Echeverria
NIQUE ESCORT	Pistol	22	Echeverria
IIS	Pistol	7.65	Pyrenees
IIS	Pistol	6.35	Santiago Salaberri
IIVERSAL	Rev	32	Hopkins & Allen
S.ARMS CO	Shotgun	Various	Crescent Firearms
S.ARMS CO	Rev	22/32/38/41RF	US Arms
S.REVOLVER CO	Rev	22/32/38	Iver Johnson
INQUER	Pistol	6.35	Aurelio Mendiola
LIANT	Rifle	22	Stevens
LOR	Rev	22	Rohm
LO-BROM	Rev	6mm/8mm	Retolaza
LO-DOG	Rev	5mm	Galand (and many others)
LO-MITH	Rev	6.35	Crucelegui
LO-MITH	Rev	6.35	Ojanguren & Marcaido
LO-MITH	Rev	7.65	Retolaza
LO-MITH ARTIAN	Rev	6.35	Arizmendi
LO-SMITH	Rev	6.35	[Spain]
VELO-STARK	Rev	6/6.35	Garate Hermanos
VENCEDOR	Pistol	6.35	Casimir Santos
VENUS	Pistol	7.65	Urizar
VENUS	Pistol	7.65	Venus Waffenwerke
VER-CAR	Pistol	6.35	Verney-Carron
VESTA	Pistol	6.35/7.65	Hijos de A Echeverria
VESTPOCKET	Rev	22	Rohm
VETERAN	Rev	32RF	Norwich Falls
VETO	Rev	32RF	[USA]
VICI	Pistol	6.35	[Belgium]
VICTOR	Pistol	6.35/7.65	Francisco Arizmendi
VICTOR	SS	38RF	Marlin
VICTOR	Rev	22/32	Harrrington & Richardson
VICTOR	Shotgun	Various	Crescent Firearms
VICTOR, THE	Pistol	22	High Standard
VICTOR No 1	Rev	22/32	Harrington & Richardson
VICTOR SPECIAL	Shotgun	Various	Crescent
VICTORIA	Rev	32RF	Hood
VICTORIA	Pistol	6.35/7.65	Esperanza & Unceta
VICTORY	Pistol	6.35	Zulaica
VIKING	Pistol	45	ODI
VILAR	Pistol	7.65	[Spain]56
VINCITOR	Pistol	6.35/7.65	Zulaica
VINDEX	Pistol	7.65	Pyrenees
VIRGINIA ARMS CO	Shotgun	Various	Crescent Firearms
VIRGINIAN DRAGOON	Rev	Various	Interarms
VITE	Pistol	6.35/7.65	Echave & Arizmendi
VOLUNTEER	Shotgun	Various	Stevens
VULCAN ARMS CO	Shotgun	Various	Crescent Firearms
VULCAIN	Pistol	6.35	[Spain]
VULKAN	Pistol	6.35	Pfannl
WACO	Pistol	6.35	SEAM
WALAM	Pistol	7.65	Femaru

Name	Type	Calibre	Maker
WALDMAN	Pistol	6.35/7.65	Arizmendi & Goenaga
WALKY	Pistol	6.35	[Spain]
WALMAN	Pistol	6.35/7.65/9S	Arizmendi & Goenaga
WARWINCK	Pistol	7.65	Arizaga
WEGRIA-CHARLIER	Pistol	6.35	Charlier
WELTWAFFEN	Pistol	7.65	MKEK
WESTERN BULLDOG	Rev	44	[Belgium]
WESTERN FIELD NO 5	SS	22	Pyrenees
WESTERN SIX-SHOOTER	Rev	Various	Weirauch
WESTERN STYLE	Rev	22	Rohm
WHEELER	RP	41RF	American Arms Co [USA]
WHITE STAR	Rev	32	Triple-S
WICKLIFFE	Rifle	Various	Hood
WIDE AWAKE	Rev	32RF	Bayonne
WINFIELD	Pistol	9S/9P	Norwich Falls
WINFIELD ARMS CO	Rev	32RF	Crescent Firearms
WINOCA ARMS CO	Shotgun	Various	Stevens
WITTES HARDWARE CO	Shotgun	Various	Lower
W.L.GRANT	Rev	22/32RF	[Spain]
WOLF PATENT	Pistol	7.65	Whitney Firearms
WOLVERINE	Pistol	22	Crescent Firearms
WOLVERINE ARMS CO	Shotgun	Various	Colt
WOODSMAN	Pistol	22	Stevens
WORTHINGTON ARMS	Shotgun	Various	Stevens
WORTHINGTON, GEORGE	Shotgun	Various	Stevens

Name	Type	Calibre	Maker
XL	Rev	22/32/38	Hopkins & Allen
XL BULLDOG	Rev	38	Hopkins & Allen
XX STANDARD	Rev	22/32/38	Marlin
YATO	Pistol	7.65	Hamada Arsenal
YDEAL	Pistol	6.35/7.65	Francisco Arizmendi
YOU BET	Rev	22	Hopkins & Allen
YOUNG AMERICA	Rev	Various	Harrington & Richardson
YOVANOVITCH	Pistol	6.35/7.65/9S	Kragujevac
Z	Pistol	6.35	Ceska Zbrojovka [Spain]
ZALDUN	Pistol	6.35	Zbrojovka Brno
ZB	Rifle/MG	Various	Zbrojovka Brno
ZENTRUM	SS	.22	VEB
ZEPHYR	Shotgun	Various	Stoeger
ZEPHYR	Rev	22	Rohm
ZOLI	Pistol	6.35	Tanfoglio
ZONDA	SS	22	Hafdasa